James Madison

Madison *James*

A Son of Virginia & a Founder of the Nation

JEFF BROADWATER

The University of North Carolina Press   Chapel Hill

This book was published with the assistance of the
THORNTON H. BROOKS FUND
of the University of North Carolina Press.

Frontispiece: Portrait of James Madison by Thomas Sully. (Virginia Historical Society)

Library of Congress Cataloging-in-Publication Data
Broadwater, Jeff.
James Madison : a son of Virginia and a founder of the nation / Jeff Broadwater.
p. cm.
Includes bibliographical references and index.
ISBN 978-0-8078-3530-2 (cloth : alk. paper)
ISBN 978-1-4696-2831-8 (pbk. : alk. paper)
ISBN 978-0-8078-6991-8 (ebook)
1. Madison, James, 1751–1836. 2. Presidents—United States—Biography. 3. Statesmen—
United States—Biography. 4. United States—Politics and government—1809–1817.
5. United States—Politics and government—1789–1815. I. Title.
E342.B76 2012
973.5′1092—dc23
[B]   2011035946

THIS BOOK WAS DIGITALLY PRINTED.

To Cyndi

Contents

Illustrations

Preface

If, save only for George Washington, he was the most indispensable of the founders, there was nothing flamboyant about James Madison. Reserved, soft spoken, and slightly built, he seemed incapable of fiery oratory. Guarded about a private life that was unremarkable except for a fortuitous marriage to the effervescent Dolley Payne Todd, he left behind no scandals waiting to be exposed. Irving Brant, who wrote a six-volume biography of Madison, once complained that nineteenth-century editors of Madison's papers had so sanitized his letters as to make him appear to be nothing more than "a disembodied brain."[1] To many historians, the intellectual creativity Madison demonstrated in helping to write the U.S. Constitution and *The Federalist* far overshadowed the rest of his career, including his two terms as a supposedly mediocre president.

Yet Madison enjoyed rare success as a practicing politician, winning election after election and holding a series of public offices. "My life," he wrote an earlier biographer, "has been so much of a public one that any review of it must mainly consist, of the agency which was my lot in public transactions."[2] How did James Madison, an unimposing speaker and an often indifferent prose stylist, with no military honors and no personal magnetism—at least in large groups or formal settings—make a career in politics?

He often worked quietly, sometimes obscuring his own accomplishments. "He is," the French diplomat Louis Otto wrote, "a man one must study for a long time in order to make a fair appraisal of him." His victories came through the familiar combination of dedication, talent, and connections, with no secret weapons or magic formulas. He worked hard, and he did his homework. He learned to accommodate himself to disappointments, and he persisted in the craft of politics when public service offered few pecuniary rewards. He brought a keen intelligence to his duties, although his mental gifts were more conceptual than pragmatic. He had a better sense of humor than did his best friend, the more charismatic Thomas Jefferson. A penchant for off-color jokes notwithstanding, Madison avoided any hint of impropriety and rarely allowed his own conduct to become an issue. He and Jefferson shared a similar commitment to the separation of church and state, but Madison never faced the charges of religious infidelity that Jefferson endured. Madison's virtues attracted Jefferson's lifelong devotion. They earned him the confidence of Alexander Hamilton and George Washington at critical periods in the nation's founding. Despite being cast as occasional rivals, he and James Monroe maintained a friendship over half a century, and Madison won the heart of Dolley Payne Todd, who became an invaluable political asset.[3]

The idea of Madison as a disembodied brain has been nurtured by modern historians and political scientists, who have often tried to make an unusually erudite politician into a more systematic thinker than he was. Most of his writings were produced for specific political purposes. Todd Estes's description of Madison's work on *The Federalist* during the debate over the ratification of the Constitution could be said of his career generally: "For all Madison's intellectual brilliance, what made him successful in these debates were his achievements as an intellectual *politician*, for Madison fused the roles of scholarly intellectual and intellectual politician as well as anyone ever has."[4]

In assessing Madison's career as a politician, his political thought cannot, in other words, be ignored. Historians who have concluded that "politics always trumped abstract ideas for Madison" go too far.[5] Madison routinely worked from a critical but not unsympathetic appraisal of human nature: people possessed enough virtue to govern themselves, but not so much that the task would be easy, and no one was so noble as to be trusted with absolute power. If allowed to select their leaders, the people would more often than not choose wisely. Majorities, to be sure, would presumably be motivated by self-interest or sometimes be carried away by momentary passions, and factions were inevitable. The people's shortcomings meant liberty could be threatened by too much democracy as well as by too little. Checks had to be placed on the legislature, the most popular branch of government. A revolutionary, a reformer, and for the most part a liberal by the standards of his day, Madison could demonstrate conservative tendencies.[6]

Government, in Madison's mind, existed to protect individual liberties, both from tyrants and from tyrannical majorities. Individual civil rights were more than a matter of personal preference or convenience; citizens had to be able to exercise their rights for a republican system to function. Political freedom required personal freedom. We remember Madison for the elaborate system of checks and balances he helped build into the Constitution. He did not, however, believe safeguards for individual liberties could be limited to structural devices. The relationship between the rulers and the ruled was fluid and mutually dependent. Influenced by the French *philosophes*, especially Brissot de Warville, Madison thought the success of republican government depended on an enlightened public opinion that could be promoted by the state. "It is the reason, alone, of the public that ought to control and regulate the government," he wrote in *Federalist No. 49*. "The passions ought to be controlled and regulated by the government."[7]

Madison's commitment to the rule of political reason injected into his thinking an element of professionalism and a preference for stability, along with a dread of war and the prospect of war. Decades ahead of his time, Madison saw the need for legislative drafting bureaus to help lawmakers prepare bills. He was an early advocate of the secret ballot. Demonstrating a professional's disdain for a dilettante, he offered no encouragement when a younger brother suddenly suggested he might seek public office. Madison rejected Jefferson's suggestion that all laws and debts expire after a generation: "A Government so often revised becomes too mutable to retain those prejudices in its favor which antiquity inspires." While generally more fearful of the legislative than the executive branch, Madison warned against the accretion of presidential prerogatives in time of war, and the "constant apprehension of war," he argued, had the same effect: "to render the head too big for the body."[8]

Without sacrificing his capacity for independent action, Madison never strayed too far from the values of his Virginia constituents. For most of his career, they generally shared his commitment to popular rule, with safeguards for individual liberty, especially for freedom of religion and the rights of property. A Virginia republican, he was also a Virginia nationalist, a term that, in Madison's case, was not an oxymoron. Despite unshakable political, economic, and familial roots in Virginia, Madison tirelessly championed the federal Union and national expansion, even as westward migration drained people and wealth from the Old Dominion. He believed, however, that the country should be governed by Virginia values. Far and away the largest state during and immediately after the American Revolution, Virginia in the 1780s expanded its sphere of influence by supporting a strong national government. Madison's native state dominated presidential politics until the last years of his life. As the nation expanded into the West, Madison expected new settlers to replicate Virginia's agrarian economy, albeit, he hoped, with less reliance on slave labor.[9]

In addition to a Virginia bias, Madison had other prejudices and blind spots. His contempt for Great Britain lingered for years after the Revolution and helped bring on the War of 1812. Despite his vaunted powers of analysis, the more he thought about American slavery, the more muddled his thinking became. For all the acclaim he has received as a political theorist, sometimes his theories failed.

Frustrated by the political instability of the 1780s, Madison pushed hard for the adoption of the Constitution and the creation of a stronger central government. Then he saw it all go wrong in the 1790s. The executive, legislative, and judicial branches of the new federal government did not check and balance one another. The various factions that Madison had foreseen in what he had called "the extended republic" did not neutralize one another's most malicious tendencies. Congressional elections, which Madison had envisioned as far more sober affairs than state legislative races, did not produce statesmen independent of parochial interests. A natural alliance between the South and West did not immediately coalesce in defense of agrarian republicanism. Fearing an excess of popular participation in the 1780s and governments too responsive to the mob, Madison saw too little democracy in the 1790s, allowing, he thought, a minority faction, the new Federalist Party, to dominate the federal government.

In response, Madison tempered his enthusiasm for an energetic national government, becoming a defender of states' rights and of a strict construction of the Constitution. He changed his tone after the Federalist threat had passed. His political shifts have created for historians "the Madison problem": Was he guided throughout his career by a consistent set of principles, or did he vacillate in response to the demands of political expediency?[10]

In a public career spanning some fifty tumultuous years, only the most intransigent ideologue could have been completely consistent. Madison lived through a period of dramatic political change. Born a subject of the British monarchy, he died during the presidency of Andrew Jackson. Madison's reversals often represented constructive accommodations to political reality. During the debate over the adoption of the Constitution, he argued against the addition of a bill of rights because he saw the fight over amendments as a ploy to derail the ratification process. After the Constitution had been approved, he almost single-handedly pushed a bill of rights through Congress in an effort to appease the more moderate critics of the new government. Madison's apparent twists and turns usually involved the scope of federal power; he sought for most of his career to maintain a proper division of sovereignty between national and state authorities.

As much as he worried about state and federal relations, he worried more about maintaining a republican system and striking a balance between majority rule and minority rights. He was probably never as much of a nationalist as Hamilton; in the heyday of his own nationalism in the 1780s, Madison valued a strong central government primarily as a check on provincial and capricious state governments. His most audaciously nationalistic proposal, a congressional veto over state laws, came at a time when Congress was at its weakest. Madison believed consolidation and aristocracy, on the one hand, and states' rights and unfettered democracy, on the other, both undermined republican government. When he saw the political currents shifting too far in one direction, he would tilt toward the other. Near the end of his life, he felt compelled to defend his own consistency, but he also recognized that a republican leader ultimately had to yield to the settled verdict of the people.

We have fine full-length biographies of Madison, shorter volumes for student readers, and brilliant expositions of his political philosophy. Only a truly gifted historian could hope to improve on the work of Irving Brant, Ralph Ketcham, Jack Rakove, Lance Banning, or Drew McCoy. This book attempts something slightly different and more modest. While trying to provide enough context to tell a coherent story, I have focused on those aspects of Madison's life that are apt to be of the most enduring interest to the most readers: his fight for religious freedom, the debates over the adoption of the Constitution and the Bill of Rights, the origins of the party system, his relationship with Dolley Madison, his performance as commander in chief during the War of 1812, and his views on slavery. Assuming that, as I recall the distinguished intellectual historian Paul Conkin once saying, "some gaps in our knowledge belong there," I have not attempted to cover everything. I have tried instead to offer my version of what might be called the essential Madison.

Even a modest book generates substantial debts. Teresa Peterson provided invaluable service in preparing the manuscript. Stuart Leibiger gave it a close and incisive reading that saved me from innumerable errors, and an anonymous reader for the University of North Carolina Press spurred me to give more thought to a number of important issues, including Madison's views on slavery. On research trips to the Alderman Library at the University of Virginia, I benefited from the hospitality and expertise of David Mattern and J. C. A. Stagg. Chuck Grench, my editor at UNC Press, was, as always, a reliable source of wisdom and encouragement. Julie Miller, a specialist in early American history in the Manuscript Division of the Library of Congress, tracked down several pieces of Madison's correspondence I had missed. Copyeditor Alex Martin straightened out my prose, and Associate Managing Editor Paula Wald oversaw the process of turning a manuscript into a book.

The Library of Congress, the Library of Virginia, and the Virginia Historical Society helped me locate illustrations for the text. Along with countless other historians, I am indebted to the Davis Library at the University of North Carolina at Chapel Hill and to the Perkins Library at Duke University for access to their rich collections.

Closer to home at Barton College, I must acknowledge the contribution made by the staff at the Hackney Library, including interlibrary loan librarian Steven Stewart, and by an undergraduate research assistant, Ashley Mahoney. Rodney A. Werline, the Leman and Marie Barnhill Professor of Religious Studies, allowed me to discuss Madison's views on church-state relations with his class on religion in America. Our late colleague, E. B. Holloway, did not live long enough to see the manuscript completed, but no one took more interest in it. I should also thank our administration for allowing me a semester with a reduced teaching load. Finally, Cyndi was my most valuable collaborator. With the charm of her fellow North Carolinian Dolley Madison, she was the model of the long-suffering academic spouse, helping me find rare books and adjusting without complaint to sharing the house with the fourth president and his rather substantial retinue. The dedication to her is long overdue.

James Madison

Religion and Revolution

*J*ames Madison was born on 16 March 1751, while his parents, James Madison Sr. and Nelly Conway Madison, were visiting his maternal grandmother on her plantation in King George County, Virginia. The young family soon returned to their own plantation, which would eventually be known as Montpelier, in Orange County. Little is known of Madison's early life, and the house where he first lived has long since disappeared. Madison's great-great-grandfather, John Maddison, had come to Virginia as a ship's carpenter in the middle of the 1600s. Maddison and his descendants prospered in America, the second *d* was dropped along the way, and by 1751 James Madison Sr. owned 2,850 acres, making him the wealthiest landowner in the county. The great house at Montpelier that would be his son's home for the rest of his life was finished when James Madison Jr. was a young boy. As an adult, Madison remembered helping move furniture into the new mansion.[1]

The house stood among wooded, rolling hills near the Rapidan River, within sight of the Blue Ridge Mountains on a clear day. The Madisons were rural people, but they were not isolated. They owned dozens of slaves, and they enjoyed the company of a handful of white neighbors; Orange County sheriff Thomas Chew and his family were the closest. Worship at the Brick Church, a nearby Anglican congregation where James Madison Sr. served as a vestryman, brought the Madisons into contact with a community beyond the plantation.[2]

The first of twelve children, James Madison saw three siblings die in infancy. Two others died young from dysentery. He probably began his education at home under the supervision of his grandmother Frances Taylor Madison, a pious Anglican. He may have gone later to a local school. The future president's reading included books from his father's modest library and articles from Joseph Addison's *The Spectator*, a popular magazine known for its elegant essays. From 1762 to 1767, Madison attended a board-

Sketch of Montpelier by J. F. E. Prud'homme after a painting by John G. Chapman. Montpelier is known as James Madison's house, but his father, James Madison Sr., was the owner until his death in 1801, well into his son's middle age. After his father's death, Madison shared the house with his mother, Nelly, who died in 1829 at the age of ninety-eight. (Library of Virginia)

ing school run by Donald Robertson in King and Queen County. Robertson was a graduate of the University of Edinburgh, and the curriculum, which included Latin, Greek, logic, astronomy, and mathematics, was demanding. Madison recalled years later, "All that I have been in life I owe largely to that man." From 1767 to 1769, Madison studied with the Reverend Thomas Martin, the new rector of the Brick Church.[3]

After two years with Martin, Madison faced the first important decision of his life. The sons of Virginia's gentry often went to the College of William and Mary to complete their education. A few traveled to England to study law at the Inns of Court. Madison chose the College of New Jersey, soon to be better known as Princeton. By eighteen, Madison was showing signs of hypochondria, and New Jersey's cooler climate seemed healthier than the coastal lowlands near Williamsburg. William and Mary suffered under a questionable academic reputation, and Martin, a Princeton alumnus himself, may have influenced Madison's decision. An Anglican's choice of a Presbyterian college raised some eyebrows, but Madison seems never to have been wholly committed to the established church.[4]

In fact, Princeton's biases, both religious and political, may have been part of the institution's appeal. A Scottish divine, John Witherspoon, had become president of Princeton in 1768 and quickly established a reputation as a champion of evangelical Christianity and religious toleration. Contemporary critics accused Witherspoon of turning the college into "a seminary of sedition."[5] A modern historian has called it "a kind of West Point for dissenting Presbyterianism."[6] Madison must have known what he was getting into, and presumably it was what he wanted. In the summer of 1769, Madison set out on horseback for New Jersey with Thomas Martin, Martin's brother Alexander, and a slave named Sawney.[7]

Madison immediately warmed to Princeton, writing Thomas Martin shortly after they parted company, "I am perfectly pleased with my present situation." Madison thrived in college, completing his coursework in two years. Princeton combined the classics with then innovative courses in history, mathematics, and science, making Madison one of the best-educated of the American founders. New Light Presbyterianism and liberal political ideas permeated the campus, but then as now college life was not interminably serious. Madison joined the Whig Society and wrote bad and slightly risqué poetry satirizing the Cliosophians, a rival social club. His fellow Whigs included William Bradford, a future attorney general of the United States, as well as Hugh Henry Brackenridge and Philip Freneau, both of whom would enjoy distinguished literary careers.[8] As college students typically do, Madison worried about money and about his appearance. "Every small trifle which I have occasion for," he wrote James Sr., "consumes a much greater sum than one wou[ld] suppose." In another letter, he sent his mother neck and wrist sizes for three or four shirts, but he implored her not to add the ruffles until he could come home and supervise the project.[9]

Madison received his undergraduate degree in the fall of 1771, but he remained at Princeton until April 1772, studying Hebrew under Witherspoon and reading law, among what he called his "miscellaneous studies." Of the twelve members of his graduating class, only Madison failed to speak at the graduation service. Although he never relished public speaking, he may have been excused for health reasons. He contracted a mysterious ailment about the time he graduated—the timing is uncertain—and the ill effects persisted for two or three years. Overwork may have been partially to blame. Madison reportedly slept only four or five hours a night while he was at Princeton. After Madison returned to Montpelier, William Bradford wrote expressing concern about his former classmate's health: "I believe you hurt your constitution while here, by too close an application to study." Another fellow student, Joseph Ross of Pennsylvania, completed his degree on the same accelerated schedule as Madison did, and Ross died a year after leaving Princeton. Madison complained of symptoms similar to epilepsy, but modern biographers have concluded he was not an epileptic. The episode may have been triggered by having to leave Princeton, which he loved, without any definite career plans. It may have been aggravated by an inordinate concern about his health. Slight, with boyish features, Madison seemed delicate. In reality, he demonstrated a remarkable resistance to diseases like malaria and smallpox, which were common in his day, and he lived to a venerable old age. He was also taller than commonly believed; one creditable estimate put him at five feet, six inches tall, short, but not unusually so.[10]

Besides his epileptic symptoms, Madison returned to Montpelier with at least an academic interest in religion. According to one report, he had been caught up in a religious revival that had swept Princeton. He led family devotionals for a time after coming home. His surviving papers from his school days include a copybook with a Socratic dialogue between an atheist and a theist in which the theist argues for the existence of God from the "Fabric of the Universe." He also took extensive notes from a popular biblical commentary.[11]

The young graduate could sound downright sanctimonious. As he wrote William Bradford in November 1772, "a watchful eye must be kept on ourselves lest while we are building ideal Monuments of Renown and Bliss here we neglect to have our names enrolled in the Annals of Heaven." He complained in another letter of the difficulty of finding printed copies of John Witherspoon's sermons in Virginia. When Bradford asked Madison's advice on the choice of a vocation, the Virginian advised him to consider the ministry, perhaps as a second career. "I have sometimes thought there could not be a stronger testimony in favor of Religion," he wrote Bradford, than for successful professionals to renounce worldly pursuits "by becoming fervent advocates in the cause of Christ." He opined to Bradford in a later letter that "the specious Arguments of Infidels have established the faith of Enquiring Christians."[12]

Madison avoided such professions of faith in later years. Seeds of skepticism were planted alongside his adolescent orthodoxy. The first entry in his commonplace book is from the memoirs of the French cleric and politician Cardinal de Retz: "Nothing is more subject to Delusion than Piety. All Manner of Errors creep and hide themselves under that veil." The second is from the essayist Michel de Montaigne and includes the observation, "People who pretend to Religion cannot help confessing in general that they are Sinners; but they conceal or disown all Particulars."[13]

Madison had been baptized as an infant, but he was never confirmed in the Anglican Church. In 1790, an unfounded rumor circulated in Virginia that he had converted to Methodism. A year later, while he and Thomas Jefferson were touring New York and New England, they attended a Congregational Church in Bennington, Vermont; when asked how they liked the music, they responded that it had been so long since they had been to church that they could make no comparisons. In middle age, Madison brought ministers to Montpelier to give the sacraments to his mother, but he did not kneel at prayer. As president, he and Dolley Madison occupied the President's Pew at St. John's Episcopal Church near the White House, and at Montpelier they worshipped at St. Thomas's Church; how often is uncertain. After dinner at the White House in 1815, the Boston Unitarian George Ticknor reported that Madison seemed sympathetic to liberal Christianity. He was more likely to refer in public to "Nature's God" than to Jehovah or Jesus.[14]

At Princeton, Madison had been impressed by the Reverend Samuel Clarke's *The Being and Attributes of God*, which argued that conclusive evidence for the existence of God could be drawn from the physical world. Clarke's brand of rationalism fell from intellectual grace over the course of the eighteenth century. Nevertheless, when Thomas Jefferson asked Madison in 1825 to suggest theological works for the University of Virginia library, Madison recommended Clarke's book. He may have failed to stay abreast of the latest thinking because of a waning interest in religion. In February 1836, a Presbyterian minister from Danville, Virginia, wrote Madison to warn him that he could not be "expected to remain much longer on this earth" and to urge upon him "the necessity of . . . Divine influence to qualify you for heaven." Madison responded with a terse reference to his "general rule of declining correspondences on the subject [of] my religion." Reluctant to discuss his own views, Madison remained throughout his life respectful of the opinions of others.[15]

The mature Madison may have been inclined toward Deism, as were many of the leading figures of his day, including Jefferson, who would become his closest political confidant. Eighteenth-century liberals sometimes shared more in common with orthodox Christians than is commonly acknowledged. Abigail Adams rejected the idea of the Trinity, but she believed that Jesus had been sent by God, crucified, and resurrected. Benjamin Franklin expressed "some doubts" about the divinity of Christ, but he believed in a divine creation, the immortality of the soul, and the vengeance of the Almighty "either here or hereafter." Madison and Jefferson subscribed to a practical faith. They had more confidence in reason than in biblical revelations, but they thought religion could help promote the public virtue they believed was essential to the success of republican governments.[16]

Hand in hand with a skepticism about orthodox Christianity—cause and effect here is hard to trace—went a hostility to the established church. Late in life Madison wrote of his "very early and strong impressions in favor of liberty both civil and religious." Prerevolutionary Virginia imprisoned almost fifty Baptist ministers for preaching without licenses or for overstepping the geographic boundaries they imposed. The persecution of religious dissenters, Madison wrote Bradford in January 1774, "vexes me the most of anything whatever." The establishment of religion had corrupted both the clergy and the people and retarded Virginia's economic development. "Poverty and luxury prevail among all sorts: pride, ignorance and knavery among the Priesthood and vice and wickedness among the Laity." Madison attributed Pennsylvania's prosperity, by contrast, to its embrace of religious freedom. "I can not help attributing those continual exertions of genius which appear among you to the inspiration of liberty and that love of fame and knowledge which always accompany it."[17]

As relations worsened between the colonies and Parliament on the eve of the American Revolution, the establishment appeared to Madison to threaten political freedom as well as liberty of conscience. The state church in Virginia was, after all, the Church of England. If the Anglican Church had been the established church "in all the northern colonies," as it had been in the South, and if religious beliefs had been uniform, he believed "that slavery and subjection might and would have been gradually insinuated among us. Union of religious sentiments begets a surprising confidence and Ecclesiastical establishments tend to great ignorance and corruption, all of which facilitate the execution of mischievous projects."[18]

Opposition to the idea of an established church and fear that British authorities would appoint an Anglican bishop for the American colonies, which would threaten the vestries' control of their local congregations, made it easier for patriots like Madison to resist imperial taxes and trade regulations. Madison enthusiastically supported the resistance movement. He visited Philadelphia in 1774 and saw two royal officials, Alexander Wedderburn and Thomas Hutchinson, burned in effigy. While he was in Philadelphia, patriot leaders met at the City Tavern and called for a continental congress to coordinate the American response to the infamous Coercive Acts. Congress eventually proposed that local committees of safety be created to enforce a boycott of British goods, and Madison was elected to the Orange County committee in December 1774.[19] His family's prominence and his college degree, a rarity in eighteenth-century America, made a position of leadership, at least at the local level, almost inescapable.

After the fighting began, Madison received a commission as a colonel, under the command of his father, in the Orange County militia. He drilled enough to boast of the Virginians' marksmanship: "The most inexpert hands rec[k]en it an indifferent shot to miss the bigness of a man's face at the distance of 100 yards. I am far from being among the best and should not often miss it on a fair trial at that distance." Poor health kept him from active duty, and he never saw combat. As he explained in his autobiography, he was disabled by "his feeble health, and a constitutional liability to sudden attacks, somewhat resembling Epilepsy, and suspending the intellectual functions."[20]

In reality, Madison's intellectual functions rarely stopped after 1775, although the outbreak of the Revolutionary War did occasionally test his patience and common sense. He initially gave credence to rumors that Benjamin Franklin was a British spy and that Richard Bland, the veteran Virginia lawmaker, was a traitor. He fumed against "selfish Quakers" who had refused to sign non-importation agreements foreswearing the purchase of British goods. His ire cooled when some of Virginia's Quakers began to join militia companies. He felt no sympathy for Anglican ministers with Loyalist leanings. Madison heartily approved when the Culpeper County committee of safety closed the church of James Herdman, stopped paying his salary, and expelled him from the parish. In Orange County, patriots burned allegedly "seditious pamphlets" belonging to the Reverend John Wingate. Shortly thereafter, he left his church.[21]

Madison had floundered professionally since leaving Princeton. He may have toyed with the idea of a career in law or the ministry, but he seems to have had no genuine interest in either. James Madison Sr., a sensible and well-respected planter, remained active and vigorous far into his son's adulthood, living until 1801. As a result, Madison was not forced to assume the patriarchal role thrust on Jefferson and so many of their contemporaries who had lost fathers early in life. The Revolution, however, created new opportunities for ambitious Americans. In April 1776, Orange County elected Madison one of its two delegates to a convention scheduled to meet in Williamsburg in May. The May gathering was the last in a series of conventions that provided Virginia with a provisional administration between the collapse of royal authority and the creation of a new state government. Madison found his calling in Williamsburg: politics. Intelligent and studious, able to grasp abstract principles without neglecting more mundane details, he was ideally suited to legislative service, notwithstanding his limitations as an orator, which included a weak voice and a less than commanding physical presence. He immediately impressed his fellow delegate Edmund Randolph, then a prominent young lawyer. Modest, principled, and apparently immune to flattery, Madison, Randolph recalled, was content "throwing out in social discourse jewels which the artifice of a barren mind would have treasured up for gaudy occasions."[22]

Madison served in Williamsburg on a committee appointed to draft a new constitution and a bill of rights for Virginia. George Mason did most of the work, and the provision on religious freedom that Mason proposed for the Declaration of Rights attracted Madison's close attention. Drawing on John Locke and English law, Mason's draft, as modified in committee, provided "that all men should enjoy the fullest toleration in the exercise of religion," consistent with the public safety. Madison's reading and experience had convinced him that "toleration" permitted too much discrimination. The English legal commentator William Blackstone had argued that religious nonconformity was technically a crime; England's Toleration Acts had only suspended the penalties. Although allowed to practice their faith, dissenters faced a series of legal restrictions. Under English law, baptisms and marriages were not recognized unless performed by an Anglican clergyman. Dissenters were barred from English universities and from civil and military offices. In America, before and after the Revolution, Catholics, Jews, Quakers, Unitarians, atheists, and agnostics were often banned by law from public office. As Thomas Paine later wrote, toleration was "not the opposite of intolerance, but . . . the counterfeit of it."[23]

Madison hoped to expand on Mason's language and to disestablish the Anglican Church. Madison apparently prevailed upon Patrick Henry to offer an amendment deleting Mason's reference to "toleration" and replacing it with the assertion that "all men are equally entitled to the full and free exercise" of their faith. No evidence exists that Mason or anyone else objected, but a second provision proved more contentious. Madison proposed that "no man or class of men ought, on account of religion to be invested with peculiar emoluments or privileges," language which presumably would have ended Virginia's responsibility for the salaries of the Anglican clergy. Conservative delegates challenged the clause, but Madison quickly responded with a second amendment that simply recognized an equal right to religious freedom for all citizens. Edmund Pendleton, a much revered conservative and a devout Anglican, introduced the revised amendment, and it passed easily.[24]

Even without language ending public support for the Anglican Church, the Virginia Declaration of Rights, in moving beyond mere toleration, represented a major step toward a modern concept of religious liberty. Reform had not been inevitable; other states would continue restrictive and discriminatory practices well into the nineteenth century. The South Carolina constitution, for example, required public officials to profess belief in the "Protestant Christian Religion." Madison had not, of course, acted alone, and it would take some time for the convention's rhetoric to become reality. The cause of reform benefited from the liberalism of a revolutionary age, Virginia's growing religious diversity, and the English origins of the Anglican Church. James Madison must share credit with George Mason and like-minded delegates who needed only a nudge to expand the rights of conscience and with ordinary church members who demanded religious equality. For purposes of understanding Madison's career, his contribution to the separation of church and state may be less important than what the struggle for freedom of religion meant to him. It led him to think more broadly about civil liberties in general. As we shall see, it turned his creative and persistent intellect to work on the problem of protecting individual rights when the majority rules.[25]

After the adoption of the new state constitution, Madison spent an uneventful term in the House of Delegates. When he ran for reelection in 1777, he refused to "treat" the voters, that is, provide them with liquor on Election Day. Madison believed the practice was "inconsistent with the purity of moral and republican principles." He lost the race, "his abstinence," he wrote later, "being represented as the affect of pride or parsimony."[26]

His colleagues, however, would not leave Madison unemployed. In November 1777, they elected him to the Governor's Council, an eight-member committee charged with advising Virginia's chief executive. The council exercised broad powers. After white residents of Monongalia County demanded protection from Indian raids, Madison, for example, signed an order to deliver 130 rifles to the county lieutenant, with instructions to sell the guns to those inhabitants "most likely to make proper use of them." As was his custom, Madison took his duties seriously, attending over 177 sessions of the council between January 1778, when he joined the body, and December 1779, when he was elected to Congress. Despite his best efforts, the council proved to be an unwieldy structure. Madison later called it "a grave of useful talents." Whatever the council's limitations, the experience allowed Madison to hone his political skills. It also marked the beginning of his friendship with Thomas Jefferson—one of the most momentous political alliances in American history—when Jefferson was elected governor in June 1779.[27] Madison's intelligence, public-spiritedness, and willingness to serve impressed Jefferson and most of Virginia's political elite.

Madison reached Philadelphia in March 1780 for his first session of Congress; the trip from Montpelier took twelve days due to the "extreme badness of the roads and frequency of rains." He moved into a boardinghouse at Fifth and Market Streets run by Mary House and her daughter Eliza Trist. They would become a virtual family; Madison lived with them off and on for the next fifteen years. Madison applied his characteristic diligence to his congressional duties. In a tenure extending from March 1780 until November 1783, he compiled the best attendance record in Congress. Although his attendance became sporadic near the end of his last term, he left Philadelphia only twice, once for a brief vacation in New Jersey and again when Congress moved temporarily to Princeton.[28]

His health held up surprisingly well. In June 1783, he complained to Edmund Randolph of "being somewhat indisposed in my head," but for the most part, his supposedly fragile constitution seemed almost impervious to the stress of service in a wartime legislature.[29] Finances were a far greater problem. A Virginia law passed in December 1779 promised Madison a salary of twenty dollars a day plus expenses, but runaway inflation and the collapse of the state's currency made the promise as worthless as a Continental dollar. All the Virginia delegates complained constantly of their financial distress. By May 1781, Theodorick Bland was reduced to offering his horses for sale to raise meal money. Joseph Jones described service in Congress to Virginia's state auditors: "The wear and tear of horses, carriages, clothing and other extra expenses necessary to the appointment renders the office by no means eligible in point of profit, whatever it may be in point of honor." The economic meltdown left Madison dependent on his family and on generous loans from a local Jewish merchant, Haym Salomon. Madison stayed in Philadelphia partly because he could not afford to go home.[30] He suffered firsthand from the collapse of public finances during the American Revolution, and the experience helps explain his later support for constitutional reform.

In Congress, Madison worked closely with Jones and Randolph, and he allied himself with a pro-French faction associated with the Pennsylvania financier Robert Morris in opposition to a rival camp led by Samuel Adams of Massachusetts and Virginia's prolific Lee family. Arthur Lee in particular had an exacting sense of rectitude that allowed him to see corruption everywhere. When Lee lambasted Silas Deane and Benjamin Franklin, the American commissioners to France, Madison defended them. "Without being a public knave himself," Lee concluded, Madison "has always been the supporter of public knaves." More common were complaints about his lack of social skills. He remained an uninspiring speaker, awkward in large gatherings. Delaware delegate Thomas Rodney found him arrogant and without the grace and "ease which sometimes makes even the impertinence of youth and inexperience agreeable."[31]

Most delegates, by contrast, recognized Madison's abilities and work ethic, and he soon found himself chairing committees and drafting major state papers. Although Madison had only read law sporadically and was never admitted to the bar, Edmund Randolph, a gifted lawyer whose nickname was "the Attorney," wrote Madison in August 1782 asking for his opinion on a matter of admiralty jurisdiction. A few months after the end of the American Revolution, Chevalier de la Luzerne, the French minister to the United States, offered this assessment of Madison: "A man of learning, who desires to do good works and to improve himself, but who is not overly ambitious." Madison's predictable prejudices in favor of Virginia notwithstanding, Luzerne said he was "regarded as the man of the soundest judgment in Congress."[32]

The Virginian generally supported a more vigorous national government, a reasonable and pragmatic stance given the military situation, the monetary crisis, and the weakness of Congress under the Articles of Confederation. Entering Congress as a twenty-nine-year-old rebel in the middle of a revolution, Madison could also show a vindictive, doctrinaire side. He demanded that public officials be held personally liable for the financial misdeeds of their subordinates, a policy that prompted the highly regarded Nathanael Greene to resign as quartermaster general of the Continental Army. Madison supported, with some reluctance, the impressment, or seizure, of private property for military use. He believed that captured Loyalists should be treated as traitors, not as prisoners of war. He balked when Congress agreed, on humanitarian grounds, to exchange two foreign officers who had been taken prisoner while serving with the British. At one point, Madison proposed that Congress order the execution of British officers held by the Americans as retaliation for the burning of American towns. After the American peace commissioner Henry Laurens was captured by the British and then successfully petitioned for his release following several months in prison, Madison wanted him disqualified from representing the United States. Madison thought Laurens's petition had been too conciliatory. Congress disagreed.[33]

Madison might best be described as a moderate, republican nationalist, at least when Virginia's interests could be reconciled with the national interest. Under the Articles of Confederation, the votes of a majority of states were required to pass routine measures. To expedite the business of Congress, Madison argued unsuccessfully that the Articles meant a majority of the states present; frequent absences made it difficult to get seven affirmative votes and hamstrung congressional deliberations.[34] On a more substantive point, he argued that Article 13 gave Congress an "implied power" to enforce its decisions, typically requests for cash or supplies, on the states. In March 1781, Madison proposed that the Articles be amended to recognize explicitly a power of enforcement. "The situation of most of the states is such," he wrote Thomas Jefferson, "that two or three vessels of force employed against their trade will make it in their interest to yield prompt obedience to all just requisitions." Politically, it was a wholly impractical idea.[35] His fellow delegates also turned down a more modest proposal to create a library of Congress containing, among other materials, books on international law and American history. "The want of this information," he argued, "was manifest in several important acts of Congress."[36]

Yet there were limits to Madison's nationalism in the 1780s. He voted, with considerable reservations, to give a charter to Robert Morris's Bank of North America. Suspicious of banks, Madison feared Congress had exceeded its authority, but he trusted Morris's financial acumen and recognized that Morris had already sold subscriptions to the bank based on a reasonable expectation, given earlier resolutions, of congressional support.[37] Madison consistently defended Virginia's prerogatives. When settlers in Kentucky, then one of Virginia's western counties, petitioned Congress for statehood, he insisted that the matter first be referred to the Virginia General Assembly. He fought doggedly to locate a permanent national capital along the Potomac.[38] Madison could support an effective central government in large part because he believed that Virginia, much the largest and most influential of the original thirteen states, would fare better as a member of a viable union than it would as a virtually independent republic. Madison believed Virginia and the southern states would be "opulent" but weak at sea, and he hoped a strong union, with a peacetime navy, could protect the South's trade from "the insults and aggressions of their N. brethren." Madison feared too weak a central government might collapse once independence was won, triggering a commercial war between North and South. In contrast, Virginia could enhance its influence within Congress by supporting the new government.[39]

The most critical issues James Madison faced as a member of Congress involved the sorry state of public finances, the disposition of unappropriated lands west of the Appalachian Mountains, and the recognition by European powers of the territorial rights of the new nation. Madison spent part of the winter of 1779–80 reducing his thoughts about the monetary crisis to writing in an essay titled simply "Money." He concluded, contrary to conventional wisdom, that confidence in the government was more important than the amount of money in circulation in determining its value. Madison favored higher taxes and spending cuts, but shortly before he arrived in Philadelphia, Congress adopted a different plan. The existing Continental currency would be devalued at a rate of forty to one; Congress would surrender the power of printing money to the states, within certain limits; old Continental dollars could be redeemed in the new state currencies; and Congress would rely more heavily on requisitions from the states for funds. The plan shifted power from Congress to the states, and when Madison entered Congress, the American Revolution entered a critical phase. "Our army threatened with an immediate alternative of disbanding or living on free quarter," was the way he described the dilemma to Jefferson. He went on: "Congress from a defect of adequate statesmen [was] more likely to fall into wrong measures and of less weight to enforce right ones."[40]

Madison feared the forty-to-one plan would fail, and it did as hard-pressed state governments continued to issue paper money that quickly depreciated. Congress attempted to stem the inflationary tide by requesting specific supplies rather than money, but it made little difference. The want of sound money, Madison lamented in November 1780, "is the source of all our public difficulties and misfortunes." He eventually came to favor an amendment to the Articles giving Congress the right to impose a tariff, or impost as it was more often called. After the Rhode Island legislature rejected one impost—amendments to the Articles required unanimous consent—and Virginia, to Madison's dismay, withdrew its earlier approval, Congress gave him the task of drafting a new plan.[41]

The assignment produced two of Madison's first important state papers, the Report on Restoring Public Credit of 6 March 1783, and the Address to the States of 25 April 1783. A compromise forged in committee, the report proposed Congress be empowered to adopt a duty of 5 percent on most imports for a period not to exceed twenty-five years. Proceeds would be earmarked for payment of the war debt, and revenues would be collected by officials appointed by the states. Madison believed the preservation of republican virtue and the survival of a national union depended on payment of the public debt. Nothing, he argued in debate, could more undermine "our republican character and constitutions, than a violation of the maxims of good faith and common honesty." If Congress could not pay its bills, creditors would look to the states for relief. Madison did not expect a financially irrelevant union to survive, and he raised again, this time on the floor of Congress, the specter of a maritime trade war between North and South. Nevertheless, the impost failed badly even in Virginia, where, Joseph Jones reported to Madison, "we are much in want of useful men."[42]

Issues related to the Revolutionary War debts would linger into the 1790s and create partisan divisions that would in turn help produce America's first political parties. Ironically, Madison in the 1780s proposed that Congress assume the war debts of the states, and he opposed discrimination between the primary and secondary holders of government securities. By the 1790s, he had changed positions, the historian Robert Rutland has suggested, as public debts became increasingly concentrated in the hands of northern speculators. Other evidence suggests Madison was less aggressive in his fiscal nationalism than were Robert Morris or New York's Alexander Hamilton. Hoping to tie investors to the national government in perpetuity, they wanted to make the national debt permanent. Madison wanted to pay it off as soon as possible. Hamilton, who would become Madison's bête noire in the 1790s, opposed the import plan of 1783 as timid and inadequate.[43]

The Franco-American victory over the British at Yorktown in October 1781 and the prospect of peace had only aggravated the financial crisis. Congress's many creditors included the officers and soldiers of the Continental Army, who were reluctant to go home without being paid. As Madison explained to Edmund Randolph, "Without money there is some reason to surmise that it may be as difficult to disband as it has been to raise an army."

A mutiny on New Year's Day in 1781 among unpaid Pennsylvania troops disgruntled with state authorities had led to two deaths. Discontent in the army continued to fester. In the spring of 1783, about a hundred men from a Virginia cavalry unit mutinied near Salem, North Carolina.[44]

Meanwhile, Madison began to hear reports of a possible revolt closer to Philadelphia. On 20 June 1783, about eighty soldiers, led by their sergeants, marched into the city from Lancaster. According to the notes Madison kept of congressional proceedings, "They professed to have no other object than to obtain a settlement of accounts." The following day, they surrounded the State House, where Congress met. "No danger from premeditated violence was apprehended," Madison noted. "But it was observed that spirituous drink from the tipling houses adjoining began to be liberally served out to the soldiers, and might lead to hasty excesses." Congress ultimately decided to abandon Philadelphia and reconvene in Princeton. Adding insult to injury, Pennsylvania officials, fearing their own troops were not entirely reliable, refused to mobilize the state militia to defend Congress.[45]

The move to Princeton meant that Madison would have to trade Mary House's hospitality for the cramped quarters of a small college town. "We are exceedingly crowded in this place; too much so both for our own comfort and for the dispatch of business," he wrote his father in August 1783. "Mr. Jones and my self are in one room scarcely ten foot square and in one bed." He resented a piqued Congress's refusal to return to Philadelphia once the apparent danger had passed, and going back to the city himself, he missed as many debates as he attended.[46]

One partial solution to its financial woes was for Congress to acquire and then sell the vast tracts of western lands claimed by several of the states, including Virginia, which asserted rights to Kentucky and hundreds of thousands of acres north of the Ohio River. In September 1780, Congress adopted a committee report calling on the states to cede their western lands to Congress. Paradoxically, Virginia had reasons to give up its claims; Joseph Jones had served on the congressional committee, and back in Virginia, George Mason had already drafted terms for a transfer of title. The area could not be effectively governed from Richmond; Virginia's pretensions only incited the jealousy of the other states; and, to the extent land sales could provide Congress with a source of revenue, they would alleviate congressional demands on the Old Dominion.

The settlement of a long-standing border dispute between Virginia and Pennsylvania seemed to have created an opportunity to solve the larger issue in the summer of 1780. But Mason, Jones, and, by September at the latest, Madison, attached several conditions to the Virginia cession, chief among them a requirement that Congress not recognize the validity of private purchases of Indian land. Such purchases were generally void under Virginia law, a technicality that had not deterred out-of-state speculators and a few Virginians. If, however, the speculators were held to own most of the land at the time it came under congressional jurisdiction, one reason for the cession would disappear, since this would deny Congress the proceeds from sales of the land the speculators claimed. Madison himself stayed clear of the land companies; he had made it a rule "never to deal in public property, land, debts or money, whilst a member of the body whose proceedings might influence these transactions."[47]

Congress initially refused to accept any conditions, and Maryland, a "landless" state where the speculators wielded considerable influence, refused to ratify the Articles of Confederation until Virginia dropped its opposition to the Indian purchases. Events pushed the parties toward a compromise. On 2 January 1781, as British raiding parties led by Benedict Arnold ravaged the Chesapeake Bay, the Virginia General Assembly approved a formal, but still conditional, cession. Shortly thereafter, Maryland, under pressure from the French minister Luzerne, who preferred a united ally to a divided one, approved the Articles. Still, Congress rejected Virginia's conditions. As the issue dragged on into the fall, Madison grew worried that the assembly would withdraw the cession and wreck any chance for an agreement. By spring, Madison had almost lost patience with Congress. If the issue were not soon resolved, Virginia's lawmakers, he decided, would "certainly be fully justified in taking any course with respect to their western claims which the interest of the state shall prescribe."[48]

His frustration notwithstanding, Madison persisted. Working with his old Princeton mentor John Witherspoon, now a member of Congress from New Jersey, Madison negotiated a compromise acceptable to Virginia and most of the states. Congress agreed to several of Virginia's conditions, including a demand that the ceded territory should eventually be divided into several new states. Virginia's claim to its remaining territory was confirmed, and Congress "tacitly" denied the validity of private purchases of Indian lands, a result suggested by language providing that the ceded lands would be held for the common benefit of all the states.[49]

In a debate that lasted for three years, Madison consistently advocated compromise. He tried to balance Virginia's interest with the national interest. When Congress drafted a statement of principles for peace talks with the British, Madison accepted the argument that, once America declared its independence, Britain's purported title to the backlands had devolved upon the United States. The position was wholly inconsistent with Virginia's claims, but Madison knew it had support among the other states; he thought it might be of use to the American peace commissioners. And as the historian Peter Onuf has pointed out, state and national interests were not wholly incompatible. It was important to the "landed" states that cessions be negotiated and not imposed. Voluntary transfers of title established the precedent that Congress would respect the territorial integrity of the states, which eventually made it a little easier to confer new powers on the national government.[50]

The cession of western lands would be meaningless unless the European powers recognized the Mississippi River as the western border of the United States, and the value of those lands would be greatly diminished unless the new republic secured the right to navigate the Mississippi. On both issues, Madison took a strongly nationalistic position and plunged into the thick of the debate. In October 1780, Congress authorized John Jay to negotiate a treaty of alliance with Spain, which then held Louisiana and the port of New Orleans. Madison drafted instructions to Jay directing him to insist on Spanish recognition of an American right to use the river. As parts of South Carolina and Georgia fell under British occupation, their delegates, desperate for Spanish assistance, proposed modifying Jay's instructions. Madison wanted to hold fast to the original instructions, but another Virginia delegate, Theodorick Bland, disagreed and wrote Governor Jefferson urging the state to support revisions. "You will readily conceive," Madison wrote Joseph Jones, "the embarrassments this affair must have cost me." In January 1781, besieged by Arnold's troops in the Chesapeake Bay, the Virginia assembly voted to demand only a right to navigate the Mississippi where it touched American territory if more extensive claims were "deemed an impediment to a treaty with Spain." Congress quickly complied, and workhorse that he was, Madison was assigned the task of drafting the new instructions to Jay.[51]

Madison tried repeatedly to revive the original American demands on Spain, but he was more deferential toward France. In some of the darkest days of the war, Congress, seeking to cement its alliance with France, instructed its diplomats to follow the lead of the French in any future peace talks with Great Britain. When American prospects brightened after the British defeat at Yorktown, some members of Congress proposed that U.S. diplomats be given the authority to act independently of the French. Admitting the original instructions represented "a sacrifice of dignity to policy,"

Madison persuaded Congress to leave them intact. He did not, he told his fellow delegates, want Europeans to believe that "we are a people unstable in our councils and measures, governed wholly by circumstances."[52]

Madison opposed the effort to amend the original charges to the peace commissioners in part because he believed it played into what he saw as a British plan to break up the Franco-American alliance. The American Revolution bred in Madison an animosity toward Great Britain that never disappeared. "No description," he wrote Philip Mazzei in July 1781, "can give you an adequate idea of the barbarity with which the enemy have conducted the war in the southern states." He wrote later that Lord Cornwallis's campaign in Virginia was "the most barbarous" in modern history.[53] In retrospect, American independence seems to have been inevitable after the capture of Cornwallis's army at Yorktown, but it took almost two years to negotiate a peace treaty. In the long interval between Yorktown and the Treaty of Paris of 1783, Madison came to suspect the British would try to achieve through diplomatic chicanery what they had not been able to win honorably on the battlefield. Consideration of a possible commercial treaty with Great Britain unnerved him. He feared discrimination against southern shipping, and he knew American interests would change over time. Commercial treaties, he believed, should be limited to "moderate periods," and he wanted to leave the door open to the adoption of a protective tariff.[54]

His suspicion of the British contrasted sharply with his affinity toward the French. Early in September 1781, he watched with other members of Congress as Comte de Rochambeau's army marched through Philadelphia on its way to Yorktown. "Nothing can exceed the appearance of this specimen which our ally has sent us of his army." After the French troops had reached Virginia, Madison's correspondents sent him glowing reports of their professionalism and civility. A year later, as French troops returned to Philadelphia on their way to New York, Madison could write, "The praises bestowed on their discipline and sobriety in Virginia, are repeated here with equal cordiality and justice." These impressions had political consequences. "Nothing but staunch republicanism," Edmund Randolph wrote Madison in January 1783, "and a due attachment to the French alliance will ever be acceptable to Virginia."[55]

Term limits imposed by the Articles of Confederation brought Madison's congressional career to a close in the fall of 1783. He seemed ready to leave Congress, although he worried that a frequent "change of members and of circumstances often proves fatal to [the] consistency and stability of public measures." Thomas Jefferson called Congress "a good school for our young statesmen," and Madison had graduated at the top of his class. An unusual combination of persistence, intelligence, revolutionary ardor, and a moderate nationalism had made James Madison the most effective politician in Congress.[56] It remained to be seen what the distinction was worth. There was, in reality, something strangely adolescent about Madison's years in Philadelphia. Unmarried and unattached, financially dependent on his parents, and with no fixed plans for the future, Madison in Congress often resembles nothing so much as a modern undergraduate, or perhaps, given his workload, a harried graduate student. In other words, he was not yet a Founding Father, and when he returned to Virginia, he would find himself, in more ways than one, back where he had begun.

At home at Montpelier, Madison resumed reading law, and he continued his studies intermittently for the next two years. It was almost as if he needed to maintain the fiction that he was preparing for a legal career. Given the lax standards of the day, a person of Madison's intelligence could have learned enough law in six weeks to be admitted to the bar.[57] In reality, he had no desire to practice law. His father gave him 560 acres, but with little real interest in farming, Madison stayed at Montpelier. Jefferson invited him to settle near Monticello; he demurred. While Jefferson was serving as American minister to France, he invited Madison to visit him. For two hundred guineas, Jefferson wrote, "you will . . . have purchased the knowledge of another world." Madison responded with a series of excuses, among them "that crossing the sea would be unfriendly to a singular disease of my constitution." In the fall of 1784, he toured upstate New York with the Marquis de Lafayette. A year later, when James Monroe suggested they make a trip west, Madison pled poverty. Among several obstacles: "My resources do not authorize me to disregard that of expense."[58]

By then he was back in his element. In April 1784, Orange County voters had elected him to the Virginia House of Delegates. Because real power under the Articles of Confederation rested with the states, Madison may have exercised more influence as a member of the Virginia assembly than he had as a member of Congress. Younger, and presumably more reform-minded, legislators looked to him for leadership.[59]

He took on a range of issues with mixed results. Convinced that Virginia's 1776 constitution did not provide for a true separation of powers or fairly apportion seats in the legislature, he pushed unsuccessfully for constitutional reform. To better control smuggling and to improve the collection of customs duties, he proposed legislation limiting foreign vessels to Norfolk and Alexandria; he was forced to accept crippling amendments. At George Washington's request, he steered to passage bills chartering corporations to improve the James and Potomac Rivers. Washington and Madison had first met in 1781 as Washington traveled from New York to Yorktown. Cooperation on the navigation bills solidified their friendship. He had less success persuading the assembly to provide Congress with a steady source of revenue or in allowing British merchants, as called for in the Treaty of Paris, to collect debts incurred by Virginians before the Revolution. He made a major effort to create courts of assize, a system of circuit courts staffed by professional judges that would have curbed the authority of the amateurs who dominated the county courts. The assembly passed an assize bill, delayed its implementation, and, in 1788, repealed it.[60]

Much of Madison's legislative work involved his efforts to resurrect a revised legal code that had been completed in 1779. Jefferson had drafted large parts of the new code, and some of it had passed quickly. Most of it had not. In the fall session of 1785, Madison introduced the outstanding bills. At first, Madison directed bill after bill through the House. "He has astonished Mankind," wrote delegate Archibald Stuart, "and has by means perfectly constitutional become almost a Dictator." But progress slowed when the debate reached Bill No. 64, which attempted to make Virginia's criminal law more humane by reducing the number of capital offenses. The legislative foot-dragging led Stuart to describe the session as "the most stupid, knavish and designing Assembly that ever sat." As proof, he offered "no other argument . . . but that Madison after the first three weeks lost all weight in the House." Madison responded by shifting tactics and concentrating on the most significant proposals. He ultimately passed over forty bills from the proposed new code. After the legislature adjourned, Madison assessed the session for James Monroe: "If its importance were to be measured by the list of all the laws it has produced, all preceding legislative merit would be eclipsed. . . . If we recur to the proper criterion no session has perhaps afforded less ground for applause."[61]

One of the bills stalled in the assembly was No. 82, the Bill for Religious Freedom. Intended to repudiate the very principle of state aid to religion, the bill had been drafted by Thomas Jefferson in 1777. It triggered what Jefferson called "the severest contest in which I have ever been engaged." The assembly had already suspended tax collections to pay the salaries of Anglican ministers, but it retained the right to license clergy and meetinghouses, and until the fall 1784 session only marriages performed by Anglican divines were recognized as valid. By the end of the Revolution, the established church rested on a shaky foundation. The number of Anglican clergy had dwindled during the war, and the so-called dissenting sects, mainly Baptists and Presbyterians, had come to represent a majority of the church-going population. Meanwhile, religion produced interminable wrangling whenever it surfaced as a political issue. In May 1783, Patrick Henry moved that the House of Delegates resume its former practice of appointing a chaplain to begin each session with a prayer. The delegates agreed, and then fell out fighting over the wording of the prayer.[62]

Many conservative Episcopalians feared their church could not survive without state support, and it had long been assumed that the social order required an established faith. Among the American colonies, only Pennsylvania and Rhode Island had lacked one. Revival of the old regime in Virginia after the Revolution was politically impossible, but the idea of a general assessment—a tax levied on behalf of all churches, or at least all Protestant denominations—enjoyed considerable popularity. Most Episcopalians, and many Presbyterians, seemed likely to support it. Distinctions between the two seemed to be eroding, especially in the Piedmont. Indeed, in the absence of an Anglican priest, the vestry of Madison's home church in Orange County had invited a Presbyterian to conduct services.[63]

In its May 1784 session, the assembly had taken up a general assessment bill and a bill effectively incorporating the Anglican Church under the control of the Episcopal clergy. Despite powerful support from Patrick Henry, both measures were deferred to the October session. Dissenters saw the incorporation bill as a backhanded attempt to revive the old establishment.[64]

As he sometimes did, Henry went home in the middle of the fall session, "a circumstance very inauspicious to his offspring." Even without Henry, the general assessment enjoyed impressive support. Richard Henry Lee, for example, argued that a nondiscriminatory assessment would not violate the provisions protecting freedom of religion in the Virginia Declaration of Rights. In reality, few of the bill's Anglican supporters envisioned supporting non-Christians; it was specifically intended to subsidize "teachers of the Christian religion." Madison spoke against the bill, but his oratory was not apt to derail a popular measure. A legislative ploy proved more effective. He agreed to support an amended version of the bill incorporating the Episcopal Church that would put the church under the control of a convention composed of clergy and laity. Madison could defend the bill on its merits: the church needed to be recognized as a legal entity in order to own property. More important, it served his tactical purposes. Defeat of an incorporation bill, Madison reasoned, would intensify the Anglican demand for tax dollars. Its passage, in contrast, seemed likely to aggravate the dissenters' anxieties about the return of the establishment and make an assessment bill look even more sinister. Unable to defeat the assessment outright, Madison persuaded the assembly to postpone a final vote until its next session.[65]

After the legislature adjourned, Madison reported to James Monroe that "the assessment was the only proceeding of the late Session of the Assembly which makes a noise thro' the country." Madison believed support for the measure was fading among Episcopalians, and among the other denominations, only the Presbyterian clergy favored it. The latter seemed, he told Monroe, "as ready to set up an establishment which is to take them in as they were to pull down that which shut them out."[66]

Madison fumed later that spring when he heard Congress was considering legislation to set aside public land in the Northwest Territory for the support of religion. "How a regulation, so unjust in itself," he wrote Monroe, "so foreign to the authority of Congress, so hurtful to the sale of public land, and smelling so strongly of an antiquated bigotry, could have received the countenance of a committee is truly [a] matter of astonishment." Madison hoped the upcoming elections would eliminate several legislative advocates of a general assessment, but he apparently intended to stay out of the public debate, until he received a letter from George Nicholas in April urging him to enter the fray.[67]

Madison responded quickly. He probably needed little encouragement, and by the end of June 1785 he had completed one of his most memorable public papers, a fifteen-paragraph petition titled the "Memorial and Remonstrance against Religious Assessments." He began by citing the Virginia Declaration of Rights, which had recognized religion as "a duty towards the creator," language he interpreted as putting religion beyond the cognizance of either civil society or the state. He invoked a familiar republican maxim: "It is proper to take alarm at the first experiment on our liberties." If the state could "establish Christianity, in exclusion of all other Religions"—and by "establish" he clearly meant provide financial aid—it could with "the same ease" establish "any particular sect of Christians, in exclusion of all other sects." State aid was inherently discriminatory; the assessment bill had exempted Quakers and Mennonites, who lacked a regular clergy, and it would force the state to define Christianity, since only recognized Christian churches could benefit from its provisions.

Some of Madison's arguments, for example that the bill would have encouraged emigration from Virginia, seem less than compelling, but he left no doubt that an alliance between church and state could corrupt both. In the past, "religion both existed and flourished, not only without the support of human laws, but in spite of every opposition from them." When the state had embraced the church, "what have been its fruits? More or less in all places, pride and indolence in the clergy, ignorance and civility in the laity, in both, superstition, bigotry and persecution." The political consequences of an alliance between religion and government were equally catastrophic. "In some instances they have been seen to erect a spiritual tyranny on the ruins of the civil authority; in many instances they have been seen upholding the thrones of political tyranny; in no instance have they been seen the guardians of the liberties of the people."

George Nicholas and others helped circulate the "Memorial and Remonstrance" in the Piedmont. George Mason had a copy printed in Alexandria. In all, thirteen copies circulated throughout the Virginia countryside, garnering 1,552 signatures, including those of eleven women in Westmoreland County. Madison had penned the classic statement, surely the most influential in American history, for the separation of church and state, but he kept his authorship secret until he disclosed it in a letter to George Mason's grandson in July 1826. The editors of the modern edition of Madison's papers speculate that he may have feared offending lawmakers whose cooperation he needed on other issues. Perhaps, but his opposition to the general assessment bill was already well known. Paradoxically, the "Memorial and Remonstrance" may have had less impact on the assembly than a petition by an anonymous evangelical that circulated more widely and attracted far more signatures.[68]

Over the summer, public opinion turned decisively against the assessment. By the middle of June, Madison expressed doubt that, if it passed, it could be enforced in the back counties. By the middle of August, he could report to Jefferson that even the Presbyterian clergy had abandoned it, "being moved either by a fear of their laity or a jealousy of the Episcopalians." Much to Madison's relief, the incorporation of the Episcopal Church had inflamed the "mutual hatred of these sects." A coalition between Episcopalians and Presbyterians, he feared, would jeopardize freedom of religion in Virginia.[69]

When the state legislature convened in the fall, the sponsors of the general assessment bill did not bring it up for a vote. So changed was the political climate that Madison went on the offensive, pushing for passage of Jefferson's long-delayed Bill for Religious Freedom. The bill consisted of three paragraphs. The first rested the case for the rights of conscience on an argument that might surprise modern advocates of the separation of church and state: "Almighty God hath created the mind free," and state regulation represented "a departure from the plan of the Holy author of our religion." Madison defeated an effort by conservatives to add a reference to Christ to the preamble. The second paragraph renounced the idea of state aid to religion. The third paragraph, written before courts had begun to strike down laws that violated constitutional liberties, tried to protect the rights of conscience by warning future lawmakers that repeal of the bill would be "an infringement of natural right."[70]

The bill passed in January 1786 with only minor amendments. Madison reported his victory to Jefferson almost immediately: "I flatter myself [that we] have in this country extinguished for ever the ambitious hope of making laws for the human mind." Jefferson ranked the bill among his greatest accomplishments, and historians have usually described it as an almost unprecedented blow for religious liberty.[71] In reality, the bill echoed principles expressed ten years earlier in the Virginia Declaration of Rights, and it codified what had become the practice in Virginia. It might best be seen as the tombstone marking the grave of the general assessment bill.

James Madison came out of the debate more convinced than ever that without freedom of religion, other rights could not long survive. A legislature that could curtail one liberty could extinguish them all. The American Revolution, he could see, had not secured individual rights, and independence had not guaranteed Americans good government. Madison's service in Congress had often been an exercise in futility, and his years in the Virginia House of Delegates had been almost as frustrating. The experiences had undermined his faith in majority rule, or at least demonstrated a need for greater checks and balances to protect individual rights and give stability to public measures. His victories in the battle for religious freedom suggested a solution. He believed the general assessment bill had failed because of jealousies among Virginia's various denominations; none of them trusted their rivals to share fairly the government largesse. In one of the most celebrated insights of his career, Madison came to believe that similar "factions," if properly harnessed, could be used at the national level to create an informal system of checks and balances that might prevent the adoption of oppressive legislation.[72]

"Conscience," Madison believed, "is the most sacred of all property," and he would return to the issue of church-state relations time and time again. He debated with his friend Jefferson the propriety of excluding ministers from the legislature. Jefferson, striving to maintain the separation of church and state, initially supported their exclusion. Madison eventually convinced him the state should not discriminate against the clergy.[73] During the debate over the ratification of the U.S. Constitution, Madison at first opposed the addition of a bill of rights, in part because he feared it would offer too little protection to religious freedom, and by implication limit the people's rights. His Baptist constituents disagreed, and mainly to appease them, he agreed, as a candidate for Congress, to support a bill of rights. After he entered Congress, he proposed a set of amendments that were more sweeping than what became the First Amendment. He wanted to protect religious freedom from state as well as federal action, and he wanted to ensure that "no person religiously scrupulous of bearing arms shall be compelled to render military service in person." He also opposed immigration policies that tended to discriminate against Catholics.[74]

In 1798, Madison criticized the Alien and Sedition Acts, which curtailed freedom of the press by restricting criticism of the federal government, as a precedent that might support laws infringing on freedom of religion.[75] When he became president in 1809, he declared that he intended "to avoid the slightest interference with the rights of conscience, or the functions of religion so wisely exempted from civil jurisdiction." In 1810, he signed legislation, over the opposition of many religious leaders, to authorize Sunday mail delivery; the practice continued until 1912. In 1811, he vetoed a bill giving public land in the Mississippi Territory to the Salem Meeting House Baptists; several Baptist churches in North Carolina wrote him to commend him for his action. He also vetoed a law incorporating an Episcopal church in the District of Columbia; it contained a provision for selecting and removing ministers that Madison believed was beyond the proper purview of Congress. He also objected to language authorizing the church to support the poor and to educate poor children. The church could undertake such charity without the blessings of the state; otherwise it "would be a precedent for giving religious societies as such, a legal agency in carrying into effect a public and civil duty."[76]

As president, Madison did not insist that the federal government divorce itself entirely from matters of faith. Because of a lack of space elsewhere, public buildings in Washington, D.C., were often used for religious services. Madison attended, at least occasionally. On 29 May 1812, the president and First Lady Dolley Madison heard Reverend James Brackinridge, a Presbyterian minister, condemn members of Congress for breaking the Sabbath.

Like "Ninevah of old," Brackinridge warned, "your palaces will be burned to the ground." After the British burned the capital during the War of 1812, Dolley Madison told Brackinridge she had "little thought [that his] denunciation would so soon be realized."[77]

As Madison grew older, he did not become more pious; he only seemed to become more committed to the separation of church and state. Scholars have debated whether his views on the issue betrayed a certain hostility to religion itself, and the evidence is mixed.[78] Back at Montpelier after leaving the White House, Madison seemed pleased with the fruits of tolerance in Virginia: "The number, the industry, and the morality of the Priesthood, and the devotion of the people have been manifestly increased by the total separation of the church from the state." Yet even his Baptist supporters would not go as far as Madison. They opposed state financial aid to churches, but they supported laws requiring church attendance and establishing religious qualifications for holding public office. Madison had doubted moral scruples could serve as a reliable check on the popular will. He wrote in 1787 that "religion in its coolest state, is not infallible." When "kindled into enthusiasm . . . it may become a motive to oppression as well as a restraint from injustice." Events made him more wary. Among his fiercest critics during the War of 1812 had been the Congregationalist and Unitarian clergy of New England. "The greater part of the people in that quarter," he complained in November 1814, "have been brought by their leaders, aided by their priests, under a delusion scarcely exceeded by that recorded in the period of witchcraft."[79]

In retirement, Madison worried about seemingly innocuous accommodations between church and state. He disapproved of the practice of putting congressional and military chaplains on the public payroll. Minority faiths would inevitably be victims of discrimination. Members of Congress, he thought, would set a better example if they paid their chaplains out of their own pockets. He worried about the days of prayer and fasting he had proclaimed as president. The practice had a long history. "But I was always careful to make the Proclamations absolutely indiscriminate, and merely recommendatory." He had several reservations. "They seem to imply and certainly nourish the erroneous idea of a *national* religion." Proclamations tended to conform "to the standard of the predominant sect," and the majority party would be tempted to use them for political purposes, as the Federalists had done in the 1790s.[80]

While Madison showed no animosity toward religion as a matter of personal faith, it seems fair to conclude that his anxieties about religion in the public realm went beyond concerns about an unholy alliance between church and state. They included the misuse of the power of entrenched, institutional religion. In a memorandum he wrote in 1819, Madison warned that incorporating churches allowed them to become "perpetual monopolies" likely over the years to acquire great wealth. He suggested that limits might be placed on the amount of property a church could own: "The danger of silent accumulations and encroachments by Ecclesiastical Bodies have not sufficiently engaged attention." In 1823, Madison defended the decision of the University of Virginia not to hire a professor of religion. "A University with sectarian professorships becomes, of course, a sectarian monopoly: with professorships of rival sects, it would be an arena of Theological Gladiators. . . . There seems to be no alternative between a public university without a theological professorship, and sectarian seminaries without a University." He also opposed hiring professors who were also members of the clergy. Teachers, he thought, ought to demonstrate "a proper respect for Religion," but if ministers joined the faculty, one sect would likely become dominant and provoke hostility toward the university from all the others.[81]

By January 1786, after a decade of almost unbroken public service, Madison's most enduring accomplishments—in particular, authorship of the "Memorial and Remonstrance," defeat of the general assessment bill, and passage of the Bill for Religious Freedom—had come in the struggle for liberty of conscience. He had learned the value of playing competing factions, in this case Virginia's rival denominations, against one another, and he would put the insight to good use as he turned to his next great challenge.

{ C H A P T E R   T W O }

A Republican Constitution

*I*n a speech in 1827, the Philadelphia lawyer and politician Charles J. Ingersoll called James Madison the "Father of the Constitution," and the appellation stuck. Madison denied it, writing another admirer, "You give me credit to which I have no claim. . . . This was not like the fabled goddess of wisdom the offspring of a single brain. It ought to be regarded as the work of many heads and many hands."[1]

He had reasons to be modest. He knew he had shared the stage at the Philadelphia convention of 1787 with a remarkable collection of political talent. His colleagues often got the better of him. The historian Forrest McDonald has calculated that of seventy-one proposals Madison supported in Philadelphia, he lost on forty. After months of preparation, he took his seat in the convention with only the vaguest notions about how a new national government might operate. He advanced some bad ideas, and he clung tenaciously to some unworkable ones. McDonald called him "an ideologue in search of an ideology."[2] If Madison had won on the issue of allocating seats in Congress, the convention probably would have broken up without reaching a consensus. If the delegates had adopted the constitution Madison wanted, it never would have been ratified by the individual states.

But Charles Ingersoll did not miss the mark by much. From supporting the idea of a constitutional convention to laboring tirelessly for ratification of the convention's handiwork, Madison remained in the thick of the battle for constitutional reform. He attended every session of the Philadelphia convention and spoke up, by one count, two hundred times. Only Pennsylvania's dapper Gouverneur Morris may have been more voluble.[3]

And the other delegates listened. Madison's blandness in formal settings served him well. As Joseph Ellis puts it, "He seemed to lack a personal agenda because he seemed to lack a personality." Madison never allowed himself to become the issue. In the opinion of Thomas Jefferson, who was not in Philadelphia, after a decade of public service, Madison had acquired a self-control and a wealth of information that "rendered him the first of every assembly . . . of which he became a member."[4] The Georgia delegate William Pierce, who was in Philadelphia, called him the "best informed man of any point in debate."[5]

To be sure, the Constitution that Madison more or less fathered was more a matter of improvisation than the result of a master plan. Contrary to Charles Beard's notorious claims a century ago, it was not a plot to protect the financial interests of delegates who held unusual amounts of government securities. Nor in Madison's case should the Constitution be seen simply as an effort to preserve aristocratic rule in the face of democratic tendencies unleashed by the American Revolution, as some modern historians might argue.[6] Instead, by 1787, Madison had become convinced that the failures of the young republic's political institutions at both the state and national levels presented a threat to minority rights and a potential hazard to the very idea of republican government. Madison's most important contributions to the cause of a republican constitution are a matter of reasonable debate, but two stand out: the insight that ideas about constitution-making that had been developed in the states could be applied at the national level and the notion that a reformed national government could be used to protect individual liberties within the states. To achieve his larger aims, Madison compromised grudgingly and accepted, however reluctantly, defeat on lesser points. Notwithstanding his occasional stubbornness and a penchant for ideologically elegant but impractical solutions, his greatest assets would prove to be his intelligence, persistence, and a rather remarkable adaptability.

The American economy struggled in the 1780s. Wages and prices fell, and the new nation suffered an unfavorable balance of trade. Before the Revolution, the British Navigation Acts protected American merchants from foreign competition. These acts went away with independence. Among other new restrictions, the British West Indies were closed to American shipping, and Great Britain prohibited its subjects from buying ships in the United States. Before the war a third of the vessels in the British merchant fleet had been built in America.[7]

The economic woes undermined an already feeble political system. Without the power to tax or to regulate trade, Congress could neither pay its bills nor protect American merchants and shippers from foreign competition. A modest tariff or duty on imports could have gone a long way toward solving both problems. There was widespread support for giving Congress the power to regulate and tax foreign trade, but amendments to the Articles of Confederation required the unanimous consent of the states, which could never agree on the details of a plan. Congress continued to rely on voluntary requisitions from the states; they typically provided less than 40 percent of the funds requested. The United States found itself borrowing money from Dutch bankers to pay the interest on earlier loans; even so, by 1785 Congress had defaulted on its interest payments to the French government. As the federal Constitutional Convention completed its work in Philadelphia in September 1787, the first principal payment on the French debt came due, and Congress had no money to pay it.[8]

"Congress," Madison wrote Jefferson in October 1785, "have kept the vessel from sinking, but it has been by standing constantly at the pump, not by stopping the leaks which have endangered her." Inaction did not help. Madison reported from New York to his brother Ambrose in August 1786, "Nothing can bear a worse aspect than our federal affairs as viewed from this position. No money comes into the public treasury, trade is on a wretched footing, and the States are running mad after paper money." In fact, "at the head" of the nation's ills, Madison "put the general rage for paper money." By 1786, seven states had issued paper currency, with Rhode Island the most infamous of the group. State paper tended to lose value quickly, allowing debtors to pay their bills in deflated dollars. Madison and others considered it a fraud on creditors that hurt the economy generally and drove specie out of circulation. Madison also feared paper emissions could create tensions among the states if they balked at accepting one another's currency.[9]

One possible solution to the crisis was the special convention. Local and regional meetings to address economic issues had been held during the Revolution; conventions in New England in 1780 and 1781 had proposed giving additional powers to Congress. In June 1784, Madison introduced in the House of Delegates a resolution calling for a meeting of representatives from Virginia and Maryland to draft an agreement regulating the use of the Potomac River. What became known as the Mount Vernon Conference, which met in March 1785, led eventually to the federal Constitutional Convention, but only by the most circuitous path. In January 1786, when the House of Delegates took up the recommendations of the Mount Vernon Conference, John Tyler, father of a future president, introduced a resolution calling for a meeting of all the states on the issue of trade regulation. It passed by large margins, and the legislature named Madison to the Virginia delegation. Although Madison later took credit for drafting the resolution, he had earlier expressed skepticism about a national convention, suspecting that some of the idea's supporters hoped more debate would forestall substantive reform. Indeed, even though the convention was to be held in Annapolis, the Maryland senate blocked that state's participation out of fear the meeting would actually undermine support for Congress.[10]

Over the next few weeks, Madison reconciled himself to the Annapolis Convention. "I almost despair of success," he wrote Jefferson, but he saw two reasons why reform could not be delayed: political instability invited "foreign machinations," and as new states entered the Union, finding a consensus on the needed reforms would become more difficult. Failure would at least let nationalists know where they stood. Efforts to amend the Articles of Confederation in the state legislatures had repeatedly been defeated. At the same time, when Charles Pinckney of South Carolina proposed that Congress call a general constitutional convention, Madison opposed the idea. Virtually simultaneous conventions struck him as impractical, but if the delegates who would meet in Annapolis on 13 September could agree to give Congress the power to regulate trade, one reform could set the stage for more.[11]

Madison's continuing caution resulted in part from the acrid controversy over the right of the United States to navigate the Mississippi River, an issue that had festered since the Revolution. Spain closed the river to American traffic in June 1784; Congress quickly responded by authorizing John Jay, the secretary for foreign affairs, to open negotiations with the Spanish diplomat Don Diego de Gardoqui to lift the ban. Talks went on for months before Jay and de Gardoqui reached a tentative agreement: the United States would accept the closure of the Mississippi for a defined period—perhaps twenty-five to thirty years—in exchange for commercial concessions from Spain. Jay made a formal proposal to Congress in May 1786. Southerners were aghast. Loss of access to the Mississippi would retard the development of the Deep South and mean fewer slave states in the immediate future. It would also reduce the value of public lands in the West, Congress's most valuable asset. "Can there be," Madison asked James Monroe, "a more shortsighted or dishonorable policy?" Congress voted seven to five to repeal its instructions requiring Jay to seek access to the river, but because it took nine votes to approve a treaty, the secretary's initiative was effectively stalled, at least temporarily.[12]

Yet the damage had been done to the cause of a more energetic national government. James Monroe, who led opposition to the Jay-Gardoqui treaty in Congress, claimed he spied a conspiracy by New England to preserve its influence by keeping the western territories out of the Union or by splitting the confederacy. For his part, Madison wondered how he could persuade Virginia lawmakers to trust the northern majority in Congress with new powers. As he wrote Jefferson, the Mississippi controversy could "be fatal I fear to an augmentation of federal authority." Madison agreed in November 1786 to return to Congress so he could carry on the battle against the Jay-Gardoqui treaty.[13]

By the spring of 1786, Madison had concluded that Americans would soon be forced to decide whether the Union was worth saving. Conditions in Virginia were as bleak as those in Congress. "The internal situation of this state is growing worse and worse. Our specie has vanished," and as tobacco prices fell, "the people are again plunged into debt to the merchants." Efforts to relieve debtors only made matters worse. Emissions of paper money and laws postponing the collection of debts and the payment of taxes, Madison believed, drove hard currency out of the market and contributed to an unfavorable balance of trade. Money collected in taxes would be put back in circulation by the state, but when taxes were deferred, those dollars went into the hands of foreign merchants and aggravated the specie shortage.[14]

To Madison, the republic's ills were all related, and they called for a comprehensive political economy. As he told Jefferson, "Most of our political evils may be traced to our commercial ones, as most of our moral may be to our political." His support for hard money ought not to be interpreted as a sign of indifference to the plight of cash-strapped farmers. He believed paper money and inflation mainly benefited speculators, even though paper might enjoy momentary popularity. His support for constitutional reform should not be seen as a scheme to shift political power from democratic state governments to a national government that would be less responsive to the people's legitimate interests. Madison rejected the widespread notion "that the interest of the majority is the political standard of right and wrong." Concerned about individual rights, Madison recognized a dilemma inherent in democracy, one the success of the Revolution forced Americans to confront. William Grayson, a future Anti-Federalist recognized it as well, writing Madison, "Montesquieu was not wrong when he said the democratic might be as tyrannical as the despotic." And Madison's sympathies for minorities extended beyond economic minorities like creditors. In his fight to end the religious establishment in Virginia, he had arrayed himself with religious dissidents. During the debate over the Jay-Gardoqui negotiations, he found himself part of a minority defined by geography.[15]

Madison had an opportunity to reflect on how a proper state government might be organized in August 1785 when the lawyer Caleb Wallace asked him for advice on a constitution for the new state of Kentucky. Wallace had prefaced his request with an invitation for Madison to join him in the West. Madison's response suggests a remarkable lack of self-awareness for a man who lived virtually his entire life in the same house: "I have no local partialities which can keep me from any place which promises the greatest real advantages."

Working from a published edition of the state constitutions, Madison recommended a two-house legislature with a senate "constituted on such principles as will give *wisdom* and steadiness to legislation." How to make the upper house a stabilizing influence bedeviled American constitution-makers for years. Madison believed senators should serve four- to five-year terms, as opposed to the annual terms in the lower house. He supported limited property requirements for voting, recommending to Wallace the North Carolina practice, in which property ownership was required to vote in state senate elections. "I see no reason why the rights of property which chiefly bears the burden of Government and is so much an object of Legislation should not be respected as well as personal rights in the choice of Rulers." From New York, he borrowed the idea of a council of revision, which could veto laws before they took effect. As a further check on lawmakers, Madison envisioned something akin to a modern legislative research bureau—a standing committee that could prepare bills for the legislature. "Our Assembly . . . give almost as many proofs as they pass laws of their need of some such assistance." To keep elections "tolerably chaste," voting should be by ballot, not orally as was the common practice, and seats in the legislature should be reapportioned periodically to reflect shifts in population. In a nod to republican orthodoxy, legislators, Madison believed, should be barred from simultaneously holding executive or judicial offices.

The legislative power of the state assemblies struck Madison as too broad to be specifically enumerated. At the same time, those rights beyond the reach of the state—freedom of religion and of the press, the right to a jury trial or to file a petition for habeas corpus, among others—should be listed. Madison took the separation of powers as an article of faith, but he expected little from the executive and judicial branches. The executive seemed barely even the second most important branch. He had no fixed ideas about how the office should be filled or constituted and apparently saw no need to worry about it. "All the great powers which are properly executive" had been transferred "to the Federal Government," an observation that should startle modern readers steeped in the feebleness of the Articles of Confederation. Madison gave the courts even less attention. Worried almost solely about the independence of the judiciary, he suggested judges should serve for good behavior, drawing fixed and liberal salaries.[16]

Establishing a republican order in national politics would be more difficult. Many of Madison's fellow Virginians, including Richard Henry Lee and George Mason, feared Congress would discriminate against the South if it were given the power to regulate trade. To Madison, the need to be able to retaliate against nations, in particular Great Britain, that discriminated against American commerce outweighed more parochial concerns, a view Jefferson encouraged. Many did not see, Madison told James Monroe, "the interests of the state as they are interwoven with those of the confederacy."[17]

Madison preferred free trade to commercial retaliation, but above all he wanted to keep foreign markets open to Americans. The sturdy yeomen who personified republican virtue to Madison and Jefferson were not subsistence farmers. In Virginia's answer to the Puritan work ethic, Madison and Jefferson believed the opportunity to produce a surplus for distant markets would encourage sound husbandry and good citizenship. By this logic, Madison could see how control of the Mississippi would not only assist U.S. expansion into the Southeast but also uplift the American character.[18]

There were other benefits in federal regulation of trade. A national tariff would shift the burden of direct taxes from farmers, and if it enabled Congress to make timely interest payments on the war debt, the market value of government securities would rise, which would help alleviate the chronic monetary shortage that underlay popular complaints about debts and taxes.[19]

The republican state could not, however, wholly eliminate poverty, and republicanism was not a panacea for every social ill. After Jefferson, writing from his diplomatic post in Paris, had described for him the wretched state of Europe's poor, Madison observed that "a certain degree of misery" seemed inevitable in heavily populated areas. Republican governments would tend to relieve the misery of the lower classes by promoting a more equal distribution of land, but there would rarely be enough for everyone. Other tendencies in republican societies might actually make life worse for those without real property. The monarchial states of Europe had made their surplus workers into "manufacturers of superfluities," household servants, soldiers, and merchants. Those occupations would virtually disappear in the peaceful, frugal, and egalitarian America of Madison's imagination. The vision hardly fit reality, making, for example, no allowance for the existence of slavery, but when slavery was not in issue, white Virginians showed a remarkable ability to forget about their slaves.[20]

As Drew McCoy has noted, Madison and Jefferson favored development over space, as opposed to development through time. Convinced that free, white farmers—stable, healthy, and independent—made the best citizens, they hoped the frontier would prevent the rise in America of industrial cities with large masses of dependent poor. Industrialization and urbanization, with their attendant ills, were almost unavoidable as societies matured, but acquiring new domains in the West would buy time for the republic. In addition to land, farmers needed markets and access to foreign manufactured goods, so territorial expansion, free trade, and republicanism went hand in hand.[21]

Jefferson and Madison exchanged more than political theories as each became the other's closest collaborator. In 1784, Madison began reading the massive writings of the French naturalist Comte de Buffon. Madison and Jefferson took offense at Buffon's claim that New World species were inferior to those of Europe. To disprove Buffon, Madison sent Jefferson measurements of American moles and weasels. Jefferson reciprocated by acting as his friend's purchasing agent in Europe, sending Madison a pocket telescope, a walking stick, a chemistry set, a portable copying machine, and, most important, books.[22]

Madison had specifically requested books, mainly on public and constitutional law and especially on the history of earlier European confederacies. By January 1786, Madison had received what he called his "literary cargo," two trunks of twenty-one separate titles, some running to multiple volumes. He spent several weeks studying the political history of the Greeks, Swiss, Dutch, and Germans, and he reduced his notes to an essay, "Notes on Ancient and Modern Confederacies." He concluded that they had usually failed because the central government had been too weak; it needed the capacity to act directly on citizens. Instead, "men too jealous to confide their liberty to their representatives, who are their equals, abandoned it to a Prince who might more easily abuse it." How much Madison's research shaped his thinking is hard to judge. Already painfully aware of the weaknesses of the Articles of Confederation, he has the appearance of a lawyer looking for arguments to bolster his case. During the debate over the ratification of the Constitution, James Wilson, the influential Pennsylvania delegate who sympathized with Madison's objectives, questioned the relevance of histori-cal analogies between the United States and earlier republics. Nonetheless, Madison's reading gave him a rich storehouse of theories, arguments, and anecdotes. Ideas from the "Notes" reappear in his speeches at the Constitu-tional Convention and at the Virginia ratifying convention and in his essays in *The Federalist*.[23] The "Notes" also suggest one reason for the unimposing but indefatigable Madison's influence: he began preparing for a constitu-tional convention before anyone, Madison included, knew there would be a constitutional convention.

James Madison attended the Annapolis Convention in September 1786. Besides Virginia, only four other states sent delegations. The convention elected John Dickinson chair, but with such a poor turnout, the delegates could hardly take up the commercial issues they had been sent to consider. Instead, New York's Alexander Hamilton prepared a draft resolution asking Congress to call a meeting in Philadelphia to consider a general revision of the Articles of Confederation. Madison urged Hamilton to temper his lan-guage—early evidence perhaps of the Virginian's more moderate national-ism—and the convention passed the revised draft. Often seen as a logical step toward an inevitable constitutional convention, "the Annapolis report was," Jack Rakove has written, "as much a desperate maneuver of politi-cians who had exhausted all other alternatives as a bold stratagem of states-men who knew exactly what they wanted."[24]

Fast on the heels of the Annapolis Convention came the fall session of the House of Delegates, and Madison soon found himself in his familiar posi-tion as a legislative dynamo. He drafted a complex bill to improve the col-lection of customs duties, and he helped pass a resolution against an emis-sion of paper money. To his chagrin, however, the assembly approved a bill permitting the payment of taxes with tobacco. He lost another round in his fight for court reform, and he fell one vote short in an effort to reduce the number of capital crimes in Virginia, part of the new legal code Jefferson had helped initiate a decade earlier. "The rage against horse stealers," Madi-son wrote his friend in Paris, "had a great influence on the fate of the Bill."[25]

Most important, Madison wrote a bill providing for the appointment of delegates to a constitutional convention. The failure of the Annapolis Con-vention and his own legislative defeats contributed to Madison's decision to abandon his earlier hesitancy and seek radical reform. He may also have feared that if more nationalistic politicians did not act quickly, the Jay-

Gardoqui controversy would split the Union before it could be reinforced. "The crisis is arrived," Madison said. Americans must now decide whether they would "reap the just fruits of that Independence which they have so gloriously acquired . . . or . . . will they renounce the auspicious blessings prepared for them by the Revolution." Ironically, in light of the acrimony the debate over the ratification of the Constitution would provoke, Madison's resolution passed without dissent. He believed the vote represented a "revolution of sentiment" over the previous year in favor of a stronger national government.[26]

More difficult than passing the resolution was filling the Virginia delegation. Madison hoped the assembly would appoint representatives "such as will give dignity to the experiment and at the same time be most likely to gain a ratification of the result." Madison himself was an obvious choice, as were George Mason, Edmund Randolph, and the revered law professor George Wythe. But Patrick Henry, increasingly suspicious of Congress because of the Jay-Gardoqui controversy, declined an appointment, as did Richard Henry Lee and former governor Thomas Nelson. John Blair, a prominent lawyer and judge, and Dr. James McClurg, a member of the governor's council, did agree to serve. Madison wanted George Washington, the biggest prize of all, to head the delegation, but Washington proved an elusive quarry, and Madison had to leave for New York to take his seat in Congress before the delegation was completed.[27]

"The extreme badness of the weather" slowed his journey north. "We had," he wrote Eliza House Trist, a "snow storm incessantly in our teeth" from Princeton to Paulus Hook. In New York, he found "our situation is becoming every day more and more critical. No money comes into the Federal Treasury. No respect is paid to Federal authority; and people of reflection unanimously agree that the existing confederacy is tattering to its foundation." As Congress struggled to maintain a quorum, John Jay reported that both the United States and Great Britain had violated the Treaty of Paris of 1783; Congress could neither retaliate effectively against the British nor compel the states to honor their obligations. From Paris, William Short, Jefferson's secretary, reported that the failure of the United States to pay its debts to France, including debts to French officers who had served in the Continental Army, was creating "an unfavorable impression."[28]

Professional politician that he had become, Madison did not take public catastrophe too personally. This equanimity was one of the secrets of his success. After a month back in Congress, he could write Eliza House Trist, "This place agrees as yet very well with my healt[h]." Others were less resilient. Madison's colleague William Grayson suffered a mental breakdown in Philadelphia in 1786 and was "often delirious . . . with strange fancies and apprehensions." On the mend in New York, "Col. Grayson damns it for the worst climate on the face of God's Earth." Madison, by contrast, often seemed immune to the hardships of legislative service, temporary quarters, and long absences from home.[29]

Madison's immediate objective was not preparing for a constitutional convention, which Congress endorsed a few days after he arrived in New York; it was ensuring that Congress did not approve John Jay's proposal to close the Mississippi River to American traffic, although the two issues were related. Madison lobbied Abraham Clark, a New Jersey politician who speculated in western lands, to use his influence to persuade New Jersey to reverse its position supporting the Jay-Gardoqui rapprochement. Eventually, New Jersey switched sides. Madison tried to transfer the negotiations to Madrid and place them in Jefferson's hands. Jay blocked the move. Madison took the unusual step of meeting personally with Gardoqui; he tried to discourage the Spanish minister by telling him Congress could never enforce a treaty closing the Mississippi. Opposition from the South and West doomed the agreement. By the middle of March, Madison could write Thomas Jefferson, "The Spanish project sleeps." When Madison left New York for Philadelphia on 2 May, he felt confident that "the project of shutting the Mississippi was at an end." It was just in time. Madison realized the southern states would never agree to augment the powers of Congress if they feared the northern majority would surrender the Mississippi in exchange for commercial concessions from Spain.[30]

In order to ensure the success of the Constitutional Convention, Madison's second most important goal, after defeating the Jay-Gardoqui treaty, was to persuade George Washington to join the Virginia delegation. The general's enormous prestige would lend credibility to an otherwise dubious undertaking. Madison, aided by Edmund Randolph, spent the winter of 1786–87 attempting to lure Washington away from Mount Vernon. Typical was Madison's letter of 7 December: "It was the opinion of every judicious friend whom I consulted that your name could not be spared."[31]

Unfortunately for Madison and Randolph, Washington had already decided to stay away from Philadelphia. After the Revolution, former officers of the Continental Army had organized the Society of the Cincinnati, and Washington had agreed to serve as the group's president. Membership in the organization was hereditary, and it drew criticism for its alleged aristocratic tendencies. The controversy embarrassed Washington, who was ever mindful of his reputation for republican rectitude. He tactfully informed the Cincinnati that he would not be able to serve another term as president or attend their upcoming convention, scheduled coincidentally for May 1787 in Philadelphia. How then could he attend the Constitutional Convention without offending his former officers? As Madison and Randolph appealed to his sense of duty in another hour of national crisis, and to his personal vanity, the general began to waver. In March 1787, he advised Randolph he would go to Philadelphia. Madison's response suggested he could sometimes be more persistent than perceptive. He suggested to Randolph that Benjamin Franklin serve as chair—Washington had seemed the most likely presiding officer—and that Washington should delay his appearance until the success of the convention was assured. It seems an all too clever and transparent attempt to protect Washington's image by not fully committing him to the cause of constitutional reform. Washington, a consummate if taciturn political actor, was hardly a man to be stage managed by others, and Madison's proposal died a merciful death.[32]

A crisis in Massachusetts helped Madison enlist Washington. Western farmers led by Daniel Shays, a former Continental Army officer, took up arms to resist the collection of state taxes. Initial reports wildly exaggerated the scope of Shays's Rebellion. Henry Lee wrote Madison in October 1786 that forty thousand of the seventy-five thousand men in the Massachusetts militia supported the insurrection. Grayson passed on rumors that the British were involved, while admitting, "I have heard no satisfactory proof." Undeterred but sincerely alarmed, Madison circulated unfounded reports of violence and foreign intrigue, suggesting the turmoil showed the need to add "vigor" to the national government. George Washington agreed. "We are fast verging," he wrote Madison, "to anarchy and confusion!"[33]

Fearful that officials would overreact, Thomas Jefferson, by contrast, counseled restraint. "Those characters wherein fear predominates over hope may apprehend too much from these instances of irregularity." Indeed, Shays's Rebellion provided the occasion for one of Jefferson's most memorable epigrams: "I hold it that a little rebellion now and then is a good thing, and as necessary in the political world as storms in the physical." Henry Knox estimated the number of armed rebels at fewer than twelve hundred, and troops led by General Benjamin Lincoln easily dispersed them. By February 1787, Madison could report to Washington that Shays's Rebellion "is nearly extinct."[34]

Because the rebellion collapsed with little bloodshed and because armed uprisings were relatively common on the early American frontier, it is tempting to ridicule the nervous response of the political elite or to suspect nationalists like Madison of manipulating the crisis to make their case for a stronger central government. Yet one can only imagine how a modern state would react if several hundred armed protestors began marching across the countryside. Local protests and isolated violence in Virginia added to the anxiety. Madison feared that, in Massachusetts, "the discontents are rather silenced than subdued." More frightening to Madison than the prospect of violence was the political success of the rebels after Shays's Rebellion collapsed. Electing supporters to local offices and replacing Governor James Bowdoin with the more malleable John Hancock, Massachusetts farmers seemed poised to force a new emission of paper money.[35] When he took his seat in Congress in February, Madison believed the young republic, buffeted by Shays's Rebellion and the Jay-Gardoqui controversy, faced two unattractive options: a monarchy, which might at least maintain order, or a partition of the confederacy, which would lessen sectional rivalries. As the Philadelphia convention approached, Madison seemed no more optimistic. Only fundamental reform could preserve the achievements of the American Revolution, but he doubted the states could reach a consensus. The options now were "general chaos or at least partition." Others saw a return to monarchy as inevitable.[36]

Madison's ideas about a new constitution began to take shape in the spring of 1787 in letters to Washington, Jefferson, and Randolph. His thinking at this point was mainly philosophical; specific details would come later. For all his historical research, he drew heavily from the states' recent experiences in constitution-making. They had established certain basic principles of American constitutionalism: constitutions were to be written documents, not amorphous collections of statutes and traditions as they were in English practice; they were to be written by conventions specifically elected for the purpose; and they had to be ratified by the people, either through a second convention or a popular vote. Power was to be separated among the courts, the executive, and, to better check the most influential branch, a bicameral legislature. Madison foresaw only a limited role for the judiciary: the right of the courts to set aside acts of the legislature as unconstitutional was not well established in the 1780s. Judicial review would eventually become the primary means of enforcing constitutional law, but in 1787 the idea played almost no part in Madison's jurisprudence. At the same time, Americans had come to assume a proper constitution would include a bill of rights to protect individual liberties, a well-established precedent that Madison and the great majority of the other delegates in Philadelphia later cavalierly dismissed. On the whole, Madison was more nationalistic than Jefferson, or many of those who became Anti-Federalists, and less nationalistic than Alexander Hamilton and many of the future Federalists who would ally themselves with him.[37]

Writing Jefferson in March, Madison laid out four fundamental principles: the new constitution must be ratified by the people; Congress must be given the power to veto state laws "in all cases whatsoever"; representation in Congress must be based on population; and power must be divided among different branches of government. Madison envisioned a central government that could circumvent obstreperous states and deal directly with individual citizens; popular ratification and proportional representation would enhance its legitimacy. A federal veto would allow Congress to protect the rights of individuals, as well as its own jurisdiction, from state encroachments.

Madison rejected Randolph's proposal for piecemeal amendments to the Articles of Confederation; he told Randolph the new government needed "positive and complete authority in all cases where uniform measures are necessary"; and he suggested to Washington that Congress be given an express power to coerce recalcitrant states. Yet Madison hoped to find a "middle way" between the "consolidation" of all sovereignty in the national government and the anarchic regime of the states. He believed the adoption of proportional representation in Congress "would not be attended with much difficulty." The northern states would likely support it because of their current numerical majorities; the southern states would go along because they expected to grow more rapidly. As a large-state delegate himself, Madison seemed strangely myopic, or perhaps simply inconsistent, about the need to accommodate state loyalties. On the one hand, he believed the larger states would not agree to transfer power to Congress unless representation was based on population. On the other hand, he apparently convinced himself that proportional representation, coupled with a reduced role for the states in the new national government, would eliminate disparities among them: "A vote in the national councils from Delaware, would then have the same effect and value as one from the largest state in the union."[38] Few small-state representatives would see it that way.

In the spring of 1787, Madison wrote, for his own use, a twelve-count indictment of the political status quo. He called it "The Vices of the Political System of the United States." By the eve of the Philadelphia convention, concerns about the failures of the state governments had become more common than complaints about the weakness of Congress under the Articles of

Confederation. Madison may have even concluded that Congress's ineffectiveness had encouraged the arbitrary actions of the states.[39] He aimed "The Vices" mainly at the "multiplicity," "mutability," and "injustice" of state laws. Breaking with conventional wisdom, Madison envisioned a national government, armed with the authority to override state laws, capable of protecting minority rights within the states. Oppressive state legislation, he argued, "brings more into question the fundamental principle of republican government, that the majority who rule in such governments, are the safest guardians both of public good and of private rights." Lawmakers, Madison reasoned, could be motivated by ambition, personal interest, or the public good. "Unhappily," he wrote, "the two first are proved by experience to be most prevalent." Unscrupulous politicians could often hide their real motives from the voters. An honest but naive representative could become "the dupe of a favorite leader." Worse yet, the people might knowingly embrace unjust policies. All societies were divided into factions based on economic interests, geography, religion, or loyalties to a particular leader. Majority factions would naturally seek their own interests at the expense of the less powerful. A recognition that pursuing the public good might best serve a faction's long-term self-interest could restrain more venal instincts. So too could a concern for one's reputation or an adherence to religious scruples. But experience taught that these self-imposed restraints were frequently inadequate.

Congress, Madison argued, would be less vulnerable to the evils of factions than were the state legislatures. Congress, in his analysis, not only could be trusted to act in the national arena but also could be used to protect citizens from their own state governments. In a larger sphere, "a common interest or passion is less apt to be felt and the requisite combination less easy to be formed by a great than a small number." In light of the primitive communications technology of his day, Madison assumed that unsavory alliances could not readily be formed on a national scale. The multitude of interests found in a national legislature would, moreover, "check each other." And there was an added safeguard; he called it "an auxiliary desideratum." The prestige of national service and the difficulty of winning elections in congressional districts far larger than state legislative constituencies would produce superior lawmakers. National elections in the new system "will most certainly extract from the mass of society the purest and noblest characters which it contains."[40]

It was a novel, but not wholly original, idea. The Scottish philosopher David Hume had challenged the conventional wisdom, best represented by Baron de Montesquieu, that republican governments could only be expected to flourish in small states where citizens shared similar interests. Madison's arguments parallel Hume's so closely that the Virginian's debt is obvious. Other influences likely pushed him in the same direction. John Witherspoon had argued at Princeton that competing interests needed to be balanced against one another, and he believed the proper equilibrium could best be achieved in an "enlarged system." The social utility of competing factions could also be inferred from Adam Smith's *The Wealth of Nations* (1776). Madison's own experience had validated the theory: jealousy among religious sects had helped kill the general assessment bill in Virginia, the republic's largest state.[41] And so he left New York for Philadelphia confident a new national government could be erected that would act with the prudence and restraint so often lacking in the states.

Madison reached Philadelphia on 5 May, the best-prepared of all the delegates and, not counting the Pennsylvanians, the first to arrive. His fellow delegates trickled into the city. As he wrote his father, "We have been here for some time suffering a daily disappointment from the failure of the delegates to assemble," but the convention had a quorum by 25 May. Beginning with procedural matters, the delegates elected George Washington president of the convention; he and Madison grew closer in the course of the debates. The delegates voted to keep their deliberations secret. Madison said years later no constitution would have been adopted if the debates had been public. The delegates held their tongues and pens, and the silence grated on the nerves of a curious populace. Madison's cousin, the Reverend James Madison, would write him later in the summer, "If you cannot tell us what you are doing, you might at least give us some information of what you are not doing."[42]

Madison's research into the history of earlier confederacies had been frustrated by a scarcity of records, and he resolved that historians of the American founding would not face the same problem. At the start of the convention, Madison took a seat in front of the presiding officer where he could hear everything and began to make notes in his own shorthand, which he rewrote in more detail at night. It helped, he wrote later, that he was familiar "with the style and the train of conversation and reasoning which characterized the principal speakers. It happened, also that I was not absent a single day, nor more than a casual fraction of an hour in any day, so that I could not have lost a single speech, unless a very short one."[43]

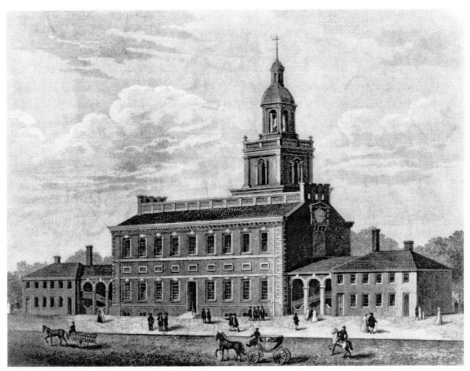

Engraving by John Serz of the Pennsylvania statehouse, better known as Independence Hall, where, in 1787, Madison would help write the Constitution. (Library of Congress)

Not only was he the best-prepared delegate in Philadelphia, his note taking made him the best-informed on the work of the convention.

He enjoyed an occasional respite. At one point Madison and several other delegates visited the botanical gardens of William Bartram on the Schuylkill River, and the Philadelphia summer was less brutal than legend would have it. "We have till within a few days had very cool weather," Madison wrote his father in the middle of August. "It is now pleasant, after a fine rain." Madison began the convention as healthy as he had ever been, but he exhausted himself with speeches and note taking. By late August his notes became noticeably less thorough.[44] Madison's letters contain remarkably few personal asides. He was a very private man or, more to the point, a man with very little private life.[45]

While they waited for the other delegates to arrive, the Virginians had prepared their own outline of a constitution. Edmund Randolph presented the Virginia Plan, largely but not entirely Madison's work, to the convention on 29 May. The plan called for a two-house legislature with representation based on "the Quotas of contribution" or "the number of free inhabitants, as the one or the other rule may seem best in different cases." The reference to "Quotas of contribution" was virtually a euphemism for slavery since slaves would presumably increase a state's tax burden. The first chamber would be elected by the people, and it would select the second from candidates nominated by the state legislatures. The legislature's powers were vague but broad. Congress could set aside all state laws that, in its opinion, violated "the articles of union," and it could use force against a state that neglected its duties under the articles.

Reflecting priorities Madison had demonstrated earlier, the plan gave less attention to the executive or the judiciary. The executive would be elected by the legislature and serve a single term. The plan anticipated the creation of a national court system and the establishment of a council of revision, consisting of members of the executive and the judiciary. The council could veto acts of Congress before they took effect, but Congress could override the veto by an unspecified majority.[46]

The delegates generally agreed that the national government needed an independent source of revenue, the power to regulate trade, and some power to enforce its decisions. In proposing that Congress be empowered to strike down state laws, however, the Virginia Plan went beyond the recommendations of the Annapolis Convention and incorporated an idea that had occurred to Madison several weeks earlier.[47]

It was a highly nationalistic agenda, but it was nationalism with a Virginia flavor. Virginia would no longer cast one vote among thirteen, as it did under the Articles of Confederation; it would now control the single largest bloc in Congress. The question of representation provoked an immediate controversy and delayed resolution of other issues, especially the matter of deciding what Congress would actually do. On 30 May, Madison suggested the phrase "number of free inhabitants" be replaced with "an equitable ratio of representation," to leave open the possibility of counting slaves on all occasions, but as contentious as the issue would be, the broader proposal to give some states more votes than others proved far more divisive. Many of the delegates had fought over the issue years ago. Pennsylvania, led by Benjamin Franklin, had objected when John Dickinson had included a provision for state equality in his draft of the Articles of Confederation. The small states, naturally opposed to proportional representation, won that round. Now Delaware urged that debate on the question of representation be postponed; its delegates had been instructed to oppose any change in suffrage. Dickinson and Connecticut's Roger Sherman proposed an obvious solution—proportional representation in one house and state equality in the other—but Madison and the majority of large-state delegates had no interest in compromise.[48]

The convention debated the issue of representation until the middle of July, and with the large- and small-state delegates committed to defending their respective positions, the speeches obscure almost as much as they reveal. Madison never explained clearly how an upper house—it was not called the Senate until later in the convention—based on population would work, but he seems to have had a radical reform in mind. He apparently intended for the lower house to select members of the upper house, from candidates nominated by the state legislatures, without regard to state boundaries. Some states, most likely the smaller ones, might not be represented in the upper house at all. On 7 June, when Dickinson moved to empower state legislators to elect senators, Madison opposed the proposal: "If the motion should be agreed to, we must either depart from the doctrine of proportional representation; or admit into the Senate a very large number of members. The first is inadmissible, being evidently unjust. The second is inexpedient." In other words, elections by state legislatures presumed each state would be represented in the Senate, and if representation were to be based on population, as Madison thought it should, giving each state a senator would make the Senate too large and unwieldy. On 30 June, James Wilson proposed there be one senator for each one hundred thousand inhabitants, with states with fewer than one hundred thousand residents receiving a single senator. Madison supported the proposal, calling it a "concession" to the small states, which again suggested he did not think the original Virginia Plan would guarantee them representation in the upper house.[49]

The small states wanted to ensure their fair share of the bounty expected to be provided by federally owned western land. Otherwise, their reasons for opposing the Virginia Plan are clear enough, but why would Madison say at one point in the debates that there was no ground for compromise on the issue of representation?[50] Parochial political interests are obvious. Virginia would have more seats in the lower house than any other state, and it would probably fare well in the election of members of the Senate, where state lines could be ignored but state loyalties would persist. Because the new government would act directly on the people, Madison believed federal lawmakers should be selected by the people or by other federal representatives; the principle of state equality symbolically interposed the states between the citizens and the national government. Madison wanted the federal government to be independent of the states, but state equality seemed to go hand in hand with allowing state legislators to select senators, a practice Madison feared would compromise the autonomy of the new government.

To Madison, that autonomy was essential. He gave one of his most important speeches of the convention on 6 June, after Charles Pinckney of South Carolina had proposed that the lower house be elected by state legislators. The national government, Madison said, needed to be able to protect private rights and the integrity of legal proceedings from state action: "Interferences with these were evils which had more perhaps than anything else produced this convention." He warned "Republican liberty" might not survive much longer in the face of the states' misdeeds. Small states especially showed little regard for legal norms, an undiplomatic remark that was a prelude to his larger point. "Were we not thence admonished to enlarge the sphere as far as the nature of Government would admit?" If Congress could be insulated from the evils of local politics, it would exercise power more responsibly than could the state legislatures. Drawing on his "Vices" memorandum, Madison argued that the only defense against "the inconveniencies of democracy consistent with the democratic form of Government" was to create a republic so large and diverse that no one faction could dictate to the rest. In a smaller state, "where a majority are united by a common interest or passion, the rights of the minority are in danger."[51]

His oratory notwithstanding, Madison suffered a major defeat the next day when all ten states present voted to allow the state legislators to elect senators. On 13 June, however, the convention, sitting more informally as a committee of the whole, approved a modified version of the Virginia Plan. It deleted the original provision authorizing the federal government to use force against a wayward state; Madison himself had abandoned the idea early in the convention. Madison, supported by James Wilson, had wanted to combine members of the executive and judiciary into a council of revision with the power to veto acts of Congress. He feared that acting alone neither the executive nor a federal court would be willing to challenge the national legislature. The delegates disagreed and vested the veto power in the executive. The 13 June report also provided for the election of the Senate by the state assemblies. On most other points, it was a victory for Madison and the larger states.[52]

The small states struck back on 15 June, when William Paterson of New Jersey introduced the New Jersey Plan. Paterson proposed that Congress be given the power to regulate trade, to collect import duties, and in an ironic brush with the revolutionary past, to impose a stamp tax. The New

Jersey Plan replaced the congressional veto over state laws with what became the supremacy clause, requiring state courts to abide by acts of Congress, state law notwithstanding. The New Jersey Plan gave the nationalists almost everything they had wanted four years earlier. But it left in place a unicameral legislature in which each state had one vote, and Madison believed it put too few checks on the states.[53]

Madison responded to Paterson on 19 June. Citing the examples of the Amphyctonic and Achean confederacies from his own research, the erudite Virginian argued that, under the New Jersey Plan, Congress would be too weak to protect itself from subversion by the states, to protect the states from one another, or to "secure the internal tranquility of the states themselves." Exasperated after a month debating the same issue, he added, "The great difficulty lies in the affair of Representation; and if this could be adjusted, all others would be surmountable."[54]

Yet the debate went on, and Madison made argument after argument against the principle of state equality. Massachusetts, Pennsylvania, and Virginia had different interests; they would not unite against the smaller states. History suggested that the most intense rivalries within a confederacy would be among the largest states. He warned the small states that if the confederacy collapsed, they would be more vulnerable; to defend themselves they would be forced to trust "great discretionary powers" to an "Executive Magistrate" and to maintain a permanent army. "A standing military force, with an overgrown Executive will not long be safe companions to liberty. The means of defence against foreign danger have always been instruments of tyranny at home." The real fault line between the states was not large versus small; it was North versus South. State interests were not defined by size "but by other circumstances; the most material of which resulted partly from climate, but principally from the effects of their having or not having slaves."[55]

On 2 July, a tie vote on a renewed motion by Oliver Ellsworth of Connecticut to give each state one vote in the Senate brought the convention to a halt. The delegates responded by appointing a Grand Committee, with one member from each state. The composition of the committee boded well for the small states. At least two of the large-state delegates, Franklin from Pennsylvania and Mason from Virginia, had indicated a willingness to compromise. On 3 July, the committee reported what came to be known as the Great Compromise, or the Connecticut Compromise, after Roger Sherman, one of its chief architects: representation in the House of Representatives would be based on population, and in the Senate the states would be equal.

As a sop to the large states, and possibly to placate Mason, tax and revenue bills would be required to originate in the lower house.[56]

Madison did not like it, and he predicted—wrongly as events would prove—that the compromise would offend most voters. "It was vain," he said, "to purchase concord in the convention on terms which would perpetuate discord among their constituents." The debate went on sporadically for days. On 14 July, he claimed state equality might be justified if Congress acted on the states, but "he called for a single instance in which the Gen. Govt. was not to operate on the people individually," an implausible argument for a delegate who wanted to give Congress authority to set aside state laws. He was a little more credible when he linked the question of representation to the division between North and South. State equality in the Senate would give the North a permanent advantage. Presently there were five slave states and eight states in which slavery had been abolished or was on its way to extinction. If representation was based on population, the disparity would be smaller, and, optimistic about the South's potential for growth, Madison predicted, "every day would tend towards an equilibrium." When the convention approved the Great Compromise on 16 July, Madison suffered, in the words of Lance Banning, "a devastating blow." At an informal caucus the next morning, Madison may have even considered leading the large states out of the convention, but there was little support for such a divisive move.[57]

Madison endured another defeat the same day, when the delegates rejected a congressional veto power over state legislation. A revised version of the supremacy clause in the New Jersey Plan went into the Constitution in its place. On 21 July, the delegates defeated his proposal for a council of revision, choosing instead to vest the power to veto acts of Congress solely in the executive. Passage of the Great Compromise caused Madison to consider new checks on Congress; he proposed a three-fourths majority as opposed to a two-thirds vote to override a presidential veto. The convention disagreed. He also lost when he proposed presidential impeachment trials be transferred from the Senate to the Supreme Court or some other tribunal.[58]

Despite his frustrations and his failures, Madison persisted and adapted, winning his share of victories and remaining, more often than not, open to compromise. Early in the convention, Madison prevailed when the states decided to trust the executive power to a single individual, as opposed to a committee. The issue split the Virginia delegation, with Mason, Randolph, and Blair dissenting. Madison successfully defended the Virginia Plan's proposal for popular election of the House of Representatives, and he helped defeat a motion by Charles Pinckney and John Rutledge of South Carolina to allow the states to regulate the "time, manner, and place" of congressional elections. He joined with North Carolina's Hugh Williamson in persuading the delegates to base population in the lower house on a periodic census; the provision would shift political power westward. He successfully struck land ownership from the qualifications for holding national office. The delegates feared the rise of a landless proletariat, but they could not agree on the appropriate requirements, and they knew the nation was moving in a more democratic direction. Wanting to minimize the influence of the states in Congress, Madison enjoyed a victory on 23 July when the convention decided senators would vote individually, not as a state bloc. To enhance their independence, members of Congress would in the future draw their salaries from the federal government, not the states. It was another reform Madison supported.[59]

Bans on state emissions of paper money and laws impairing contracts, his two main grievances against the states, went into the Constitution with almost no debate. A near riot in Philadelphia had forced local merchants to accept state paper. As he wrote Jefferson in July, "Nothing but evil springs from this imaginary money wherever it is tried."[60]

Madison could also applaud the convention's decision to seek ratification of the Constitution in special state conventions. A convention elected to consider the specific issue would better represent the views of the people and would give the act of ratification the popular sanction a state legislature could not. Madison believed legislative ratification would make the Constitution legally analogous to a treaty in which a breach by one party absolved the other parties from their obligations, an interpretation he hoped to avoid. Ratification by convention also offered tactical advantages. State legislatures, whose prerogatives were being circumscribed by the Constitution, would be less friendly, and since most state legislatures were bicameral, requiring their approval would give opponents of the Constitution almost twice as many opportunities to defeat it.[61]

After the convention approved the Great Compromise, with what Madison saw as a malapportioned Senate, he worked, with considerable success, to strengthen the presidency as a check on Congress. To protect the independence of the executive, Madison backed away from the proposal in the Virginia Plan that Congress fill the office. He saw merit to the popular election of the chief executive, although it favored the North to the extent that southern slaves would never be allowed to vote. Ultimately he agreed to the creation of the Electoral College, where the three-fifths compromise, counting a slave as three-fifths of a free person, would benefit the South. He proposed that the president, not Congress, be given the power to appoint judges and to negotiate treaties. He persuaded his colleagues to revise Congress's power to "make" war to "declare" war, thus shifting the responsibility for managing military operations to the president.[62]

If the Great Compromise tempered Madison's faith in Congress, he did not intend to cripple the institution. He waffled on the issue of giving Congress a broad, general grant of authority or enumerating its powers specifically. He said in later years that the broad grant in the Virginia Plan had been a placeholder for a list of enumerated powers, and perhaps it was. In Philadelphia, he ultimately supported an expansive list of specific powers. Unlike many other southern delegates, he defended Congress's power to tax exports, a potential burden on the tobacco trade. The revenue, he suggested, could finance the navy the South would need to protect its commerce. He challenged the conventional wisdom more starkly when Charles Pinckney and George Mason argued that a two-thirds majority should be required to pass legislation regulating foreign and interstate trade. Many southerners feared a narrow northern majority would impose an American-style navigation act on southern planters, forcing them to use American ships and driving up freight rates. Madison disagreed. He believed it might encourage the development of a shipping industry in the South. And most important, he did not want to curtail Congress's ability to retaliate commercially against Great Britain.[63]

Adamant as he was on the problem of representation, he compromised without great angst on other issues. He had demonstrated flexibility on the method of selecting a president. He indicated support for a property requirement for voting for members of at least one house of Congress, but when the decision to let state legislators elect senators made the issue irrelevant with regard to the Senate, Madison did not pursue it. He supported a compromise on the issue of multiple office holding: members of Congress could not hold other federal offices while serving in Congress or accept positions created or given raises while they were serving in the national legislature. He complained when the convention voted to allow the foreign slave trade to continue for another twenty years, but he acquiesced in the three-fifths compromise. In 1783, he had proposed that the Confederation Congress use the same ratio to determine its requisitions on the states.[64]

Despite his successes, Madison feared, as the delegates completed their work, that they had failed. "I hazard an opinion," he wrote Thomas Jefferson on 6 September, "that the plan should it be adopted will neither effectively answer its national object nor prevent the local mischiefs which everywhere excite disgust against the state governments." The convention adjourned on 17 September, and a few weeks later, Madison explained his reservations to Jefferson in more detail. By refusing to adopt a congressional veto of state legislation, the Philadelphia convention had failed to subordinate state to federal authority. In other words, the delegates, by leaving sovereignty divided, had backed into the principle of federalism, and Madison disapproved. He doubted the federal courts would strike down unconstitutional state laws, and he deplored the inefficiency of attempting to enforce the Constitution through ad hoc lawsuits against bills that had already become effective. Without a federal veto, the new government could not protect individuals from the injustice of state laws that had "contributed more to that uneasiness which produced the Convention, and prepared the public mind for a general reform, that those which accrued to our national character and interest from the inadequacy of the Confederation to its immediate objects." A national body politic, with its greater number of competing interests, would be a safer custodian of individual liberty.[65]

Yet Madison never considered opposing the Constitution. He saw nothing better on the horizon, and the odds that the Constitution would be ratified even in what he considered its existing tepid form were none too good. Alexander Hamilton, representing New York, had wanted a far more high-toned government, one modeled on the British system, but most of the criticism came from those who believed the new regime would be too powerful and too remote. Two or three delegates had left Philadelphia prematurely and in anger. Mason, Randolph, and Elbridge Gerry of Massachusetts stayed until the end and then refused to sign the finished document. Patrick Henry had been hostile from the beginning. William Grayson "disliked" the end result. In Congress, Richard Henry Lee went to work immediately on amendments.[66] The Reverend James Madison wrote Madison to complain that the convention had not fully separated the legislative, judicial, and executive functions. Joseph Jones and others complained about the Senate, although, ironically, not about the principle of state equality.[67]

Madison suspected that nine states, the number required for the Constitution to take effect, would ratify it, but if New York and Virginia stayed out of the new Union, it would not be worth much, and they were divided. Enthusiasm for the Constitution seemed to wane in Virginia after the fall legislative session. James Monroe predicted that "there will be a greater division among the people of character than . . . took place" even during the Revolution. It is difficult to imagine James Madison missing a political meeting, but he told his brother Ambrose in November 1787 that he had not initially intended to seek a seat in the convention elected to consider ratification in Virginia. He thought the Philadelphia delegates should step aside. But others did not share his scruples, and he believed he would be well equipped to dispel misconceptions about the Constitution.[68]

He certainly was. Madison considered his fellow delegates to have been "in general . . . the best contribution of talents that the states could make for the occasion," and he has long been considered the most influential of them all.[69] That influence owed more to his work ethic than to his political instincts. He failed to recognize that the Great Compromise was necessary to win the support of the small states for a stronger central government. His theory that a multitude of competing factions in an extended republic would preclude arbitrary legislation collided with his admission that the real divide in American politics pitted the North against the South. Overly optimistic about the South's future, Madison's argument that state equality in the Senate would put the South at a disadvantage proved to be exactly wrong. As the South fell farther behind the North in population, the Senate Madison had so strenuously opposed would become a bastion of southern power.

From Paris, Jefferson could see the obvious practical and political weaknesses in Madison's scheme for a congressional veto of state laws. It "proposes," Jefferson wrote his friend in June 1787, "to mend a small hole by covering the whole garment." Congress could not reasonably be expected to review the hundreds of state laws passed every year when barely 1 percent of them would touch on matters of national interest. To Irving Brant, "Most remarkable of all, in so realistic a student of politics, was his failure to realize that if his idea had prevailed, the Constitution never would have been ratified."[70] Madison may not have been the realist Brant thought he was, and he performed with mixed results as a prophet. He failed to anticipate the emergence of a vigorous Supreme Court. With the first great chief justice, John Marshall, only beginning his political career, the oversight can be forgiven. Madison also failed to foresee the rise of a strong presidency; with Washington the consensus choice to assume the office, his myopia on that point is a bit more curious.

Yet Madison had helped frame the debate in Philadelphia, he had pushed the convention to create a new government as energetic as the people might possibly accept, and he had acted from the purest of motives, colored as they might have been by class and place. Archibald Stuart, a member of the House of Delegates, wrote Madison in November 1787 worried "less the weakness and inefficacy of the state governments should become so notorious and so disgusting to the people as to drive them into concessions of liberty much beyond the point which is actually necessary for Good Government."[71] Stuart aptly summarized Madison's fears. And so Madison put aside his own defeats, recognized the Constitution as the best available alternative to the decrepit Articles of Confederation, and, his reservations notwithstanding, committed himself, with his characteristic diligence, to its ratification.

From Ratification to the

Bill of Rights

hortly after the Philadelphia convention adjourned, the Virginia legislature reelected James Madison to Congress by a vote of 126 to 14. Broke by the end of the convention, Madison borrowed one hundred dollars from fellow delegate John Blair and left for New York. Madison's return to Congress broke a deadlock in the Virginia delegation. Richard Henry Lee and William Grayson opposed the Constitution; Henry Lee and Edward Carrington supported it. Richard Henry Lee wanted to amend the Constitution, or at least send it to the states with proposed amendments. Madison hoped Congress would recommend it be approved as written. The eventual compromise favored the Federalists, as supporters of the Constitution would be called. Without endorsing the substance of the document or proposing changes, Congress voted unanimously to ask the states to call conventions to consider ratification of the new charter.[1]

As the ratification debate began, articles in the New York newspapers criticizing the Constitution provoked Alexander Hamilton to plan a series of essays in its defense. His first essay appeared in the *New York Independent Journal* on 27 October 1787, but busy with his law practice and hoping to publish several articles a week, Hamilton needed help. Gouverneur Morris turned him down. William Duer wrote several essays, but they proved unusable. The capable John Jay was a better choice, but bad health and bad luck limited his contribution. After Jay wrote Nos. 2 through 5 of what history knows as *The Federalist*, he was disabled by a bout of rheumatoid arthritis. Jay recovered to write No. 64, which appeared on 5 March 1788, and then he was badly injured in April defending a group of doctors, wrongly accused of grave robbing, from a mob.[2]

Madison also agreed, apparently early in November 1787, to contribute.

He had known Hamilton since November 1782, when the New Yorker first entered the Continental Congress. Eventually, Madison wrote twenty-nine essays. Hamilton wrote the remaining fifty-one. As was the custom of the day, all the pieces appeared under a pseudonym, in this case "Publius," from Publius Valerius, an early Roman politician who, as a sign of his commitment to republicanism, tore down his forbidding mansion on a hill and built a more modest dwelling below. Rumors of Madison's involvement in *The Federalist* began to circulate immediately; his authorship was not publicly acknowledged until 1792, when a French edition of the papers appeared. Historians once debated the authorship of some of the essays, but it now seems certain that Madison wrote Nos. 10, 14, 18–20, 37–58, 62, and 63.[3]

Madison, Hamilton, and Jay churned out *The Federalist* over a ten-month period, with a break in the spring and early summer of 1788. To publish three or four articles a week in an era when there were no New York dailies, they used four papers: the *Independent Journal*, the *Packet*, the misnamed *Daily Advertiser*, and the *New York Journal*. From 11 January to 20 February, Madison wrote all the essays. The first thirty-six articles were published in a bound volume in March, when Madison returned to Virginia to run for a seat in the state ratifying convention. The rest of the essays appeared in a second volume in May, with the last seven essays appearing first in book form. What Thomas Jefferson called "the best commentary on the principles of government which ever was written" has since been reprinted in twenty foreign languages and roughly a hundred English editions.[4]

Madison recalled years later that most of the essays were written "in great haste." His intimate knowledge of the Philadelphia convention allowed him to work quickly, and he drew on his earlier writings. *Federalist No. 10* repeats arguments from "The Vices of the Political System of the United States." Madison lifted material for Nos. 18, 19, and 20 from his "Notes on the Ancient and Modern Confederacies." At first Madison worked closely with Hamilton. The Virginian could walk from his rented room at 19 Maiden Street to Hamilton's house on the corner of Wall Street and Broadway. An aggressive publication schedule ultimately made close cooperation impossible. As Madison wrote Jefferson in August 1788, "The writers are not mutually answerable for all the ideas of each other, there being seldom time for even a perusal of the pieces by any but the writer before they were wanted at the press." After a chasm opened between the two principal authors, Madison offered another reason for distancing himself from Hamilton: "a known difference in the general complexion of their political views."[5]

In the winter of 1787–88, Madison and Hamilton, however, still had much in common. Both had originally believed the Constitution had left the national government too feeble. As Hamilton described his own feelings, according to Madison's notes on the convention, "No man's ideas were more remote from the plan than his own were known to be." While they presented a generally united front in *The Federalist*, Madison worried more about preserving a representative, republican system; Hamilton cared more about conferring sufficient "energy" on the national government. He argued in *Federalist No. 9* that the new government would be able to suppress divisive factions, a suggestion Madison repudiated in *Federalist No. 10*. In his support for a strong but virtuous, republican state, Madison stood between more assertive nationalists like Hamilton and moderate Anti-Federalists like his fellow Virginian George Mason. It seems likely that writing his *Federalist* essays contributed to the evolution of Madison's views and helped reconcile him to a Constitution creating a new government of limited powers.[6]

Madison shared Hamilton's contempt for the parochialism of the state legislatures. The debate over the general assessment bill in Virginia and the issue of religious freedom had forced Madison to confront the problem of protecting minority rights when the majority rules. The performance of the Virginia assembly in the fall of 1787 only heightened his fears. He fumed when Virginia lawmakers voted to permit the collection of prewar British debts only if the other states permitted it and only if Great Britain fulfilled all its obligations under the Treaty of Paris. He reported to Thomas Jefferson that "the Assembly . . . is engaged in several mad freaks," including a draconian ploy to prohibit the importation of "foreign spirits" and its customary refusal to honor the financial requests of Congress. The irresponsibility of "the present Assembly," he told George Washington, made a strong case for a new government and for "the necessity of some such anchor against the fluctuations which threaten shipwreck to our liberty."[7]

Scholars have struggled to identify the political philosophy behind Madison's *Federalist* essays. Writing in the shadow of the New Deal, Irving Brant attributed to Madison a desire to use government to protect the poor from economic exploitation. More recently, Madison has been seen as an apostle of a classical liberal regime, devoted to individual interests, especially property rights, and the pursuit of private gain at the expense of the engaged citizenship and public virtue associated with an older republican tradition. The historian Lance Banning, in the most intensive study of Madison's thought, proposed a more nuanced interpretation, arguing that Madison did not want to "reduce the *current* scope of popular participation." Yet, it seems clear, Madison feared democratic institutions were so prone to abuse, even in the United States, that they could prosper only within carefully circumscribed limits. "The Americans are an enlightened and a liberal people, compared with other nations," he wrote one correspondent, "but they are not all philosophers." In writing *The Federalist*, Madison faced what the historian Jack Rakove has called an "ironic dilemma." He was attempting "to appeal to the same public opinion whose excesses" the Constitution was intended to curb.[8]

As the ratification debate went forward, the Constitution's greatest weakness became its lack of a bill of rights. Even Thomas Jefferson complained. Writing from Paris, where he was still the American minister, Jefferson found much to like in the new Constitution, but he also had reservations, and the first one he mentioned to Madison was "the omission of a bill of rights. . . . Let me add that a bill of rights is what the people are entitled to against every government on earth, general or particular, and which no just government should refuse or rest on inference."[9]

All the Anti-Federalists wanted amendments of some kind. Patrick Henry and many others demanded a second constitutional convention. Madison recognized the depth of the opposition, especially in New York and Virginia, but he felt certain the Anti-Federalists were too divided to agree on a workable alternative to the Constitution as it had been submitted to the states. Northern and southern Anti-Federalists had different interests, and even in Virginia, opponents of ratification were divided. Moderates, among whom Madison placed Edmund Randolph and George Mason, wanted amendments to protect the rights of individuals and of the states. Others, including Henry, demanded more substantial changes and seemed willing to risk the Union in their effort to secure them. Madison supported the Constitution because he concluded that neither the Union nor republican government could long endure under the Articles of Confederation and because he believed the Constitution was the only alternative that could command the support of a majority. The "question on which the proposed Constitution must turn," he wrote Edmund Pendleton in February 1788, "is the simple one whether the Union shall or shall not be continued. There is in my opinion no middle ground."[10]

In his first and most famous essay, *Federalist No. 10*, Madison challenged conventional wisdom, exemplified by Montesquieu, that republicanism could only flourish in a small state where citizens would most likely share a common interest. Accordingly, Anti-Federalists argued that sovereignty ought to remain with the states. Madison's reply began by identifying what he described as the greatest threat facing popular governments, the presence of "factions." He defined a faction as "a number of citizens" united by a common interest "adverse to the rights of other citizens, or to the permanent and aggregate interests of the community." Factions could arise around differences in religion, the personalities of individual leaders, or "the most frivolous and fanciful distinctions." Yet, Madison wrote, "the most common and durable source of factions, has been the various and unequal distribution of property."

The influence of factions in government created a "distrust of public engagements, and alarm for private rights." When citizens attempt to confront factions, self-interest corrupts reason. The state could try to eliminate the differences that produce factions, but differences are inevitable in a free society. Madison dismissed that cure as worse than the disease. Lawmakers — and for Madison real authority resided in the legislature — could attempt to resist and control special interests, but the people's representatives could not always be trusted.

The problem became especially acute if a faction represented a majority of citizens, which could easily happen in a small, direct democracy. What could restrain the arbitrary majority? "We all know," he wrote, "that neither moral nor religious motives can be relied on as an adequate control." Here Madison showed the ingenuity that made *Federalist No. 10* the most important work of political theory ever written by an American. He defined a republic as a representative government, and by emphasizing the idea of representation, and thereby removing the citizen from a direct role in policymaking, overturned the conventional wisdom. "A republic, by which I mean a government in which the scheme of representation takes place, opens a different prospect and promises the cure for which we are seeking." In a large republic, no one faction would be likely to seize power. "Extend the sphere, and you take in a greater variety of parties and interests; you make it less probable that a majority of the whole will have a common motive to invade the rights of other citizens." One religious sect could be checked by another; no one cause would command majority support. "A rage for paper money, for an abolition of debts, for an equal division of property, or for any other improper or wicked project, will be less apt to pervade the whole body of the union, than a particular member of it." An extended republic provided "a republican remedy for the diseases most incident to republican government."

The extended republic offered another benefit. As the electorate expanded "it will be more difficult for unworthy candidates to practice with success the vicious arts by which elections are too often carried."[11] In *Federalist No. 14*, Madison returned to the theme of the extended republic, defending it now on practical grounds. Improvements in communications, for example, would make a more centralized administration possible. And recognizing the novelty of his arguments, he appealed to America's revolutionary heritage. "Is it not the glory of the people of America, that whilst they have paid a decent regard to the opinions of former times and other nations, they have not suffered a blind veneration for antiquity?"[12]

Madison's next essays, Nos. 18, 19, and 20, drew on his "Notes on the Ancient and Modern Confederacies" and narrated the misfortunes that had befallen the Greeks, Germans, and Dutch because they lacked strong central governments.[13] By mid-January 1788, he was receiving letters praising the first Publius essays, but as the debate went on he grew more defensive. "A faultless plan was not to be expected," he wrote in No. 37. Given the "inherent" difficulties facing the Philadelphia delegates, including the "novelty of the undertaking," its complexity, and conflicts between the large and small states, "the real wonder is, that so many difficulties should have been surmounted."[14] In *Federalist No. 38*, Madison argued, plausibly enough, that the Anti-Federalists could not agree in their criticisms of the Constitution, and less persuasively, that the Articles of Confederation suffered from some of the same defects as those attributed to the new charter. The Articles, for example, also lacked a bill of rights.[15]

In *Federalist No. 40*, Madison gave a somewhat strained reading of the instructions the Philadelphia convention received from Congress in an effort to answer the charge that the delegates had exceeded their authority. More effective was his appeal, once again, to the revolutionary tradition. The delegates, he wrote, "must have reflected, that in all great changes of established governments, forms ought to give way to substance; that a rigid adherence in such cases to the former, would render nominal and nugatory, the transcendent and precious right of the people" to "abolish or alter their governments as to them shall seem most likely to effect their safety and happiness."[16]

The next few essays, all appearing in the last half of January, defended the broad powers to be conferred on the new government, including the power to tax and to maintain a standing army, both sensitive points in republican theory.[17] Madison defended the federal government's right to regulate foreign and interstate commerce. The Constitution would empower Congress to eliminate trade barriers that would otherwise create tensions among the states.[18] He dwelt at some length on the clause guaranteeing the states "a republican government." It would permit Congress, he believed, to suppress "domestic violence"—he referred obliquely to Shays's Rebellion, or even a slave revolt.[19]

In *Federalist No. 44*, Madison warmed to a defense of the ban on state bills of credit and state laws impairing contracts. "The loss which America has sustained since the peace, from the pestilent effects of paper money . . . constitutes an enormous debt against the states." Laws impairing contracts violated "personal rights" to benefit "enterprising and influential speculators" at the expense of "the more industrious and less informed part of the community." The same essay discussed the grant to Congress of the power to pass laws "necessary and proper" to implement its enumerated powers. The provision only stated explicitly what could reasonably be inferred: "Wherever the ends are required, the means are authorized." It was a commentary he would live to regret when he later opposed Hamilton's effort to charter a national bank. If Congress abused its authority, it would, "in the first instance," be checked by the executive and judicial departments. "In the last resort," the people can elect "more faithful representatives." When Congress threatens to overstep its bounds, the state legislatures "will be ever ready to sound the alarm."[20]

Suggesting that the states could serve as a check on the national government was a far cry from Madison's original proposal to give Congress a veto over all state legislation, and the *Federalist* essays often found Madison modifying his positions or setting old ideas aside. In *Federalist No. 39*, responding to Anti-Federalist claims that the Constitution would create an all-powerful consolidated state, Madison described a federal system in which sovereignty would be shared. The Constitution itself was to be ratified "by the people, not as individuals composing one entire nation; but as composing the distinct and independent states to which they respectively belong." With its members elected by the people, the House of Representatives could be called a truly national institution; the Senate, elected by the state legislatures, was federal. The executive was "of a mixed character," but in later essays Madison stressed the role of the state legislatures in selecting presidential electors. The Constitution would be national in "the operation of the government on the people in their individual capacities," which had been one of his chief objectives, but it was federal in the extent of its powers. "Its jurisdiction extends to certain enumerated objects only, and leaves to the several states a residuary and invisible sovereignty over all other objects." With broader responsibilities and the larger number of officeholders, state governments would enjoy an advantage in competing for popular support, and state interests could be expected to prevail in Congress.[21]

The Constitution's treatment of slavery obviously troubled Madison. "It was doubtless to be wished that the power of prohibiting the importation of slaves had not been postponed until the year 1808," but he consoled himself with the thought that "it ought to be considered as a great point gained in favor of humanity" that the foreign slave trade would ultimately be banned. He devoted *Federalist No. 54* to the issue of counting slaves, albeit as three-fifths of a free person, for purposes of representation in Congress. Slaves could not be counted for tax levies, as northerners demanded, and excluded in determining the size of a state's congressional delegation. Arguing that "government is instituted no less for protection of the property, than of the persons of individuals," Madison suggested counting slaves was a way to give additional protection to property rights, although he admitted that the argument "may appear to be a little strained in some points."[22]

He undoubtedly felt most strained in attempting to defend equality of representation in the Senate. Rationalizing what had been his most bitter defeat at the Constitutional Convention, Madison suggested in *Federalist No. 62* that a House of Representatives elected by the people and a Senate selected by the state legislatures, and representing the states as equals, was not unreasonable "in a compound republic partaking both of the national and federal character." It was, however, "superfluous" to test by theory a clear product of compromise. Madison preferred to justify the Senate as a stabilizing influence in the new government. With their longer terms and fewer numbers, senators would feel a sense of individual responsibility lacking in the House. The volume and fickleness of state legislation appalled Madison; he hoped the Senate could help the federal government avoid a similar fate. "It will be of little avail to the people that the laws are made by men of their own choice, if the laws be so voluminous that they cannot be read, or so incoherent that they can not be understood; if they be repealed or revised before they are promulgated, or undergo such incessant changes that no man who knows what the law is today can guess what it will be to-morrow."[23]

Madison's essays treating the separation of powers were less defensive, and they rivaled *Federalist No. 10* in their creativity. Critics complained that the Constitution, contrary to the teachings of Montesquieu, failed to separate cleanly the legislative, executive, and judicial functions. The Senate would usurp the proper role of the courts when it heard cases of impeachment, and the president's veto power would intrude on the prerogatives of the legislature, to cite but two examples of an allegedly improper inter-mingling. In *Federalist No. 47*, Madison redefined what the separation of powers meant. It existed when no one branch exercised the "whole" of two powers.[24]

"Parchment barriers," he wrote, would not keep power within its proper channels. The authors of the Articles of Confederation, recalling the dangers of a hereditary monarch, failed to foresee that, in a republican system, the most assertive branch would be the legislature.[25] Officeholders in each branch had to be given the "constitutional means, and personal motives, to resist the encroachments of the others. . . . Ambition must be made to counteract ambition." Designing a government forced lawgivers to confront human nature. As he famously observed in *Federalist No. 51*: "If men were angels, no government would be necessary. If angels were to govern men, neither external nor internal controls on government would be necessary. In framing a government which is to be administered by men over men, the great difficulty lies in this: you must first enable the government to control the governed; and in the next place, oblige it to control itself. A dependence on the people is no doubt the primary control on the government; but experience has taught mankind the necessity of auxiliary precautions."[26]

Dividing the legislative functions between two houses provided one "auxiliary precaution"; fortifying the executive with a limited veto provided another, as did the division of sovereignty between the state and national governments. Madison seemed to suggest in *Federalist No. 39* that the federal courts could resolve conflicts between the different levels of government, but he said little about their role in maintaining the separation of powers at the federal level. He generally deferred to Hamilton on issues of judicial review. For Madison, the surest safeguard "for civil rights must be the same as that for religious rights. It consists in the one case in the multiplicity of interests, and in the other, in the multiplicity of sects," circumstances that "render an unjust combination of a majority of the whole very improbable" in a large republic.[27]

Madison devoted several essays to the claim the Constitution favored the wealthy, an allegation that went to the core of the ratification debate. Madison himself had argued that congressional elections would eliminate the coarser politicians who often won state legislative seats. Worse yet, the upper classes seemed to lean heavily Federalist, creating a fear among many citizens of more modest means, as Rufus King reported from Massachusetts, "that some injury is plotted against them, that the system is the production of the rich."[28]

Charges of elitism, and possible remedies, took several forms. Some proposed frequent popular conventions to resolve constitutional disputes. Madison demurred, arguing for the advantages of stability: "Frequent appeals [to the people] would in great measure deprive the government of the veneration which time bestows on everything."[29] The House of Representatives, supposedly the people's branch, ironically presented a tempting target for Anti-Federalists. Its two-year terms violated the republican maxim "Where annual elections end, tyranny begins." Madison responded with a series of arguments: representatives needed time to travel, to resolve elections disputes, to learn their jobs, and so on. Anti-Federalists commonly argued House members, elected as they were from large districts, would not understand local conditions. Madison replied that Congress would not be regulating local affairs. More representatives would not necessarily be better. "In all numerous assemblies, of whatever characters composed, passion never fails to wrest the scepter from reason," he wrote in *Federalist No. 55.* "Had every Athenian citizen been a Socrates, every Athenian assembly would still have been a mob." In any event, the Constitution would mandate an increase in the number of representatives as the population grew.[30]

Madison also attempted to turn the tables on the Anti-Federalists. Their predictions of political disaster under a new government betrayed doubts about "the capacity of the people to choose their own rulers." Madison knew minority rights could not be trusted to the good faith of the majority, but he also understood that republican governments presupposed "qualities in human nature, which justify a certain portion of esteem and confidence." Could, Anti-Federalists wondered, an aristocratic Congress exempt itself from oppressive laws? Republicanism ultimately rested on the people's love of liberty, Madison answered. "If this spirit shall ever be so far debased as to tolerate a law not obligatory on the legislature as well as on the people, the people will be prepared to tolerate anything but liberty."[31]

Delaware, Pennsylvania, and New Jersey ratified the Constitution in December 1787, and Georgia and Connecticut joined them early in January 1788. In New Hampshire, however, a convention adjourned without reaching a decision. In Massachusetts, where Anti-Federalists were strong, Federalists secured ratification only after agreeing to recommend amendments to Congress. Madison considered the amendments to be "a blemish, but . . . in the least offensive form."[32] He attempted to monitor the ratification debate elsewhere, with mixed results. He wrote George Washington in February 1788 that North Carolina was leaning toward ratification; in reality the state was an Anti-Federalist redoubt.[33] Madison received conflicting reports from Virginia; public opinion there was divided and volatile. Jefferson suggested that nine states, the minimum number required, should ratify the Constitution, and the remaining four withhold their assent until a bill of rights was added. Patrick Henry, who wanted more sweeping amendments, reportedly hoped to force the other states to accept Virginia's terms.[34]

In Madison's own Orange County, Baptists were "much alarmed fearing religious liberty is not sufficiently secured." Anti-Federalist candidates emerged for the county's two seats in the state ratifying convention. Madison's father and others urged him to come home and campaign for a delegate's position. Professing reluctance to enter yet another campaign, Madison wrote his last *Federalist* essay and left New York in March.[35]

In recent years, historians have tended to discount the impact of *The Federalist* on the ratification debate. The initial circulation of the essays was too late and too local to influence events in many of the states. Nevertheless, Madison, Hamilton, and Jay provided much appreciated arguments to Federalists in the critical states of New York and Virginia. "*The Federalist*," moreover, "may fairly enough be regarded as the most authentic exposition of the text of the Federal Constitution, as understood by the Body which prepared and the authority which accepted it." Or so Madison wrote in 1825, and history has generally concurred.[36]

James Madison arrived at Montpelier on 23 March to find Orange County "filled with the most absurd and groundless prejudices against the Federal Constitution." The next day, he wrote Eliza House Trist, he was forced "to mount for the first time in my life, the rostrum before a large body of the people, and to launch into a harangue of some length" as a cold wind blew and a light snow fell. Citizens cast their votes one by one with the sheriff, and the Federalist ticket prevailed by a decisive margin. Madison received 202 votes; his Federalist colleague James Gordon Jr. got 187. Anti-Federalist Thomas Barbour won 56 votes, and Charles Porter, who had defeated Madison years earlier in a legislative race after Madison refused to ply the voters with rum, got only 34.[37]

Statewide, the vote was closer. The debate over ratification divided a political elite that had usually been united on the great issues of the revolutionary era. Federalist Cyrus Griffin rejoiced at Madison's election: "We consider you as the main pillar of the business on the right side."[38] The elections gave the Federalists a slight majority in the upcoming convention. A few delegates were truly undecided; some owed their election to their personal popularity, not their stand on the Constitution. The Anti-Federalist William Grayson predicted that the decision of the convention would rest with "seven or eight dubious characters, whose opinions are not known." Although towns, with commercial interests tied to broader markers, leaned more strongly toward the Constitution than did remote rural areas, Virginia was an overwhelmingly agricultural society dominated by a planter aristocracy. Competing economic interests cannot wholly explain the division of opinion. The Northern Neck and the Tidewater north of the James River were Federalist. The Southside, under the sway of Henry, was Anti-Federalist. The Piedmont was divided. The Great Valley had favored the Federalists. The western counties in the Ohio Valley leaned Federalist; Kentucky tilted in the opposite direction. A handful of undecided western delegates held the balance of power.[39]

And then there was Edmund Randolph. The Virginia governor had reservations about the Constitution; he had refused to sign it in Philadelphia, but he disliked Patrick Henry, its most outspoken Virginia critic, even more. "The Governor is so temperate in his opposition and goes so far with the friends of the Constitution," Madison wrote Thomas Jefferson, "that he cannot be properly classed with its enemies." Madison spent the spring of 1788 trying to cultivate Randolph's active support. He ultimately succeeded. Randolph feared that for Virginia to reject the Constitution after eight states had approved it would be to risk disunion. Robert Rutland described Randolph as "everything that Madison was not—tall, handsome, a glib speaker, and essentially a weakling." Yet Randolph projected the appearance of substance, and his endorsement would give the Federalists a psychological edge once the convention began.[40]

Virginia's Anti-Federalists feared a new national government would allow British creditors to collect their prewar debts, uphold the western land claims of out-of-state speculators, and above all else close the Mississippi River to American traffic in exchange for commercial concessions from Spain. The controversy over the Jay-Gardoqui negotiations left many westerners wary of Congress, and the slow pace of a Kentucky statehood bill fed their resentment.[41]

The Mississippi issue troubled Madison enough that shortly before the convention began he wrote fellow Federalist George Nicholas a long letter in which he attempted to develop an argument why American navigation rights would be safer under the new government than under the old one. Madison suggested that a stronger national government would encourage a new sense of American nationalism that would chafe at the compromise of western interests, or those of any other section. The new government would secure western land titles, which would encourage westward migration and strengthen the kinship ties between East and West. The new government would protect Americans' right to use the Mississippi in order to maintain the value of public land needed to retire the public debt. He saw little material difference between requiring a two-thirds vote in the Senate to approve a treaty under the Constitution, and the need for the approval of two-thirds of the states represented in Congress, as required by the Articles of Confederation. More important, under the Constitution, the president would serve as a check on the treaty-making power, and, in an argument to which he would return during the partisan wars of the 1790s, so too could the House of Representatives. Its approval could be necessary to implement a treaty even though the Constitution gave it no explicit role in the treaty-making process. Larger than the Senate and popularly elected, the House would better represent the local interests of the majority of citizens, who would demand access to the Mississippi. The members of the Senate, in contrast, would more likely be taken "from the commercial and maritime situations, which have generally presented the best choice of characters."[42]

In March, a referendum in Rhode Island defeated the Constitution by a vote of 2,945 to 237; the state's embattled Federalists boycotted the election. New Hampshire, New York, and North Carolina remained in doubt. Madison could expect the struggle for ratification in Virginia to receive a boost from Maryland and South Carolina, where conventions would approve the Constitution shortly before the Virginia convention met. Yet Virginia itself would be pivotal and not only because it might be in a position to provide the last of the nine votes needed to organize the new government. A letter from Hamilton implied that defeat in Virginia would doom Federalist efforts in New York. Without New York and Virginia, which together contained almost one-third of the American population, and an even larger share of its political talent, the new republic would not be viable.[43]

The Virginia convention met in Richmond on 3 June. Madison arrived that evening, unusually late for him, but he had not expected a quorum to be present the first day. The delegates immediately elected the venerable Edmund Pendleton, crippled by a carriage accident, as chair, and they voted to relocate from the state capitol to the larger New Academy on nearby Shockoe Hill. Founded by the Frenchman Alexandre Marie Quesnay de Beaurepaire on the European model, the academy was to teach everything from fencing to foreign languages. Shortly after it opened, Quesnay returned to France to raise money. Caught up in the French Revolution, he never came back, and the school failed, but the building survived until it was destroyed by fire several years later.[44]

Richard Henry Lee, who was not a delegate, advised George Mason to propose a clause-by-clause debate of the Constitution. He did and the delegates agreed, a move that has often been seen as a tactical blunder by the Anti-Federalists because it played to Madison's forte—a mastery of detail—and to the incomparable legal skills of allies like George Wythe and John Marshall. In reality, the formidable Mason could argue anything with anyone, and Patrick Henry's gasconade could not be limited by the rules of debate. Madison, moreover, had at least one reason to dread a prolonged convention: the General Assembly was scheduled to meet in three weeks, and its members would swell the ranks of Richmond's Anti-Federalists.[45]

Randolph stunned Anti-Federalist delegates by announcing his support for ratification at the start of the convention, but Madison, once he recovered from "a bilious attack," carried the rhetorical burden for the Federalists. As he wrote Rufus King on 18 June, "I have been much indisposed and continue so in a degree which barely allows me to co-operate in the business." George Washington offered fatherly advice from Mount Vernon: "Moderate exercise, and books occasionally, with the mind unbent, will be your best restoratives." Undoubtedly, Madison's illness made his usually indifferent oratory even less compelling. The convention's official secretary, David Robertson, sometimes inscribed in his notes, "Here *Mr. Madison* spoke so low that he could not be distinctly heard." Rocking back and forth when he was excited, Madison, according to nineteenth-century Virginia historian Hugh Grigsby, "always rose to speak as if with a view of expressing some thought that had casually occurred to him, with his hat in his hands and with his notes in his hat."[46]

With most of the delegates committed to one position or the other, the Virginia deliberations failed to demonstrate the intellectual creativity that had characterized the federal Constitutional Convention in Philadelphia. The delegates debated a host of issues. The most contentious did not necessarily raise the most vexing issues of constitutional interpretation, and they would not be of the greatest interest to later generations. Madison spent much of his time defending Congress's power to tax. Anti-Federalists argued that Congress should be allowed to tax only when a state refused to honor voluntary requisitions. Some wanted to limit the federal taxing power to a levy on imports. Requisitions had worked badly in the past, Madison replied, and a federal power of taxation would make the United States less dependent on foreign aid. As the country grew, moreover, manufacturing would increase, making imports a relatively less lucrative source of revenues.[47] Preserving American access to the Mississippi River was another sensitive issue; here Madison repeated the arguments from his letter to George Nicholas.[48]

Equally worrisome was the jurisdiction of the new federal courts, which raised the always explosive issues of British debts and out-of-state land claims. In a major speech late in the convention, Madison assured his fellow delegates that Congress would show restraint in creating federal trial courts. When Anti-Federalists complained about having to travel to a distant national capital for sessions of the Supreme Court, he wrongly predicted that the court would meet in different locations to better accommodate litigants. He also told the convention, again wrongly as it turned out, that a citizen would not be able to sue a state in federal court.[49]

Although the Anti-Federalists' demand for a bill of rights constituted their most appealing argument, the issue hardly dominated the debate. Madison bristled when, on 12 June, Patrick Henry cited Jefferson's letter suggesting that four states should withhold ratification until amendments protecting civil liberties were added. "Is it come to this then, that we are not to follow our own reason?" Madison asked. "Is it proper to introduce the opinions of respectable men not within these walls?" He was a trifle inconsistent—Madison himself had noted Washington's support for the Constitution—but in fairness to Madison, Jefferson had more recently tempered his reservations. According to Irving Brant, Henry's attempt to defend a bill of attainder passed by the Virginia legislature against Josiah Phillips during the Revolution "virtually destroyed the bill-of-rights issue as an argument against ratification." Madison did confront the specific charge that the Constitution failed to protect religious freedom, and he offered a familiar response: "That multiplicity of sects, which pervades America . . . is the best and only security for religious liberty." With the people clearly opposed to a religious establishment, "there is not a shadow of right in the general government to intermeddle with religion."[50]

There were other issues. Madison defended the Electoral College and the president's power to grant pardons. He spoke up for Congress's authority to maintain a standing army and to regulate the state militias. When Mason complained that the Constitution lacked specific protections for slavery but permitted the notorious foreign slave trade to continue, Madison kept his remarks brief. The Constitution gave Congress no control over slavery within the states, and the slave trade compromise, allowing the trade to continue for another twenty years, preserved the Union without making the problem worse.[51] Repeatedly he returned to fundamental themes in responding to claims that the Constitution was elitist or undemocratic. In a republic, the gravest threats to individual rights came from the majority. Under the Articles of Confederation, the nation appeared headed toward anarchy, and "anarchy ever has, and I fear ever will, produce despotism." Anti-Federalists supposed "that the general legislature will do every mischief they possibly can." Madison disagreed: "I go on this great republican principle, that the people will have virtue and intelligence to select men of virtue and wisdom." He found the work as tedious as any he had ever done. "My health is not good," he wrote Alexander Hamilton, "and the business is wearisome beyond expression."[52]

Anti-Federalists knew they could probably not defeat the Constitution outright. Federalists wanted to avoid any conditions or modifications. Madison, for example, objected when Hamilton indicated an openness to compromise in New York: the state might reserve the right to secede if certain proposed amendments were not acted on within a specified period. Madison believed attaching conditions would invalidate the ratification. Massachusetts had approved the Constitution and simply recommended amendments. In April, George Nicholas had suggested the Massachusetts model as the only safe compromise, and Madison seemed to agree.[53] Recognizing "the nice balance of numbers, and the scruples entertained by some who are in general well affected," Madison and other Federalist leaders now decided to offer a version of the Massachusetts plan as a compromise. Madison apparently feared the Federalists' initial edge had disappeared and hoped coupling ratification with a request, not a demand, for amendments would give them at least a three- or four-vote majority.[54]

The convention completed its clause-by-clause debate on the Constitution on 23 June. The next day, George Wythe proposed that the delegates ratify the charter and recommend amendments be considered under Article 5, which required the approval of a two-thirds majority of both houses of Congress and three-fourths of the states. Wythe also proposed adding a caveat to the act of ratification providing that rights not granted to the federal government were retained by the people and could not be abridged. Patrick Henry responded with a motion to refer a bill of rights and other amendments to a second convention of the states before the Constitution could take effect. "I can never consent to his previous amendments," Madison said during the ensuing debate, "because they are pregnant with dreadful dangers." Madison feared that a second convention would unduly weaken the national government or end in discord, which would threaten the Union itself. On the afternoon of 29 June, the convention defeated Henry's motion by a vote of 88 to 80, and then voted 89 to 79 to approve Wythe's, with David Patteson of Chesterfield County changing sides. Madison was then appointed to committees to prepare a formal instrument of ratification and a set of proposed amendments.[55]

The Federalists could be accused of playing a cynical, almost desperate, game. On 25 June, George Nicholas had presented a list of amendments he said Federalists would support, but the Federalists had little interest in them, and few seemed likely to clear the hurdles imposed by Article 5. The amendments eventually approved by the convention included one requiring a two-thirds vote to pass legislation regulating trade. It was evidence of widespread distrust of northern commercial interests; Madison had long opposed it. He voted with the minority in an unsuccessful effort to strike another amendment allowing a state to devise its own method of collecting any direct taxes or excises imposed by Congress. Of the forty amendments approved by the convention, "several of them," Madison wrote Washington, were "highly objectionable." But they had secured a handful of wavering and undecided votes, and they allowed the Federalists to offer voters an alternative to a dreaded second constitutional convention.[56]

Notwithstanding the particularly bruised feelings of George Mason, Madison believed the convention ended well, with most Anti-Federalists accepting the result. The outcome certainly enhanced Madison's prestige. "I confess I have also attributed to you the glory of laying the Foundation of this great fabric of government," John Page wrote in August. A French diplomat who had watched the convention reported to his superiors: "Mr. Maddisson is the one who, among all the delegates, carried the votes of the two parties. He was always clear, precise and consistent in his reasoning, and always methodical and pure in his language. He certainly would have convinced his Antagonists if they had not already had a predetermined plan."[57] The convention demonstrated once again Madison's capacity for effective service in a deliberative assembly, his ability to endure the occasional defeat, and his willingness to persevere in the interest of a larger objective.

Yet even with the ratification of the Constitution in South Carolina, New York, and New Hampshire, the debate continued. North Carolina and Rhode Island remained outside the Union, and as Madison wrote Tench Coxe, "The conspiracy [against] direct taxes is more extensive and formidable than some gentlemen suspect." Madison feared New York's decision to ratify the Constitution and call for a second national convention had done more harm than good. His feckless ally Edmund Randolph seemed to support a second convention; Madison warned him it would be "the offspring of party & passion." When Madison returned to Congress, he was appalled by the sectional tenor of the debate over a permanent location for the national capital. Convinced future growth in the South and West would make a site on the Potomac River ideal, Madison vehemently protested the efforts of northern members to keep the capital in New York City. The debate, he thought, fueled, if it did not justify, the paranoia of southern Anti-Federalists. Then in early November, the Virginia assembly passed, by a decisive vote of 85 to 39, a resolution introduced by Patrick Henry calling for a second convention.[58] The Constitution had been ratified; whether the government it created commanded enough popular support to survive remained to be seen.

Writing from Paris in July 1788, Thomas Jefferson seemed pleased with the ratification of the Constitution. "It is a good canvas," he told Madison, "on which some strokes only want retouching." Jefferson suggested adding a declaration of rights to protect the right to a jury trial, the writ of habeas corpus, freedom of the press, and freedom of religion, as well as amendments to ban monopolies and standing armies in peacetime. Originally opposed to any amendments, Madison now preferred to wait a year or so, until experience would expose the Constitution's real deficiencies. Yet Madison ultimately came to see a bill of rights, as opposed to more sweeping structural amendments, as a harmless device to make a second convention unnecessary and to appease moderate Anti-Federalists. Such a conciliatory gesture could "extinguish opposition to the system, or at least break the force of it, by detaching the deluded opponents from their designing leaders." Within a few months, moreover, even Madison began to see the need for changes. Tench Coxe suggested to him an amendment protecting religious freedom from state action, an issue that had long concerned Madison. For his part, Madison wanted to expand the House of Representatives and to restrict the jurisdiction of the Supreme Court to eliminate "superfluous appeals."[59]

In a letter written in October 1788, Madison attempted to explain his original position to Jefferson. "My own opinion," he wrote with less than complete candor, "has always been in favor of a bill of rights; provided it be so framed as not to imply powers not meant to be included in the enumeration." He considered its absence not to be "a material defect" for several reasons. Congress had only the powers delegated to it, and they did not extend to individual rights. Rights reduced to paper, especially freedom of religion, might be too narrowly drawn. The "jealousy" of the states would better check federal power. More important, Madison doubted that "parchment barriers" could control prevailing prejudices. "In Virginia I have seen the bill of rights violated in every instance where it has been opposed to a popular current." The House of Delegates would have passed the general assessment bill if the people had favored it. Admittedly, a bill of rights could help educate citizens about their rights, and in a monarchy it could serve to rally public opinion against arbitrary action, but how, Madison wondered, could a declaration of basic freedoms be enforced in a republic, when oppressive legislation typically reflected the wishes of the majority?[60]

The value of a bill of rights hinged on its enforceability and went to a fundamental cause for Madison's interest in constitutional reform, the protection of minority rights. He had assumed at the Constitutional Convention in Philadelphia that judges would reject ex post facto laws. More often, however, Madison seemed skeptical, if not hostile, as American courts groped toward what in hindsight seems to be the obvious solution, the power of judicial review. In the 1780s, American judges began to strike down laws they held to be unconstitutional. Because British judges were often seen as agents of the crown, and because American judges had been unprofessional amateurs, the tendency in the colonies had been to defer to juries, which reflected public opinion, on questions of both law and fact. After the Revolution, increasingly professional judges became more assertive. Alexander Hamilton, a practicing attorney, argued in *The Federalist* that a bill of rights was unnecessary because federal judges, whom he assumed would be lawyers, would keep Congress within its constitutional limits. Madison saw a similar trend developing in Virginia, and he recognized, "in the ordinary course of government, that the exposition of the laws and constitution devolves upon the judicial branch," but he believed that Congress and the president were equally competent to define the scope of their powers. How that was supposed to work, he never explained. Jefferson had to make the connection between civil liberties and judicial review for him. "In the arguments in favor of a declaration of rights," Jefferson wrote in March 1789, "you omit one which has great weight with me, the legal check which it puts in the hands of the judiciary."[61]

The debate over amendments intruded into the elections for members of the first Congress to serve under the Constitution. In the fall of 1788, the General Assembly elected Anti-Federalists Richard Henry Lee and William Grayson to Virginia's two Senate seats. Madison finished third in the vot-

Portrait of James Monroe. Madison and Monroe were occasional rivals and lifelong friends. (Library of Congress)

ing. Critics claimed he would oppose any amendments and would not follow legislative instructions to resist federal taxation of ordinary citizens. Madison would surely serve in the new government; he heard indirectly that George Washington intended to offer him a post in the executive branch if Madison were not elected to Congress. Madison said he preferred a place in the House of Representatives to the Senate. He thought it would be less expensive to maintain and, presumably, would offer him more independence.[62] Patrick Henry hoped to thwart his ambitions. Under Henry's leadership, the legislature placed Madison's Orange County in a gerrymandered congressional district with counties, in the words of Madison's ally George Lee Turberville, "most tainted with anti-federalism." Anti-Federalists also supported a twelve-month residency requirement for congressional candidates to prevent Madison from running in a more hospitable district. Worse yet, he would face a formidable opponent, his old friend James Monroe.[63]

Madison's supporters urged him to return to Virginia and campaign. He hesitated; he disliked electioneering, and he feared the show of ambition might be counterproductive. He was sick again, and he had hoped to remain in New York City for "a task," which he never explained, that required access to the papers of Congress. But the race divided the district. "Upon the whole," Madison was told, "the Baptist Interest seems everywhere to prevail," and Baptists chafed at the omission of a specific provision in the Constitution protecting religious freedom. Voters reportedly complained most about the lack of a bill of rights and the threat of new federal taxes.[64]

Reluctantly, Madison came home and waged the most aggressive campaign of his career, writing letters explaining his positions and debating Monroe at courthouses and churches throughout the district. Riding home after a debate at a Lutheran church in January, Madison suffered frostbite on his nose; he carried a slight scar for the rest of his life. Madison wrote one long letter defending a broad federal power to tax. Relying on requisitions created resentments among the states, as some states complied with congressional requests and others did not. Direct taxation was needed to support a creditable national defense and to allow the federal government to borrow money abroad. Import duties, the likely alternative, would fall most heavily on the South.[65]

The issue of a bill of rights proved even more critical, and it led Madison to announce his change of position. In a letter to George Eve, the sympathetic pastor of the Bull Run Baptist Church in Orange County, Madison explained that he had opposed amendments before ratification as likely to produce "dangerous contentions." A second constitutional convention would be slow and unpredictable and might attract "insidious characters." With ratification accomplished, "circumstances are now changed." Proper amendments should reassure "well meaning opponents" of the Constitution and provide additional safeguards for individual liberties, especially "the rights of Conscience in the fullest latitude." Madison's promise to support amendments satisfied the Baptists, and on 2 February, he defeated Monroe in the eight-county district by a vote of 1,308 to 972. An almost unanimous vote in Orange County, where he beat Monroe 216 to 9, and two-to-one landslides in Culpeper and Louisa carried the election for Madison.[66] He confided to Edmund Randolph that he was unsure if he should be "satisfied or displeased with my success." He expected Congress to be bitterly divided between Federalists and Anti-Federalists and North and South, and he feared he saw in the new House of Representatives "a very scanty proportion who will share in the drudgery of business."[67]

Once Congress convened in March, Madison took on much of the drudgery himself, speaking 124 times in the five-month session, twice as often as anyone else. He served as an informal adviser to President Washington and drafted his first inaugural address. He inserted one substantive provision, a call for amendments demonstrating "a reverence for the characteristic rights of freemen, and a regard for the public harmony." He also drafted the House's response to the message and Washington's reply to the House.[68] He supported the president's decision to make Jefferson secretary of state, which was no surprise, but ironically, in the light of history, he recommended Hamilton for secretary of the treasury as "best qualified for that species of business."[69]

When a Senate committee recommended that the president be called "His Highness the President of the United States of America and Protector of the Rights of Same," Madison argued successfully for something simpler. If Congress invented an elaborate title, it was likely to sound "ridiculous and absurd." If Congress borrowed one from Europe, "the servile imitation will be odious."[70] When it was proposed that all members of Congress be paid six dollars a day, Madison supported an amendment by Theodore Sedgwick of Massachusetts to pay House members a dollar less. Madison believed the Senate's supposedly greater prestige justified the disparity, but the amendment lost badly. Frederick Muhlenberg of Pennsylvania, eager to move the capital to Philadelphia, complained that members could not live in New York City for less than six dollars a day. "It is vain at this place to talk of frugality."[71]

Madison introduced legislation to create executive departments of war, treasury, and state. Creation of the departments raised a constitutional issue. A presidential appointment of a department head clearly required Senate approval; did the president need the Senate's approval to remove one? Madison, arguing Senate involvement in the removal process would mainly serve to protect ineffective officeholders, favored unfettered executive discretion. He also believed Congress was competent to settle the question: "The meaning of the Constitution may as well be ascertained by the legislative as by the judicial authority."[72]

At the beginning of the session, Madison introduced a revenue plan based on the aborted import of 1783. He proposed specific duties on certain luxury goods and an ad valorem duty on other imports. He wanted a tariff high enough to minimize the need for unpopular direct taxes. Northern delegates preferred higher levies, but more controversial was Madison's call for tonnage duties that discriminated against foreign ships and those of nations that did not have commercial treaties with the United States. The Senate deleted the second condition, and Congress passed a modified version of Madison's plan. He had hoped to use the discriminatory duties to retaliate against Great Britain and force it to open British markets to American goods. The revenue plan exposed some of his less useful convictions: that Great Britain was invariably hostile to American interests, that British prosperity depended on access to American markets, and that American imports from Britain were all "either superfluities or poisons."[73] In Madison's world, theory sometimes outran common sense.

"I never had less time that I could truly call my own," he told Edmund Randolph at the end of May, and Madison's surviving correspondence contains remarkably few personal references. In a letter to his father, he mentioned his "anxiety for the state of my mother's health." In a letter to Jefferson, he expressed relief that the congressional race had not damaged his friendship with James Monroe. In a sign it had not, Monroe bought four lottery tickets for Madison as part of a fundraiser for Fredericksburg Academy, where Monroe was a trustee. Madison's ticket No. 69 won three pounds. He probably needed the money; he professed a lack of ready cash when Henry Lee invited him to join a real estate partnership.[74]

Despite his heavy workload, Madison appeared content with the progress of the session. The sectional differences many had feared seemed manageable, the difficulties inevitable. He complained late in the session that Congress proceeded "with a mortifying tardiness"—partly the result of poor committee work and long-winded speeches—"but principally resulting from the novelty and complexity of the subject of Legislation. We are in a wilderness without a single footstep to guide us. Our successors will have an easier task."[75]

The Frenchman Brissot de Warville described the Madison of 1788–89 as tired, but confident, with "the thoughtful look of a wise statesman."[76] Admirers like Tench Coxe praised Madison for balancing state and national interests, but there were a few dissenters. The Massachusetts Federalists Fisher Ames and Theodore Sedgwick shared similar assessments of Madison. While respecting his integrity, intelligence, and knowledge of public affairs, they feared he worried too much about popular opinion in Virginia. "I think him a little too much of a book politician," Ames wrote, "and too timid in his politics." Sedgwick put it succinctly: Madison seemed "constantly haunted with the ghost of Patrick Henry."[77] Other critics could be more petty than perceptive. After Madison introduced what became the Bill of Rights, Noah Webster published a letter in a New York newspaper criticizing him for wasting Congress's time simply to fulfill a campaign promise to his constituents.[78]

Madison did feel obligated by tacit commitments made at the Virginia ratifying convention and by the explicit pledge he made in his congressional race. On 4 May, he gave notice he intended to introduce proposed amendments on 25 May. He hoped to preempt Theodorick Bland and John Laurance, who were carrying petitions from Virginia and New York, respectively, for a second convention. Something like a bill of rights, he wrote one confidant, would "kill the opposition everywhere" and probably secure ratification of the Constitution in North Carolina, which remained out of the Union. More fundamental, Madison wanted to create a genuine consensus in support of the new government. As the political scientist Robert Goldwin has noted, Madison must have understood that for his theory of factions to work, the different factions would have to feel enough loyalty to the new regime to submit willingly to its decisions.[79]

Few of Madison's colleagues shared his concerns.[80] On 25 May, he agreed to postpone the debate on amendments until 8 June "in order that more urgent business may not be delayed." On 8 June, when Madison proposed that the House meet as a committee of the whole to debate amendments more freely, he encountered spirited objections. James Jackson of Georgia suggested that the debate be postponed until March 1790. Madison responded, in the words of the *New York Daily Advertiser*, with a "long and able speech." He did not intend to reconsider "the whole structure of government" but only planned to take up amendments that could win the support of two-thirds of both houses of Congress and three-fourths of the states. "The great mass of the people" who opposed ratification did so because there was no bill of rights, an objection which could now be eliminated without "endangering any part of the Constitution."[81]

The time spent on the procedural skirmish frustrated Madison, but the maneuvering did give him an opportunity to introduce his amendments, and the House scheduled a substantive debate for 21 July. After promising the Baptists he would support a bill of rights, Madison had started a scrapbook of newspaper articles about proposed amendments and had begun making a list of possible changes to the Constitution. Madison submitted to the House nineteen amendments culled from two hundred—there was some duplication—recommended by the state conventions. He deleted the ones that were controversial and that would have unduly weakened the federal government, and he added two of his own. One prevented the taking of private property for public use without just compensation; the other prohibited the states from infringing on freedom of religion, freedom of the press, or the right to a jury trial in a criminal case.[82]

He began with a preamble, borrowed in part from the Declaration of Independence, that recognized, among other general rights, the right of the people "to reform or change their government." He proposed expanding the House of Representatives to include one representative for every thirty thousand citizens, up to an unspecified limit, and he suggested that no congressional salary increase could take effect until after the next congressional election. A separate section, including most of what eventually became the Bill of Rights, encompassed protections for freedom of speech, press, and religion; procedural safeguards for criminal defendants; and recognition of the right to bear arms, with the caveat that "no person religiously scrupulous of bearing arms, shall be compelled to render military service in person." Other amendments attempted to limit the appellate jurisdiction of the Supreme Court to legally significant cases and issues, to guarantee the right to a jury trial in criminal cases, and to require a grand jury indictment for serious criminal prosecutions. The last two amendments committed the three branches of the federal government to respect the separation of powers and declared that all powers not delegated to the federal government or denied to the states were retained by the states.[83]

Besides introducing the amendments, Madison repeated the now familiar arguments in favor of a bill of rights, and echoing Jefferson's language, he addressed the problem of enforcement. "Independent tribunals of justice will consider themselves in a peculiar manner the guardians of those rights; they will be an impenetrable bulwark against every assumption of power in the legislative or executive." He made the argument, but he may not have meant it. The exalted role it envisioned for the judiciary conflicted with the position he took in the debate over the president's power to dismiss subordinates and with reservations he expressed elsewhere about the potentially overarching power of the courts.[84]

If Madison's amendments failed to generate great enthusiasm in Congress, they had the desired effect elsewhere.[85] To be sure, there were critics. Madison's cousin the Reverend James Madison complained about the lack of structural amendments. Before he saw Madison's proposals, George Mason suspected "some milk & water propositions may be made by Congress to the State Legislatures by Way of th[r]owing out a Tub to the Whale; but of important & substantial Amendments, I have not the least Hope." After he saw what the House passed, Mason concluded, "With two or three further amendments . . . I could cheerfully put my hand & heart to the new

Government."[86] Reports reaching Madison suggested that the introduction of amendments had markedly improved the prospects for ratification in North Carolina. Washington believed the amendments would "quiet the fears of some respectable characters and well meaning men."[87]

As a guide to the intent behind the Bill of Rights, the House debates can be frustrating. At times, the representatives seemed to debate everything but the substance of the amendments. On 21 July, they debated again, to Madison's dismay, how to proceed, and then voted 34 to 15 to refer his amendments to a select committee consisting of one member from each state. On 13 August, John Vining of New York presented the committee report. It made few significant changes to Madison's draft, but the report triggered a debate on the propriety of amending the preamble of the Constitution and about the placement of the other amendments. The changes to the preamble went by the wayside. Madison wanted to incorporate the substantive amendments into the text of the Constitution for, he thought, clarity's sake, and his colleagues defeated a motion by Roger Sherman to add them to the existing document as a supplement. On 19 August, the House reversed itself, approved Sherman's motion, and thereby recast the amendments as a literal, more visible, and more dramatic bill of rights.[88]

The House defeated Anti-Federalist amendments to recognize the right of voters to "instruct" their representatives, to limit the power of Congress to regulate congressional elections, and to provide that powers not "expressly" delegated to Congress were reserved to the states. Madison argued, in language that would later prove to be an embarrassment, "It was impossible to confine a government to the exercise of express powers." The phrase "or the people" was added to Madison's recommendation that powers not delegated to Congress were reserved to the states. The members did not, however, attempt to nail down the meaning of every clause. When the debates reached a would-be ban on "cruel and unusual punishment," Samuel Livermore, a New Hampshire Federalist, said he liked the clause because it "appears to express much humanity," but he confessed that "it appeared to have no meaning. . . . The truth is, matters of this kind must be left to the discretion of those who have administration of the laws."[89]

Madison probably preferred a statement of general principles over specific guarantees, except on the question of religious freedom. Madison's draft of 8 June provided that "the civil rights of none shall be abridged on account of religious belief or worship, nor shall any national religion be established, nor shall the full and equal rights of conscience be in any manner, or on any pretext infringed." The select committee report expressed the same ideas more concisely: "No religion shall be established by law, nor the equal right of conscience be infringed." During the debate of 15 August, Madison explained "the meaning of the words to be, that Congress should not establish a religion, and enforce the legal observation of it by law, nor compel men to worship God in any manner contrary to their conscience." When the objection arose that the clause seemed hostile to religion itself— the implicit threat was to the state establishments—Madison proposed adding "national," to modify the word "religion," but sitting as a committee of the whole, the members adopted language proposed by Livermore: "Congress shall make no laws touching religion, or infringing the rights of conscience." A few days later the House adopted another version, this one from Fisher Ames and probably Madison: "Congress shall make no law establishing religion, or to prevent the free exercise thereof, or to infringe the rights of conscience."[90]

By the middle of August, Madison was referring in private correspondence to "the nauseous project of amendments." After a week of debate, he wrote Edmund Randolph, "Progress has been exceedingly wearisome." Legitimate differences of opinion divided members of Congress. Some Anti-Federalist leaders, undoubtedly aware of Madison's effort to use a bill of rights to prevent more radical reform, wanted to squash the initiative.[91]

By 25 August, however, the House had passed the amendments and sent them on to the Senate. The senators deleted Madison's exemption for conscientious objectors from military service, the statement on the separation of powers, and his attempt to limit the appellate jurisdiction of the Supreme Court. The Senate also discarded the amendment protecting freedom of the press, freedom of religion, and the right to a jury trial from state action. An effort to turn the demand for amendments to his own purposes—limiting the power of the states—Madison considered "this to be the most valuable amendment on the whole list." None of the state conventions had proposed it; it was largely his invention. In all, the Senate rewrote the seventeen House amendments into twelve, achieving greater brevity with no serious loss of substance except, perhaps, for a weaker clause on religion. Madison served on the House-Senate conference committee that worked out the acceptable, final language on that issue: "Congress shall make no law respecting an establishment of religion, or prohibiting the free exercise thereof." By December 1791, three-fourths of the states had approved ten of the amendments. The ones expanding the House of Representatives and delaying any congressional pay raise to the subsequent term failed.[92] Ratification of the Bill of Rights in Virginia came in December after considerable debate and delay.[93]

Although James Madison has been called the Father of the Constitution, he played a larger role in the adoption of the Bill of Rights. At the time, his success was more political than legal. The Bill of Rights produced little litigation until the twentieth century. The amendments possessed largely, in the words of Richard Labunski, "symbolic value" in the 1800s. Yet Madison achieved his principal objective, skillfully taming opposition to the new government, and shrewdly making new allies among the more malleable of Virginia's Anti-Federalists, without demanding real concessions from the Constitution's original supporters. The introduction of amendments and their passage by Congress had reassured many skeptics; by the time they took effect, according to Robert Goldwin, "the amendments were the solution to a problem that had ceased to exist."[94]

Beginning with the appearance of the "Memorial and Remonstrance against Religious Assessments" in 1785, Madison had enjoyed five years of remarkably productive statecraft and compiled a record of political and legislative accomplishment rarely equaled in American history. The struggle for the Bill of Rights exemplified Madison's political style and helps explain his success. He shifted positions as circumstances changed, from opposing a bill of rights before ratification to supporting one afterward. He endured frustrating defeats, the death in the Senate, for example, of his amendment curbing the states' discretion over religion, the press, and the right to a jury trial. Yet once committed to the task, he never wavered in his larger goal of securing amendments that would bind the great majority of white Americans to the new regime without undoing the work of the federal Constitutional Convention. Despite shifts and reversals, he maintained a fundamental consistency, projecting his Virginia republicanism on a national stage.

The Origins of the Party System

"*I*f I could not go to heaven but with a party," Thomas Jefferson once said, "I would not go there at all." Jefferson was given to hyperbole, but the framers generally took a dim view of political parties. "Party spirit," Abigail Adams said, "sees not that wisdom dwells with moderation." Madison believed parties were at best a necessary evil. The Constitution made no provision for them, and Madison hoped its elaborate system of checks and balances would mitigate their unwholesome tendencies.[1]

To Madison's dismay, a new Federalist clique soon gained control of the national government. Convinced that the Federalists, despite their electoral successes, represented a minority of the population, Madison justified the creation of his own Republican Party as a way to preserve popular government, and, in fact, fewer than one eligible voter in four may have voted in the national elections of the 1790s. The Federalist ascendancy forced Madison to confront an issue he had never squarely addressed: the problem of minority tyranny within a republican state.[2]

Members of Congress split initially over the fiscal policies of Alexander Hamilton, the first secretary of the treasury. The partisan divide widened during the debate over the Jay Treaty with Great Britain and became unbridgeable after the XYZ Affair with France. A common theme ran through all the contests: How friendly should the United States be to Great Britain, and how closely should American society resemble British society?[3] The debates were bitter because the issues were fundamental and because neither side accepted the idea of a loyal opposition. "My imagination will not attempt to set bounds to the daring depravity of the times," Madison wrote to Jefferson in August 1791. He typically referred to his Federalist rivals as "anti-republicans," or as "the British party." He thought many of them wanted to transform the United States into a monarchy.[4] The paranoia ran high. By November 1791, Edmund Randolph was warning Madison that

George Washington had joined the Federalist conspiracy "to destroy the republican force in the U.S." In turn, the Federalist Rufus King suspected Madison of "some deep and mischievous design," perhaps an independent southern confederacy.[5]

A party system developed gradually and from the top down. Most elections, especially in the South, were local affairs dominated by local issues and personalities, making organization from the grass roots to a broader arena difficult. Party development reached a certain milestone in 1792 when Republicans nominated George Clinton, the governor of New York, for vice president; the incumbent John Adams was clearly identified with the Federalists. Party organizations remained embryonic, however, until the presidential campaign of 1800.[6]

No single variable explains party loyalties. The historian David Hackett Fischer found the best predictor of voting behavior in 1800 to be rates of population growth, with the fastest-growing regions most likely to be Republican. Motives, of course, could vary from voter to voter. One Washington barber held Madison's hairstyle against him. "Little Jim Madison, with a queue no bigger than a pipe stem," he complained, lacked the presence required for national office. Sectional differences explain the most; the South and West became Republican strongholds. New England was a bastion of Federalism.[7] Historians have debated the degree of continuity between the Federalist supporters of the Constitution and the Federalist Party on the one hand, and between Anti-Federalists and Republicans on the other. Recent scholarship has tended to minimize the connections, but in Virginia many of the Federalists of 1787–88 were Federalists in the 1790s. Most Anti-Federalists became Republicans. On balance, changes of allegiances from the 1780s to the 1790s favored the Republicans. Madison, nevertheless, feared being linked to the Anti-Federalists.[8]

Nor did Madison care to be identified with the Democratic-Republican societies that sprang up around the country in the 1790s, even though he shared many of their views. Elite factions were bad enough; popular factions enjoyed even less legitimacy. Madison chafed in late 1794 when President Washington publicly condemned the societies. He believed they had helped incite the Whiskey Rebellion, a short-lived uprising against a federal tax on distilled liquor. Few of the societies survived beyond 1796.[9]

Madison's more eloquent and charismatic friend Thomas Jefferson would come to overshadow him as a party leader, and later historians would write of Jeffersonian, not Madisonian, Republicans. Yet as a member of the first federal Congress, Madison laid the foundation for a new party and was

Cornelius Tiebout engraving of Thomas Jefferson after a painting by Rembrandt Peale. The iconic Jefferson overshadowed the diminutive Madison in the popular imagination, but they worked together as equals. (Library of Congress)

initially a more aggressive partisan than Jefferson. In the interim between Jefferson's resignation as secretary of state in 1793 and his return to politics as vice president in 1797, Madison was the undisputed leader of the Republican opposition.[10]

Alexander Hamilton submitted his First Report on the Public Credit to Congress in January 1790. Continental securities had been trading at a fraction of their face value. At least 80 percent of the federal debt had been sold by the original holders, typically at no more than fifty cents on the dollar. Hamilton proposed refinancing the debt, which carried an interest rate of 6 percent, at lower rates; he suggested a menu of payment options, each of which would yield slightly varying effective returns. Creditors would benefit because federal revenues from import duties and a tax on whiskey would be pledged to pay the interest. A sinking fund, supported by postal revenues, would be established to retire a small portion of the federal debt each year. The treasury secretary also proposed that the national government assume the outstanding Revolutionary War debt of the states. Hamilton did not want Congress competing with the states for revenue, and he wanted to ensure the loyalty of creditors to the new national government. Hamilton realized Congress could create wealth by restoring the public credit and increasing the market value of government securities, which would create capital for, among other projects, a national bank. Madison resisted the idea. Hamilton's plan had foreign policy implications that troubled Madison. The treasury secretary's scheme would require the United States to maintain friendly relations with Great Britain. Interest payments would be largely funded by import duties, and most American imports came from Britain.[11]

On 8 February, the House, sitting as a committee of the whole, took up the First Report. There had been talk of discriminating between original and secondary holders of government obligations, and Madison embraced the idea. He advocated paying the highest market value to the secondary holders and face value to the original holders. As a sort of indemnity, original holders who had sold out to speculators would be paid the difference between the highest market price and the face value. Madison also proposed paying the debt at the original 6 percent interest rate, and he wanted to retire it as quickly as possible. He had, he said, "never been a proselyte to the doctrine, that public debts are public benefits."[12]

As the debate continued through February, Madison complained that Hamilton's plan would provide a windfall to speculators. He could not agree "that America ought to erect the monuments of her gratitude, not to those who saved her liberties, but to those who had enriched themselves in her funds." Part of the debt consisted of certificates issued in lieu of cash to soldiers and private citizens who then sold the steeply discounted paper under financial duress. Ignoring them, as Hamilton's plan did, would only compound an injustice. To Hamilton, discrimination would constitute a breach of contract and limit the transferability, and hence the value, of public securities. It would also disperse government revenues. Hamilton wanted to concentrate wealth in the hands of a relatively few speculators, where it could more readily be invested. The treasury secretary envisioned a future characterized by intensive economic development as already settled areas industrialized, and industrialization would require capital.[13]

Madison also objected to Hamilton's assumption plan, but here his motives were clearly more political and his position more nuanced. Virginia had paid much of its own debt and would gain little through assumption. The states, he argued, drew on different sources of revenue than did the federal government; the total public debt could better be managed if it remained divided between Congress and the states. But in a speech on 24 February, he suggested a basis for compromise: any assumption plan should be based on the state debts at the end of the Revolution, in other words, before Virginia had retired the bulk of its obligations.[14]

Some historians have questioned Madison's motives and his judgment. Critics doubted the feasibility of identifying the original owners of securities that had been transferred, and Madison's plan would have increased the total federal debt. The leading student of Revolutionary-era finance concluded that Madison's proposal seemed "on the whole, to have been little more than a political maneuver designed, among other things, to make a show of opposition without offering a real alternative and to court favor among Virginians who had sold out to Northern speculators."[15] That judgment is too harsh. Pennsylvania had distinguished between original and later purchasers in retiring its state debt, so the idea was not unprecedented.[16] Madison's correspondents almost universally condemned assumption,[17] but opinion on discrimination was mixed, and there Madison was not yielding to popular pressure.[18]

Instead, Madison's opposition to Hamilton's funding plan and his reservations about assumption reflected the republican values of rural Virginia. Chafing under their debts, Virginia's planters resented their dependence on British credit. In republican theory, finance had long meant speculation, which yielded an enervating luxury and a dissipated idleness. Little more than gambling, "stock jobbing" discouraged honest labor, fostered a lust for wealth that distracted citizens from their civic duties, and created extremes of wealth and poverty that shattered notions of a common public good. Attempts to profit from public debts produced the greatest dangers: political corruption, unnecessary government spending, and oppressive taxes. Exaggerated as they were, the critics' fears were not wholly unfounded. The majority of the senators and representatives who voted for assumption stood to benefit from the plan, and Hamilton's chief assistant, William Duer, was himself speculating in government securities.[19] Speculators, Madison told Jefferson, were "exploring the interior and distant parts of the union to take advantage of the ignorance of holders."[20]

Madison's hostility surprised Alexander Hamilton; the secretary of the treasury said later he would not have taken the position if he had known Madison would challenge his economic policies. In 1783, Madison had called for assumption and opposed discrimination among debt holders. To Federalists like Theodore Sedgwick, Madison now appeared to be "an apostate from all his former principles."[21] But in the intervening seven years, much of the original Continental paper had been acquired by northern speculators, and Virginia had retired most of its debt. Late in 1789, Madison had given Hamilton signs of an impending disagreement. When Hamilton solicited his thoughts for the Report on Public Credit, Madison observed the debt should be set "in a manifest course of extinguishment." Both men had taken what they liked from the English philosopher David Hume. Hamilton concurred in Hume's argument—unusual in its day—for the aesthetic advantages of commercial, urbanized society. Hume, however, warned that a public debt could become unmanageable; ministers could not be trusted to administer it prudently forever. Hamilton believed British history had proved Hume wrong; Madison believed it had vindicated him.[22]

Although he did not question Madison's integrity, Hamilton complained, "the truth is, that although this gentleman is a clever man, he is very little acquainted with the world." For his part, Hamilton understood international finance better than he understood American politics. Ambitious, thin-skinned, and high-strung, Hamilton by the late 1790s would be willing to use force and various legal stratagems to quash his political opposition. He really did want to model the American economy after the British system; his plans for American banking did not include loans to ordinary citizens. An émigré with no state loyalties, Hamilton at one point proposed breaking up the large states into smaller ones, and his prickly sense of honor would lead to a fatal duel with Aaron Burr.[23]

Whatever Hamilton's shortcomings, most members of Congress feared redeeming the public debt at less than face value to its current holders would be a poor way to instill faith in the new government. The administrative problem of distinguishing among holders seemed overwhelming, and the House defeated Madison's proposal for discrimination, 36 to 13, with 9 of the favorable votes coming from Virginia. Assumption, however, proved more divisive, and on 12 April 1790, the House voted it down 32 to 29.[24]

Yet as Madison later wrote Edmund Pendleton, recorded votes could be misleading. In deciding who would pay the state debts, dollars counted for more than political principle. Madison admitted privately that much in Hamilton's report was "supported by very able reasoning." Madison merely wanted some protection for Virginia in the final settlement. "A simple un-qualified assumption of the existing debts," he wrote Pendleton, "would bear particularly hard on Virginia." Even after the initial defeat of assumption, Madison continued to hope for a compromise; there "threatens a very un-happy issue to the session, unless some scheme of accommodation should be devised."[25]

According to a familiar story, a dejected Alexander Hamilton intercepted Thomas Jefferson on the steps of the Executive Mansion and persuaded Jefferson to host a dinner at which the secretary of state ultimately medi-ated a compromise. The dinner apparently formalized an agreement that had been in the works for several weeks. Madison agreed to accept a Senate amendment reducing the debt to be assumed, thus reducing the burden to Virginia. Hamilton, in turn, would not actively oppose a southern location for a permanent national capital. Madison would not be required to endorse assumption publicly; in fact he attacked the Senate amendment on the floor of the House. Privately, he lobbied Alexander White and Richard Bland, two Virginia congressmen whose districts bordered the Potomac, to vote for it. He confided to his father that as amended "assumption is no longer of much consequence to Virginia."[26]

Finding a home for the new government involved more than regional pride or even a possible real estate bonanza. The issue had bitterly polarized the First Congress. Madison remarked during a debate in September 1789 that if Virginians could have foreseen the sectional animosities it generated, they would not have joined the Union. Madison and his allies believed local interests would influence national policy. The defeat of Madison's proposal to discriminate among debt holders, Benjamin Rush told him, "would not have taken place had the Congress been seated on the Banks of the Dela-ware or the Potomac." Condemning Hamilton's financial plan as "a system calculated only for a commercial society," Henry Lee warned that unless the capital is brought "near the center of territory . . . we southern people must be slaves in effect." Madison agreed. "Nothing is more contagious than opinion," he wrote. "It is extremely difficult . . . to avoid confounding the local with the public opinion."[27] If the United States were to remain a vir-tuous, agrarian republic, it could not be governed from a great commercial city.

In the Compromise of 1790, Madison demonstrated a capacity for hard-nosed political maneuvering. Undoubtedly, he believed he was acting in the public interest. Convinced too much power was being concentrated in the central government, Madison later came to resent the deal, but ironically, it would be one of the last legislative accomplishments of his congressional career.[28]

On 14 December 1790, Hamilton had submitted his Second Report on the Public Credit, which called on Congress to charter a Bank of the United States (BUS). Hamilton envisioned the BUS as a joint undertaking of the federal government and private investors. Madison bided his time, but on 2 February 1791, he made a long speech attacking the BUS on multiple grounds. Bank notes issued by the BUS would drive specie from circulation. Given the risk of a bank run, encouraging several small banks would be safer than chartering one large bank. Under Hamilton's plan, the BUS would benefit private investors, as opposed to the government, more than did its European counterparts. But Madison's case against the BUS quickly came down to the constitutional authority of Congress to charter a bank.

Hamilton argued that Article 1, Section 8, of the Constitution, giving Congress authority to adopt legislation "necessary and proper" to implement its enumerated powers, was broad enough to include the BUS. Madison could reply that the Philadelphia convention had considered and rejected giving Congress the discretion to grant charters; Madison had made the proposal. It was a slightly disingenuous argument. He argued elsewhere that the relevant intent was that of the state ratifying conventions. More consistently, he argued the necessary and proper clause was "merely declaratory of what would have resulted by unavoidable implication. . . . In this sense it had been explained by the friends of the Constitution, and ratified by the state conventions." Endorsing a strict construction of the Constitution, the Federalists of 1787 and 1788 had excused the absence of a bill of rights by pointing to Congress's lack of any express or implied powers to restrict individual liberty. "The essential characteristics of the government, as composed of limited and enumerated powers, would be destroyed," Madison told the House, by a broad construction of the necessary and proper clause.[29]

Jefferson agreed, but historians, perhaps unfairly, have tended to dismiss Madison's constitutional arguments, and the House passed a Senate version of the BUS bill by a vote of 39 to 20. Madison concluded that the bank bill was too arcane to incite public indignation.[30] He drafted a veto message for Washington and hoped the president might adopt it, but Washington, who generally deferred to Hamilton on financial matters, demurred. When BUS stock went on sale, a disgusted Madison wrote Jefferson, "The subscriptions are . . . a mere scramble for public plunder." Most shocking was to see "the members of the Legislature who were most active in pushing this Jobb, openly grasping its emoluments. . . . Stock jobbing drowns every other subject."[31]

In May and June 1791, Madison and Jefferson toured the Hudson River Valley. They said it was a vacation; skeptics saw a conspiracy to solidify a political alliance with sympathizers in New York. Later in the summer, Madison recruited his Princeton classmate Philip Freneau to come to Philadelphia and launch the *National Gazette* as a counterweight to John Fenno's proadministration *Gazette of the United States*. Jefferson subsidized Freneau by giving him a part-time job at the State Department.[32] As Washington's first term neared its end, partisans could identify a "republican faction" in Congress and in the state legislatures. The South Carolina Federalist William Loughton Smith, underestimating Madison's importance, labeled the diminutive Virginian "the General," and Jefferson "the Generalissimo."[33]

The nascent party organizations reached a new plateau during the presidential election of 1792. In a bitter debate in March, Madison helped defeat a bill to put Washington's image on U.S. coins; he believed the idea was unduly monarchial. Yet Madison urged the president not to retire. At Washington's request, Madison reluctantly helped him draft a farewell address. Despite Washington's Federalist predilections, Madison feared the likely alternatives could be far worse, and no one could openly challenge the old hero. Vice President John Adams commanded considerably less affection, and in 1792, Republicans made a half-hearted effort on behalf of their own vice presidential candidate, Governor George Clinton of New York.[34]

Meanwhile, Madison attempted to articulate the philosophy of the new Republican Party in eighteen essays he wrote for the *National Gazette* between November 1791 and December 1792. Convinced now that Hamilton and the Federalists did not represent a majority of Americans, Madison revised his ideas about the advantages of an extended republic. "The larger a country, the less easy for its real opinion to be ascertained, and the less difficult to be counterfeited." Bribes, partisanship, propaganda, and "the terror of the sword . . . may support a real domination of the few, under an apparent liberty of the many." Schemes, like the assumption of state debts, that consolidated power in the federal government would undermine the states and pile on Congress more responsibilities than it could manage. The influence of the presidency would inevitably expand "whilst the increasing splendor and number of its prerogatives . . . might prove excitements to ambition too powerful for a sober execution of the elective plan." Consolidation, he warned, "is the high road to monarchy."[35]

More than ever, Madison connected a nation's capacity for self-government to its economic pursuits. "Of all occupations those are the least desirable in a free state, which produce the most servile dependence of one class of citizens on another." Great Britain, as usual, provided Madison with his best example of the worst in political economy: English buckle makers had recently petitioned the Price of Wales to wear shoe buckles because the popularity of shoestrings and slippers had endangered more than twenty thousand jobs. By contrast, "The life of the husbandman is pre-eminently suited to the comfort and the happiness of the individual." Echoing Jefferson's observation in his *Notes on the State of Virginia* that "those who tilled the soil were the chosen people of God if ever he had a chosen people," Madison went on: "'Tis not the country that peoples either the Bridewells or the Bedlams. These mansions of wretchedness are tenanted from the distresses and vices of overgrown cities." Madison did not blame the victims of the financial-industrial complex; he condemned the state that sustained it: "That is not a just government, nor is property secure under it, where arbitrary restrictions, exemptions, and monopolies deny to part of its citizens that free use of their faculties, and free choice of their occupations, which not only constitute their property in the general sense of the word; but are the means of acquiring property strictly so called."[36]

An essay appearing on 22 September 1792 addressed the current state of partisan competition. Three party alignments had existed in American history, beginning with the Tories and the Whigs during the Revolution and continuing with the Federalists and Anti-Federalists during the debate over the ratification of the Constitution. Creation of the new government, Madison claimed, had extinguished the latter division. From it "has arisen a third division," one "natural to most political societies." Some individuals by nature or circumstance "are more partial to the opulent than to other classes of society." They believe "mankind are incapable of governing themselves," and they prefer government by the few "approximated to an hereditary form." Outnumbered, "the anti-republican party" would try to exploit "all prejudices, local, political, and occupational" to thwart the popular will. The Republican Party had been formed to defend liberty against its almost inevitable foes. Madison's rationale for the Republican Party prevented him from making a case for a truly modern party system because he did not recognize the legitimacy of a political opposition. Rather, it was the opposition's hostility to republicanism that justified the creation of a new political organization. Nor did he believe the party system would be permanent. He expected the Republicans, the faction with a more populist appeal, eventually to prevail.[37]

Some of his own contemporaries accused Madison of being both fickle and inflexible, and historians have occasionally agreed. When Hamilton's funding bill was pending in the House of Representatives, Madison rejected a compromise bill offered by William C. Maclay of Pennsylvania. Maclay fumed that Madison's "pride seems of that kind which repels all communication. . . . The obstinacy of this man has ruined the opposition."[38] A once popular textbook concluded "Madison was stubborn to the point of stupidity."[39] In a leading, modern study of the politics of his era, Madison is "stubborn and willful . . . quietly, implacably determined to have his way."[40]

Like most politicians, Madison hated to admit he ever changed positions, and like most people, he hesitated to admit a mistake. He had not been a force for compromise at the Constitutional Convention. He clung resolutely to a particular set of prejudices toward Great Britain: that the British were implacably committed to the destruction of American liberty, that British prosperity depended on access to American raw materials and markets, that Americans had little need for British trade or capital, and that American economic sanctions could shape imperial policies. Madison assumed that the United States had the advantage over Great Britain because, he thought, America was essentially self-sufficient in producing the necessities of life. Provincialism exaggerated his sense of American superiority, and he had little feel for commercial realities. Until Anglo-American relations deteriorated to the point that war seemed likely, Madison had nothing to fear from the failure of his economic policies. If restrictions on British trade did not lead to a liberalization of the imperial commercial system, American sanctions would, supposedly, reduce British influence in the new republic.[41]

He could be a stickler for constitutional niceties. He opposed allowing the president to designate post roads; he argued this was an unconstitutional delegation of legislative power. He opposed, again on constitutional grounds, a bounty to the cod industry, but not a tax rebate. He objected to putting the president pro tem of the Senate and the speaker of the House in the line of succession behind the president and the vice president; he argued they were not "officers" of the federal government within the meaning of the Constitution. He did not believe Cabinet heads should report in person to Congress, but he complained that a written report from the secretary of the treasury recommending a plan to reduce the national debt violated the constitutional requirement that appropriations bills originate in the House. Madison claimed a federal tax on carriages violated Article 1, Section 2, which provided that direct taxes had to be apportioned among the states based on population. The Supreme Court upheld the tax.[42]

Yet Madison seemed to switch sides often enough that obstinacy was surely only part of his political personality. His conversion from an outspoken nationalist in the 1780s to a defender of states' rights and a strict construction of the Constitution in the 1790s has perplexed historians. Contemporaries saw the dilemma as well. In February 1795, a sympathetic Federalist, Samuel Dexter, requested a private meeting with Madison so he might better understand "the motives for your present line of politics, when compared with your former measures." Madison invited Dexter to dinner but protested impressions "may not do justice to the consistency between my present and former line of politics."[43] Irving Brant, however, concluded that in opposing the BUS, Madison "was arguing against himself." In *Federalist No. 44*, Madison had given the necessary and proper clause of the Constitution an interpretation not unlike the one Hamilton used to justify a national bank. Other historians have accorded Madison's later and narrower reading little credence.[44]

Politics must have played a part in moderating Madison's nationalism. Virginians routinely complained that Hamilton's fiscal policies taxed them to enrich northern speculators. Madison was capable of small hypocrisies; for all the praise he heaped on the yeoman farmer and the virtues of country life, he never got his own hands dirty, and he spent most of the decade from 1786 to 1797 in New York or Philadelphia.[45] At the same time, the essentials of Madison's republican philosophy remained largely unchanged. He was above all a Virginia nationalist. He believed the survival of the republic depended on a viable national government, but one founded on Virginia principles, chief among them the conviction that agrarian societies best nurtured the virtue necessary for republican government. High finance undermined it. One of Madison's correspondents called Virginia "the great repository of republican principles," and he never disagreed.[46] However primitive Madison's theories may seem today, the unsavory speculation he deplored was real, and Hamilton's economic policies did not ignite a massive surge of industrialization. The United States of the 1790s lacked the necessary managerial and technological expertise.[47]

Madison's apparent conversion to strict construction can best be explained as an attempt to apply his republican philosophy to a new political and constitutional order. Madison always believed individual rights could be jeopardized by both "an excess of power" and "an excess of liberty." In the 1780s, when the pendulum had swung toward too much liberty, he had called for a stronger national government. By the 1790s, Madison feared a building momentum toward an excess of centralized power. In part because he saw government as an impartial judge among competing interests, Madison shifted positions in an attempt to maintain the proper balance between freedom and authority.[48]

Madison's thinking, it seems reasonable to conclude, evolved with the fluid constitutional doctrine of the post-Revolutionary era. Madison went to the Philadelphia Convention in May 1787 committed to a congressional veto over state laws and a broad delegation of powers to the new government, but he got neither. He reconciled himself to the proposed Constitution, and if he put a broad construction on the necessary and proper clause in *Federalist No. 44*, he was forced to argue elsewhere that the new charter created a government of only limited powers. Virginia ratified the Constitution with that understanding. After Madison realized he could use a bill of rights to deflate the Anti-Federalist opposition, he drafted what became the Ninth and Tenth Amendments, reserving unspecified but potentially broad privileges to the people and to the states. Intimately involved as he was at every stage of the debate, Madison could easily have come out of it with an altered view of the acceptable scope of federal authority.[49]

The issue of congressional subsidies for new technologies illustrates the process. At the Philadelphia convention, Madison had proposed that Congress be allowed to grant bounties to encourage "the advancement of useful knowledge and discoveries," but the measure was defeated. In March 1790, Tench Coxe suggested to Madison that Congress dedicate certain public lands for the support of new inventions. Madison liked the idea, but he reluctantly concluded that it violated the intent of the Constitution. "This fetter on the National Legislature tho' an unfortunate one, was a deliberate one."[50] A moralist at heart, Madison felt obligated to honor the understanding of the Constitution that had emerged during the struggle over ratification.

As congressional debates became more partisan, and as Madison became increasingly identified with the Republican faction, his influence in the House declined. He spoke less in the Second Congress, which convened in October 1791. His position as a party leader did not offset a loss of deference among the membership at large. In March 1792, Madison failed to defeat a congressional apportionment bill that, he claimed, discriminated against "the southern states and particularly Virginia." In the first ever presidential veto message, Washington vetoed the bill; it violated the constitutional provision limiting the House to no more than one representative for every thirty thousand people.[51] The veto reflected Madison's continuing, if declining, influence with the president.

Republicans did well in the 1792–93 congressional elections, winning a majority in the House, but party discipline remained weak, and Madison was not particularly effective in the new environment, marked as it was by bitterly divided but internally unstable factions. In February 1793, Virginia's William Branch Giles, working from a draft Jefferson had prepared and Madison had reviewed, introduced nine resolutions censuring Alexander Hamilton. Madison defended them on the House floor and claimed Hamilton had wrongly diverted funds to the BUS that should have been used to pay the Revolutionary-era debt to France. The resolutions lost badly. Madison was one of only five House members who voted for all nine. Privately, he expressed regret for the episode. He thought "the Session was too near its close for a proper discussion [and] it is very unfortunate that they were offered," but the debate over censure may have prevented passage of any Federalist initiatives before Congress adjourned early in March.[52]

Disagreements over foreign policy dominated Washington's second term. Republican enthusiasm for the French Revolution knew no bounds. Reporting to Madison on the new National Assembly in August 1789, Jefferson opined "it is impossible to desire better dispositions toward us." Two years later, Madison wrote Edmund Pendleton, "The French Revolution seems to have succeeded beyond the most sanguine hopes." George Lee Turberville predicted "the Reign of Despotism" in Europe was not likely to survive the eighteenth century. As late as December 1794—after the Reign of Terror and on the eve of the triumph of the conservative Directory—James Monroe could write from Paris, "the affrs. of the republick are in every respect in the most flourishing condition: wise, humane, and just in its councils, and eminently successful in its armies."[53]

In a kind of egocentrism, or perhaps paranoia, gone amok, many Americans identified the struggle between France and its enemies, chiefly Great Britain, with the battle over the meaning of republicanism at home. The conviction that the British and French were fighting by proxy the war between Federalists and Republicans helps explain the salience foreign policy issues acquired in the 1790s. "We have every motive in America to pray for

[France's] success, not only from a general attachment to the liberties of mankind, but from a peculiar regard for our own," Madison wrote in March 1793. A "miscarriage" in France, "would threaten us with the most serious dangers to our present forms and principles of our Governments." A resolution Madison coauthored with Monroe for Virginia Republicans explained the risk: "All attempts which may be made in whatever form or disguise to alienate the good will of the people of America from the cause of liberty and Republican Government in France have a tendency to weaken their affection to the free principles of their own Governments."[54]

Madison had long favored commercial sanctions against Great Britain. He resented British restrictions on the ability of American ships to carry American goods to British ports. Ironically, for all his Anglophobia, Madison's proposals, had they worked, might have tied the United States even more closely to the British economy. Yet Madison made some of the longest—and least memorable—speeches of his career in defense of economic reprisals against the British.[55]

After Great Britain declared war on France, Washington on 22 April 1793 issued what came to be known as the Neutrality Proclamation, which expressed an intent to remain aloof from the European conflict. Hamilton followed up with his "Pacificus" essays, defending the president's right to make foreign policy without congressional authorization. Madison believed that the proclamation ignored America's responsibility, under a 1778 treaty with France, to defend the French West Indies, and he thought the president, ill advised by Hamilton, had inadvertently usurped the power of Congress. In the summer of 1793, while Madison was at Montpelier enjoying the congressional recess, Jefferson urged him to respond to Hamilton. "For god's sake, my dear sir, take up your pen, select the most striking heresies, and cut him to pieces in the face of the public. There is nobody else who can and will enter the lists with him."[56]

Relatively isolated at home, Madison hesitated. Republicans did not want to challenge George Washington directly. The excesses of the newly arrived French envoy Edmund Genet, who was licensing privateers and generally compromising American neutrality, complicated Madison's task. Genet's behavior threatened to provoke a backlash against France; Madison would welcome Washington's decision in August to demand his recall.[57] Ultimately, however, Madison yielded to Jefferson's entreaties and produced, in August and September 1793, his five "Helvidius" essays. To avoid criticizing Washington, Madison strained to read the Neutrality Proclamation narrowly as a statement of fact, not a declaration of policy. The power to declare war or to make treaties, Madison argued, was legislative, not executive, because "the executive is the department of power most distinguished by its propensity to war: hence it is the practice of all states, in proportion as they are free, to disarm this propensity of its influence." Madison's strictures on the dangers posed by a strong executive repeated familiar republican themes, but elsewhere the Helvidius essays were difficult to digest, overwrought in tone, and overly technical in substance. Their author may have recognized as much. "I have forced myself into the task" of replying to Hamilton, he wrote Jefferson. "I can truly say I find it the most grating one I have ever experienced."[58]

Madison returned to Philadelphia for the Third Congress late in 1793, shortly before Jefferson's resignation as secretary of state. Washington offered the job to Madison. He declined it. Having listened to Jefferson's complaints about the administration, Madison dreaded being outvoted by a Federalist majority in the Cabinet. Partisan divisions could now be more sharply drawn. When Jefferson left office on 31 December, Madison became the undisputed leader of the Republican faction in the capital. In January, Madison introduced nine resolutions, prompted by an earlier report from Jefferson as secretary of state, calling for higher duties on ships and goods from countries that did not have commercial treaties with the United States or that discriminated against American trade. The fees would fall primarily on British shipping. After Great Britain began seizing neutral ships trading with the French West Indies, public sentiment seemed to turn in favor of more drastic action, but Madison opposed even a modest program of naval construction as likely to provoke a war. "Not that the Monocrats and Papermen in Congress want a war," he told Jefferson, "but they want armies and debts." The House passed a non-intercourse bill, only to see it die in the Senate, with Vice President John Adams casting a rare, tie-breaking vote.[59] Madison's pacifism in the face of British affronts did not, paradoxically, rehabilitate his reputation in the eyes of the supposedly pro-British Federalists. To the opposition press, as he put it, he remained "a corrupt tool of France."[60]

Madison defended his position in an essay, "Political Observations," which appeared in pamphlet form in New York and in serial form in Philadelphia in Benjamin Franklin Bache's *Aurora General Advertiser*. Madison claimed that "the first, and most contemplated" object in drafting the Constitution had been to empower Congress to regulate foreign trade. It was an exercise in revisionist history as far as his own motives were concerned, but he could deny with complete sincerity any desire to go to war against Great

Britain. "Of all the enemies of public liberty war is, perhaps, the most to be dreaded, because it comprises and develops the germ of every other. War is the parent of armies; from these proceed debts and taxes; and armies, and debts, and taxes are the known instruments for bringing the many under the domination of the few." War expands executive prerogative and encourages profiteering. "No, nation," Madison wrote, "could preserve its freedom in the midst of continual warfare."[61]

If Congress had reached an impasse on foreign policy, Madison and the Republicans survived a political threat. In his annual message to Congress, Washington had seemed to blame the Democratic-Republican societies for inciting the Whiskey Rebellion, a short-lived uprising in western Pennsylvania against a federal excise tax on distilled liquors. Having voted for the levy, Madison had no sympathy for armed resistance to taxation with representation. Fearful the rebellion would be used to justify a standing army, Madison complained privately that the whiskey rebels were inadvertently "doing the business of Despotism." The House tied itself in knots attempting to draft a reply to Washington. Pennsylvania's Thomas Fitzsimons proposed that the House denounce "self-created societies." Madison objected. He had hoped to avoid the issue altogether. As much as he disliked the rebels, he believed Washington had blundered in attempting to implicate local Democratic-Republican clubs in the rebellion. "If we advert to the nature of republican government," Madison told the House, "we shall find that the censorial power is in the people over the government and not in the government over the people." The House eventually agreed on more ambiguous language apparently aimed at the whiskey rebels rather than local Republican activists.[62] Madison believed the fall congressional elections went well despite the controversy; he was especially pleased by Edward Livingston's victory over incumbent Federalist John Watts in New York City.[63]

The foreign policy crisis, however, remained. By March 1794, Great Britain had seized more than 250 American merchant ships. Hoping to avoid war, Washington appointed Chief Justice John Jay as a special envoy to Great Britain, and Jay proceeded to negotiate one of the most unpopular treaties in American history. After he returned from London, Jay remarked he could have traveled the length of the republic at night by the light of the bonfires burning him in effigy. Historians have disagreed on the merits of the treaty and even over whether it deserved the attention it attracted. The British agreed to abandon seven western forts they occupied in violation of the Treaty of Paris of 1783 and to open the British West Indies to some American ships. Commissions would mediate disputes over pre-

Revolutionary British debts, claims arising from the seizure of American vessels, and the exact location of the Canadian border. The treaty, however, ignored southern claims for slaves lost to the British during the Revolution. Expanding the definition of contraband, it did little to protect neutral rights. The treaty also eliminated discriminatory duties on British ships and granted Great Britain most-favored-nation status.[64]

The Senate, meeting in a secret session on 24 June, ratified the treaty by a vote of 20 to 10. The treaty did enjoy support from merchants in Boston, New York, and Philadelphia; their profits came largely from the British trade. Senator Pierce Butler from South Carolina had been sending pages of the treaty to Madison as fast as his secretary could copy them, and there were other leaks. Madison had suspected Jay of pro-British sympathies, and Jay's concessions appalled him and most other Republicans. The treaty, Robert Livingston wrote from his Clermont estate in New York, "sacrifices every essential interest and prostrates the honor of our country." It also killed Madison's dream of using economic pressure to force changes in British policy.[65]

Because the Senate had not approved Article 12, regulating trade with the West Indies, Madison assumed the treaty would have to be renegotiated and submitted to a second vote. Madison entered the debate with a petition to the Virginia General Assembly; since it elected Virginia's senators, the assembly had some claim to a right to address the issue. Madison warned that the elimination of discriminatory duties would allow the British to dominate the carrying trade now dominated by U.S. ships. He also questioned the assertion the Jay Treaty was needed to avoid war. History provided no evidence that what later generations would call appeasement could preserve the peace. But George III accepted the treaty without Article 12, and it was never put to a second vote in the Senate.[66]

The debate over the treaty moved next, and somewhat awkwardly, into the House of Representatives, when the administration requested $80,000 to establish the commissions the agreement had anticipated. Madison was apparently caught by surprise on 2 March 1796, when Edward Livingston moved that the House ask President Washington to produce Jay's correspondence and instructions. Livingston later amended his motion to exempt papers that might prejudice ongoing negotiations. The House passed the amended motion; Madison, hesitant to risk a confrontation with Washington, had tried unsuccessfully to further narrow the request. The president's response surprised Madison again. Washington refused to produce the documents on the grounds that the framers of the Constitution had intended to put treaty negotiations beyond the jurisdiction of the House, and the request did not explain the relevance of the documents to that body's legitimate duties. Madison blamed the rebuff on Alexander Hamilton, who had weakened Jay's position by privately sending the British conciliatory messages during the course of the negotiations.[67]

In a speech on 6 April, Madison observed that it had not been the practice of the House to explain its requests for documents. Its inquiries were proper "where treaties embraced legislative subjects, submitted by the Constitution, to the power of the house." Washington's reference to the Philadelphia convention particularly offended him. He had mentioned the intent of the framers during the debate over the BUS and had been rebuked. The Constitution produced by the convention, he said now, "was nothing more than the drought of a plan, but a dead letter" until approved by the required number of states. The Virginia convention had ratified the document with the understanding "the treaty making power was a limited power." Many of the state conventions had been concerned lest the Senate use its authority to make treaties to usurp the power of the House of Representatives and of the state legislatures.[68]

When the House began debate on legislation to implement the Jay Treaty, Madison attacked the merits of the treaty itself, which may have been a tactical blunder. He complained that the treaty did not compensate slave owners for slaves who fled to British lines during the Revolutionary War, although he did not belabor the point. The treaty, he noted, ignored the British practice of impressing American merchant sailors into the Royal Navy. He complained more vigorously that British agents would be allowed to continue in the Indian trade and, presumably, to incite the tribes. It was "singularly reprehensible" to open ports on the eastern bank of the Mississippi River to Great Britain. Jay had abandoned the American position that "free ships make free goods," and accepted the British view that American naval stores could be considered contraband, which Madison claimed was almost unprecedented. The treaty surrendered the young republic's most effective economic weapons: its ability to sequester British debts or accounts and to impose discriminatory duties. And Britain received most-favored-nation status without making corresponding concessions.[69]

Despite Madison's opposition, the House passed the implementing legislation in late April by a vote of 51 to 48. "The progress of this business throughout has to me been the most worrying and vexatious that I ever encountered; and the more so," he wrote Thomas Jefferson, "as the causes lay in the unsteadiness, the follies, the perverseness, and the defections among our friends, more than in the strength or dexterity, or malice of our opponents."[70] As early as December 1795, Madison had expected the original majority against the treaty to dwindle under pressure from northern commercial interests. Maritime insurance companies, for example, refused to write new policies until the treaty took effect. By April Madison feared the antitreaty majority had "melted" to eight or nine votes. Federalists had successfully persuaded much of the public to think defeat of the treaty "was the same thing, with a declaration of war." Washington's endorsement was, as usual, critical.[71] Western Republicans had their own reasons to support the treaty. They wanted the British out of the frontier posts, and they feared Federalists would retaliate for the defeat of Jay's Treaty by acquiescing in the Spanish threat to close the Mississippi to American traffic.[72]

The controversy over Jay's Treaty marked a critical step in the evolution of a party system. Both sides tried to mobilize and manipulate public opinion. In Congress, sectional interests prevailed and laid the foundation for the partisan divide. Almost 80 percent of the votes for the Jay Treaty came from New England and the mid-Atlantic states; almost three-quarters of the opposition came from the South. After the March 1795 elections, Federalists held only one of Virginia's nineteen House seats.[73]

Madison throughout analyzed the struggle in starkly political terms. He believed from the beginning that the treaty's Federalist supporters were "a British party, systematically aiming at an exclusive connection with the British Governt."[74] He suspected that Hamilton had urged Washington to deny the House request for documents pertaining to the treaty simply to embarrass New York Republicans by forcing them into an open breach with the president. The Jay Treaty did lead Washington to make a final break with Madison. The incessant partisan wrangling and Madison's role in founding the antiadministration *National Gazette* had already undermined his confidence in the Virginia congressman. For his part, Madison blamed their differences on the Federalists around the president.[75]

Republicans won seven roll-call votes on procedural issues relating to Jay's Treaty before losing on the final vote, which raises questions. Did Madison really want to defeat the treaty and risk being blamed for triggering a war with Great Britain, or was he a sincere but ineffectual legislative tactician? Madison's bookish and unassuming style had worked well in earlier, less partisan assemblies; it proved less useful in the more polarized atmosphere of the Third and Fourth Congresses. Congressman Zephaniah Smith of Connecticut assessed his strengths and liabilities. Possessed of "infinite prudence and industry," Madison was the most influential man in the House, but he suffered from "a hollow, feeble voice" and lacked "energy or imagination." Smith offered a backhanded compliment: "I never knew a man that better understood [how] to husband a character and make the most of his talents; and he is the most artificial, studied character on earth." Edward Livingston admired Madison, but complained, "He never determines to act until he is absolutely forced by the pressure of affairs and then regrets that [he] has neglected some better opportunity." For almost eight years, Madison lost every major foreign policy battle he fought in the House.[76]

Madison's personal limitations surely played a role in his defeat, and he had no legal or political tools with which to control his colleagues. As we have seen, powerful forces were at work in support of the Jay Treaty. His correspondence with James Monroe and Thomas Jefferson, his closest political collaborators by 1795, suggests he might have been satisfied by passage of an amendment condemning the Jay Treaty but allowing it to take effect. Republicans could make their point and saddle a Federalist administration with responsibility for implementing an unpopular agreement. "But," he wrote Monroe, "before some were ripe for the arrangement others were rotten." Ultimately, he viewed congressional approval of the Jay Treaty as a partisan defeat. He wrote Jefferson in May 1796, "A crisis which ought to have been so managed as to fortify the Republican cause, has left it in a very crippled condition." The affair took its toll on Madison. He complained privately in the middle of the treaty debate, "I have never been more occupied with the drudgeries of my station, than at this moment." Although he surely could have been reelected, he decided not to seek another term in Congress.[77]

In December 1794, Thomas Jefferson had subtly expressed a wish to see Madison elevated to the presidency; in their day no one would have talked of campaigning for the office. "Reasons of *every* kind, and some of them, of the most *insuperable* as well as *obvious* kind," Madison replied, "shut my mind against the admission of any idea such as you seem to glance at." Jefferson continued to raise the possibility of a Madison candidacy occasionally, but by February 1796, Madison could write James Monroe, "The republicans knowing that Jefferson alone can be started with hope of success mean to push him."[78] No movement developed on Madison's behalf. Given Madison's resume, the seeming inevitability of Jefferson's nomination suggests the limits of Madison's appeal. Madison himself appeared to have no interest in higher office and worried Jefferson's own diffidence might undermine the Republican cause. Jefferson, in fact, had expressed a willingness to serve as vice president under the leading Federalist candidate, John Adams.[79]

Adams defeated Jefferson in a close vote along sectional lines. Madison considered Adams less sympathetic to the British than most other Federalists and preferable to Thomas Pinckney, whom Alexander Hamilton had supported. The election results partially assuaged the partisan rancor engendered by the Jay Treaty. Yet the always circumspect Madison had never really liked the volatile Adams. When Adams suggested sharing real power with Jefferson, the Republican leader drafted a conciliatory letter to the president-elect. Madison recommended he not send it, effectively vetoing any idea of a copresidency. The letter, he warned, could prove an embarrassment should the administration "force an opposition to it[self] from the Republican quarter."[80]

Madison soon found himself in that opposition. In the wake of the Jay Treaty, the French had seized alleged contraband from roughly three hundred American ships sailing in the West Indies. Adams decided to send a diplomatic mission to France and hoped to include Madison in the delegation. Settling into the life of a gentleman farmer at Montpelier, Madison declined the offer; he never would leave the country, and he seems to have had a morbid fear of the ocean. Madison's rejection of the assignment probably ended the possibility of any meaningful cooperation between Adams and Jefferson. John Marshall, Charles Pinckney, and Elbridge Gerry did go to France, but their mission failed when representatives of the French foreign minister, Talleyrand, demanded $250,000 to begin negotiations.[81]

Bribes were common in European diplomacy, but Talleyrand's price was high. When Adams informed Congress of the XYZ Affair—from his designation of the French agents—it unleashed a wave of anti-French sentiment. Adams persuaded Congress to cut off trade with France, to terminate the 1778 treaties, and to authorize the seizure of armed French ships. Congress passed legislation establishing a Department of the Navy and a ten-thousand-man New Army, nominally under the command of George Washington, but effectively under the leadership of Alexander Hamilton. It was a condition Washington had demanded against Adams's better judgment. In 1798–99, the new republic found itself in the Quasi-War with France, an undeclared naval war in which the United States seized eighty-five French ships.[82]

Historians have generally praised Adams's handling of the affair. He resisted pressure from more militant Federalists for a formal declaration of war, and he continued to pursue negotiations, which ended the crisis by 1800, in the midst of considerable hysteria. When he declared 9 May 1798 a day of prayer and fasting, fighting broke out between pro- and anti-French mobs in Philadelphia. Rumors circulated that the French intended to burn the city on fast day. Republicans claimed the British were planning to send troops to the United States.[83]

Madison treated Adams less charitably than history has. Talleyrand's "unparalleled stupidity" appalled him, but he believed Federalist criticism of the French government went too far.[84] He wrote Jefferson contrasting Adams to the sainted Washington, highlighting the second president's shortcomings, "the one ever scrutinizing into the public opinion, and ready to follow where he could not lead it: the other insulting it by the most adverse sentiments and pursuits." Madison believed that Hamilton dominated Adams and that both of them wanted to enter the war in Europe on the side of Great Britain. Adams's messages to Congress proved a fundamental maxim of republican theory: the president could not be given broad discretion to manage foreign policy because the executive would be too prone to lead, or manipulate, a nation into war. Military conflict always threatened republican institutions. Wars encouraged secrecy, profiteering, higher taxes, greater debts, and the consolidation of power in the executive. America's likely ally added to the risk. "Warm and well informed friends of Republicanism," Madison wrote Jefferson, see "in a war on the side of England, the most formidable means put into the hands of her partisans, for warping the public mind toward Monarchy."[85]

Federalists responded to such criticism by passing the Alien and Sedition Acts of 1798. The Alien Act authorized the president to deport suspicious foreigners without due process of law. The Sedition Act prohibited "false, scandalous and malicious writings" against the president or Congress. Because Federalists did not recognize the idea of a loyal opposition, the law did not extend to criticism of the vice president, the Republican Jefferson, and it was set to expire on 3 March 1801, when Adams's term would end. About two dozen Republicans were arrested under the Sedition Act, and eleven were convicted, including Representative Matt Lyon of Vermont. Federalist prosecutors targeted the opposition press. William Duane, publisher of the *Philadelphia Aurora*, was charged for reporting that the Pennsylvania senator James Ross had drafted a bill to replace the Electoral College with a committee of Federalist officials. Madison called the Alien Act "a monster that must for ever disgrace its parents," and he considered the Sedition Act to be a flagrant violation of the First Amendment. Local Republican groups condemned the acts for abridging freedom of speech and for unconstitutionally expanding the power of the federal government.[86]

Madison and Jefferson turned to the states for relief, not to the federal judiciary as a modern litigant would do. In the 1790s, Federalists controlled the federal courts, the right of judges to strike down unconstitutional laws was yet to be clearly established, and neither Madison nor Jefferson wanted to expand their jurisdiction. In the summer and fall of 1798 the two Virginians met first at Montpelier and later at Monticello. Madison began work on a statement denouncing the Alien and Sedition Acts for the Virginia House of Delegates. Jefferson drafted a separate resolution that was eventually adopted by the Kentucky legislature. He believed a state legislature could declare an unconstitutional federal law null and void. Madison favored a more moderate approach, finding the Alien and Sedition Acts unconstitutional but seeking relief through the ordinary political channels. Wilson Cary Nicholas and John Taylor of Caroline added the stronger language Jefferson preferred to Madison's draft before it was introduced in the House of Delegates. The amendments, however, were trimmed in the course of debate, and the Virginia Resolutions adopted on 21 December largely followed Madison's recommendations.[87]

Passage of the Alien and Sedition Acts tested Madison's nationalism more than did any other event in his political career. He wanted to express Republican outrage and mobilize public opinion against the laws without jeopardizing the Union. The Virginia Resolutions declared the acts unconstitutional but proposed only "that the necessary and proper measures" be taken by each state "for cooperating with this State in maintaining unimpaired the authorities, rights, and liberties, reserved to the States respectively, or to the people." The vagueness of the remedy invited confusion. Although Madison began by pledging loyalty to the Constitution and to the Union, he also referred to the Constitution as a compact among the states, which suggested a contract that could be dissolved upon a breach by one of the parties to it. Equally ominous language called on the states "to interpose for arresting the progress of the evil, and for maintaining within their respective limits, the authorities, rights and liberties appertaining to them." Madison's attempt at moderation went largely unappreciated. To many he had raised the specter of secession. A majority of the states expressly rejected the resolutions; none but Kentucky adopted anything comparable.[88]

Whatever the response to the Virginia Resolutions, Madison could not stay out of politics. Early in 1799, he published two essays in the *Philadel-*

phia Aurora General Advertiser. One warned of the pernicious influence of British money, best exemplified by British investors in the BUS, in American society. The other attempted to turn Federalist criticisms of the French Revolution against the Federalist Congress. If French lawmakers had become tyrants, this only proved that the people's representatives should be kept under constant scrutiny. Given the external threats it faced, the members of France's current executive department, "the Directory[,] are models of virtue." Military conflict typically inflated executive power, but, Madison added, in a thrust at the Federalist defense buildup, "actual war is not the only State which may supply the means of usurpation. The real or pretended apprehensions of it, are sometimes of equal avail to the projects of ambition."[89]

In April, Orange County voters returned Madison to the House of Delegates without opposition. When the assembly convened in December, Madison immediately asserted himself, nominating James Monroe for governor. His old friend won easily; Madison received two votes. His service in the 1799–1800 session is best remembered for his defense of the much maligned Virginia Resolutions. Early in the session he wrote a lengthy "Report" on the relatively brief resolutions at Watson's Tavern in Richmond while suffering from a "dysenteric attack which laid me up for about a week." On 23 December, Madison moved that a committee be appointed to report on the response to the Virginia Resolutions. The House agreed, named him chair, and by the next day the committee had submitted its report. Both houses approved a slightly amended version in January.[90]

If Madison wanted to convince skeptical readers of the essential moderation of the Virginia Resolutions, he probably made few converts. He returned to the idea that the Constitution was a compact among the states and expanded on it. When parties to a contract could not resort to a superior tribunal, they had to decide for themselves if the agreement had been breached. Federal courts, he argued, could resolve constitutional disputes between departments of the federal government, but as creatures of the Constitution themselves, they could not decide controversies between the national government and the states. States can "interpose" themselves where there has been "a *deliberate, palpable* and *dangerous* breach of the constitution, by the exercise of *powers not granted* by it." Madison's propositions were hardly self-evident, and he would eventually conclude that the Supreme Court could resolve such disputes. Even in the "Report of 1800," Madison struggled to find a remedy to the current crisis. The Virginia Resolutions, he readily admitted, were not comparable to a judicial finding of unconstitutionality. They "are expressions of opinion, unaccompanied with any other effect, than what they may produce on opinion, by exciting reflection."

Madison reached surer and more familiar ground when he assailed the substance of the Alien and Sedition Acts. Unwarranted expansions of federal power generally—he cited the BUS and the carriage tax as particularly egregious examples—inadvertently exalted the executive and could lay the foundation for monarchy. Congress could not manage all the duties it would assume once it moved beyond its delegated powers, responsibilities would shift to the president, and as the status of the executive office rose, it would excite the ambitions of self-seeking politicians. Presidential elections could become so violent and corrupt, the voters might come to prefer a monarchy. By allowing the president to order deportations without legislative or judicial oversight, the Alien Act accelerated the trend toward what Arthur M. Schlesinger Jr. would later call "the imperial presidency." Madison turned next to the Sedition Act, which had drawn on the common law doctrine of seditious libel. His prose was turgid and technical, but here the report had its most lasting significance: Madison made the case that the framers of the First Amendment had not intended for freedom of the press to be limited to its common-law meanings, a position the Supreme Court would later adopt.[91]

The General Assembly had five thousand copies of the report printed, and if Virginia Republicans heartily embraced Madison's arguments, the latter's immediate impact is dubious. Madison did, however, provide Republicans with a rationale for their existence as a political faction—the defense of constitutional liberty—and a platform—a strict construction of federal power coupled with a broad view of individual rights—as they entered the presidential contest of 1800.[92]

Jefferson was the almost inevitable Republican candidate. Federalists renominated Adams with considerably less enthusiasm. In January, Madison met with Virginia Republicans in Richmond to organize a campaign. He also agreed to serve as a Republican elector. As a member of the legislature he supported a bill to select electors on a statewide basis rather than by district, a move that typified the ruthless politics of the era. The Republican majority wanted to ensure that a few Federalist strongholds would not give Adams a handful of electoral votes. Madison otherwise played a relatively limited public role in what was one of the nastiest races in American history. To some the country teetered on the brink of civil war. Alexander Hamilton drew up plans for an invasion of Virginia. Governor Monroe was relieved the sedition trial of Richmond's Republican editor James Thomas Callender proceeded without incident; he did not want to provoke federal intervention.[93]

Although both parties fielded presidential and vice presidential tickets, under the system then in effect, the second-place finisher in the presidential race became vice president. Each elector cast two votes, so for a party's ticket to be elected as intended, at least one elector had to throw away his vote for vice president. The possibility of a tie between candidates of the same party existed, but lax party discipline had made the issue moot in earlier elections—thirteen candidates had received votes in the Electoral College in 1796. The hardening of party lines by 1800 changed the situation. In 1800, Republicans awarded the vice presidential nomination to New York's Aaron Burr, who had been their vice presidential candidate in 1796. That year Burr had been embarrassed by a poor showing in Virginia. In 1800, Madison worked to ensure that all Virginia's electors cast a vote for Burr, partly out of deference to Burr's feelings and surely to nurture a New York–Virginia alliance. Madison had reason to believe that several Republican electors elsewhere would throw away their vice presidential votes. The prevailing etiquette condemned honest discussions of such maneuvering. In November 1800, New York Republican David Gelston wrote Madison, "We will not . . . *even think* of taking a vote from Mr. J. We should consider it as a sacrilege—we are all well aware from good information that three states, two at least, will give Mr. J. 3 or more votes than Mr. B will have, but I trust that it never will be said that either Virginia or New York could be guilty of such a subterfuge."[94]

"The republic is saved," John Dawson reported to Madison from Philadelphia in May 1800. "Our ticket has succeeded in the city of New York by a majority of about four hundred." As we shall see, Dawson celebrated prematurely, but not without cause. The spring elections gave Republicans control of the state legislature, and in New York the legislature selected the presidential electors. Running against Jefferson in 1796, Adams had carried New York. Losing the state in 1800 cost him the election and gave Republicans a narrow 73 to 65 victory in the Electoral College.[95]

Jefferson and Burr, however, had tied, and Burr sent mixed messages about his willingness to accept the presidency. As provided for in the Constitution, the deadlock went to the House of Representatives, where neither Jefferson nor Burr could assemble the required majority of the states. Federalists considered legislation to confer the presidency on a Federalist, and they attempted to make a deal with Burr that would have elevated the malleable New Yorker to the executive office. Jefferson alerted Madison to "the certainty that a legislative usurpation would be resisted by arms." Madison suggested that Jefferson and Burr convene the new Congress, which Republicans would control, and let it select a president. He admitted that the procedure might not be "strictly regular," but it would reflect the popular will. Jefferson asked Madison to come to Washington. He demurred. "I cannot but think, and feel that there will be an awkwardness to use the softest term, in appearing on the political theatre before I could be considered as regularly called to it."[96]

Ultimately, enough Federalists relented to give Jefferson the presidency. Hamilton himself had called Burr the "most unfit man in the U.S. for the office of president." Madison believed the lack of a standing army had prevented the Federalists from attempting a coup.[97] His constitutional arguments had been vindicated through the new medium of ordinary party politics. If Madison struggled as a legislative tactician, he had identified himself with the popular tides, maintained his unshakable alliance with the shrewdest politician of the era, and provided a platform for a new majority party. It had taken a decade, but Madison would never again be on the losing side in a major election.

The Politics of Charm and the

Limits of Diplomacy

artha Bland, the wife of Virginia congressman Theodorick Bland, knew James Madison when he served in the Continental Congress. He was, she thought, "a gloomy, stiff creature . . . the most unsociable creature in existence." Edward Coles, who served as Madison's personal secretary in later years, recalled a man habitually dressed in black, with knee breeches and silk stockings. His hair was powdered, tied in back, and combed to a peak on his forehead, presumably to cover a bald spot. A small frame, weakened by chronic intestinal problems, and his natural reserve made him physically unimposing. As Coles described Madison around the time he became secretary of state, "His ordinary manner was simple, modest, bland, and unostentatious, retiring from the throng and cautiously refraining from doing or saying anything to make himself conspicuous."[1]

Those, like Louisa Catherine Adams, wife of the rising political star John Quincy Adams, who penetrated the Madison exterior found a dry wit, and as the Virginian George Tucker put it, "a lively relish for the ludicrous." Some found Madison more engaging than Thomas Jefferson. A sympathetic Washington hostess, Margaret Bayard Smith, best described Madison in society. He was charming among friends but "mute, cold and repulsive" if a single "indifferent person" was present. It made him awkward with strangers and uncomfortable in large groups.[2]

Madison remained single into middle age, and almost no evidence exists of romance in his earlier years, but he was hardly a misogynist. In January 1788, when the Count de Moustier, a French diplomat, arrived in New York with his mistress, the artist Madame de Brehen, a minor scandal erupted. Madison remained nonplussed, and he and de Brehen became good friends.

While Congress was meeting in New York, one report linked Madison to a Henrietta Colden, a smart, handsome widow. A Scot with Loyalist connections, she was friends with Light Horse Harry Lee and his wife, Matilda. In the fall of 1786, another rumor circulated, with less detail, of an impending marriage to an unidentified fiancée.[3]

One name we know: Kitty Floyd. Madison apparently met Kitty in the winter of 1782–83. She was then the fifteen-year-old daughter of William Floyd, a member of Congress from New York. Floyd stayed at the same Philadelphia boardinghouse where Madison lived. Madison would have been in his early thirties when the courtship began, but the age difference raised few eyebrows in that day. One of his colleagues, Francis Kinloch, a South Carolina delegate born in 1755, had recently married Milly Walker, the teenage daughter of a prominent Virginia family. Thomas Jefferson knew Kitty and encouraged the relationship. When Jefferson heard the lovesick Madison had been ribbed by his boardinghouse friends, he wrote his fellow Virginian hoping "there were some foundation for it." A marriage to Kitty, Jefferson told Madison, "would give me a neighbor whose worth I rate high" and "will render you happier than you can possibly be in a single state."[4]

By spring 1783, Kitty and Madison were engaged. She turned sixteen on 24 April. A few days later, Madison made a brief trip to New Jersey with Kitty and her family, one of his rare vacations while serving in Congress. They exchanged miniature portraits by the famous artist Charles Willson Peale, and Madison went to Virginia to make arrangements for a wedding. They planned to marry after Congress adjourned in November.[5]

Separation and delay proved fatal. Madison had not vanquished his chief rival, a nineteen-year-old medical student named William Clarkson. Kitty broke off the engagement and married Clarkson two years later. Madison could scarcely bring himself to explain his disappointment to Jefferson, writing him obliquely that his plans had been disrupted "by one of those incidents to which such affairs are liable." Jefferson tried to be supportive, recommending "firmness of mind" and "steady employment," and writing Madison, "the world still presents the same and many other resources of happiness, and you possess many within yourself."[6] The breakup dealt Madison a painful blow; how deep the scars ran is hard to judge. Madison had written to Jefferson in cipher and, after he recovered the letter years later, tried to cross out the coded language. Kitty's marriage proved ill starred. Clarkson died young from yellow fever. She survived until 1832. Despite the age difference, Madison outlived her by four years.[7]

Dolley Payne was born in a log cabin on 20 May 1768, in what is today Guilford County, North Carolina. Her parents, John and Mary Coles Payne, had moved to North Carolina from Virginia in 1765. The Coleses were Quakers; John Payne joined the faith after he married. About a year after Dolley's birth, the family returned to Virginia under suspicious circumstances: Payne sold a considerable amount of land in North Carolina at a substantial loss before they moved. Mary and John both held positions of responsibility among the Quakers, and he eventually became a "Public Friend," or lay minister. During the Revolution, Payne freed his slaves and after the war moved to Philadelphia, the site of a vibrant Quaker community. He had tried unsuccessfully to operate a store in North Carolina; in Philadelphia he went broke trying to sell laundry starch. To Quakers insolvency constituted a moral lapse, and they expelled Payne from the Pine Street Meeting.[8]

Dolley Payne had arrived in Philadelphia a vivacious teenager. Tall with blue eyes, dark hair, and a porcelain complexion, "she soon raised the mercury there in the thermometers of the heart to fever heat," in the words of one family friend. Dolley did not openly rebel—she never liked conflict—but her natural exuberance chafed under the modesty and restraint of her faith. Meanwhile, the family's woes mounted. In addition to John Payne's business reversals, Dolley's oldest brother, Walter, disappeared at sea in 1785. Four years later, Virginia Quakers excommunicated Dolley's younger brother Isaac for allegedly "dissolute behavior."[9]

John Payne died in October 1792, but he apparently arranged Dolley's marriage to a promising young lawyer, John Todd. He may not have been Dolley's first choice for a husband, but the couple enjoyed a comfortable living—John was not a particularly strict Quaker—and they had two sons: John Payne Todd, born in February 1792, and William Temple Todd, born in September 1793. Tragedy struck shortly after William's birth. A yellow fever epidemic raging through Philadelphia killed the baby, John Todd, and Todd's mother and father, all within a matter of weeks. A lawsuit against Todd's brother over her husband's estate left Dolley Payne with a small fortune.[10] That bit of good luck aside, a woman who would become famous for her gaiety and love of life had experienced almost unimaginable grief by age twenty-five. The ebullient Washington hostess of the early 1800s had a lonely and fretful side, and its source should be no mystery.

Dolley Payne may have first seen James Madison in 1789, when he spent several days in Philadelphia on his way to New York for a session of Congress. Madison's traveling companion was Isaac Coles, another Virginia congressman and Dolley's uncle. She definitely knew Aaron Burr. Then a New York senator, Burr roomed in a boardinghouse operated by Mary Payne after her husband's death. When John Todd died, Dolley asked Burr to serve as the guardian of her son, and Madison asked Burr, in the spring of 1794, to introduce him to Dolley. He was forty-three; she was twenty-five, a greater age difference than the one between Madison and Kitty Floyd. Madison fell hard, telling Dolley's cousin Catherine Coles she could write Dolley "he thinks so much of you in the day that he has Lost his Tongue, at Night he dreames of you and Starts in his Sleep a calling you to relieve his Flame for he Burns to such an excess that he will be shortly consumed and he hopes that your heart will be calous to every other swain but himself."[11]

Dolley felt considerably less feverish. She solicited the advice of her lawyer, William W. Wilkins, a former suitor himself. Wilkins found Madison "good and amiable" and encouraged the marriage. The two were married on 15 September 1794 at the Harewood, Virginia, plantation of Dolley's sister Lucy and Lucy's husband, George Steptoe Washington. A letter Dolley wrote on her wedding day disclosed a continuing ambivalence. She professed her admiration, not affection, for Madison. She expressed confidence that he would be "a generous and tender protector" for "my little Payne," and then signed the letter, "Dolley Madison! Alass!" Happily, they were kind, even-tempered people who complimented each other well, and they grew closer over time.[12]

In December, the Quakers expelled Dolley. She had not observed the traditional year of mourning before her second marriage, and worse yet she had married an Anglican, albeit a nominal one. For his part Madison groused about the expense of supporting a family; he had to move out of a boardinghouse and rent more spacious quarters. At least one fellow member of Congress, the Connecticut Federalist Jonathan Trumball, believed marriage had improved Madison's disposition. He seemed, Trumball thought, less irritable and more sociable.[13]

The nation's capital had moved to Washington, D.C., during the last year of John Adams's presidency, while Madison was enjoying his semiretirement at Montpelier. When the Madisons arrived in Washington early in 1801 so Madison could assume his new duties as secretary of state, the city resembled a frontier county seat. Beyond public officials, the population numbered about thirty-one hundred, of which almost a quarter were slaves and free blacks. The president's house and offices for the Treasury, War, and State Departments stood at one end of an unpaved Pennsylvania Avenue.

The Capitol Building was at the other end, a mile and a half away. There were scattered clusters of construction elsewhere, including the so-called Six Buildings, which served as the temporary home of the State Department; Washington's residents banded together for protection from robbers. Heat, humidity, and mosquitoes were harder to avoid. Albert Gallatin, the incoming secretary of the treasury, considered the city an unhealthy swamp. To republican theorists, the distance between the executive branch and Congress may have suggested the separation of powers; Washington's open spaces could symbolize its transparency in conducting the public's business. To northerners and Europeans accustomed to real cities, the ramshackle capital raised questions about the viability of the new government.[14] Washington's founders had high expectations, "but never was so magnificent a design for a capital," wrote Augustus John Foster, a British diplomat, "so wretchedly and shabbily executed."[15]

American manners, heavily influenced by life in the backcountry, did not help the national image. Foster found American women especially repulsive. They were, he wrote his mother, "a spying, inquisitive, vulgar and most ignorant race. They are many of them daughters of tavern keepers, boarding housekeepers and clerks' wives and yet as ceremonious as ambassadresses." Margaret Bayard Smith, at a dinner given by the wife of another British minister, found a woman with an arm elbow deep in a salad bowl, "only rollicking," the woman said, "for an onion." Smith also recalled entertaining two senators who had never before seen a piano.[16]

Washington, in other words, enjoyed a meager social life, which suited the new president perfectly well. Looking forward to Madison's arrival, Jefferson wrote him in March 1801, "We shall have an agreeable society here, and not too much of it." Republicans disliked overly refined and extravagant entertainment because they believed luxury undermined civic virtue. The formal levees George Washington had begun bore too close a resemblance, in their eyes, to ceremonies of the English court. Jefferson replaced formal dinner parties with small, casual dinners at which guests were seated pell-mell in no particular order. Larger events required a hostess as well as a host. Jefferson's daughter, Martha Jefferson Randolph, occasionally served as the unofficial First Lady for her widowed father, but the Randolphs were frequently away, and Dolley Madison filled the potentially treacherous void. Rosemaire Zagarri has argued that the American Revolution created new political opportunities for women that were soon squelched by a backlash against "female politicians." Women, male critics claimed, valued personal comfort over the public good. Jefferson's experience as minister to France convinced him that politically active women had exerted a detrimental impact on French policy. When Albert Gallatin proposed that the administration hire women to fill vacant clerical positions, Jefferson said no.[17]

Yet Dolley Madison stayed on cordial terms with the president, and Jefferson's faith in her husband never faltered. Madison had declined the secretary of state's job under the Federalist George Washington, but he had no qualms about accepting the position in a Republican administration. The Madisons lived briefly with Jefferson until a place was ready for them in the Six Buildings. Five years later, Martha Jefferson Randolph and her husband, Thomas, would name a child after James Madison. Shrewd but essentially apolitical, Dolley Madison did not challenge Jefferson directly, and as a hostess she adopted a less formal style than she would assume after her husband became president. Jefferson gave few formal parties, and from 1801 to 1809, the secretary of state's house—the Madisons eventually settled into a three-story brick house on F Street—became the center of Washington's social life. She impressed even the acerbic Augustus John Foster, who found her "so perfectly good-tempered and good-humored that she rendered her husband's house as far as depended on her agreeable to all parties."[18]

"I am not much of a politician," Dolley once wrote Madison, but she liked to stay informed about current events.[19] She networked incessantly, calling on prominent local families and wives of politicians and members of the diplomatic corps, and forming useful alliances. She became close friends with Margaret Bayard Smith, the wife of Samuel Harrison Smith, the editor of the influential *Daily Intelligencer*. Margaret Bayard Smith was an important writer herself. Dolley and Hannah Nicholson Gallatin, wife of the treasury secretary, were also close. She had known Sally McKean, wife of the Spanish minister Yrujo, from Philadelphia. Despite the language barrier— Dolley's French was spotty—she enjoyed immensely the company of the wife of the French minister, Marie-Angélique Lequesne Ronsin Turreau. "I never visit her," Dolley said, "but I crack my sides a laughing." Madame Turreau improved her taste in clothes. Adopting a trademark turban, Dolley dressed well by American standards, but she recognized the danger in a democratic society of looking too aristocratic, and so she wore pearls instead of diamonds. She still commanded attention. Madison, in contrast, was said to look "like a schoolmaster dressed for a funeral."[20]

Dolley used her charm and connections to raise money for worthy causes, including the Lewis and Clark expedition; to find jobs for friends

Engraving of Dolley Madison from a painting by Gilbert Stuart. Dolley's marriage to James Madison illustrates the maxim that opposites attract. Personally and politically, she was an enormous asset to her husband. (Library of Congress)

and relatives; and, more broadly, to promote bipartisanship and national unity. Martha Washington and Abigail Adams had remained in the background; Dolley worked on her image. She never complained or criticized in public, and she never forgot a name or a face.[21] In an era of bitter factionalism, when political conflicts could easily become violent, Dolley showed hospitality to all, first as a Cabinet wife and later as First Lady, and she became the most popular woman in America. Before returning to Europe, the Dutch diplomat Peder Blicherolsen wrote Madison to express his appreciation for the Madisons' hospitality and apparently for the quality of their food and wine: "I should most probably without Mrs. Madison's generosity have been poisoned." One biographer has wisely observed, "As is true of other geniuses, nothing in her background can account for her accomplishment."[22] At a practical level, her lack of a political agenda, apart from promoting Madison's career, allowed her to pursue harmony as an end in itself.

Perhaps earlier disappointments bred an insecurity she assuaged by seeking to please. Perhaps the deaths in her own family made her more appreciative of other relationships.

Fame did not insulate Dolley Madison from new griefs and bouts of depression. She worried about Madison's workload, and spending most of the year in Washington, she missed Montpelier. Madison enrolled John Payne Todd in St. Mary's College in Baltimore, but Dolley's son neglected his studies and wasted his money. Neither his mother nor his stepfather could discipline him, and Payne became a permanent liability.[23] In July 1805, a nasty tumor on her leg forced Dolley to go to Philadelphia for treatment. A reoccurrence of Madison's intestinal problems on the trip north terrified her. Dolley's treatment left her bedridden for months. Madison had to return to Washington alone. When two Quaker visitors complained she was having too much company, the lecture brought back unpleasant memories: "I really felt my ancient terror of them revive to a disagreeable degree." Her mother died in 1807, her sister Mary the next year. Several siblings survived, but her brother John was a gambler and an alcoholic. "When I trace the sad events that have happened to me," she wrote Eliza Collins Lee in February 1808, "I feel as if I should die." She survived, but in June, she came down with rheumatism.[24]

For all Dolley's goodwill, moreover, she could not heal the new republic's political fissures. Radical Federalists proved incorrigible. In 1804, they entertained fantasies of electing the renegade Republican Aaron Burr governor of New York, and then leading New York and New England out of the Union. Differences among Republicans seemed even more menacing. Virginians John Randolph of Roanoke and John Taylor of Caroline complained the administration had embraced too much of the Federalist program. Pennsylvania representative Michael Leib believed Madison had been too slow in replacing Federalist officeholders with Republicans. The influential editor William Duane had not gotten all the public printing business he wanted. In politics, hospitality and good manners could only go so far.[25]

Bad manners accomplished even less. On 28 November 1803, Secretary of State Madison accompanied the new British minister, Anthony Merry, on his first visit to the White House. Merry wore the diplomatic regalia appropriate for the occasion, which included a plumed hat and a sword. Jefferson greeted him in worn, casual clothes and during the interview dangled a frayed slipper on his toe. The president's apparent indifference offended

Merry, and his irritation grew when Madison told him he would be expected to pay the first visit to the other Cabinet secretaries, which was a departure from previous practice. Later in the year, at the first White House dinner attended by Merry and his wife, Elizabeth, protocol demanded that Jefferson escort Mrs. Merry to her seat. Instead, Jefferson took Dolley Madison's arm. She recognized the faux pas, whispering to Jefferson, "Take Mrs. Merry," but the president ignored her. When Elizabeth Merry attempted to take a seat by Sally McKean, the wife of the Spanish minister, a congressman pushed her aside. In a report dated 7 December, Merry complained to his government about the Americans' boorish behavior, and Madison had an etiquette war on his hands.[26]

It could easily have been avoided. A year earlier, when Merry's name had emerged as a possible replacement for Robert Liston, the incumbent minister, Rufus King, then representing the United States in London, expressed his approval. James Monroe concurred: "From everything I can hear Mr. Merry is a candid worthy man."[27] The son of a London merchant who went bankrupt, Merry was an experienced diplomat with a reputation for honesty, affability, and a careful attention to his duties, but he was also unimaginative and overly cautious. Because Anglo-American relations deteriorated precipitously during his tenure, historians have tended to treat him harshly; the most thorough study of his career is, however, sympathetic. Merry probably would have performed perfectly well in a secondary role at a traditional European court. Merry's relatively modest background may have made him especially sensitive to snubs, and Elizabeth Merry complicated the picture. An intelligent, attractive woman who had inherited a considerable estate from her first husband, Elizabeth Merry undoubtedly expected more deference in America than she received. In public gatherings, she overshadowed her husband the way Dolley Madison overshadowed James. When news of the Merrys' travails reached England, an opposition newspaper, *Cobbett's Political Register*, blamed Elizabeth for starting the flap.[28]

Having spent several years in Paris, Jefferson understood the demands of polite society, so in snubbing the Merrys, what was the president thinking? The evidence suggests more than an innocent gaffe. Jefferson sincerely disliked formality, but he seemed to go out of his way to insult the British minister, even urging Louis André Pichon, the French chargé d'affaires, to cut short a trip to Baltimore so he could attend the White House dinner for the Merrys. The ongoing war between England and France made Pichon a most awkward dinner guest. With few other tools at his disposal, Jefferson apparently wanted to reaffirm America's independence from Britain at Merry's expense.[29]

Contrary to his own instincts, Madison felt compelled to follow Jefferson's lead. The very day Merry sent his angry report to London, he and Elizabeth attended a dinner at the Madisons' where the secretary of state, in another breach of etiquette, ignored Mrs. Merry and began the meal by escorting Hannah Nicholson Gallatin to her seat. Mrs. Merry, in turn, insulted Dolley Madison by comparing her table to a farm kitchen spread. After that disaster, the Merrys and Edward Thornton, the secretary of the British legation, temporarily boycotted administration social events, as did Yrujo, the Spanish minister.[30]

Dolley Madison tried to heal the breach as best she could. She encouraged Cabinet wives to visit Mrs. Merry. One wonders how that went. Anthony Merry, in a letter to George Hammond in the Foreign Office, described them as "a set of beings as little without the manners as without the appearance of Gentle Women." After Dolley heard Elizabeth favored Dolley's "Essence of Rose" perfume, she sent her a bottle. Dolley found the minister's wife strangely introverted. "The manners of Mistress Merry disgust both sexes and all parties," James Madison wrote Monroe.[31] Yet Dolley's persistence triumphed. By June 1805, she could write Anna Cutts about her "intimate" friendship with Elizabeth Merry.[32]

Madison meanwhile struggled with the affair, and he worried about "what complexion this nonsense may wear" on Merry's dispatches to London. He wrote Rufus King, just home from England, for advice on etiquette: "I am mortified at troubling you on a subject which more than any other, is in itself unworthy of either of us." English practice varied too much from occasion to occasion, King replied, to provide much guidance; "it is Title and not office which is chiefly regarded in the ceremonial of England," and he added, "the English though a cold and a proud people, place little value amongst themselves upon the knowledge or observance of mere ceremony." Attempting to clarify expectations, the administration, in January 1804, issued its own written "Cannons of Etiquette."[33]

At times, Madison found Merry "at bottom a very worthy man, and easy to do business with," but outbreaks of harmony never lasted long. When Henry Scott, an alleged runaway slave working for the British ministry, was arrested without notice to Merry, the minister complained of a violation of diplomatic immunity. White servants being in short supply, it was necessary, Merry observed, to "use People of Colour for all Purposes." Madison suggested he be more careful in selecting his staff, chiding Merry "for the want of regularity in the manner in which the hireling in question entered into your service." Ever prickly, Merry even complained when Jacob Wagner, the State Department's chief clerk, wrote to him directly during one of Madison's absences from Washington. Merry believed a group of Indians visiting the White House on New Year's Day 1806 received more respect than he did; at least Jefferson donned a black suit to meet them.[34]

Officials in London appeared to brush aside Merry's complaints about his mistreatment, and it would surely be an overstatement to suggest that the Merry affair led to the War of 1812. Anglo-American relations in a broad sense remained civil during Merry's tenure, and American trade flourished.[35] Yet the British minister failed at first to give credence to the administration's humanitarian objections to impressment. Merry proved so unresponsive to American complaints about the Royal Navy's practice of seizing alleged deserters from American ships that Madison fumed he was "a mere diplomatic pettifogger" and began pursuing individual cases through James Monroe in London. For his part, Merry urged his government to take a firm stand against the United States on trade and maritime issues. His influence is difficult to judge, but Merry's reports contributed to an image of America as an unstable, irresolute republic. He exaggerated its political divisions and doubted that its citizens, because of "the predominant passion of avarice," would ever pay enough taxes to support a viable national government. In short, Britain should feel no need to appease its former colonies.[36] We can only speculate at how different the next few years might have been if Jefferson and Madison had shown the Merrys the normal courtesies and then forged a closer relationship with the British minister.

James Madison inherited a small Department of State. Seven clerks and one messenger worked in Washington. Roughly seventy ministers, counsels, commissioners, and commercial agents were scattered across the globe. As secretary of state, Madison largely abstained from party politics, and he retained most of his Federalist subordinates. When a Federalist was dismissed, fellow party members would complain, but Republicans rarely believed they received all the patronage they deserved.[37] Republican editor William Duane called Daniel Brent, one of Madison's Federalist clerks, "a nincompoop." If Brent was not a model of efficiency, he and Madison formed a respectful relationship, and Brent stayed in his job for years. Madison relied even more heavily on his chief clerk, Jacob Wagner, another Federalist.[38] Although Madison can probably not be called a pioneer in civil service reform, his ability to work with a Federalist staff suggests a capacity to operate within a party system that recognized the legitimacy of the opposition. When Madison kept Wagner in his post after a long illness temporarily disabled the chief clerk, he won praise for his kindness from the Federalist press. Partisan differences would not, however, fade away. Wagner eventually resigned and became an antiadministration editor.[39]

Madison's office managed a host of responsibilities. In addition to supervising American representatives abroad, the State Department issued passports and oversaw the publication of federal laws. In the absence of a Department of Justice—the attorney general was essentially a lawyer retained by the government—legal matters went through Madison's office, as did commissions for federal jobs, which is how Madison became the nominal defendant in the landmark case *Marbury v. Madison* (1803). With no central purchasing office, the State Department bought its own supplies, including the red tape which with documents were bound and oats for the departmental horse. Beginning in 1802, the able William Thornton operated the Patent Office, technically a division of the State Department, as virtually a separate agency. By 1807, impressment cases were probably becoming an administrative burden as well as a diplomatic irritant.[40]

Much of the work was routine. Only the ministers to Great Britain, France, and Spain and the consuls to the pirate states on Africa's Barbary Coast faced major crises while Madison served as secretary of state. Diligent as he was, Madison did not stay in close contact with all the American officials under his jurisdiction. He took office distracted by the settlement of his father's estate and an ensuing feud between his brother William and sister Frances. Frequent sick spells and anxieties about money continued. "My expenses here," he wrote Joseph Jones in 1804, "devour my private as well as public resources."[41] Madison tried to spend July through October every year at Montpelier. The trips to and from Washington could be harrowing, fraught "with every difficulty which bad roads and bad weather could inflict." Coming home in May 1808, Madison had to disassemble his carriage and, in three trips, float "it over Porter's mill pond in something like a boat." Fortunately for Madison, he could not have been closer to the president. Loyal, serious, and unassuming, Madison could advise the more mercurial Jefferson without threatening to upstage him. When they were both in Virginia, they saw each other frequently, and special couriers regularly rode the thirty-mile circuit between Montpelier and Monticello.[42]

Both Madison and Jefferson viewed the world through what Madison scholar Marvin Meyers has called "the narrow frame of Virginia Republican doctrine," a perspective that minimized conflict within the administration while limiting the range of policies likely to be debated. They took office accused by the Federalists of being overly sympathetic to France; in reality, Napoleon's coup d'état had shattered any illusions Madison might have held about Franco-American relations. He clung, however, to certain principles—and misconceptions—that often undermined his diplomatic efforts. He hoped to pursue an idealistic foreign policy: "It is impossible that the destinies of any nation, more than an individual, can be injured by an adherence to the maxims of virtue." Leaders usually claim to act from the purest motives. Madison admitted elsewhere that "the business of Government is not transacted with the celerity which is expected in the concerns of individuals."[43]

Committed to foreign trade and commercial expansion, he consistently exaggerated the effectiveness of economic sanctions. Committed to territorial expansion but fearful of war as a threat to republican institutions, he had a grasp of military matters that was superficial at best. On lesser issues, he could be deliberate and flexible, traits that occasionally made him appear indecisive, and he did not understand how his country looked to foreigners. The Frenchman Turreau, for example, believed Americans were too devoted to individual gain to support an offensive war, but if they were attacked, their materialism would cause them to fight ferociously in defense of their possessions.[44] At the same time, Madison's talents were considerable, and his philosophical predilections were widely shared. They would not be political liabilities.

Conflict with the Barbary states illustrated the limits of American power. Treaties negotiated in the 1790s obligated the United States to pay tribute to Algiers, Tripoli, and Tunis. In exchange, the Barbary states agreed not to attack American shipping. Finding it cheaper to pay bribes than to wage war, many of the European powers had signed similar agreements. By the time Madison took office, the United States had fallen behind in its payments to Algiers and Tunis. Meanwhile, an increasingly assertive Tripoli, technically a protectorate of Algiers, was restive because its treaty entitled it to less loot than its neighbors received. On 14 May 1801, the bashaw of Tripoli declared war on the United States by chopping down the flagpole at the American consulate. Whenever one Barbary state negotiated a more favorable treaty, the others would up the ante. Their demands could be shameless and insatiable. As William Eaton, the American counsel in Tunis, wrote Madison, "The restless spirit of these marauders cannot be restrained." After a fire destroyed fifty thousand small arms owned by the bey of Tunis, the bey demanded that the Western powers replace his arsenal and imposed an assessment of ten thousand muskets on the United States. American officials abroad repeatedly recommended military action to end the extortion.[45]

In the spring of 1801, Madison signed the paperwork sending a small naval squadron to the Mediterranean to protect American shipping from Tripoli's corsairs, but he hoped for a negotiated settlement, and he was not above attempting to appease the Barbary pirates. Madison was willing to continue paying the bashaw if it could be done secretly.[46] The United States sent cannon and powder, among other gifts, to Tunis and gun carriages to Morocco, a fourth Barbary state. America's initial military efforts against Tripoli proved ineffective; the frigate *Philadelphia* ran aground on the North African coast, and the ship and its crew were captured. A daring raid led by Stephen Decatur destroyed the ship, preventing it from being used against the United States.[47]

In the summer of 1804, the Jefferson administration escalated the naval war; the president actually worried that European and Turkish diplomats might secure the release of the *Philadelphia*'s crew before the United States could strike a decisive blow. An aggressive American blockade and an invasion organized by Eaton produced a peace treaty abrogating Tripoli's right to tribute but allowing other forms of piracy—specifically kidnapping Americans for ransom—to continue. Elsewhere, the administration kept paying tribute and endured other indignities. When the Tunisian ambassador Sidi Suliman Mellimelli visited Washington in the winter of 1805–6, Madison had to provide him with a prostitute; the State Department's accounts reflected an entry for the services of "Georgia, a Greek."[48]

A slave revolt led by Toussaint L'Ouverture in the French colony of Saint-Domingue presented Madison with another kind of dilemma and an unexpected opportunity. Madison felt no regret over the decline of European influence in the New World, but the prospect of a successful slave revolt horrified white southerners. Madison expected a government under L'Ouverture to be "pure Despotism."[49] At the same time, Americans saw money to be made in trading with the rebels, and that commerce strained American relations with French officials attempting to maintain control of the island. When the Baltimore merchant Samuel Smith heard the administration intended to send warships to Saint-Domingue to protect American trade, he warned Madison against provoking the French: "We know our risqué [sic] and take it at our peril, we know we have no right to trade there, but the profit is *tempting*—the loss we can *Insure against*." War could make business more difficult.[50] Although Congress eventually prohibited the trade, the issue soon became irrelevant. In December 1801, Napoleon had sent General Charles Leclerc and twenty-eight thousand soldiers to Saint-Domingue to restore French rule. The fighting and yellow fever decimated the French army; its losses included Leclerc. The French finally abandoned the island in 1809, long after their cause had become hopeless.[51]

The French debacle in Saint-Domingue created unexpected opportunities for the United States in Louisiana. By June 1801, Madison had heard rumors of a Spanish cession of Louisiana to Napoleon. Fearful of antagonizing the United States, Spain and France hesitated to confirm the transfer. The Pinckney Treaty of 1795 supposedly guaranteed American access to Spanish port facilities in New Orleans, and if Spain disagreed, American officials, including Madison, assumed they could take the city by force. France, in contrast, had made no commitments to the Americans and could not be easily pushed aside. Madison told Robert R. Livingston, then the American minister in Paris, that the cession was of "momentous concern." Madison envisioned the West becoming a battleground between British Canada and French Louisiana, with the French colony serving as a haven for runaway slaves. After meeting with Madison, Pichon, the French chargé d'affaires, warned his government that its acquisition of Louisiana would painfully embarrass the Jefferson administration and sow the seeds of a future conflict.[52]

Madison hoped he could somehow "turn the present crisis to the advantage of the United States" by persuading Spain to cede Florida, essentially the modern state of Florida and a strip of land running along the Gulf Coast westward to New Orleans, to the United States. He hoped to take Florida as compensation for American ships condemned in Spanish ports during the Quasi-War with France in the 1790s. Uncertain of the boundaries of Louisiana, Madison also instructed Livingston to find out what France would take for New Orleans and Florida—if it had been included in the cession—and the administration sent James Monroe to Paris to assist in the negotiations.[53]

In October 1802, the Spanish intendant in New Orleans, still nominally in command of the city, revoked the right of Americans to store goods there, effectively closing New Orleans to American shipping. Madison complained to the Spanish minister of "a direct and gross violation of the terms as well as the spirit of the Treaty of 1795." Rumors circulated that frontiersmen in western Pennsylvania were planning to march on New Orleans, and Congress debated a bill to expand the army. Madison and Jefferson, meanwhile, authorized Monroe and Livingston to negotiate an agreement for the purchase of New Orleans and for "West and East Florida, or as much there of as the actual proprietor can be prevailed to part with."[54] France's tenuous hold on Saint-Domingue, the putative centerpiece of Napoleon's New World empire, had reduced Louisiana's value to him, and the resumption of war with Great Britain after a brief peace made New Orleans a vulnerable luxury. When Napoleon offered to sell all of Louisiana to the United States, Monroe and Livingston, departing from their instructions, agreed. Livingston advised Madison that, according to the Spanish ambassador in Paris, Spain had not ceded Florida to France. When Livingston pressed Talleyrand, after the fact, on the eastern boundaries of the Louisiana Purchase, the French foreign minister, as Livingston reported his remarks, responded famously, "I can give you no clear direction. You have made a noble bargain for yourselves and I suppose you will make the most of it." With that encouragement, the American diplomat then concluded it was "incontrovertible that West Florida is comprised in the cession of Louisiana."[55]

The administration had backed into its greatest diplomatic achievement, and it might have backed out. Monroe reported from Paris that he and Livingston would never have purchased all of Louisiana if they could have bought only a part. Early in the crisis, Pichon concluded that Madison considered American acquisition of territory west of the Mississippi River to be "a chimera." In May 1802, when Madison could still hope the transfer of Louisiana from Spain to France might be undone, he suggested the United States guarantee Spanish territory west of the Mississippi if Spain would sell West Florida to the American government. After Madison learned of their agreement with Talleyrand, he wrote Monroe and Livingston and readily excused them for exceeding their authority. Their instructions had not mentioned "the country beyond the Mississippi" because no one thought it might be for sale, and no one wanted to be "suspected of a greedy ambition."[56] Livingston, moreover, advised the secretary of state that even New Orleans would "be of little consequence if we possess the Floridas," with their own extensive river system. As late as February 1804, Livingston suggested the United States keep New Orleans but swap the area west of the Mississippi with Spain in exchange for Florida.[57]

Jefferson's constitutional scruples could have quashed the transaction just as easily. The president worried that the federal government lacked the authority to acquire new territory or to organize it into new states. Madison argued the treaty-making power authorized the annexation of territory by agreement with a foreign power. He and Jefferson tinkered with a proposed constitutional amendment to remove any doubts, but they abandoned the project. Convinced a further delay might allow Napoleon to renege on the sale, they decided to send the treaty to the Senate, where it was approved by a vote of 22 to 7. "I infer the less we say about constitutional difficulties respecting Louisiana the better," Jefferson concluded, "and that what is necessary for surmounting them must be done sub silento."[58]

As striking as the indifference to the larger part of Louisiana is the administration's apparent willingness to use force to achieve its objectives. After the Spanish revoked the American right of deposit, Madison wrote, grandiloquently, "there are now or in two years will be, not less than 200,000 militia on the waters of the Mississippi, every man of whom would march at a minute[']s warning to remove obstructions from that outlet to the sea." If negotiations with France failed, he considered war to be inevitable and authorized Monroe and Livingston to seek a rapprochement with Great Britain. Later he consoled them for their failure to obtain a clear title to Florida. "The Floridas," he reasoned, "can easily be acquired, especially in the case of war, and perhaps by arrangements involving little or no money." When Spanish officials seemed laggard in vacating New Orleans, Madison instructed American authorities in the area to use force if necessary to occupy the city, but the Spanish proved less obstinate than he had feared.[59]

The peaceful transfer notwithstanding, the Louisiana Purchase produced a crisis with Spain. In addition to the dispute over West Florida, Spain claimed its cession to France had been conditioned on a pledge from Napoleon not to alienate the territory. Madison believed that objection was intended to bolster Spain's bargaining position in negotiations over the boundaries of Louisiana. Meanwhile, American saber-rattling, the American consul Sylvanus Burke wrote Madison from Amsterdam, was "betraying symptoms of undue ambition in our country." Livingston reported from Paris that the fixation on Florida "has greatly hurt our character for moderation." European diplomats believed "we will buy Territory that is convenient to us, but if the owner does not choose to sell, we will take it by force." In the words of Charles Pinckney, the American minister to Madrid, the Spanish foreign minister Pedro de Cevellos had condemned Americans "as a Nation of Calculators, entirely bent on making money and nothing else."[60]

Much of the acrimony centered on the Mobile Act of 1804, which empowered the president to establish a revenue office in the disputed territory; Yrujo called it "an atrocious libel" against the government of Spain. The Spanish minister's tone infuriated Madison, and their shaky relationship collapsed.[61] Madison wanted Spain to recognize the Rio Bravo River as the western border of Louisiana, to accept American occupation of West

Florida, to sell East Florida, and to settle American spoliation claims arising from the Quasi-War. As negotiations went on in Madrid, Madison shifted positions slightly, but he consistently instructed American representatives to take a hard line, suggesting, for example, the creation of a temporary buffer zone in Texas, which would simply delay the date on which Mexican territory would be swamped by a burgeoning American population. "No guarantee of the Spanish possessions," he told Monroe, "is to be admissible." Diplomacy, understandably, went nowhere, and by October 1805, Jefferson and Madison were considering whether the United States should seek a "provisional alliance" with Great Britain in the event of war with Spain. Madison was cool to the idea. In December, Jefferson proposed to Congress an ambitious defense plan that included construction of six seventy-four-gun warships. Privately, the president preferred diplomacy, and he got from Congress what became known as the Two-Million-Dollar Act, essentially an appropriation to bribe France to pressure Spain to sell Florida.[62]

Relations with Spain continued to deteriorate. Relations with Yrujo became so strained that the administration asked for his recall and considered removing him by force if he did not leave the country voluntarily. Yet, for all their bold rhetoric, Jefferson and Madison hesitated to act and continued to talk. War threatened to frustrate the Republican commitment to cut federal taxes and the national debt. As they waited, the Spanish crisis was overtaken by an even more ominous challenge from Great Britain. In April 1807, Jefferson fumed to his secretary of state, "I had rather have war against Spain than not, if we go to war against England," because, he claimed, American volunteers could easily take Florida, Mexico, and probably Cuba. War seemed imminent to Madison, but caution and common sense prevailed, and the administration merely suspended negotiations with Spain as it turned to face another crisis.[63]

Only a few months after taking office as secretary of state, Madison complained to Rufus King about the "wanton abuse of power on the part of Great Britain," and especially "the spoliations on our trade, and the impressment of our seamen." At war with Napoleon, the British attempted to interdict American trade with France and seized British subjects from neutral vessels for service in the Royal Navy. Many of the impressed men were deserters, but even British subjects who had become American citizens were subject to impressment because British law did not recognize the legality of foreign naturalization proceedings. The Treaty of Ameins brought a brief respite later in 1801, but when the hostilities resumed in 1803, so did the practice of impressment. An Anglo-American agreement banning impressment on the high seas seemed within reach, but the two sides never agreed on the final details. Madison estimated that in 1803 and 1804, approximately seventeen hundred men had been impressed from American ships. War in Europe benefited the American carrying trade, which increased the demand for merchant seamen at the same time that it strained the resources of the Royal Navy. The impressment issue represented a tug-of-war between an expanding British navy, where discipline was strict and danger abounded, and the growing American merchant fleet, which offered safer and more lucrative employment. Both sides drew so heavily on the same manpower pool that compromise proved elusive.[64]

Albert Gallatin calculated in April 1807 that, much to his surprise, British subjects might constitute half of all able-bodied seamen employed in the American foreign trade. Gallatin's report startled Madison. He had entertained the idea of a prohibition on British sailors serving on American ships. Now, even though he believed Gallatin's figures to be too high, he suggested limiting the ban to men who had been out of the Royal Navy for less than two years. Jefferson cut off the debate, at least temporarily. The treasury secretary's "estimate of the number of foreign seamen in our employ," he wrote Madison, "renders it prudent I think to suspend all propositions respecting our non employment of them."[65]

As cases of impressment mounted, British restrictions on American trade, mainly in the form of cabinet decisions known as orders in council, hit Madison in the sorest of spots. He had long resented America's exclusion from direct trade with British colonies and discriminatory duties imposed on American shipping. In one of the longest letters he wrote during his first year as secretary of state, he complained to Rufus King that British tonnage duties worked against the United States because American exports were bulkier than British exports. Judging from his correspondence, Madison raised the issue on his own initiative, not in response to political pressure. Whatever advantages British shippers enjoyed, American commerce boomed in the early 1800s, and the Anglo-American trading relationship was the largest in the world.[66] Amid the fighting in Europe, a series of orders in council gradually erected new barriers. In an effort to punish Britain, Napoleon eventually adopted his own Continental System regulating neutral trade, but as Britain was the greater sea power, its policies were more onerous.

British and American officials quarreled over the definition of contraband, war matériel legally subject to seizure, and over the validity of paper blockades: blockades of enemy ports that even the Royal Navy could not consistently enforce and that were therefore in violation of international law. The legality of the American carrying trade between the French West Indies and the European mainland, however, generated the most controversy. Britain's Rule of 1756 prohibited in wartime trade not permitted in peacetime, which included the West Indian carrying trade. With the Royal Navy sweeping French merchantmen from the seas, Napoleon opened the commerce to ships from the United States. British authorities generally tolerated the trade under the "broken voyage" doctrine, holding the Rule of 1756 did not apply if an American ship stopped at an American port on its way, for example, from the French West Indies to France. Under this loose interpretation of the rule, "American re-exports soared from $2 million in 1792 to $53 million in 1805." Then in 1805, a British court decision threatened the American bonanza. The *Essex* case held that a token call at an American port could not be used to circumvent the Rule of 1756, and the Royal Navy began seizing more American ships.[67]

The opinion, Madison wrote James Monroe, "has spread great alarm among the merchants, and has had a grievous effect on the rate of insurance." It was, he concluded, a "new and shameful depredation." He responded with "An Examination of the British Doctrine, which Subjects to Capture, a Neutral Trade, Not Open in Time of Peace," a seventy-thousand-word, 204-page attack on the Rule of 1756. Displaying Madison's customary command of international law, European history, and minute detail, the treatise delivered a devastating blow to the rule, for anyone who managed to read it. Senator William Plumer tried: "I never read a book that fatigued me more than this pamphlet has done." Making odd use of a Cabinet officer's time, Madison had returned to the scholarly approach that had served him brilliantly during domestic debates over questions of constitutional theory. Unfortunately for him, legal arguments would not alter British policy.[68]

Congress responded to British insults by passing the Non-Importation Act, restricting the sale of British goods that had American counterparts, and then delayed the effective date of the measure pending the outcome of further negotiations. It was a timid gesture, unlikely to impress the British. A change in administrations in England, however, had placed the supposedly pro-American Charles James Fox at the head of the Foreign Ministry and encouraged hopes for a diplomatic solution. Jefferson sent the Baltimore Federalist William Pinkney, a highly regarded lawyer, to London to assist the ubiquitous James Monroe in representing the United States.

Madison's instructions, dated 17 May 1806, contained a long list of American demands and an unconvincing claim that the Non-Importation Act was not intended to penalize Great Britain. Some evidence suggests that Monroe believed the instructions doomed his mission from its outset, but Madison probably believed his proposals were reasonable. Within the administration, Madison, to be sure, became the chief advocate of a tough British policy. Jefferson, for example, rejected his proposal that British ships be barred from using the Norfolk naval yard for repairs. When the Monroe-Pinkney mission initially made little progress, Madison advocated an economic boycott of Great Britain.[69]

Monroe and Pinkney signed an agreement with their British counterparts on 31 December 1806, and the draft reached Washington on 3 March, shortly before Congress was to adjourn. The American diplomats had won some concessions, including a virtual repeal of the *Essex* decision, a narrow definition of contraband, and a reduction in British tonnage duties on American ships, among others. But they had made concessions as well. Lords Holland and Auckland, the British negotiators, had refused to address impressment in the treaty; the practice enjoyed too much political support in Great Britain. Instead, they provided Monroe and Pinkney with a note promising greater care to prevent the impressment of Americans and pledging to release promptly any American citizens who were wrongly seized. The note lacked specifics, but the negotiations convinced Monroe and Pinkney that British officials intended to restrict impressment. The Americans agreed to forego commercial retaliation against Great Britain for ten years, and another clause prohibited the United States from engaging in indirect trade with the British East Indies, that is, from stopping in European ports to trade for the specie required to purchase East Indian exports. The provision was intended to limit competition with Britain's East India Company.[70]

Jefferson elected not to submit the treaty to the Senate. The president and the Cabinet had already agreed they could not accept a treaty surrendering the right to impose commercial sanctions, one of Madison's favorite projects, without ending impressment. The restrictions on the East Indian trade, a seemingly obscure issue, drew fire from Republican merchants. Historians have debated the merits of the treaty, but Monroe had firsthand knowledge of the political situation in Britain, and Pinkney had more practical experience with trade issues than either Jefferson or Madison. Many in England saw it as a surrender to the Americans. The administration's rejection of the treaty angered and embarrassed Monroe and created a rift with Madison that took years to heal. Monroe believed ratification of the agreement would have encouraged trade with Great Britain and led to improved Anglo-American relations. One modern study has concluded that the Monroe-Pinkney Treaty offered the United States substantial advantages for "little more than a promise of benevolent neutrality."[71]

A myriad of considerations, however, worked against the treaty. The note on impressment lacked the legal authority of a treaty provision. Tending to exaggerate the effectiveness of economic weapons, Jefferson and Madison made too much of Monroe and Pinkney's concessions on that point. Timing worked against careful consideration of the treaty; it arrived in Washington just as Congress was preparing to go home and while Jefferson was suffering from a bout of disabling migraine headaches. Meanwhile, a respiratory infection left Madison barely able to conduct routine business. The old, unlamented Jay Treaty, moreover, had left Jefferson and Madison wary of commercial accords with England. Unable to predict the future, they also failed to foresee the risks of rejecting the new agreement. Administration officials, including Monroe and Pinkney, expected to be able to renegotiate the treaty and obtain more favorable terms. As late as July 1807, John Jay, who should have known better, advised Madison that the British could be easily intimidated; their economy, he suggested, depended too heavily on American trade for them to risk war with the United States.[72]

Events appeared to vindicate an assertive diplomacy, or more precisely, a British blunder left Americans in no mood to compromise. On 22 June 1807, the *H.M.S. Leopard* opened fire on an American frigate, the *Chesapeake*, off Hampton Roads, Virginia, after the commander of the *Chesapeake*, James Barron, had refused to allow a British boarding party to search his ship for deserters. Repeated broadsides from the *Leopard* killed three Americans and wounded several others, including Barron. Caught by surprise, the *Chesapeake* was forced to strike its colors and to surrender four crewmen—two whites and two blacks. British officials claimed Barron had knowingly accepted British deserters. The men seized may have represented only a small percentage of the British subjects onboard the American vessel. After a court-martial in Halifax, Nova Scotia, one of the men taken from the *Chesapeake*, Jenkin Ratford, was found to be a British-born citizen who had volunteered for the Royal Navy and then deserted. He was executed.[73]

The removal of sailors by force from an American warship, although not authorized by London, escalated the impressment crisis and triggered a wave of outrage against Great Britain. The incident, John Dawson wrote Madison from Fredricksburg, Virginia, "has excited an indignant feeling, which extends to every description of persons in this place." In Philadelphia, a mob attacked a British brig, the *Fox*, removed its sails and rudder, cut its rigging, and broke its gun carriages. Madison drafted a presidential proclamation barring British ships from American ports. Jefferson toned down Madison's prose slightly; a reference to the *Leopard*'s "lawless and bloody purpose" became simply "purpose." The people, Madison assured Monroe, stood behind the president and demanded "Reparation or War."[74]

His instructions to Monroe, dated 6 July, asserted that "this enormity is not a subject for discussion." The United States demanded a disavowal of the attack and the return of the captured men—Ratford had not yet been executed. Apparently against the advice of the Cabinet, Jefferson and Madison also made the end of impressment a condition for settlement, although Madison resurrected his earlier proposal permitting impressment of sailors who had deserted within the last two years. The nationality of the men seized was irrelevant to Madison; he came to consider deserters to be akin to political exiles. Talks on other issues would be suspended pending a resolution of the *Chesapeake* affair, and if it could not be settled quickly, Madison, anticipating war, urged Monroe to advise American ships abroad to return to the safety of their home ports. Meanwhile, the Cabinet made secret plans for an invasion of Canada, but the federal government lacked the legal authority to mobilize the state militias on which the operation depended.[75]

The British offered to recall Vice-Admiral George Berkeley, the Royal Navy commander at Halifax, return the three surviving captives, and compensate the families of those killed or wounded on the *Chesapeake*. Whether in London or in Washington, however, British officials refused to discuss impressment from merchant ships as part of the *Chesapeake* settlement. As the diplomatic efforts floundered, the delay dissipated the war fever. Madison seemed strangely optimistic, or complacent, about the prospects for ultimate success. George Rose, the British envoy to Washington during the crisis, concluded that Madison wanted to keep the controversy alive in order to build public support for more aggressive commercial sanctions against Great Britain. Irving Brant agreed, even suggesting that Jefferson and Madison saw an advantage to war: they could justify seizing Florida as a preemptive strike to prevent Britain from occupying the territory. If Madison saw any benefits in a war, it seems unlikely he actually wanted one. He had always seen military conflict as a threat to republicanism. Impressment infuriated his Republican constituents, and he surely hoped British embarrassment over the *Chesapeake* might lead to an agreement to end the practice. In any event, he had an opportunity to settle the *Chesapeake* affair quickly, and he did not take it. By January 1808, Jefferson and Madison would agree to separate the *Chesapeake* negotiations from the broader issue of impressment, but by then it was too late. British attitudes had stiffened.[76]

In the absence of an agreement, British ships continued to harass American shipping. "Merchant vessels arriving and departing," Madison reported to Monroe, "have been challenged, fired at, examined and detained within our jurisdiction, with as little scruple as if they were at open sea. Even a Revenue cutter conveying the Vice President and his sick daughter from Washington to New York and wearing her distinctive and well known colours did not escape insult."[77]

Madison received mixed reports from American agents abroad about the effect of the European war on the young republic's trade,[78] but in November 1807, a new round of orders in council and royal proclamations declared a blockade of all French-controlled ports and reaffirmed the right of impressment. The British blockade was especially galling because it seemed to be motivated by greed rather than military necessity. British regulations were designed less to starve Napoleon than to allow British businesses to monopolize whatever trade that did reach the continent. Jefferson asked Congress for $850,000 to build a fleet of small gunboats and to return three decommissioned frigates to active duty, but earlier budget cuts had left the country woefully unprepared for war.[79]

The Non-Importation Act of 1806 finally took effect on 14 December 1807, and a few days later Jefferson sent Congress a proposal, drafted by Madison, for a trade embargo. The Senate passed the bill the day it received it, and the House of Representatives approved it three days later. The Embargo Act generally prohibited American ships from engaging in foreign trade, and although it did not prohibit foreign ships from entering American ports, they could not take on American cargo. Madison had been contemplating an embargo for years. During a similar crisis in the 1790s, he had written Jefferson, "What a noble stroke would be an embargo? It would probably do as much good as harm at home; and would force peace, on the rest of the world, and perhaps liberty along with it." He was not alone. Russia declared an embargo for a few months in 1801, and in February 1806, Elbridge Gerry had written Madison to recommend one. In August, Monroe reported that the British were considering an embargo of their own. Despite the familiarity of the concept, the Embargo Act itself was hastily conceived and so ill considered that it did not originally provide penalties for violations. Albert Gallatin told Jefferson and Madison that its consequences would be hard to predict. The New York Republican Morgan Lewis warned Madison the act would leave four thousand New York City seamen unemployed and encourage them to leave the country; Lewis also feared that the embargo would hurt the state Republican Party at the polls.[80]

Historians have sometimes criticized the Jefferson administration for making matters worse by failing to explain publicly the purpose of the Embargo Act, although Madison tried. Jefferson first saw it as a defensive measure that would give American ships time to return home before the start of hostilities. It also served as a diplomatic tool: it supposedly signaled a willingness to go to war if the nation's demands were not met. Gradually, Jefferson came to see the embargo as an offensive weapon and as a substitute for war, which was closer to Madison's position. In the last week of December, the *National Intelligencer* published three essays, generally attributed to Madison, defending the embargo. In the first essay, Madison argued that rather than provoking war or precluding negotiations, the embargo would make it the interest of Great Britain and France to alter their policies. Dependent on American foodstuffs, Spain, he asserted, would suffer the most under the blockade, a surprising aside that suggests Madison continued to worry about Spanish spoliations and the Floridas even while the nation was on the brink of war with Britain.[81]

In a second essay, Madison admitted the embargo would temporarily reduce the value of American exports, but the burden of lower prices would fall chiefly on planters, who, having already sold the summer's crops and bought supplies for the winter, could bear it most easily. If that argument demonstrated a capacity to rise above local self-interest, his cavalier dismissal of the effects on merchants betrayed his Virginia biases. "It will separate the wheat from the chaff." Honest, prudent merchants would survive. "The merchant, who has been fraudulently trading on another's capital, may sink. And will not this be just." The final essay minimized the risk of war and the nation's vulnerability to attack and repeated now familiar arguments: economic warfare with European powers favored the United States because Americans sold "necessaries" and bought "superfluities," which could easily be abandoned; an embargo would encourage frugality; and it would stimulate "household manufactures."[82]

Of course, the American economy could not tolerate an embargo indefinitely. "I take it to be an universal opinion," Jefferson wrote Madison in March 1808, "that war will become preferable to a continuance of the embargo after a certain time."[83] New England Federalists had opposed the embargo from the beginning, and in Massachusetts the issue helped them regain control of the state legislature. Smuggling flourished along the Canadian border and in foreign ships leaving American ports. Hundreds of American vessels exploited loopholes in the Embargo Act. One clause permitted American ships to visit foreign ports to retrieve goods supposedly bought before the embargo took effect. Another allowed ships engaged in the coasting trade to seek refuge from bad weather in foreign ports. Rampant smuggling led the administration to send troops to the New York–Canada border and to seek additional, draconian legislation vesting in federal agents new prerogatives, including broad powers of search and seizure. The administration had underestimated the importance of exports to the American economy and had failed to anticipate Great Britain's ability to draw on existing reserves of wheat and cotton or to find new markets in Latin America.[84] Jefferson and Madison "have been greatly perplexed," Dolley Madison wrote Anna Cutts, "at the remonstrances from so many Towns to remove the Embargo." The secretary of state had expected Americans to rally around the law.[85]

Louis-André Pichon believed the Louisiana Purchase had ensured Thomas Jefferson's reelection in 1804. Jefferson enjoyed such popularity, and the Federalists were so disorganized and ineffective, that his diplomatic triumph may not have been a political necessity. The only suspense in the 1804 election came from the decision to replace Vice President Aaron Burr. On 25 February 1804, the Republican caucus in Congress unanimously nominated Jefferson for a second term and chose George Clinton, the former governor of New York, to be his running mate. Clinton's appeal was a matter of geography and, according to the political gossip, age. Virginia Republicans supposedly supported the elderly New Yorker because they suspected he would be unable to mount a serious challenge to a Virginia candidate if Jefferson decided to retire in 1808. The Federalist candidates, Charles Cotesworth Pinckney and Rufus King, ran no real campaign, and Jefferson won in the Electoral College by a vote of 162 to 14, losing only Connecticut, Delaware, and two electoral districts in Maryland.[86]

Madison had long been seen as a possible candidate for higher office, and his close relationship with Jefferson made him a logical successor. Initially divisions among Republicans presented a greater obstacle to a Madison presidency than did the Federalists. George Clinton had his supporters in New York, and there was some noisy opposition to the administration among Pennsylvania Republicans. Jefferson's popularity often precluded direct attacks on the president; the less regal Madison made a more tempting target. Moderate Republicans, many of them voters who had supported the Constitution during the ratification debates of 1787–88, would rally around Madison. The more doctrinaire, often southern slave owners with Anti-Federalist leanings, proved troublesome. These "Old Republicans" included John Taylor of Caroline and the brilliant but unstable John Randolph of Roanoke.

Randolph in particular developed a personal contempt for Madison. Randolph's animosity fed in part on Madison's role in the infamous Yazoo case, in which a supine Georgia legislature had been bribed to make massive land grants to four groups of speculators. After the fraud was exposed, Madison served on a commission appointed to sort through the legal wreckage; the commissioners recommended a compromise settlement that included some compensation for investors who had purchased bad titles. Randolph furiously assailed the government's intervention, and the case was an unholy mess. Once the Supreme Court ruled in *Flechter v. Peck* (1810) that Georgia could not simply set aside the original grants, however, Madison's commission looked to have made the best of a bad situation. Yet Randolph's antipathy to Madison went beyond any single issue; he may have seen in Madison the professional politician who was anathema to pure republicanism. That Randolph circulated salacious rumors about Dolley Madison during the campaign of 1808 suggests the lengths to which he would go.[87]

For his part, Madison professed to believe "candid people will be sensible that the greater part of political management consists rather in taking advantage of events as they occur, than in precisely foreseeing or inviting them." In 1808, as the most prominent prospect within the majority party, Madison benefited from the natural course of events. Republicans probably would have supported a third term for Jefferson, but exhausted by seemingly insolvable foreign policy crises, the president barely had the stamina to complete his second term. A Clinton faction in New York hoped to nominate the vice president for president while Randolph and other Old Republicans encouraged James Monroe, embittered by the rejection of the Monroe-Pinkney Treaty, to run.[88]

In addition to a long record of public service and his close association with a popular incumbent, Madison possessed another important advantage. In an era when officeholders did not routinely speak to large audiences or sit for interviews, Dolley Madison's parties and receptions gave Madison a unique opportunity to cultivate public support. Margaret Bayard Smith believed Dolley Madison's hospitality "won a popularity for her husband which his cold and reserved manners never could have done."[89] One Washington wit compared him to "a country schoolmaster in mourning for one of his pupils who he had whipped to death." Dolley helped soften that image. The nominating process of the day enhanced her influence; the Republican members of Congress she entertained constituted the party caucus that would select the Republican nominee. Samuel Latham Mitchill, a Republican senator from New York, believed Dolley's socializing gave Madison an advantage over Clinton because the vice president, a widower, stayed "snug in his lodgings and keeps aloof." Meanwhile, as one Delaware congressman reported, Dolley "spoke very slightly" of her husband's other rival, James Monroe.[90]

On 24 January 1808, the Republican caucus voted overwhelmingly to nominate Madison for president, and in an effort to forestall his presidential bid, nominated Clinton for a second term as vice president. The vote did not heal the divisions within the party. Randolph's faction and the New York delegation boycotted the caucus. Clinton, while remaining on the ticket, allowed his supporters to organize an independent candidacy for president. It was an act of disloyalty that Madison tolerated, setting a precedent that would not bode well for his presidency. In Virginia, meanwhile, dissident Republicans nominated Monroe.

Clinton and Monroe remained regional candidates representing disgruntled minority factions. More formidable opposition came from a respectable Federalist ticket, presidential candidate Charles Cotesworth Pinckney of South Carolina and vice presidential nominee Rufus King of New York. Madison benefited from an early tactical blunder by the Federalists. In February, Senator Timothy Pickering of Massachusetts demanded that Jefferson release copies of Madison's diplomatic correspondence. He did, and the papers showed Madison pursuing American interests aggressively and, at first blush, evenhandedly, against both Great Britain and France. However counterproductive the Embargo Act may have been, it did not bring on an economic disaster sufficient to change large numbers of votes. Madison profited, ironically, by the administration's inability to enforce the act more thoroughly. Outside the seaports, the embargo may have been felt only indirectly by the average Republican voter. In the end, the Federalist ticket improved on the party's showing in 1804, but not by nearly enough. Madison received 122 electoral votes to 47 for Pinckney and 6—all from New York—for Clinton. Republican Party loyalty in the South and West, abetted by Madison's résumé, Jefferson's panache, and Dolley Madison's charm, proved too much for Pinckney. "I was beaten by

Mr. and Mrs. Madison," he said. "I might have had a better chance had I faced Mr. Madison alone."[91]

Paradoxically, just as Madison was winning a decisive victory, congressional support for the Embargo Act started to collapse. On 15 November 1808, Madison and Gallatin wrote Jefferson urging him to make some new recommendations to Congress: divisions among Republicans and "the apparent public opinion may on consideration induce a revision of our own." The president believed that the nation had three options: continuation of the embargo, war, or "submission and tribute." His earlier militancy had disappeared. Fearful war would end for the foreseeable future his dream of eliminating the national debt, he hoped to continue the embargo. Jefferson, however, had shown little leadership since December 1807, when he announced his decision not to seek a third term, and now he felt he could defer to the president-elect.[92]

Jefferson's deference may have frustrated Madison. He feared Congress would likely declare war on Great Britain by May if relief could not be obtained from some quarter. Madison wanted to increase defense spending while escalating the economic warfare, virtually cutting off all trade with Great Britain and France. At first Congress seemed cooperative, passing new legislation to enforce the embargo; extending non-importation to France; barring armed French ships from American ports; and, in the Senate, defeating a Federalist effort to repeal the Embargo Act. It may have been too much success; the flurry of activity energized administration critics in New England, creating political difficulties for New England Republicans. As Orchard Cook, a Republican representative from the region, put it, "The genius and duty of Republican Government is to make laws to suit the people, and not attempt to make people suit the laws." John Quincy Adams and Joseph Story warned of civil unrest if the embargo remained in place. With Jefferson inactive, the president-elect hesitated. Madison did not believe New England would push its opposition to the point of secession, and he continued to favor some form of economic coercion, but Madison did not assert himself. On 20 January 1809, Wilson Cary Nicholas introduced a motion to repeal the embargo by 1 June 1809, and to issue letters of marque and reprisal against the European belligerents, a final step, unless they altered their policies, toward a formal declaration of war.[93]

The motion opened the door to a direct attack on the embargo. On 2 February, New England Republicans, Clintonites from New York, antiadministration Republicans in Pennsylvania, Randolph's faction, and the Federalist minority joined forces in the House to make repeal of the embargo effective in March. Madison attributed the decision to an odd coalition of disgruntled New Englanders and War Hawks "hoping to provoke [a] backlash against new British spoliations." The House then adopted a bill banning trade with Britain and France. The Senate added an amendment allowing the president to lift restrictions on either belligerent that might repeal its restrictions on American trade. The Non-Intercourse Act of 1809 represented, not a coherent policy, but a nervous improvisation by a factious Congress and a weak executive in transition between administrations. "Certain it is," Madison wrote William Pinkney, "that no measure was ever adopted by so great a proportion of any public body which had the hearty concurrence of so small a one." The new president would have to make the best of it.[94]

Jefferson and Madison have to share the blame for the nation's diplomatic drift. An earlier and more systematic boycott of British goods might have been more effective than the embargo. Great Britain needed American markets more than it needed American raw materials. Republican fiscal policies, however, left the federal government dependent on import duties. Republicans abhorred debt and internal taxes, which helps explain why Congress and the administration could rattle sabers without ever actually preparing the country for war. They left themselves few options.[95]

Nevertheless, Jefferson and Madison had an exaggerated sense of American might, and they defended American interests aggressively. They fixated on the American carrying trade between the French West Indies and Europe, which was a wartime phenomenon of less permanent value to the United States than its direct trade with Great Britain. The administration effectively collaborated with France to undermine the British blockade of the continent, without much regard for Britain's legal claims or for the utility of maintaining a balance of power between the European superpowers. As offensive as impressment was, it too was a transitory issue, and one aggravated by the American willingness to recruit British deserters.[96]

The historian Gordon Wood has rightly described as "bizarre" the juxtaposition of a feisty commitment by southern and western Republicans to maritime rights with the more conciliatory attitudes of New Englanders directly engaged in foreign commerce. The Republicans' relative detachment from trade allowed Jefferson and Madison to stand on principle. They knew Europeans did not share their high opinion of America's place in the world; European visitors routinely castigated Americans for their obsession with making money. Asserting the young republic's maritime rights enabled Jefferson and Madison to reaffirm the independence of the United States from Great Britain. Self-imposed restrictions on American trade provided a rejoinder to allegations of American materialism. Tied to Great Britain in a generally profitable trading relationship, New England Federalists felt less resentment; they also understood that pressing the British on the West Indian trade jeopardized commerce elsewhere. For Republicans, the political potential of trade outweighed its economic benefits. Republicans hoped free trade would bind nations together economically and end war, which spawned taxes, debts, and standing armies, which in turn jeopardized republican governments. When that vision failed, economic coercion became the republican alternative to war.[97]

A Founder as Commander in Chief

Thomas Jefferson worried about James Madison as the new president took office. "If peace can be preserved, I hope and trust you will have a smooth administration," Jefferson told his old friend. But he warned him, "I know no government which would be so embarrassing in war as ours." Jefferson blamed "the lying and licentious character" of American newspapers and "the wonderful credulity" of Congress for the nation's military incompetence. Unfortunately for Madison, a war with Great Britain would dominate his presidency, and he would struggle in the White House with a host of problems. Some were of his own making; many were not. While Madison is considered one of the most creative and productive of the founders, he has not been ranked, in recent times, among the greatest of American presidents.[1]

Madison articulated an orthodox republican agenda in his inaugural address. He pledged to keep the peace, to maintain the Union, to support the Constitution, and to respect the people's liberties. He promised specifically "to avoid the slightest interference with the rights of conscience or the functions of religion." He endorsed frugality in government. He made a commitment "to keep within the requisite limits a standing military force, always remembering that an armed and trained militia is the firmest bulwark of republics—that without standing armies their liberty can never be in danger, nor with large ones safe."[2] The speech contained nothing new, but Madison took republican principles seriously, and they compromised his ability to function as a dynamic commander in chief. Although he could act decisively, he did not believe he should dominate Congress or even his Cabinet. Although he could take risks, he believed war corrupted republican states. As a result, he pursued diplomatic solutions and experimented with economic sanctions until, in the face of repeated failures and provocations, he acquired a reputation for weakness and vacillation. Once the War of 1812 began, the nation's heavy reliance on the state militia proved ill considered at best. Yet Madison's contemporaries did not consider his presidency a failure. Sharing his values, they showed him more sympathy than have historians.[3]

Madison was not wholly unsuited to the presidency. Facing threats to the nation's territorial integrity during the War of 1812 that were comparable to those faced by Abraham Lincoln during the Civil War, Madison remained composed and confident.[4] Confronting an intractable Federalist opposition, he avoided personal vendettas.[5] A conscientious administrator, he nevertheless saw the need to delegate authority, and he allowed himself some understandable diversions. Madison rarely left the White House grounds while he was in Washington, but he tried to visit Montpelier in the spring and late summer, although the war occasionally disrupted his travel plans. He found time to exchange letters with Jefferson about the optimum plow design; Jefferson had won a gold medal from the Agricultural Society of the Seine for his improved mould board. They also spent time on a plan to improve the quality of sheep in Virginia by importing Merino and other breeds from Iberia and North Africa.[6] Reserved, if not dour, in public settings, however, Madison lacked the personal traits to either inspire or intimidate, and he managed subordinates and members of Congress less adroitly than Jefferson had. He and Dolley Madison hosted the first inaugural ball, but when invited to a late supper afterward, Madison confided to Margaret Bayard Smith that he "would much rather be in bed."[7]

In fairness to Madison, the political factionalism of his day would have tested the skills of the most accomplished politician. Divisions among Republicans may have done more damage to Madison's presidency than did his Federalist opponents. After the Senate, with a Republican majority, defeated an administration bill to impose another embargo in July 1813, Senator Jesse Bledsoe of Kentucky complained, "The friends of this administration will put it down faster than its enemies." Most regular Republicans supported Madison, but three troublesome factions did not. A New York clique associated with Vice President George Clinton and his nephew, DeWitt Clinton, the mayor of New York City, wanted more patronage and resented Virginia's dominance of the party. The "Old Republicans," or "Quids," from the Latin *tertium quid* for "odd third," believed Jefferson and Madison had abandoned the cause of states' rights and limited government. John Randolph of Roanoke, who had initially cooperated with the administration, became their most prominent, and shrillest, voice. Michael Leib of Pennsylvania, newly elevated from the House to the Senate, and editor William Duane of the *Philadelphia Aurora* represented another dissident faction known as "the Invisibles," or sometimes simply "the malcontents." Their ranks also included Senator Samuel Smith of Maryland and, ironically, two key supporters from Madison's 1808 campaign, Senator William Branch Giles and Representative Wilson Cary Nicholas, both from Virginia. Among other grievances, they had lost faith in Madison's effort to use economic coercion to stop British harassment of American trade. For his part, Madison blamed the internal bickering for the ineffectiveness of American foreign policy since the outbreak of the Napoleonic wars.[8]

Madison's tendency to try to work around his opponents, rather than confronting them directly, helps explain his lackluster Cabinet, which contributed to his difficulties. Madison wanted to nominate Albert Gallatin, who had been Jefferson's secretary of the treasury, to be secretary of state, but Samuel Smith and others objected, so Madison, warned that the Senate might not confirm Gallatin, left him at the Treasury Department. Madison then made a politically expedient and disastrous appointment, nominating Senator Smith's brother Robert to be secretary of state. Despite having served as secretary of the navy under Jefferson, Robert Smith turned out to be wholly incompetent at the State Department. Madison had to write his diplomatic dispatches for him, while Smith undermined administration policy by contradicting the written record in his private conversations.[9]

The secretary of war, William Eustis, was a former Massachusetts congressman and Revolutionary War surgeon with no significant administrative experience. Paul Hamilton, the secretary of the navy, had been governor of South Carolina and was now an alcoholic. Eustis and Hamilton provided sectional balance in the Cabinet and not much else. Vice President Clinton was obviously unreliable. The attorney general, Caesar Rodney, another holdover from the Jefferson administration, was competent enough, but he was distracted by a private law practice.[10] Postmaster General Gideon Granger, yet another holdover, created almost as much trouble as Robert Smith. The administration did not use patronage effectively, and Granger, who favored the Invisibles in filling post office jobs, deserves some of the blame. Madison finally fired him when Granger made Michael Leib postmaster in Philadelphia after Leib had lost a bid for reelection.[11]

Meanwhile, one more incumbent, the quarrelsome John Armstrong, continued to represent the United States in Paris; Jefferson called him "cynical and irritable, and implacable." Closer to home, Madison's secretary, cousin Isaac Coles, stirred up a minor scandal in November 1809 when he slapped Maryland representative Roger Nelson while carrying Madison's annual message to Congress. Isaac's brother Edward quickly replaced him.[12]

The army presented another set of personnel problems. Military commissions were highly political, and the partisanship produced hard feelings and questionable appointments. As the army added new officers on the eve of the War of 1812, one disgruntled New Yorker complained to Madison that "the minions and sycophants of DeWitt Clinton have been taken up to the total exclusion of men capable of rendering service to their country. . . . Imbecility, Ignorance, and Vanity, are their chief characteristics." James Wilkinson, once a partner in Aaron Burr's conspiracy to establish a private fiefdom in the Southwest, stands out as the worst of the American generals. Wilkinson, who secretly took payments from Spain, was commanding American troops in Louisiana when Madison became president. Disobeying an order to move his camp from Terre aux Boeufs, an unhealthy swamp south of New Orleans, Wilkinson lost over half the men under his command to disease. Throughout his career, Wilkinson demonstrated a remarkable capacity to escape scandal. After an inconclusive court-martial, Madison decided not to punish him. A Maryland native, the general enjoyed the support of Republicans in his home state, despite his ill repute elsewhere. James Monroe once said "he would sooner be shot than take a command under Wilkinson." General Winfield Scott, a true professional, called him an "unprincipled imbecile."[13]

After Associate Justice William Cushing died in September 1810, Thomas Jefferson, sensing an opportunity to move the Supreme Court in a more Republican direction, sent Madison his "congratulations." In reality, vacancies on the court created more embarrassments for the president. Madison felt obligated to replace Cushing, who was from Massachusetts, with another New Englander. His options were limited since Federalists dominated the New England bar. He chose Levi Lincoln, a Massachusetts lawyer who had served as attorney general under Jefferson, and the Senate confirmed Lincoln, only to have him decline the appointment because of his failing eyesight. Some New England Republicans preferred Gideon Granger for the court, but Madison appointed Alexander Wolcott, an unpopular and highly partisan Connecticut Republican. The Senate rejected the nomination by a better than two-to-one margin. Madison eventually made a much better choice: the Federalist-turned-Republican John Quincy Adams, who was then the American minister to Russia. Adams won immediate confirmation, but he refused to leave St. Petersburg. Adams did not want to risk a transatlantic crossing with his pregnant wife, Louisa.[14]

Finally, a desperate Madison turned to Joseph Story, a Massachusetts state legislator and a former member of Congress. Jefferson doubted Story's commitment to the Republican Party and warned Madison against putting Story on the court. Madison disregarded the advice, and Story went on to an impressive career as an ally of the Federalist Chief Justice John Marshall. As Madison suffered through the ordeal of replacing Cushing, another vacancy occurred with the death of Samuel Chase. On the same day in November 1811 that he nominated Story to replace Cushing, he nominated Gabriel Duvall of Maryland, who was comptroller of the treasury, to replace Chase. The Senate quickly approved both nominations. Nothing, however, came easily for Madison. The appointment of Duvall, a party regular of no particular distinction, so offended Caesar Rodney that he resigned as attorney general.[15]

A few loyal and able subordinates brightened an otherwise dreary landscape. Madison deeply respected Albert Gallatin, and he could not have managed the government's finances without the treasury secretary's fiscal acumen. Gallatin's support, however, came at a cost. His commitment to austerity in government complicated efforts to prepare for war, and he became a magnet for controversy. He carried with him political baggage from his earlier days in Pennsylvania's party battles, and as a native of Geneva, Switzerland, he was mistrusted by more provincial politicians. Gallatin's presence in the administration helps explain why some of Madison's early supporters quickly turned against him.[16] As soon as he returned to Monticello, Jefferson began attempting to effect a rapprochement between Madison and James Monroe, the erstwhile friend who had opposed Madison in 1808. Monroe bore Madison no animosity, and he saw political advantages to cooperating with the administration. In March 1811, Robert Smith's malfeasance as secretary of state provoked Gallatin into threatening to resign. Madison, in response, forced Smith out of office and replaced him with Monroe, who served dutifully in multiple roles until the end of Madison's presidency.[17]

As we shall see, other personnel changes eased Madison's burden slightly near the end of his first term. One of the most impressive appointees was William Pinkney, the American minister to Great Britain. Honest, sensible, and unusually perceptive, Pinkney worked effectively with opposition leaders to mobilize British opinion against the orders in council. When Rodney resigned as attorney general, Madison named Pinkney to replace him; the president might well have given Pinkney even more responsibility. Madison might likewise have used John Quincy Adams closer to home, but Adams did valuable work as a member of the American delegation that negotiated the Treaty of Ghent ending the War of 1812.[18]

The brightest spot in the Madison administration was, undoubtedly, the First Lady. With only two predecessors in the history of the young republic, Dolley Madison inherited a role that was largely undefined. Even her title remained unsettled; she was sometimes called "Lady Presidentess." As First Lady she strove for greater dignity than she had demonstrated as a Cabinet wife, so she played cards less, and she did not dance at the inaugural ball. One petty vice she retained; she could still be seen sharing a snuffbox at social functions with South Carolina's John C. Calhoun and Kentucky's Henry Clay, two rising stars in Congress. She wanted to make events at the White House more elegant without appearing aristocratic. Egalitarianism, at least in theory, prevailed in the new nation, and Americans chafed at any trace of snobbery or elitism. William Pinkney's wife, for example, drew criticism from the press for allegedly appearing at the British court dressed in diamonds. A few curmudgeons complained about Dolley's extravagance, but Louisa Catherine Adams expressed the prevailing view: "There was a frankness and ease in her deportment that won golden opinions from all."[19]

The Madisons hosted a state dinner about once a week. The president planned the events, and the First Lady managed them. They put her at the head of the table and Madison's secretary, Edward Coles, at the foot, with Madison at the side. The odd arrangement relieved Madison of the social responsibilities he disliked and worked well enough, even if it reinforced his unprepossessing image. Dolley did have "Hail to the Chief" played when Madison entered the room at formal receptions because, she feared, he did not otherwise command sufficient respect. Dolley typically served southern food in the old English style—simple meats with separate vegetables—but she experimented with French cuisine, and the Madisons hired a French doorman and chef, Jean Pierre Siousatt. They called him "French John." Nevertheless, "the style of Dolley's socializing," Catherine Allgor has written, "was southern, specifically Virginian." Dolley exchanged recipes with prominent women across the country, although she did not, contrary to myth, invent ice cream or serve it in the White House for the first time. She did win praise for ice cream served in a warm pastry, a dish similar to baked Alaska.[20]

More important politically than the White House dinners were Dolley's Wednesday evening receptions, also known as "the crush" or "the squeeze" for the large crowds they attracted. Dolley Madison's squeezes brought together men and women; Federalists and Republicans; and national politicians, local elites, and foreign dignitaries. Less formal than the levees hosted by Martha Washington and Abigail Adams, Dolley's receptions resembled a modern cocktail party. Access required only a perfunctory introduction to the First Lady. Wednesday nights offered Madison a rare opportunity to meet with members of the public, and they allowed the administration to project a clearly exaggerated image of competence, civility, and bipartisanship. Federalists attempted to boycott "Mrs. Madison's drawing room" during the campaign of 1812, but they soon returned to the festivities.[21]

Dolley's duties as First Lady went beyond her role as a hostess. She worked with architect Benjamin Latrobe to redecorate the White House after years of neglect under Thomas Jefferson. She favored American-made furniture where it was available and art depicting American scenes and heroes, and she installed the first bathtub in the White House.[22] People wrote her for presidential pardons and for federal jobs, and she functioned as a power broker in her own right. Both Madison and the First Lady came from large families, and they were surrounded by nieces, nephews, and cousins in the White House, some of whom were on the federal payroll. After Richard Cutts, the husband of Dolley's sister Anna, lost his congressional seat in Massachusetts, Madison made him superintendent of military supplies.[23] Despite the apparent gaiety, Dolley felt the strains of office as much as did James Madison. "I never felt the entertainment of company oppressive until now," she wrote one confidant in November 1811. She fumed privately when administration measures met defeat in Congress. Her spendthrift son John remained an emotional and financial burden; she had to borrow money to pay his debts, presumably from gambling.[24]

If not for the outbreak of hostilities in 1812, Madison almost certainly would have been content to continue the low-tax, balanced-budget policies of the Jefferson years. His domestic agenda was modest, with a few exceptions. In December 1810, his second annual message to Congress called for the creation of a national university in Washington. In an age when Americans argued passionately about constitutional limits on federal authority—some critics attacked Madison for holding Cabinet meetings since the Constitution did not authorize them—he justified the proposed institution as an exercise of the congressional power to administer the District of Columbia. A somewhat uncharacteristically expansive reading of the Constitution, the proposal reflected his commitment to higher education, a commitment Congress did not share.[25]

Far more significant, and only grudgingly acknowledged by the president, was his acceptance of a federally chartered central bank. As the expiration of the original charter of the Bank of the United States neared in

1811, Albert Gallatin recommended its renewal. The treasury secretary had come to see the BUS as a safe place for government deposits, a convenient receptacle for customs revenue, and a reliable source of loans to the federal government. Madison allowed Gallatin to proceed with a recharter bill, but the president stayed out of the fight in Congress. He rarely lobbied lawmakers, and he never liked to appear inconsistent. Hostility to the BUS had been a founding principle of the Republican Party, and the recharter bill drew opposition from Samuel Smith, William Duane of the *Philadelphia Aurora*, Thomas Ritchie of the *Richmond Enquirer*, and others. The House of Representatives postponed action on the bill by one vote, but with Madison remaining aloof, the recharter initiative died in the Senate when Vice President Clinton broke a tie by voting against it.[26] When the bank issue next appeared, Madison would deal with it more forthrightly. In the meantime, a worsening international crisis overshadowed domestic politics.

The United States initially profited from the Napoleonic wars. American neutrality allowed American ships to transport goods that would have been subject to seizure onboard a vessel sailing under a belligerent's flag. After the Peace of Amiens brought a temporary end to hostilities in late 1801, the value of American exports fell from $94 million in that year to $54 million in 1803. Fortunately for American farmers and merchants, the fighting in Europe quickly resumed. By 1807, the value of American exports reached $108 million.[27]

Both sides tried to interdict the flow of goods to the other. In May 1806, Charles James Fox, then the British foreign minister, announced a naval blockade of northern Europe from Brest to the Elbe River. The Fox Blockade also effectively overturned the 1805 *Essex* decision, in which a British court outlawed the American practice of shipping exports from the French West Indies through ports in the United States before sending them on to France. Americans nevertheless complained that Fox was attempting to maintain an illegal paper blockade. British restrictions were enforced consistently only between the Seine and Ostend. British and American officials further disagreed over the definition of contraband. The status of French-owned cargo on American ships produced less controversy than historians, recalling the slogan "Free ships make free goods," once thought. By the early 1800s, American merchants took title to most of the goods they shipped.[28]

Napoleon responded to the Fox Blockade with what came to be known as the Continental System. Beginning with the Berlin Decree of November

1806, Napoleon proclaimed a blockade of the British Isles and threatened to seize any ship sailing to or from a British port. The French navy lacked the resources to enforce the Continental System on the high seas, but Napoleon could confiscate ships visiting French-controlled ports. Great Britain retaliated against the Berlin Decree on 7 January 1807 with an order in council banning neutral ships from trading between ports within Napoleon's European empire. After Napoleon attempted to apply trade restrictions to Russia, an order in council of 11 November 1807 extended the British blockade to all countries in the Napoleonic system. Napoleon, in turn, escalated the commercial war on 17 December with the Milan Decree. It threatened to seize any ship that cooperated with the orders in council or that submitted to a search by the Royal Navy.[29]

The dueling blockades left little room for legal and wholly unfettered American trade, and when James Madison became president in March 1809, efforts to wring concessions from either belligerent had been largely futile. Great Britain had virtually ignored the Non-Importation Act of 1806, which banned a select list of British imports. Efforts at a negotiated settlement failed when Jefferson refused to submit the Monroe-Pinkney Treaty to the Senate for ratification. The Embargo Act of 1807 caused more hardship in the United States than it did in either Great Britain or France. In fact, it gave Napoleon an excuse to issue the Bayonne Decree of April 1808: He would help Jefferson enforce the embargo by seizing any American ships in European ports. They must, he presumed, be there illegally. Over the next two years, the French emperor's supposedly friendly seizures yielded him a windfall of $10 million. From 1807 to 1812, more than nine hundred American ships were captured by one belligerent or the other. Yet all the blockades contained legal loopholes, and even illegal trade could not be completely suppressed. American merchants calculated they could make money if only one ship in three reached its destination.[30]

Madison appeared to have broken the diplomatic deadlock early in his presidency. For all the shortcomings he would demonstrate — a preternatural patience with diplomacy; a legalistic, if not doctrinaire, approach to foreign policy; and an inability to mobilize the nation for a long-anticipated war — Madison never flinched in his commitment to seeing the orders in council repealed, and he had a strategy. Fearful of military conflict as a menace to republican government, he was nevertheless willing to use the threat of war as a bargaining chip, and he told William Pinkney that, unless the orders in council were repealed, "war is inevitable." Madison hoped, however, to extract some concessions from one belligerent and use them as leverage to win more concessions from the other.[31] Madison had begun talks with Britain's minister plenipotentiary, David Erskine, during his final months as secretary of state. Robert Smith continued the discussions after Madison entered the White House. Young, inexperienced, and married to an American, Erskine seemed conciliatory.

On 7 April 1809, a new British legation secretary arrived in Washington with instructions, Erskine said, that gave him authority to settle everything. Erskine promised reparations for the attack on the *Chesapeake* and the return of its impressed sailors.[32] Erskine also indicated that his government would withdraw its orders in council if the United States would resume normal commerce with Great Britain while maintaining non-intercourse with France; renounce wartime, direct trade between France and its colonies; and allow the British navy to seize American ships trading with Britain's enemies in violation of American law. When Smith suggested deferring the issue of the Franco-American colonial trade to a separate commercial treaty and objected to British enforcement of American law as an affront to national sovereignty, Erskine abandoned these proposals. With Madison deeply involved, Erskine and Smith quickly reached an agreement: the orders in council of January and November 1807, as they applied to the United States, would be repealed on 10 June, and the United States would lift its restrictions on trade with Britain. The Non-Intercourse Act of 1809, which had replaced the Embargo Act the day Madison became president, prohibited trade with Great Britain and France, but authorized Madison to lift the ban on either belligerent that withdrew its own restrictions on the United States. On 19 April, Madison issued a proclamation providing that "on the said 10th day of June next . . . the trade of the United States with Great Britain . . . may be renewed."[33]

In hindsight perhaps, Madison should have realized that the agreement with Erskine had come too easily. The British minister had, rather oddly, praised the Non-Intercourse Act for putting Great Britain on an equal footing with the other belligerents. In reality, non-intercourse affected Britain more that it did Napoleon because Anglo-American commerce dwarfed American trade with France and because the Royal Navy had almost swept the French merchant fleet from the seas. In a message to Congress, Madison suggested that the Non-Intercourse Act had brought the British to heel and expressed hopes the agreement would force concessions from France. Privately, Madison believed military reversals in Spain had put the British government in a mood to compromise, and with the orders in council out of the way, he thought the issue of impressment could be resolved quickly.[34]

Madison received his first hint of trouble on 10 June when the *Pacific* arrived with news of a new order in council. Dated 26 April, it presented, he wrote Jefferson, "a curious feature in the conduct" of the British cabinet, but Erskine assured Secretary Smith the new order "has no connection whatever with the overtures I have been authorized to make." Erskine promised Smith that his majesty's government would honor their agreements. Madison hypothesized that Britain wanted to conceal the Anglo-American rapprochement from France.[35]

Diplomatic—and, one would think for Madison, political—disaster struck on 21 July when word reached New York that the British government had rejected the Erskine agreement. Erskine had mangled and exceeded his instructions from George Canning, the British foreign secretary. Canning considered the conditions Erskine had blithely discarded as prerequisites for a settlement. On 9 August, an embarrassed president reinstated the economic boycott of Great Britain.[36]

Paradoxically, George Canning, a relative moderate by British standards, had hoped to improve relations with the United States. Reporting from London, William Pinkney believed that the 26 April order created an opportunity to make peace. It opened Russian and German ports to American ships, permitted neutrals to carry enemy products, and eliminated certain duties on American vessels. Of the commerce that remained closed to the United States, only trade with Holland and its colonies was not already banned by the Non-Intercourse Act. Pinkney, unaware of the ill-fated Erskine agreement, expected the British to make further concessions before the American law expired.[37]

The 26 April order, in other words, constituted a significant change in the British position, but disappointment over the rejection of the more generous agreement with Erskine prevented most Americans from appreciating it, and the affair brought the two nations closer to war. Madison concluded that Canning had deliberately sabotaged Erskine. The president did not believe that the British effort to exclude the United States from the Dutch trade, which now seemed to be the only commercial issue in dispute, could be justified by military necessity. Canning, he thought, only wanted to protect "London smugglers of sugar & coffee" from competition.[38]

Worse yet, Canning had recalled Erskine and replaced him with Francis James Jackson, also known as "Copenhagen" for his role in the bombardment in 1807 of the Danish capital. No one expected much from the haughty Jackson, who, it can fairly be said, hated Americans. Jackson did not disappoint. He began his mission by engaging Madison and Smith in a pointless debate over whether the Americans knew or should have known Erskine had violated his instructions. Madison broke off all talks with Jackson in November.[39] Madison had hoped the Erskine agreement would damage the Federalists; Jackson's implacable boorishness helped blunt the political impact of its failure, and something of a war fever swept the country in the fall of 1809. William Duane, for example, suggested that the United States take British subjects as hostages for impressed seamen and take British ships in retaliation for the seizure of American ships.[40] Adding insult to injury, a British cruiser seized a ship sailing from Bordeaux with a "pipe of Brandy" intended for the president. An English court condemned the ship, but the brandy was released.[41]

With the Non-Intercourse Act set to expire in 1810, Representative Nathanial Macon of North Carolina introduced a new bill on behalf of the administration. Macon's Bill No. 1 left American trade unrestricted but banned British and French ships from American ports. If Britain or France retaliated by excluding ships from the United States, belligerent goods would be barred from American ports unless they were carried on American ships. Debate over the bill left Congress confused and divided. Few members wanted war, Madison wrote William Pinkney, and few wanted to submit, but intermediate measures seemed inadequate. Macon's Bill No. 1 passed the House of Representatives, only to be defeated in the Senate. Madison apparently preferred, as an alternative, to renew the Non-Intercourse Act after a brief suspension. He continued to hope he could use the threat of sanctions for diplomatic leverage, but he did not pressure Congress.[42]

Republican leaders in the House seized the initiative and introduced Macon's Bill No. 2, attributed to John Taylor of South Carolina. Macon's Bill No. 2 reopened trade with Great Britain and France with the provision that if one belligerent would lift its restrictions on American trade, the United States would refuse to do business with its enemy. As the measure worked its way through Congress, Madison complained to Jefferson that its members "remain in the unhinged state which has latterly marked their proceedings." When Congress finally passed Macon's Bill No. 2, Madison resigned himself to using it against the belligerents as best he could. "However feeble it may appear," he wrote Pinkney, "it is possible that one or other of those powers may allow it more effect than was produced by the overtures heretofore tried."[43]

Madison's relative inaction owed more to his respect for the separation of powers than it did to an inherent passivity. He could act with a calculated aggressiveness. Madison had long coveted Spanish-held Florida, especially West Florida, which Republicans claimed had been part of the Louisiana Purchase. Most of the settlers there were Americans, and with Spain a battleground between British and French armies, Spanish officials in West Florida seemed unlikely to offer much resistance to annexation by the United States. Madison wanted to preempt a takeover by Great Britain or France, and he sent agents to both East Florida and West Florida to prepare the way for a future American occupation. In September 1810, settlers in West Florida revolted, seized the Spanish garrison at Baton Rouge, and declared their independence. Although American officials had encouraged anti-Spanish sentiment, Madison opposed the revolution. He did not want to provoke a war, and he wanted to ensure that title to unoccupied land in West Florida passed to the U.S. government, not to the rebels. His hand forced by events, on 27 October, Madison issued a proclamation announcing the occupation, pursuant to the Louisiana Purchase, of the territory between the Mississippi and Perdido Rivers. When he ordered American soldiers into the region, he instructed them not to attack the few positions still held by Spanish troops.[44]

In January 1811, Congress granted Madison's request for temporary authority to occupy thinly settled East Florida should occupation be necessary to prevent foreign intervention in the event Spanish rule collapsed. The Spanish proved more resilient than Madison had anticipated, and once again, the administration's agents overstepped their bounds, encouraging the handful of American settlers to rebel. Resistance from Spanish officials, Indians, and runaway slaves, abetted by British warships, led Congress to abandon efforts to annex the region the following year, much to Madison's dismay. Unauthorized military expeditions by American army and militia officers who saw East Florida as, in modern terminology, a failed state, continued to the end of Madison's presidency.[45] For his part, Madison had underestimated the Spanish and overestimated his ability to use distant American settlers to pressure the Spanish to make concessions to the United States. The Adams-Onis Treaty of 1819 would finally bring the area under American control.

Florida, in any event, was a sideshow compared to efforts to liberate the nation's wartime trade, and here Madison gambled for higher stakes. Napoleon's response to Macon's Bill No. 2 came in August 1810 when the French foreign minister, the Duke de Cadore, sent John Armstrong a note stating that the Berlin and Milan Decrees would be withdrawn effective 1 November if Great Britain repealed its orders in council or if the United States effectively asserted its rights against the British. Administration officials assumed they could satisfy Napoleon's second condition by breaking off trade with Great Britain, as authorized by the Macon bill. It was a debatable assumption, and even more ambiguous was the intent of the Cadore letter. Had the decrees actually been repealed, or had Napoleon only promised to repeal them, and if so, could he be trusted to keep his promise? In truth, Napoleon hoped to entangle the United States in a war with Britain without opening the continent to unrestricted American trade or allowing the Americans to market British colonial goods in Europe. He had decided to keep American ships seized while the Non-Intercourse Act had been in effect and to use a licensing system, justified as mere "municipal regulations," to control American trade.[46]

Eager to leave France with a success in hand, Armstrong did not probe French intentions too deeply; Napoleon once told Cadore to "write to America in such a way that the President may know what an imbecile he has sent here."[47] Albert Gallatin said later the United States never would have gone to war with Britain if it had understood Napoleon's strategy.[48] Yet Madison was not, as has often been said, duped by Napoleon. He knew that evidence of the repeal of the decrees was sketchy at best. He recognized that other issues remained between the United States and France, and he was certainly no more confused than others closer to the scene. The Marquis de Lafayette wrote him from Paris on 25 August to celebrate "the Happy Repeal of the two Milan and Berlin decrees."[49] Madison was, however, willing to act quickly, if not rashly, to exploit whatever opportunity the French emperor had given him to put pressure on the British. When they refused to blink, Madison, on 2 November 1810, issued a proclamation reimposing non-intercourse on Great Britain.[50]

"I know," Dolley Madison wrote, "by intense study of Mr. M and his constant devotion to the cabinet, that affairs, are troublesome and difficult."[51] For the next several months, the administration seemed simply to be waiting for British concessions to save it from war. Lord Wellesley, the current British foreign secretary, complained to Pinkney in December that he "had not been able to obtain any authentic intelligence of the actual repeal of the French decrees."[52] Robert Smith reported to the president that so many ships had been seized by the European powers that appropriations for the relief of stranded seamen had been exhausted; Congress allocated another $76,000. The new French minister to the United States, Louis-Charles-Barbé Sérurier, seemed honestly in the dark about his government's policies. By spring, Pinkney and Armstrong had left Europe, leaving the United

States without ministers in London or Paris, and Britain had no minister in Washington.[53] Madison, meanwhile, received conflicting advice from his Cabinet and from Americans abroad. He hoped the ascension of a new prime minister, Lord Holland, might lead to a change in British policy. In April 1811, as the crisis dragged on, Madison dismissed Secretary of State Robert Smith after a brutal interview involving allegations of disloyalty and incompetence.[54]

While the politicians waited, a Norfolk mob burned a French privateer. In May, the *President*, an American frigate, exchanged fire with a British sloop-of-war, the *Little Belt*, and killed nine British sailors. In July, a British ship attacked the American brig *Vixen* on a voyage to New Orleans, slightly injuring the son of Attorney General Caesar Rodney. For his part, Madison continued to talk of the repeal of the French decrees, but he admitted, "We remain without authentic information of a decisive character." To his mind, these "obscurities" did not justify British intransigence.[55]

The arrival of a new British representative, Augustus John Foster, in July 1811 only drove the two sides farther apart. Foster now demanded not only more convincing evidence of the repeal of the French decrees, but he also insisted that the Berlin and Milan Decrees be repealed as they applied to all neutrals, not just the United States, before Great Britain would revoke its orders in council. Foster quickly fell under the influence of Madison's Federalist critics. They flattered him and told him what he wanted to hear: the president was weak and indecisive and only threatened war to rally Republican voters for the 1812 elections. Foster passed the misinformation along to his superiors in London.[56] After James Monroe replaced Smith as secretary of state, his instructions to Joel Barlow, Armstrong's successor in Paris, revealed the depths of the American dilemma. Skeptical of the Cadore letter, Monroe complained that France still exposed American ships "to great and expensive delays, to tedious investigations in unusual forms, and to exorbitant duties." Madison tried to remain cautiously optimistic. Napoleon's behavior remained inconsistent at best. French naval vessels and privateers continued to attack American merchant ships on the high seas, but other American ships visited French ports without incident.[57]

Although Madison continued negotiating with Napoleon, by November he was ready to make his annual message to Congress a request for a virtual declaration of war against Great Britain. Fearful of the "uncertainty" war created as opposed to the known problems of economic coercion, Albert Gallatin urged Madison to soften his rhetoric. The treasury secretary warned, prophetically, that mobilizing "men and money" to fight would be harder than might be expected. An unpopular war and the associated debt could bring to power men subservient to Great Britain and lead to "substantial alterations in our institutions." The expense of a navy would drain the treasury. If war came, Gallatin preferred that it be fought by privateers, who would finance their own operations and reap most of the profits: "In a country where the resources and spirit of enterprise are great, and the command of Government over those resources extremely moderate, it is necessary as far as practicable to induce individuals to apply those resources of their own accord against the enemy."[58]

Gallatin's reservations had some effect. The message Madison sent to Congress on 5 November did not call for war. Madison ignored impressment and barely mentioned Canada, despite War Hawks and expansionists in Congress who blamed British agents there for inciting Indian resistance along the American frontier. Madison emphasized British violations of America's maritime rights. He called for the expansion of the regular army, the creation of a new fifty-thousand-member volunteer force, and the mobilization of units from the state militias. He also recommended appropriations for naval repairs, and he proposed arming merchant ships.[59]

With war seeming imminent—Madison told Anna Cutts in December that he saw no alternative—the public divided along predictable lines. Republicans pledged their support. As a petition from a Virginia militia regiment put it, "The crisis has come. . . . Our swords leap flaming from their scabbards and cannot be returned unappeased."[60] A Federalist minority, centered mainly in New England, dissented. From Chittenden, Vermont, Samuel Harrison, a veteran of the American Revolution, complained to Madison, "It will take twenty years of . . . unexampled prosperity . . . to remedy one single year of war."[61]

Madison made one clumsy effort to discredit his Federalist critics and solidify antipathy toward Britain. Working through Paul-Emile Soubiron, a French confidence man who used the alias Edward de Crillon, he and Monroe paid $50,000 for a series of letters from John Henry, a former British spy. The Henry letters were supposed to expose a scheme in which New England would secede from the Union. Instead, they revealed what was already public knowledge: New England Federalists disliked Madison and his policies. The ensuing flap over Madison's gullibility and his waste of federal dollars hampered efforts to prepare for war, as did a continuing stream of mixed messages from France, which created, Madison said, as much "irritation and disgust as possible."[62]

The controversy and confusion hampered the drive to war, but they did not stop it. On 1 April, Madison proposed a sixty-day embargo on American shipping in an effort to confine ships to the safety of their home ports before the fighting began. Congress extended it, and on 5 April, Madison signed a ninety-day embargo law. Both Madison and Monroe assured Augustus John Foster that the embargo was not a step toward war, misinformation which suggests they were now more interested in concealing military plans than in negotiating. Foster concluded the embargo was another in the Americans' interminable experiments with economic sanctions, and getting similar messages for once from the administration and its critics, he assumed Britain had nothing to fear.[63] Madison, Monroe, and Madison's secretary Edward Coles all said later that Foster's arrival in July 1811 with new demands, in particular the insistence that all neutrals be allowed to market British goods in Europe, made war unavoidable. Also in early April, General Henry Dearborn sent Madison a plan for the invasion of Canada. Later in the month Madison wrote Jefferson that the only issues that remained, and they were considerable, were the timing of a declaration of war and deciding if the fighting could be limited to the high seas. Republican leaders agreed to wait for the return of the *Hornet*, an American warship, with the latest news from Europe, but to consider a formal declaration before Congress adjourned for the summer. Monroe may have preferred a naval war, but Madison, believing the British to be more vulnerable in Canada, assumed the decisive fighting would take place on land.[64]

After the *Hornet* arrived in New York on 19 May with no significant news from Europe, Madison's message to Congress on 1 June was in a sense anticlimactic. He began by deploring impressment, and he blamed the British for the renewal of hostilities "by savages on one of our extensive frontiers," although he showed no interest in the annexation of Canada. As he had done for most of his presidency, he stressed commercial issues and seemed most bitter that Great Britain "carries on a war against the lawful commerce of a friend that she may better carry on a commerce with an enemy." In deference to Congress's constitutional prerogative to declare war, Madison made no specific recommendations, but his intent was clear.[65]

Splitting along partisan lines, the House passed a declaration of war on 4 June by a vote of 79 to 49. The Senate passed it on 13 June by a vote of 19 to 13. Opposition came from Federalists; Clinton Republicans from New York and New Jersey; and a few scattered Republicans, including John Randolph, elsewhere. Some of the Invisibles voted for war.[66]

President Madison signed the declaration of war on 18 June. Unknown to anyone in the United States, the British government, responding to domestic pressure, had decided on 16 June to rescind the orders in council. Suffering through a severe recession, British manufacturers hoped the restoration of normal trade with the United States would contribute to an economic recovery. Madison said later he would not have gone to war if he had known the orders had been withdrawn. He always believed the issue of impressment could be resolved through negotiations. Often criticized for vacillation, the president could have avoided an unnecessary war if only he had dithered a little longer.[67]

How had the war happened? Early in his presidency, Madison rejected the option of leaving "commerce to shift for itself." A laissez-faire approach would have favored Great Britain, because of the superiority of the Royal Navy, and penalized France. Madison acknowledged the expediency of remaining above the fray, but he dismissed that course as dishonorable. Although Madison dreaded hostilities because he feared they could corrupt the republic's political system, he did not dwell on the horrors of war. Indeed, the potential human carnage did not seem to weigh heavily on his mind. Given the nation's lack of preparedness, he approached the possibility of war with a strange confidence in an ultimate American victory.[68]

With France rivaling Great Britain in its assaults on American trade, why not, considering the other extreme, fight them both? The idea of a triangular war enjoyed considerable support; in June 1809 John Armstrong recommended to Madison "a war with both the great belligerents." The idea encountered even more considerable opposition. A triangular war, Jefferson warned, would make privateering impossible—American ships would be denied safe havens in Europe and the West Indies—and it would kill the American export trade. Madison suspected it would fail to appease Federalists, who would oppose war with Great Britain in any case, and if he had an exaggerated sense of the nation's military potential, he had not totally lost touch with reality.[69]

Yet if Madison could fight only one war, did it have to be against Great Britain? By 1812, Napoleon arguably presented a greater threat to American trade than did the British, and he certainly exceeded them in duplicity.[70] In reality, Madison never seriously considered sparing Britain and going to war with France. Madison and the vast majority of Republicans managed to convince themselves that Britain's constitutional monarchy posed a graver threat to republican institutions than did Napoleon's dictatorship. Madison's distrust of the British went back to the American Revolution.

He believed "the original sin" against neutrals lay with Britain, but he was motivated by more than a lingering bias, real as his prejudices might have been.[71]

The practice of impressment helped tip the scales against the British and probably offended ordinary voters more than did the orders in council or the Continental System. "Free trade and sailors' rights," as the slogan of the day went, became a bedrock principle of Republican foreign policy. On the eve of war, friendly Republican groups routinely complained to Madison about the French, but they were ready to fight the British.[72] The proximity of Canada played a part, not because Madison was interested in conquest, but because he saw it as a valuable hostage in peace talks with the British. In contrast, the United States, as William Pinkney noted, had no effective way to make war against France.[73]

The quality of leadership made a difference, and luck played its part. If David Erskine had not violated his instructions, the subsequent liberalization of the orders in council might have led to fruitful negotiations. As it was, mediocrity and constant turnover in key positions plagued the British government. Blinded by confidence in their own good intentions, British officials routinely misjudged the impression they made on Americans. The thoroughly cynical Napoleon, with no illusions about his own good faith, manipulated events more effectively, making just enough concessions to keep Madison at bay.[74]

Finally, Madison believed that Great Britain threatened American independence in a way that France could not. Many of his Federalist opponents identified with Great Britain, and some of them subjected Madison and his supporters to hysterical criticism; Republicans did not have to be too paranoid to imagine a Federalist cabal returning the republic to a virtual colonial status. Because American trade with Britain dwarfed the Franco-American trade, market forces always threatened to keep the United States within the British orbit. The nation could not trade freely with Britain and do business elsewhere on British terms, Madison concluded, because the result would be an unfavorable balance of trade that would drain specie from the United States and retard economic development. To Madison, economic, and possibly political, independence required an assertive commercial diplomacy and, eventually, war.[75]

When news of the declaration of war reached Providence, Rhode Island, church bells rang in protest, shops closed, and flags flew at half-mast. After fighting erupted, New England farmers continued to send beef and flour to British armies in Canada. The war's opponents in New England became known as "Blue-Light Federalists" for the signals they sent to British warships waiting offshore. The governor of Massachusetts refused Madison's request to mobilize the militia; seventy thousand state troops never saw combat. Connecticut rebuffed a call to provide militia for coastal defense. Madison complained to Congress that if the states could ignore an order of the commander in chief in wartime the United States was hardly one nation, but he did not force the issue, and he probably avoided a civil war.[76]

The long-standing debate between Federalists and Republicans over foreign policy ensured opposition to the war, and the repeal of the orders in council raises the question of why peace was not quickly restored. Madison indicated a willingness to suspend hostilities if the British would agree to serious negotiations on the issue of impressment, and he proposed legislation to ban American ships from hiring foreign seamen. Diplomacy, however, went nowhere. Lord Castlereigh, the British foreign secretary, would not compromise on impressment, and Madison had his own reasons for opposing a speedy settlement. He mistrusted the British. His military plans called for American forces to move quickly against Canada; he feared a cease-fire followed by fruitless negotiations would rob his armies of the initiative. Madison also believed peace with Britain would only trade one war for another. If the United States reached a settlement with the British, the public would demand war with France. After disappointing campaigns in the first months of the war, Madison accepted an offer from Czar Alexander I of Russia to mediate the conflict, but the British said no.[77]

Madison can be fairly criticized for leading the nation into war unprepared, although Congress was at least equally negligent. The president and his fellow Republicans, the historian Bradford Perkins wrote, "often spoke loudly and carried no stick at all." In June 1812, the seven-hundred-vessel Royal Navy had three warships for every gun in the seventeen-ship American navy.[78] Republican theory condemned large navies and professional armies, and Albert Gallatin had argued against more defense spending, which would have meant more debt and higher taxes. In November 1810, William Eustis, moreover, had warned Madison that Congress's ostensible authority over the state militia "has hitherto failed to provide the desired effect of rendering them an efficient force on which to rely in cases of emergency."[79]

Before the war, Congress had ignored Madison's pleas to reorganize the militias in order to readily identify men who could most easily be mobilized for extended periods. Congress also rebuffed his efforts to establish a volunteer ready reserve force. In November 1811, with war imminent, Madison proposed comprehensive preparedness legislation that included expanding the regular army by ten thousand men and building twenty-two new warships. Congress defeated the naval bill but voted to add twenty-five thousand soldiers to the army, a force larger than the administration could recruit or equip.[80]

Madison complained to Jefferson that Congress, "with a view to enable the Executive to step at once into Canada[, has] . . . provided after two months delay, for a regular force requiring 12 to raise it, and after 3 months for a volunteer force, on terms not likely to raise it at all for that object." Jefferson tried to console him: "That a body containing 100 lawyers in it, should direct the measures of a war is, I fear, impossible." Nathaniel Macon of North Carolina and several other Republican representatives ultimately voted for the war after voting against every effort to prepare for it. Congress did approve new taxes to take effect on the outbreak of hostilities. It was a modest step. With much of the nation's capital sequestered in hostile New England banks, Gallatin and his successors struggled constantly to borrow enough money to finance the war.[81]

Madison later explained privately that Congress would not seriously consider the nation's defense needs until after a war had begun. Republicans vastly overrated the republic's military capacity. Jefferson said famously that the conquest of Canada would be "a mere matter of marching." Poorly trained and recalcitrant state militia forced the administration to rely at the start of the war on a regular army that numbered fewer than seven thousand men. The exact number is uncertain; slipshod recordkeeping prevented Madison from knowing how many troops were at his command. Aging veterans who had not seen action since the Revolution dominated the army's senior leadership. Most younger officers had no experience in conventional warfare. The army had no intelligence service and only a rudimentary supply system. Without a general staff, the military lacked the capacity for long-range planning, and it had no ability to coordinate multiple offensives.[82] Judging from letters from Cabinet officers urging the president to return to Washington, Madison's summer vacation in 1812 probably did not help matters.[83]

Military operations in 1812 met predictable results and only encouraged Madison's critics. War plans called for a three-pronged attack on Canada: toward Montreal along Lake Champlain and the Richelieu River; across the Niagara peninsula; and at the western tip of Lake Erie. William Hull commanded the western offensive and in July crossed the Detroit River into Canada. As his army neared the British garrison at Fort Malden, Hull, unnerved by Indian attacks on his supply lines, retreated across the border to Detroit. Surrounded by a smaller British force led by Isaac Brock, Hull suffered a mental breakdown and surrendered his army. The American capitulation came so unexpectedly that Brock, in the words of Irving Brant, "sent an officer to inquire what the white flag meant."[84]

Another decrepit general, Henry Dearborn, produced similar results in the Northeast. With vague orders from Washington, Dearborn hesitated to take command of a front stretching from Niagara to New England. Dearborn deferred to Stephen Van Rennselaer, a major general in the New York militia, who approved an attack on Queenston Heights, between Niagara Falls and Lake Ontario, in October. Regular army units under then lieutenant colonel Winfield Scott gained a foothold across the Niagara River after bloody fighting, but when New York militia units refused to cross into Canada, Rennselaer had to abandon the operation. The Queenston Heights debacle led to Van Rennselaer's replacement by Alexander Smyth of the regular army; Smyth spent the rest of the year preparing to launch an invasion that never came. Closer to Montreal, Dearborn marched an army a few miles north of Plattsburgh, New York, and then turned around after the militia decided they had gone far enough. Only a series of spectacular and unexpected victories by American frigates over British warships saved the nation from total humiliation.[85]

Madison realized that isolated triumphs at sea could not undo the damage inflicted by defeats and squandered opportunities on land. If Hull's offensive in the Northwest had succeeded, Madison believed, it would have given the United States control of Lake Erie, neutralized Britain's Indian allies, promoted enlistments, and marginalized opposition to the war. Defeat put the nation on the defensive and left it as divided as ever.[86]

Meeting in May, the Republican congressional caucus had nominated Madison for a second term by a vote of 82 to 0. Despite the apparent unanimity, the president faced several political problems even before disappointing news from the front lines became a regular occurrence. A third of the Republican members of Congress had boycotted the caucus. Vice President George Clinton had died in April; Elbridge Gerry of Massachusetts was picked to replace him in an effort to boost the Republican ticket in New England. Benjamin Stoddert, who had been secretary of war under John Adams, helped lead a movement to draft Chief Justice John Marshall as the Federalist nominee for president. To defeat Madison, however, a challenger would need to carry New York, which made Dewitt Clinton, a Republican native son and nephew of the late vice president, a viable candidate.[87]

Federalists reluctantly supported Clinton as their best bet to end the war while Clinton Republicans argued he would be a more effective commander in chief than Madison. The president's own postmaster general, Gideon Granger, reportedly supported Clinton. Madison did not actively campaign, but Dolley Madison worked harder than ever, and attendance at her Wednesday night "squeezes" swelled from two or three hundred to five hundred people. As election returns trickled in during the fall, Clinton carried New York and all of New England except Vermont. Pennsylvania proved decisive. Madison won the state and defeated Clinton 128 to 89 in the Electoral College, and Republicans retained substantial, if unmanageable, majorities in Congress. The returns reflected voters' respect for Madison; their loyalty to the Republican Party; and, in the first months of the war, a certain patience with military reversals.[88]

Personnel changes beginning late in 1812 marginally improved Madison's prospects for success in his second term. In December, he forced Paul Hamilton out as secretary of the navy and replaced him with William Jones, a level-headed Philadelphia merchant, and William Eustis resigned as secretary of war.[89]

Replacing Eustis proved difficult. William Crawford of Georgia declined the post, as did Monroe. The War Department's imposing responsibilities severely taxed its limited resources. The department appeared to be a political liability. Monroe, with his eye on the presidency in 1816, had dreamed of winning glory with a military commission, and in the fall of 1812, Madison had seriously considered putting him in command of American forces in the West. Monroe's ardor seemed to cool after the governor of Kentucky made William Henry Harrison a major general in the state militia. Monroe may not have wanted to share the stage with the popular hero of the Battle of Tippecanoe. Henry Dearborn was an uninspiring possibility for the War Department post, but he was not interested. Madison's options came down to Governor Daniel Tompkins of New York and John Armstrong, recently retired as minister to France. Albert Gallatin advised the president that while Tompkins would be "more accommodating," Armstrong, notwithstanding a reputation for "indolence," enjoyed more public support and possessed "greater talents and military knowledge." Madison took Gallatin's advice.[90] Meanwhile, the commissioning of several new major generals and an American defeat at the Battle of Beaver Dams allowed the president to relieve Dearborn of his command in the Northeast.[91]

Madison won few victories in 1813. A near-fatal bout of the flu incapacitated him for several weeks that summer. When he proposed a new embargo law to prevent trading with the enemy, the Senate killed it. He tried to achieve the same result by executive order. He refused, on constitutional grounds, to meet with a Senate committee to discuss appointments, and he paid a price. The Senate rejected Jonathan Russell's appointment to be minister to Sweden. Even minor appointments became contentious, and Madison met defeats when he nominated Tench Coxe to be a federal tax collector in Pennsylvania and Paul Hamilton to be commissioner of loans in South Carolina. For all his intelligence, Madison sometimes made strangely ill-informed decisions. After he responded to the Russian offer of mediation by naming Gallatin to the peace commission, the Senate indicated it would confirm Gallatin only if he resigned his Cabinet post. Madison refused the deal: "Besides the degradation of the executive it would have introduced a species of barter of the most fatal tendency." In reality, Gallatin probably wanted to step down, and he would not remain at the Treasury Department much longer.[92]

By late September Madison knew the public was unhappy with the progress of the war in Canada, but he believed success would silence most of his critics. Privately, he blamed Congress for nearly losing the war before it started by authorizing a dramatic expansion of the army and then refusing to pass legislation to make the new force a reality. On the Canadian border the Americans continued to win victories they could not fully exploit and to suffer embarrassing defeats. Fortunately for the United States, able young officers like Winfield Scott and Jacob Brown were beginning to displace the incompetents. In the Northwest, James Winchester lost much of his army at the River Raisin. William Henry Harrison pursued the British into Canada, defeated General Henry Proctor at the Battle of the Thames, killed the great Indian leader Tecumseh, and then retreated. Oliver Perry destroyed a British squadron on Lake Erie. An American raid on York, the Canadian capital, left the city in flames and responsibility for the fire in dispute; it also cost the life of one promising young officer, the explorer Zebulon Pike. Going from bad to worse, James Wilkinson succeeded Henry Dearborn. Wilkinson led an American army up the Saint Lawrence River only to be turned back in November by a smaller British force at the Battle of Chrysler's Farm. Wilkinson was relieved of his command, as was South Carolina's Wade Hampton after he led another American army to defeat at Chateauguay in October.[93]

The administration's inability to deploy well-trained troops under competent commanders in a consistent fashion culminated in the burning of most of Washington's public buildings by the British in August 1814. The historian James Morton Smith has called it "the most humiliating episode in American history."[94] Uncertainty about British intentions virtually paralyzed efforts to defend the capital. Raids in the Chesapeake, perhaps the most vulnerable coastal area, by Rear Admiral George Cockburn in April 1813 had destroyed military supplies, public buildings, and a few private homes at Frenchtown, Havre de Grace, Fredericktown, and Georgetown. Slaves often left with the British. "The spirit of defection among the negroes," Walter Jones wrote Madison, "has greatly increased since the former visit of the enemy." William Jones complained to Madison that the preoccupation with offensive operations in Canada had left other areas unprotected by requiring "one fourth of our naval forces [to be] employed for the defense of a wilderness." Even Jones, however, doubted the British would be so bold as to attack the capital; he believed local troops stationed in Annapolis would intercept them before they marched too far inland.[95]

Area field officers, meanwhile, warned Madison that, if challenged by British regulars, the available militia "will become an almost useless sacrifice." Others agreed. The defeat of Napoleon in 1814 made more British soldiers available for service in North America. Madison warned James Monroe the United States should "be prepared for the worst measures of the enemy and in their worst forms."[96]

Uncertainty, of course, is inherent in war, and Madison's administration might have overcome the confusion had it not been for its internal bickering. Monroe and Armstrong, rivals for the Republican presidential nomination, had been feuding since Armstrong entered the Cabinet. Expanding on Gallatin's opinion, Monroe told Madison that the secretary of war was "indolent except for improper purposes."[97] Madison had his own differences with Armstrong. In May 1814, he complained to Armstrong about long delays in paying soldiers and about their lack of serviceable clothes. In August he encouraged Armstrong to improve communications among American generals on the Canadian frontier. He also upbraided the secretary of war for making major decisions—consolidating regiments, issuing general regulations, and the like—without consulting the White House. Madison gave Armstrong a list of actions requiring presidential approval. His passivity during the British attack on Washington suggests that a resentful Armstrong had decided he would do nothing he was not ordered to do.[98]

On 5 July, Madison placed General William Winder in charge of Washington's defenses. Armstrong apparently concluded that Winder's appointment relieved him of any responsibility for the city, and he gave Winder no staff support beyond an assistant adjutant and a chaplain. Winder's qualifications were suspect—he had walked into British lines during fighting on the Canadian front and had been taken prisoner—but his uncle was governor of Maryland, and Madison hoped his family connections could help ensure the cooperation of the state's militia. Winder spent the next several days frantically inspecting the local terrain, without any clear strategy. Armstrong, convinced the British would never attack a city of no real military value, hesitated to incur the cost of mobilizing the militia. Madison felt less sanguine, but he believed militia units could be assembled after the British appeared, and he did not closely supervise military preparations. On 19 August, Admiral Cockburn began landing forty-five hundred men under General Robert Ross at Benedict, Maryland, on the Pawtuxet River. Even then administration officials remained in doubt about the enemy's objectives. Baltimore seemed a more valuable target than did the capital. The president told Dolley Madison that the invading force, lacking cavalry and artillery, was "not in a condition to strike at Washington." William Tatham, a War Department cartographer, after surveying the area, concluded that Bladensburg, Maryland, the site of a river crossing on the road to Washington, was the obvious spot to make a stand. His advice was ignored.[99]

As British troops converged on Bladensburg, Winder rushed a motley force of militia, regulars, and sailors to the town. In the confusion, Secretary of State Monroe, who had been scouting British troop movements, made some ill-considered deployments of American forces, placing men beyond the natural cover of nearby woods and arranging them in lines too far apart to support each other. Madison rode out to Bladensburg with a small party on the morning of 24 August, where he tried without success to engage Armstrong in the town's defense. Although the Americans actually outnumbered Ross's army, a fact Madison later denied, American resistance quickly collapsed.[100]

Cockburn and Ross reached Washington that evening. They burned the White House; the Capitol building; the offices of the State, Treasury, and War Departments; and the offices of the *National Intelligencer*, the administration's semiofficial newspaper. William Thornton, director of the Patent Office, persuaded the British to spare it. They left the next day. The operation and the pointless destruction tarnished the reputation of almost everyone connected with the affair, including Cockburn and Ross. Madison, who had spent four days on horseback before returning to the city, put much

"The fall of Washington—or Maddy in full flight," an editorial cartoon published in London by S. W. Fores. One of the most ignominious defeats in American military history, the sacking of the capital, rather remarkably, did not lessen popular support for Madison. (Library of Congress)

of the blame for the debacle on Armstrong. After Madison suggested that the secretary of war take a leave of absence, Armstrong resigned. Monroe's blunders at Bladensburg ended his hopes for a military commission; he agreed to become acting secretary of war. Only Dolley Madison grew in public stature during the crisis. Assisted by Jean Pierre Sioussat and two slaves, her maid Sukey and fifteen-year-old Paul Jennings, she coolly supervised the evacuation of the White House, saving the silver, Cabinet documents, and a painting of George Washington. Sioussat took Dolley's pet macaw to the Octagon House, then serving as the French ministry, for safekeeping.[101]

James Madison and the people around him, however, deserve credit for quickly restoring Washington to its normal routines. If Madison's bland demeanor could not inspire the masses, he never publicly displayed a sense of despair. William Jones promptly produced a plan to continue government operations while the major public buildings were being rebuilt. Congress could meet in the patent building and the post office. The Madisons lived briefly at the Octagon House and then moved into rooms at the Seven Buildings at the corner of Pennsylvania Avenue and Nineteenth Street, where Dolley entertained until the end of Madison's presidency. For his part, Madison resisted efforts to move the capital to Philadelphia. Less than a month after the British left Washington, he sent his annual message to Congress. The enemy's "transient success," he said, "interrupted for a moment only the ordinary business at the seat of Government."[102]

William Jones said of Madison in the fall of 1814, "The president is virtuous, able and patriotic, but . . . he finds difficulty in accommodating to the crisis some of those political axioms which he has so long indulged, because they have their foundations in virtue, but which from the vicious nature of the times and the absolute necessity of the case require some relaxation." Before the war began Madison summarized for Richard Rush the essential difference between a republican system and all others: "Elsewhere government had an easy time and the people bear and do everything." In the United States, "the government had an anxious and difficult task . . . while the people stood at ease."[103]

Madison had never believed the executive should be the dominant force in a republican system, and, as we have seen, he had given the proper scope of executive power relatively little thought until the 1790s. After the Great Compromise created, in his mind, a badly apportioned national legislature, Madison become convinced of the need to create a stronger presidency if the central government was to serve as an effective check on the states. He saw at first only one situation in which the executive might threaten the people's liberties: concerns about national security seemed invariably to enhance the prerogatives of the chief magistrate. "A standing military force, with an overgrown executive," he had told the Philadelphia convention, "will not long be safe companions to liberty. The means of defense against foreign danger have always been the instruments of tyranny at home." He had initially seen little to fear in peacetime. During the First Congress's debate over how the president ought to be addressed, Madison was reassuring: "I believe a president of the United States, clothed with all the powers given in the Constitution would not be a dangerous person to the liberties of America, if you were to load him with all the titles of Europe or Asia." Hamilton's proposals for a permanent national debt, for a national bank, and for a protective tariff raised, however, the specter of a "consolidated" government too large for Congress to manage. Representative government could become a sham as power flowed to the executive. Washington's Neutrality Proclamation, his criticism of the Democratic-Republican societies after the Whiskey Rebellion, Adams's Quasi-War with France, and the passage of the Alien and Sedition Acts heightened Madison's concerns.[104]

The War of 1812 tested his commitment to limited government and a less than imperial presidency, in large part because he faced the prospect of civil unrest from the war's very beginning. In the summer of 1812, mobs in Baltimore twice attacked the offices of the antiwar *Federal Republican*. After the paper's editor, Alexander Hanson, and several supporters were placed in protective custody, a mob attacked the jail, killing General James M. Lingan and badly beating "Light Horse" Harry Lee. James Monroe warned Madison that "if some distinguished effort is not made, in favor of the authority of the law, there is danger of a civil war."[105]

The greater threat came from opponents of the war. John Randolph predicted they would spur Madison to establish a dictatorship and turn the country into "one vast prison-house." The president and his fellow Republicans faced endless provocations. In July 1812, opponents of the war in Providence, Rhode Island, attempted to sink a ship being outfitted for service as a privateer. Benjamin Waterhouse lost his position as a Harvard medical professor because of his Republican political views.[106] Madison heard regularly from Republicans that there were Americans "not only at Boston but every where else who would sacrifice their country to the interest of Great Britain."[107] Federalists seemed eager to confirm the charges against them. The Connecticut General Assembly sent Madison a petition condemning the war as "unnecessary" and approving the governor's refusal to mobilize the state militia for federal service.[108]

Supporters constantly urged Madison to suppress dissent. Even Jefferson recommended he crack down. From Connecticut came a proposal to stockpile weapons for the use of an ad hoc republican militia. Fears of a plot in Federalist New England to leave the Union and form a northern confederacy persisted throughout the war. Madison was encouraged to support laws prohibiting the expression of ideas that might tend to promote secession. States that refused to provide militia for federal service, one irate Republican proposed, ought to be incorporated into loyal states, and their "Tories" ought to be disenfranchised.[109]

Supreme Court Justice Joseph Story proposed legislation giving the federal courts broad discretion to punish common-law crimes committed "to the prejudice or injury of the U.S.," essentially what Federalists had done with the Sedition Act of 1798.[110] The Philadelphia editor Mathew Carey wrote Madison repeatedly to demand strong measures against the opposition. "A law of ten lines, making any attempt to dissolve the union, a high crime and misdemeanor," he wrote in August 1812, "subject to severe penalty, would have probably arrested the evil in an early stage." When Madison refused to curtail free speech or to censor the press, Carey despaired, decided all was lost, and condemned the president. "None of the human race," he wrote Madison in November 1814, "without positive guilt, ever made so awful, so deplorable, so irrevocable a sacrifice of human happiness as you have done."[111]

Madison concluded early in the conflict that the "rancorous opposition" had crippled the war effort and discouraged the British from negotiating. Yet Madison always found reasons for optimism. Economic interests, he thought, doomed any secession movement in New England. Merchants there made too much money exporting staple crops from the South and West to break up the Union. After the 1813 elections, he believed an expanded Republican minority in Massachusetts had acquired "sufficient weight" to check Federalist extremism. After the 1814 elections, he told Jefferson he believed Republican successes in New York's congressional races ended any danger of that state's joining a northern confederacy.[112] Confident in the political process, Madison ignored demands for repressive legislation. When a military tribunal convicted Elijah Clark of espionage, Madison overruled the conviction. Clark was an American citizen living in Canada who had served in the British army. Madison insisted that civilians be tried in civilian courts. Perhaps Madison's only antilibertarian decision as commander in chief was his veto of legislation allowing aliens to become naturalized citizens during wartime, a practice forbidden by an older statute.[113]

Yet by the fall of 1814, Madison's patience seemed almost exhausted. Delegates from New England planned to meet in Hartford, Connecticut, in December, presumably to call for secession. The Maryland lawyer William Wirt visited Madison in October and found him looking "miserably shattered and woe-be gone." Wilson Cary Nicholas urged him to prepare for an armed rebellion. Madison attributed the opposition to the machinations of Federalist politicians, abetted by the New England clergy. When the Federalists met in Hartford, Madison sent a Colonel Jessup to Connecticut, supposedly to recruit volunteers for his regiment, but especially to monitor the convention, and if necessary, to coordinate a military response with Governor Tompkins of New York.[114]

"The Hartford Convention, or Leap or No Leap," William Charles's satiric attack on antiwar Federalists. They tested Madison's patience, but his commitment to free speech did not falter. (Library of Congress)

Fortunately for Madison, persistence, luck, and a new willingness to compromise in both London and Washington would soon bring the war to an end. In the main theaters of combat, the American army was far better led than it had been two years earlier. Of the eight generals with whom Madison had started the war—their average age then was sixty—all were inactive by May 1814. The army now had nine new generals, with an average age of thirty-six. In July, American forces on the Canadian front won a victory at the Battle of Chippewa, and a few days later American soldiers fought experienced British regulars to a bloody stalemate at Lundy's Lane. After burning Washington, Admiral Cockburn's fleet moved on to Baltimore, where it failed to take Fort McHenry and where Robert Ross died in an unsuccessful infantry assault. In September, Thomas Macdonough's triumph at Plattsburg Bay on Lake Champlain led British General Henry Prevost to abandon his invasion of New York. Later in the year, relative moderates gained control of the Hartford Convention, and when the delegates adjourned in January they demanded not secession but a series of constitutional amendments designed to limit the political influence of Virginia and the South. They wanted, for example, to end the practice of counting a slave as three-fifths of a free person for purposes of determining a state's representation in Congress.[115]

After rejecting the Russian offer of mediation, the British proposed bilateral talks in November 1813. Formal negotiations to end the war began in Ghent, Belgium, the following August. For all Madison's travails in finding loyal and able subordinates, he assembled an impressive delegation that included Albert Gallatin, Henry Clay, and John Quincy Adams, as well as the veteran diplomat Jonathan Russell and a moderate Federalist, James Bayard. The Americans, predictably, hoped to win concessions on impressment and neutral rights, although by the time the negotiations began, Madison and the Cabinet had already decided to accept a treaty that deferred settlement of the impressment issue. The British demands surprised the Americans. The British wanted extensive territorial concessions along the Canadian border, the right to navigate the Mississippi River, safeguards for Indian lands, and an end to American fishing rights off Canada's Grand Banks. Defeats at Plattsburgh and Baltimore, however, soured British public opinion on the conflict, and the Duke of Wellington, the hero of the Napoleonic Wars, gave his government a pessimistic assessment of its military prospects in America. In November, the prime minister, Lord Liverpool, concerned about the cost of the war and the need to focus on the pacification of Europe after the defeat of Napoleon, instructed the Foreign Office to settle the American contest. On Christmas Eve 1814, the delegations signed the Treaty of Ghent, which provided for the end of hostilities, the return of prisoners of war, and the restoration of prewar borders. Joint commissions were created to resolve long-standing boundary disputes between the United States and Canada, but the treaty ignored the issues that had produced the war.[116]

As the treaty made its way across the Atlantic, Madison began receiving reports of disaffection even in Virginia. Disease ravaged the militia stationed at Norfolk. Officers in the Northern Neck complained about the escape of one thousand to twelve hundred of "our primest Negroes" to the British. With the loss of slaves, the spread of disease, and the destruction of property by British raiding parties, "the whole face of the country presents one melancholy aspect of chilling devastation."[117] Everyone was ready for peace.

Madison welcomed the treaty when it arrived in Washington on 14 February, and he almost immediately sent it to the Senate, which quickly ratified the agreement. Many Americans realized it had, strictly speaking, resolved nothing. One contemporary described the treaty realistically as "such as could be obtained at that time." In his message submitting the treaty to the Senate, Madison called the war a "success." The nation, he said, "can view its conduct without regret and without reproach."[118] Because news of Andrew Jackson's defeat of the British at New Orleans in January 1815 reached Washington before the December treaty, the War of 1812 felt like an American victory. James Madison believed he had vindicated the nation's honor, reaffirmed its independence, and demonstrated the viability of republican government. Most Americans agreed.

Peace with Great Britain meant, in a sense, a return to business as usual. Less than a week after President Madison sent the Treaty of Ghent to the Senate, he asked Congress for a declaration of war against Algiers. It was a resumption of the campaign against Barbary piracy that had begun while he was secretary of state. By the end of the year, a naval expedition led by Stephen Decatur had forced Algiers to abandon its demand for annual tribute.[119]

Madison bungled another appointment. In March, he nominated Henry Dearborn, without telling him, to be secretary of war. Presumably, Madison thought the well-meaning but ineffectual old general could handle the job in peacetime, but when opposition developed in the Senate, Madison decided to withdraw the nomination. The Senate, however, rejected Dearborn before Madison could act. He got the vote expunged.[120]

At the same time, much had changed. The end of the War of 1812 marked the beginning of a new era of economic growth, territorial expansion, and, relatively speaking, political stability. The war had illustrated the limits of limited government. In 1812, the federal government still competed with the states for legitimacy. Its lack of political authority and its primitive bureaucracy would have bedeviled a politician more adroit than James Madison. New attitudes toward the navy reflected the shift in public opinion; the victories of Perry, Macdonough, and others had helped erode old republican prejudices against naval power and naval officers.[121]

Madison embraced a more nationalistic agenda in his annual message to Congress in December 1815. He suggested that Congress consider the creation of a new national bank, and he proposed a protective tariff. He called again for the establishment of a national university in the District of Columbia, and he wanted additional federally sponsored military academics. He spoke of the need to reform the state militias and to support internal improvements.[122] Congress responded, chartering the Second Bank of the United States and adopting a protective tariff, although the president never got the militia reform or the national university he wanted.[123]

Madison's transformation from strict constructionist to liberal nationalist during the war should not be exaggerated. He had quietly acquiesced in Albert Gallatin's unsuccessful effort to renew the charter of the original BUS in 1811. In January 1815, Madison vetoed a bill to charter a new bank on practical grounds; he believed the proposed bank did too little to support the public credit. Deferring to "the general will of the nation," he did not, however, resurrect his constitutional objections from the 1790s. Widespread acceptance of the BUS, he conceded, had made them irrelevant, and in 1816 he signed legislation chartering a second BUS. If there was expediency here, Madison never jettisoned all his constitutional scruples. When he proposed that Congress fund internal improvements, he suggested a constitutional amendment might be necessary. The amendment never came, and on his last day in office he vetoed, on constitutional grounds, an internal improvements bill.[124]

The publication in 1891 of Henry Adams's history of the Jefferson and Madison administrations marked the beginning of a long decline in Madison's reputation. Many historians came to see him as a mediocre chief executive, if not as "an indecisive bungler, an almost colossally inept president." Contemporaries and earlier writers—among them Charles J. Ingersoll, John Quincy Adams, James Barbour, Daniel Webster, and Henry Clay—had been far more charitable.[125] When Madison left office, his popularity rivaled George Washington's. "Notwithstanding a thousand faults and blunders," John Adams said, Madison "has acquired more glory, and established more union; than all his three predecessors . . . put together." Madison reminded Abigail Adams of "what [Alexander] Pope called the noblest work of God: an honest man." Louis Sérurier, the French minister in Washington at the end of the war, gave Madison high marks for unifying the country and enhancing its international stature.[126]

Madison's generation valued fidelity to republican principles more than it did efficiency; for his contemporaries muddling through to a respectable result was good enough. At Washington's Fourth of July celebration in 1816, Madison won praise for waging war without "one trial for treason, or even one prosecution for libel." He authorized no internments, no torture, no eavesdropping, and no censorship. He had directed an army of fifty thousand men, Washington mayor James H. Blake said, "without infringing a political, civil or religious right." Measured by his respect for civil liberties,

James Madison was the greatest wartime chief executive in American history. Madison believed he had gone to war to protect republican institutions, and he refused to compromise them once the war commenced.[127]

He left office in March 1817 popular, relieved, satisfied with his own performance, and eager to return to Virginia. He went part of the way by boat. "During the voyage he was as playful as a child," one eyewitness remembered. He "talked and jested with everybody on board, and reminded me of a school boy on a long vacation."[128]

Slavery, Sectionalism, and the Decline of the Old Dominion

The Harvard professor George Ticknor visited Montpelier in 1824 and found James Madison looking younger than he had seemed, as a wartime president, ten years earlier. Madison enjoyed good health for the first decade of his retirement, entertained an almost constant stream of admirers and relatives, and kept busy with a variety of tasks. "I have rarely during the period of my public life," he told one correspondent, "found my time less at my disposal than since I took my final leave of it." Family occupied much of his time. Madison remained close to his sister Sarah and a small army of nieces and nephews; he was especially fond of his brother William's son Robert. While Madison was president, he had put the boy through Dickinson College. He and Dolley Madison treated her youngest sister, Anna, as a virtual daughter. Dolley's brother John C. Payne lived on a small farm in Orange County and sometimes served as Madison's secretary.[1] Madison's stepson, John Payne Todd, by contrast, offered no help. He would come and go, and mainly go, drifting from city to city drinking and gambling. The Madisons, and family friends, would pay his bills and try to keep him out of debtor's prison. They did not always succeed, and he often disappeared for long stretches at a time.[2]

Visitors found in Madison a man of regular habits: breakfast at nine, dinner at four, tea at seven, and bedtime at ten. Paul Jennings, who attended to Madison at Montpelier, later recalled the ex-president chopping wood for exercise. Neat but not extravagant, Madison, Jennings thought, "never had but one suit at a time." He wanted to set a frugal example for his poor relatives.[3]

Madison did spend money on Montpelier. He had enlarged the house after retiring from Congress in the 1790s, and then undertook another round of improvements in 1808. Montpelier was essentially a magnificent duplex. He and Dolley lived on one side of the house; his mother lived on the other. Far less obsessed with architecture than was his friend Jefferson, Madison gave more attention to his farm. A postwar drop in European wheat prices forced Madison to rely more heavily on tobacco as a cash crop. He experimented with an improved plow design, tried out a wheat-threshing machine, and imported Merino sheep to improve his flock. John Quincy Adams called Madison "the best farmer in the world," and his neighbors elected him president of the Agricultural Society of Albemarle. In May 1818, he gave a long and well-publicized speech to the group in which he endorsed the principles of scientific agriculture, including contour plowing and the use of chemical fertilizers.[4]

Madison also worried about history. He answered dozens of inquiries from historians and archivists, including Jonathan Elliot, the editor of the earliest printed collection of the debates of the state ratification conventions. He took a special interest in the work of Jared Sparks, providing the young historian with over twenty letters from George Washington. Madison tried to retrieve his own correspondence and, as he put it, "employ[ed] a portion of my leisure" preparing his papers for publication. When Jacob Gideon published a one-volume edition of *The Federalist* which wrongly identified the authors of several essays, Madison wrote him to set the record straight. In a letter to Henry Wheaton, who was writing a biography of William Pinkney, Madison defended the Embargo Act and his administration's restrictions on trade. In his opinion, commercial warfare would have forced quicker concessions from Great Britain, making the War of 1812 avoidable, had Republican efforts not been sabotaged by New England Federalists. In a letter to Henry Lee, he defended his mixed record in making presidential appointments. Admitting a few mistakes, he pleaded several mitigating circumstances, including the need for Senate confirmation of Cabinet members, which sorely limited his options.[5]

Madison found the publication in 1821 of Robert Yates's notes on the Constitutional Convention especially irritating. The ex-president believed that the former New York delegate had made mistakes, and his notes exposed the strongly nationalistic views Madison had brought to Philadelphia. Madison intended for his own, more comprehensive, notes to be published posthumously. Mindful of the failures of the state governments and shaken by Shays's Rebellion, all the delegates, he wrote his brother-in-law John G. Jackson, wanted "to give to a new system all the vigor consistent with Republican principles." Fearful that instability could pave the way to monarchy, Madison admitted he had been among those "most anxious" to preserve self-government by giving the new government "as much energy as would insure the requisite stability and efficacy." In an uncharacteristic admission, he conceded he might have been too worried about the weakness of the central government, but whatever his intentions were, it remained the duty of all citizens to support the Constitution as it was "understood *by the nation* at the time of its ratification."[6]

Madison, however, did not live in the past. He saw the Constitution's distribution of powers among the different branches and levels of government as an ongoing experiment; he remained confident that the multitude of interests in an "extended republic" would prevent any one faction from becoming oppressive. Admirers regularly solicited his advice on current events, and if he avoided some issues, he spoke out on others.[7] He suggested that naturalization laws should provide for degrees of citizenship to better regulate foreign merchants who "have found it more easy than native ones to practice certain frauds." In a change of position from earlier years, he proposed that presidential electors be chosen everywhere by electoral districts, a reform he believed would appeal to the small states, and that disputed elections be decided by a joint ballot of both houses of Congress, which would favor larger states. He urged President James Monroe to oppose Spanish efforts to recolonize Latin America, and he advocated close cooperation with Great Britain. The Monroe Doctrine ultimately reflected Madison's objective, but the administration acted unilaterally.[8]

The popularity of internal improvements, the demand for a more robust protective tariff, the transition from Jeffersonian Republicanism to Jacksonian Democracy, and the emergence of a less deferential and more rambunctious popular culture tested Madison's brand of constitutionalism. Madison accepted the Supreme Court's decision in *M'Culloch v. Maryland* (1819), which struck down a state tax on the Bank of the United States, but he worried that Chief Justice John Marshall's interpretation of the Constitution's "necessary and proper" clause left "no practical limit" on legislative discretion. Even so, Marshall's judicial activism agitated Madison less than it did Jefferson or their fellow Virginian, Judge Spencer Roane, a leading critic of Marshall's jurisprudence. The Supreme Court needed the ability to resolve disputes between state and federal authorities, Madison argued, because otherwise, "the end must be a trial of strength between the posse headed by Marshall and the posse headed by the Sheriff." Madison concluded the Supreme Court might be a wiser guardian of the Constitution than Congress could be. How could legislators be expected to resist unconstitutional measures that enjoyed broad popular support?[9] He complained repeatedly about politicians who found an unlimited source of federal authority in the "general welfare" clause of the Constitution, and he believed federal support for internal improvements needed the sanction of a constitutional amendment. Yet minority rule, or transient majorities inflamed by momentary passions, presented more fundamental threats to republican government. On matters of constitutional interpretation, Madison felt compelled to defer to the popular will once it had become clear and well established.[10]

The growing force of public opinion helps explain the elder statesman's interest in education. "A popular Government, without popular information, or the means of acquiring it, is but a prologue to a farce or a tragedy; or, perhaps both," Madison wrote in 1822. "Knowledge will forever govern ignorance: and a people who mean to be their own Governors, must arm themselves with the power which knowledge gives." Largely at Jefferson's initiative, construction of a school that became the University of Virginia began in October 1817. Madison worked with Jefferson in making plans for the new institution, and after the university received a formal charter from the state legislature, Madison was appointed to its board of visitors. Jefferson became rector and functioned as the university's chief executive officer until his death on 4 July 1826. Madison replaced him, and although he delegated day-to-day responsibilities for the school to subordinates in Charlottesville, he devoted considerable energy to the position until 1834, when failing health forced him to resign.[11]

The university's affairs dominated letters between Jefferson and Madison in the early years of Madison's retirement. The two friends hoped the university would form the apex of a comprehensive system of public education, and they wanted to convert William and Mary, a private institution, into a state school. Legislators did not share their vision, and much to their chagrin, the *Dartmouth College* case (1819) held that the charters of private colleges were virtually inviolable. Undeterred, Jefferson forged ahead in bringing the university to life, with Madison as his chief adviser. Madison provided Jefferson with a list of "theological works" for the university's library and, always interested in issues of religious freedom, defended the board's decision not to hire a professor of religion.[12]

The university struggled to find qualified faculty. Skeptical of the quality of American scholars, Jefferson sent Francis Walker Gilmer to Europe on a recruiting mission. When Gilmer reported the University of Virginia could not compete with the salaries paid by European universities, Jefferson was crushed. Jefferson suggested to Madison that they settle for second-rate foreigners and try to pass them off as something more. Their stature, he rationalized, "would be unknown [in America], and would be readily imagined to be of the high grade we have calculated on." Madison urged a more prudent course, which he often did when working with Jefferson, suggesting comparably mediocre Americans might be tolerable if they should "be of good dispositions better ascertained." Fortunately for the university, Gilmer persisted until he secured the services of five eminently qualified Europeans. Their relative youth, in addition to their credentials, pleased Madison. "They will be less inflexible in their habits, the more improvable in their qualifications, and will last the longer."[13]

Consistent with their vision of the university as a nursery for sound republicans, Jefferson and Madison hoped to fill positions in law and ethics with Americans. George Tucker, a member of Congress, accepted their offer to teach "moral philosophy." A law professor proved more elusive. They wanted Thomas Cooper of Philadelphia, a brilliant and versatile scientist and jurist, but Cooper's Unitarianism ignited conservative opposition. Cooper seemed willing to come to Virginia, but when the board of visitors hesitated in approving his appointment, he accepted the presidency of the University of South Carolina.[14]

For Jefferson and Madison, law meant constitutional law, which meant political controversy, and when it came to politics, no one gave much thought to academic freedom. Worried about "the Richmond lawyers, who are rank Federalists," Jefferson began by proposing a soundly republican reading list for law students. Madison demurred, suggesting that, in the interest of balance, Jefferson delete the Virginia Assembly's Report on the Alien and Sedition Acts and add Washington's Farewell Address. Madison also suggested that the instructor be given some discretion in assigning texts. Republican principles would be best safeguarded, he implied, not by prescribed readings, but by "an Able and Orthodox Professor." Jefferson agreed, but he fumed that the ubiquitous commentaries of the English lawyer William Blackstone had led American lawyers "into Toryism." Young lawyers "suppose themselves, indeed, to be whigs, because they no longer know what whigism or republicanism means." Six candidates rejected the position; the salary was not attractive. At one point the board offered the chair in law to Henry St. George Tucker, even though he believed that Congress had the power to build canals. The painful ordeal ended when John Tayloe Lomax, a respectable Fredericksburg attorney, accepted the position.[15]

In Madison's mind, economic and social change had enhanced the value of education, especially in the principles of republican government. Two years after Madison left office, the Panic of 1819 marked the beginning of a long depression. Initially, Madison blamed "the multitude and mismanagement of the Banks. . . . Hawking their loans at every man's door they became a real nuisance." Easy credit encouraged risky ventures, overspending, and an unfavorable balance of trade. Economic hardship did not spare Madison. When he retired in 1817, his assets included five thousand acres in Virginia, more than one thousand acres in Kentucky, stock in a turnpike company, and a house in Washington. Low commodity prices, poor harvests, and Payne Todd's debts forced Madison to liquidate holdings to raise cash.[16] Blaming insects, drought, and floods, Madison complained in July 1826 that he had raised only one good crop of tobacco and one of wheat since returning to the farm. He tried to put off creditors and renegotiate loans.[17] When he asked Nicholas Biddle, president of the Bank of the United States, for a $6,000 loan, Biddle said no: the bank did not make long-term mortgages secured by land. It is no wonder Madison considered corporations to be "a necessary evil only," and suspected that banks, in part because of the self-dealing of their directors, did more harm than good.[18]

Madison did not suffer alone. Economic conditions in Virginia were even worse than those in the nation as a whole. When he learned in 1826 that Jefferson planned to hold a lottery to raise money to pay his staggering debts, Madison commiserated: "Having no resources but in the earth I cultivate, I have been living very much throughout on borrowed means." When George Ticknor visited Virginia in 1824, he found that "in general things had a very squalid appearance." Besides the Panic of 1819, bad weather, poor harvests, and soil exhaustion, Virginia's planters faced keen competition from more fertile western farms. Young people, many of them related to the Madisons, left Virginia for the North or West.[19]

Amid the economic decay, Madison began to reconsider his theories of political economy. He had long believed that the United States, because it produced necessities, had a natural advantage in trading with Europe, which he believed produced mainly luxuries. He was no longer so confident. The luxury market seemed to possess an unlimited capacity for growth. The demand for necessities, he wrote in December 1819, "never exceeds what may be deemed real and definite wants." In contrast, items "merely of fancy and fashion" are "wants of a nature altogether indefinite." Madison doubted that the nation's unfavorable balance of trade could be cured by expanded domestic manufacturing, but "it would be completely redressed by a change in the public preferences and habits."[20]

Madison may have hoped the schools would teach frugality; he surely expected them to inculcate in their students a respect for individual initiative and private property. He continued to support westward expansion—even as it drained people and dollars from Virginia—because it was essential to his vision of an extended republic. He preferred, however, the enterprise associated with commercial agriculture on a modest scale to the poverty and isolation of subsistence farming. At the same time, he expected more and more Americans would inevitably be drawn to manufacturing, and fewer, just as inevitably, would own land. The specter of a landless proletariat with no tangible stake in society had haunted republican philosophers for ages. Given the franchise, the urban masses would presumably vote to limit property rights and redistribute wealth. Madison concluded, however, that a republican system could not long endure if only a minority of male citizens enjoyed the right to vote. Public education offered a solution to the dilemma. The schools would instill a respect for property rights in citizens for whom such sentiments might not naturally arise.[21]

While Madison attempted to reconcile change and traditional values, Virginia's leaders preferred reaction. They resisted progress, embraced the past, and clung ever more defensively to slavery, even as Virginia's decline accelerated. Jefferson's granddaughter Ellen Randolph, living in Boston with her wealthy husband Joseph Coolidge, wrote the Madisons about New England's good schools, growing economy, snug houses, and warm, practical clothes. Massachusetts had abolished slavery, and was, she wrote, better off without it.[22] Madison recognized the need for change, but slavery presented an insurmountable obstacle.

Madison could never escape the dilemma of American slavery. In 1732, three slaves, Pompey, Turk, and Dido, had been accused of conspiracy in the murder of his grandfather, Ambrose Madison. Virginia authorities executed Pompey; Turk and Dido each received twenty-nine lashes. In 1767, Madison's father, as a member of the county court, sentenced a slave named Tom to death for stealing twenty-five cents' worth of goods from a storehouse. When James Madison was eight, his grandmother gave him a young slave, Billey, who would be raised alongside him. As the years passed, Madison inherited more slaves, and these slaves produced more slaves. By 1787, he held sixteen people in bondage. As other slave owners sometimes did, he referred to them as members of the family.[23]

Even as he settled into a career as a professional politician, a career that would not support him financially, Madison expressed a wish "to depend as little as possible on the labour of slaves." Yet Madison did little to make that wish a reality. Expressing frequent reservations, he routinely went about the business of slavery. In 1782, when Edmund Pendleton wrote Madison, who was in Philadelphia, for help recapturing a runaway slave, Madison promised to "take every step in my power to have him found out and secured." It was a delicate affair; the fugitive was apparently traveling with an officer in the French army. Madison seemed relieved when someone else seized the runaway.[24]

In 1790, Madison instructed his overseer "to treat the Negroes with all the humanity and kindness consistent with their necessary subordination and work." Visitors to Montpelier often found the slaves to be well housed and well treated. When James Madison Sr. died in 1801, his eldest son distributed his slaves among members of the family. Montpelier's slave population peaked then at slightly over one hundred. Madison's holdings declined in the 1820s and 1830s as mounting debts forced him to sell land and slaves. He owned thirty-eight taxable African Americans when he died in 1836.[25] Madison presumably considered blacks to be inferior, although his biases were not immutable. He never questioned the racial prejudices Jefferson expressed in his *Notes on the State of Virginia*, but he never defended them either, and he could demonstrate a certain open-mindedness on the question of race. A prosperous black farmer he met while exploring upstate New York with Jefferson greatly impressed him. Years later, he graciously entertained Christopher McPherson, a mixed-race former slave, at Montpelier. McPherson had learned to read and write, acquired his freedom, and moved to Richmond, where he worked as a clerk in the High Court of Chancery.[26]

African Americans at Montpelier had stories of their own. Sawney went to Princeton with Madison in 1769, returned to Montpelier, and served Madison's mother until Nelly Conway Madison's death in February 1829 at the age of ninety-seven. Sawney somewhere learned to read, and he bought a coffeepot and other items at the estate sale held after mother Madison died. Billey, Madison's childhood companion, accompanied him to Philadelphia during the American Revolution and tried unsuccessfully to escape. Madison refused to send him back to Virginia "merely for coveting that liberty . . . which we . . . have proclaimed so often to be the right, and the worthy pursuit, of every human being." Instead, Madison sold him in Philadelphia, and, since Pennsylvania had adopted a law to end slavery gradually, Billey soon acquired his freedom. He went to work for a Philadelphia merchant and was later swept overboard and drowned on a voyage to New Orleans.[27]

Another slave, John, accompanied Madison to New York in 1788, where they shared the "bilious" fever. Anthony ran away from Montpelier, at least twice. Sukey went to work for Dolley Madison during the War of 1812, if not earlier. They quarreled, and Dolley exiled her to Black Meadow, a Montpelier farm some distance from the main house, but they eventually reconciled, and Sukey stayed with Dolley Madison for another thirty years. Sawney managed the Black Meadow farm, had his own house and garden, and sold chickens and eggs to Dolley. As the Madisons aged, so too did Montpelier's slaves. When Lafayette visited in the mid-1820s, he found 104-year-old "Granny Milly" living in a log cabin with her daughter and granddaughter; they were all retired. One younger slave published a brief memoir years later. "Mr. Madison," Paul Jennings said, "was one of the best men who ever lived." Madison never lost his temper, struck a slave, or permitted slaves to be whipped. He would merely reprimand, and then only in private to spare them embarrassment. "They generally served him very faithfully."[28]

Madison's relatively benign regime at Montpelier may have blinded him to the most oppressive features of slavery. If it did, he did not believe the majority of slaves were content, and he never defended the institution. At the beginning of the American Revolution he worried the British might mobilize Virginia's slaves against the patriot cause. It "is the only part in which this colony is vulnerable." When Virginia lawmakers considered offering a slave as a bounty for enlistment, Madison suggested it would be "more consonant with the principles of liberty" to free slaves who agreed to fight for American independence.[29] Toward the end of the Revolution, Madison fumed about American slaves' being carried away by British forces, but so did Alexander Hamilton.[30] In the Virginia House of Delegates after the Revolution, Madison could condemn slavery, while doing nothing to end it; in all fairness, he had few opportunities. He endorsed in theory Jefferson's bill for the gradual abolition of slavery. The plan, however, had no support in the legislature and was never formally introduced. Madison was barely able to defeat a measure to prohibit private manumissions. He called it a "retrograde step" that would "dishonor us extremely."[31]

Ever mindful of nuance, Madison tried to keep references to slave ownership out of state papers, and it is partly due to his influence that the Constitution does not expressly mention slavery. In formulating a tax plan for Congress in the 1780s, Madison deleted the word "slaves" from an earlier draft, replacing it with a reference to those "who are bound to servitude for life." The provision in the Constitution counting a slave as three-fifths of a free person for purposes of determining a state's congressional representation can be traced to Madison's suggestion in 1783 that the same ratio be used to allocate federal requisitions among the states. He criticized slavery, without reservation but with minimal effect, at the Philadelphia convention. As large- and small-state delegates wrangled over how their constituents were to be represented in Congress, Madison argued the real division in the nation was between slave and free states. That argument, Jack Rakove has noted, could not easily be reconciled with his emphasis on a self-regulating multitude of factions within an extended republic.[32]

He complained in Philadelphia that "where slavery exists, the Republican Theory becomes still more fallacious." He told his fellow delegates, "We have seen the mere distinction of colour made in the most enlightened period of time, a ground of the most oppressive dominion ever exercised by man over man." When Charles C. Pinckney proposed that a constitutional ban on congressional prohibition of the foreign slave trade be extended from 1800 to 1808, Madison objected, unsuccessfully: "Twenty years will produce all the mischief that can be apprehended from the liberty to import slaves. So long a term will be more dishonorable to the National character than to say nothing about it in the Constitution."[33]

Slavery became a peripheral issue during the debate over ratification. In *Federalist No. 42*, Madison defended the slave-trade compromise; giving the new Congress the power to prohibit the importation of slaves at some point in the future represented progress over the status quo. He suggested in *Federalist No. 54* that the three-fifths compromise might be seen as a reasonable device to protect the property rights of slave owners. At the Virginia ratifying convention, Anti-Federalists attempted, as we have seen, to use the issue of slavery for their own purposes. George Mason, for example, complained that the Constitution allowed the slave trade to continue for another twenty years while failing to protect slavery within the state. The Philadelphia delegates, Mason said, paraphrasing the *Book of Common Prayer*, "have done what they ought not to have done, and have left undone what they ought to have done." Madison and his Federalist allies managed to brush the issue aside. None of the amendments that the Virginia convention endorsed after approving the Constitution involved slavery.[34]

Slavery occasionally surfaced as a point of contention during the first sessions of the new Congress. Madison's antislavery sentiments seemed constrained by political reality, the fear of encouraging slave resistance, and concern about provoking a backlash from slave owners who did not share Madison's reservations about the institution. In 1789, he supported a proposed ten-dollar tax on imported slaves; he saw it as a step toward abolition, which would "save . . . our posterity the imbecility ever attendant on a nation filled with slaves."[35]

Madison and most of his like-minded contemporaries exaggerated the role of the foreign slave trade in keeping slavery alive in the United States, and as a result, expected too much from restricting or ending it. The greatest of the failed panaceas, however, was colonization. In October 1789, Madison reduced his thoughts to writing in an unpublished memorandum. Establishing an African colony for freed slaves might be the "best hope yet presented of putting an end to the slavery in which not less than 600,000 unhappy negroes are now involved." Private manumissions were inhibited by "the ill effects suffered from freedmen who retain the vices and habits of slaves." What he described as "permanent and insuperable" white prejudice made coexistence with former slaves impossible. If relocated to the frontier, ex-slaves would soon collide with expanding white communities. If sent too far west, they would be massacred by Indians. The only option left, Madison concluded, was a settlement "on the Coast of Africa or in some other Foreign situation." Madison clung to the chimera of colonization for years, despite its obvious and overwhelming difficulties. Promoting colonization gave him a sense of acting against slavery and helped him avoid hard choices and painful realities.[36]

Madison rarely went beyond rhetorical attacks on slavery and hesitated to discuss antislavery legislation, which he argued would only make matters worse for all concerned. On 11 February 1790, Thomas Fitzsimons of Pennsylvania and John Laurence of New York presented Congress with petitions from Quaker groups calling for the abolition of the foreign slave trade. South Carolina's delegation bitterly objected to considering the petitions. Noting that Congress could not prohibit the trade for another eighteen years, Madison said he saw no harm in referring the petitions to a committee, and he thought the protests from South Carolina had inflated their importance. The House tabled them, but tempers flared again the next day when Congress received a petition from the Pennsylvania Abolition Society, signed by Benjamin Franklin, that called for legislation to discourage human trafficking. After the debate took "a serious tone," Madison complained "had the memorial been treated in the usual way . . . a report might have been made, so as to have given general satisfaction."[37]

After the House had debated the petitions for at least a week, Madison wrote Benjamin Rush that "the Gentlemen from South Carolina and Georgia are intemperate beyond all example and even all decorum." He believed their uncompromising defense of slavery would encourage abolitionist sentiment. Madison said little during the debates, but as chair of a committee appointed to consider the issue, he supported measures prohibiting American citizens from taking slaves to foreign ports and requiring the "humane treatment" of slaves in transit. At the same time, he helped pass a resolution acknowledging that Congress could not outlaw the slave trade before 1808 or regulate slavery within the states. He also proposed that the debates be published, so the public could see that Congress would do what it legally could to police the slave trade, but no more. In the end, lawmakers adopted no new regulations.[38]

By the time Quaker abolitionists began writing Madison for help, he had heard enough. In June 1791, Robert Pleasants, a Quaker merchant in Virginia who had freed his slaves, asked Madison to present another memorial against the foreign slave trade. Pleasants also proposed that Virginia adopt a law freeing slaves when they reached adulthood. Madison tried to ignore him. Pleasants persisted, and an exasperated Madison finally responded. He would not present an antislavery petition to the House of Representatives out of deference to "those from whom I derive my public station." He also recommended against submitting an antislavery petition to the Virginia assembly. Put on the defensive, slave-owning lawmakers might respond by repealing the manumission law or by requiring all freed slaves to be colonized.[39]

Madison generally managed to avoid the issue of slavery for the balance of his congressional career. In a footnote to an anonymous essay in the *National Gazette*, he observed that slaves brought to the Americas from Africa suffered higher mortality rates than did European immigrants. He started a more provocative essay on the threat slavery posed to republicanism. Slave ownership, he wrote sometime during the winter of 1791–92, created a wealthy elite with inordinate political power. In Virginia, the freehold requirement for voting reinforced the tendency toward aristocracy. As population grew and land became more dear, the Old Dominion would become even less democratic. The stranglehold on political power held by its great planters made the South less open to reform than was the North. A plausible critique of Virginia's political culture, the article apparently never saw print. Feeling trapped between a slave population primed to rebel and reactionary slave owners ready to make war on free blacks, Madison temporized and vacillated. Typical was his response when, during debate on a naturalization bill, Samuel Dexter of Massachusetts proposed that prospective citizens be required to renounce slavery. Madison said he would be inclined to support the amendment, except "the mention of such a thing in the [H]ouse had . . . a very bad effect on that species of property. . . . It has a dangerous tendency on the minds of these unfortunate people."[40]

Meanwhile, northern states, where slavery was of marginal economic importance, began to eliminate it, and new southern states, where the institution would become critical to the economy, embraced it. The Northwest Ordinance of 1787 banned slavery in territory north of the Ohio River, but south of the river, Kentucky entered the Union as a slave state in 1792, and another slave state, Tennessee, followed it four years later. In 1800, Virginia authorities thwarted a planned rebellion by the slave Gabriel.

As secretary of state and as president, Madison, preoccupied first with a foreign policy crisis and then with a war, largely managed to ignore the issue of slavery. It was a topic on which neither he nor Jefferson would take unnecessary political risks. In December 1806, President Jefferson asked Congress to ban the importation of slaves into the United States, effective 1 January 1808. Congress complied, but remedial measures could never quite check slavery's relentless expansion. On the eve of the War of 1812, Madison had been warned the British might attempt to inspire a slave revolt. Organized resistance never materialized, but Monroe estimated in 1815 that six thousand to eight thousand slaves, a relatively small number compared to the total enslaved population, had been "taken off" by the enemy during the war. Congress granted statehood to another slave state, Louisiana, in 1812; slaveholding Mississippi entered the Union in 1817. Early in 1819, while politicians in Washington debated the fate of Missouri, Congress defeated an amendment to bar slavery from the Arkansas Territory, and later in the year, admitted Alabama as a slave state.[41]

Madison took pride in the strict enforcement of Virginia's ban on the foreign slave trade, which had been enacted during the Revolutionary War, even as the nation's slave population almost doubled. He believed that the condition of slaves had improved since the American Revolution. A variety of factors shaped their fate, including the type of work they did, the temperament of the master, and, most important, Madison believed, the size of individual slaveholdings. In Virginia, slaves were now "better fed, better clad, better lodged, and better treated in every respect." He attributed the progress to a new respect for human rights engendered by the Revolution and to the abolition of primogeniture and entail, which tended to break up the large estates where Madison believed slavery was the most brutal. He did not see similar advances in the status of free blacks. Segregated from the broader society by white prejudice, they were "generally idle and depraved; appearing to retain the bad qualities of the slaves with whom they continue to associate, without acquiring any of the good ones of the whites."[42] The marginal benefits freedom offered to former slaves did not, in Madison's mind, justify the risk to the Union that immediate abolition presented.

In retirement, Madison gave more thought to a colonization plan. Emancipation, he believed, would have to be gradual and would require the consent of all concerned. Compensation should be offered to slave owners. He calculated that the nation's 1.5 million slaves were worth, on average, $400 a person, or $600 million in total. Selling 200 million acres of government land, less than one-third of the public domain, at three dollars an acre, would produce the needed revenues. Madison foresaw a few difficulties. Some masters might refuse to sell their slaves, and freed slaves would have to agree to what the twentieth century would call "ethnic cleansing." Even Madison's own slaves did not want to go to Liberia, the one success story of the American Colonization Society (ACS). He later conceded that the African experiment could not be more than "a very partial success." While he never questioned his conviction that white prejudice precluded integration, Madison otherwise seemed blithely optimistic. He assumed that northern voters would support compensated emancipation. If a federally subsidized colonization plan would require a constitutional amendment, "it can hardly be doubted that the requisite powers might readily be procured." If it proved impractical to move more than 1 million ex-slaves to Africa, once another place was found for them, "all other obstacles would yield to the emancipating disposition."[43]

Madison gave lukewarm support to more zealous opponents of slavery, mixing praise with warnings whenever some emancipation plan seemed about to take effect. When Edward Coles, Madison's former secretary, manumitted his own slaves and tried to help them make the transition to freedom, the ex-president commended him, and then lamented, "I wish your philanthropy could complete its object, by changing their colour as well as their legal condition." As free blacks they seemed destined to be denied the equality that gives "to freedom more than half its value." When fellow Virginian Francis Corbin despaired of farming profitably with slave labor and threatened to move to the North, Madison agreed that slavery was a "moral, political, and economical" evil, but consoled Corbin that improvements could be made where slaves worked in small groups under good managers. And using tenant farmers or transferring capital from land and slaves to other investments presented their own risks. When the reformer Frances Wright discussed with Madison her plan for a slave commune in which slaves could work for their freedom, he conceded that "the magnitude of this evil among us is so deeply felt, and so universally acknowledged, that no merit could be greater than that of devising a satisfactory remedy for it." Yet he feared the prospect of emancipation would not induce many slaves to cooperate with Wright. He also wondered who would do their work if they left Virginia.[44]

Madison believed enslaved Africans and African Americans were best treated where slavery was the rarest. Experience in the North also suggested that slavery could be abolished by state law where slave owners represented only a small minority of the population. As a result, when controversy arose over Missouri's application to enter the Union as a slave state, Madison found himself allied with proslavery forces. Madison argued that the "diffusion" of slavery would ultimately lead to its extinction; if slaves were widely but thinly dispersed geographically, no one locale would have a compelling interest in keeping the institution alive. Madison likely underestimated slavery's capacity to adapt and expand, but as a painless solution to the problem of human bondage, diffusion was no less plausible than colonization or banning the foreign slave trade.[45]

In 1790, during the congressional debates over petitions from antislavery Quakers, Madison had said Congress could limit slavery in the western territories and in new states. Twenty years later, he expressed doubts that the power of Congress to regulate the territories went so far. He dismissed the Northwest Ordinance as a precedent, arguing circumstances had changed since 1787. Then the foreign slave trade lay beyond the jurisdiction of Congress; banning slavery in the West was the only weapon lawmakers had to strike a blow for the freedom of all people. Madison also suspected the motives of politicians who wanted Missouri to become a free state. Unreconstructed Federalists, he suggested to James Monroe, intended to use Missouri to divide northern and southern Republicans and then "form a new state of parties founded on local instead of political distinctions."[46]

In the Missouri Compromise, Congress ultimately admitted Missouri as a slave state and, in order to maintain a balance between North and South in the Senate, brought Maine into the Union as a free state. The compromise also prohibited slavery north of the 36° 30′ line in the remainder of the Louisiana Territory. With the larger issue decided, Congress blocked an attempt by Missouri to ban explicitly free blacks from the state, an effort that clearly irritated Madison when he reported the affair to the fervently antislavery Lafayette. It was hardly consistent with the idea of diffusion.[47]

Thomas Jefferson famously called the Missouri crisis "a fire bell in the night." Madison, typically more optimistic, expected passions to cool and the wounds opened by the debate to heal. Despite his own misgivings about the constitutionality of the compromise, Madison understood that it enjoyed broad support. As he had done before, Madison elected to defer to the popular will, but other considerations were in play. Limits on the spread of slavery would further undermine Virginia's already anemic economy; selling slaves in the interstate slave trade may have been the state's most lucrative business. It was colonization without emancipation.[48]

If Madison advocated acquiescence, the Missouri controversy provoked him to attempt an uncharacteristic literary form and to display an unusual level of bitterness and sarcasm. In the story of Jonathan and Mary Bull, Madison spun an allegory of a married couple. After years of marital bliss following the union of their estates, Jonathan begins to object that Mary's tenants are settling on his land. Mary also has a black left arm, and Jonathan threatens to divorce her if she does not skin it or cut it off. Mary protests that Jonathan knew of her infirmity before they married, that she cannot be blamed for it, and that she is as eager to remove the stain as he is, if only there were a practical way to do it. Apparently intended for a small circle—it was not published until 1835—Madison's one attempt at fiction saw years of antislavery rhetoric finally give way to defensiveness and self-pity.[49]

Madison's reluctance to challenge slavery, and by extension, slave owners, helps explain his performance at the Virginia constitutional convention of 1829–30. Virginia's first state constitution, hastily written in 1776 in the middle of a war, had attracted criticism as soon as it was adopted. Each county, regardless of size, elected two members of the House of Delegates, and state senators were elected by districts drawn with little regard for population. The system produced a badly apportioned General Assembly. Only male property owners could vote, but they could not elect a governor or members of the powerful county courts; these officials were selected by

George Catlin's painting of Madison at the Virginia constitutional convention of 1829–30. Madison's attempt to find a compromise between eastern slave owners and small farmers in the West led him to compromise his own republican principles. (Virginia Historical Society)

the legislature. Worse yet to reformers, the constitution's defects could not easily be remedied. It provided no process for amendments.[50]

In 1784, Madison had proposed that the assembly call a constitutional convention, but eastern conservatives benefited from the status quo, and they stymied repeated efforts at reform. As the Tidewater stagnated and the population west of the Blue Ridge Mountains exploded, the state legislature became even more undemocratic, and the problem was more than a matter of simple equity. Small farmers in the West wanted the state to build roads; some even wanted schools. To Tidewater planters, with easier access to the sea and less interest in overland transportation, more government meant higher taxes, especially on slaves, their most valuable asset. The historian Susan Dunn has argued that Virginia's illiberal constitution discouraged political engagement and inhibited the rise of a new generation of progressive leaders. Perhaps it did. Antebellum Virginia would produce no one of Madison's stature and no cadre of public figures comparable to those of his era. Clearly, Virginia had ceased to lead the way in political innovation. By 1829, besides Madison's home state, only North Carolina still had property requirements for voting.[51]

After years of debate, the General Assembly finally submitted the call for a constitutional convention to a popular referendum, and the voters approved it. They also elected an illustrious group of delegates, including James Monroe, John Marshall, William Branch Giles, John Randolph of Roanoke, the future president John Tyler, and the sole survivor of Virginia's 1776 convention—James Madison. He had told Monroe that he might be defeated because his writings in defense of the protective tariff "have made me such a heretic in this quarter." He worried for no reason. Orange County voters did not forget his past services, and they chose Madison to represent them. In October 1829, the Madisons made the ninety-mile trip to Richmond, their longest journey since leaving Washington, D.C. They stayed with Dolley's cousin, Sally Coles Stevenson, who was married to Andrew Stevenson, the speaker of the U.S. House of Representatives. Dolley enjoyed the return to urban high society. At seventy-eight and long retired, Madison, by contrast, approached his new duties under "disqualifications . . . of which I am deeply sensible, though perhaps less sensible than others may perceive that I ought to be."[52]

This convention was more diverse than the 1776 meeting had been. Few westerners were planters, college graduates, or Episcopalians. Over a quarter of the mountain delegates were immigrants to Virginia. None of the delegates from east of the Blue Ridge came from immigrant families. Confronted by opponents with little interest in slavery, the eastern delegates would demonstrate what the historian Robert P. Sutton has called "the fatal southern neurosis: no change could be tolerated if it appeared to tamper with the slaveowner's control over his human property." Madison deferred to the younger delegates through most of the convention, but he was not invisible. On 5 October, Madison called the convention to order and nominated Monroe for president. No one dissented; who would dare? Yet disabled by age, Monroe was quickly replaced by Philip Barbour. The delegates made Madison chair of the committee on legislative affairs. Two issues dominated the debates: voting rights and the composition of the legislature. More specifically, the convention had to decide whether to extend the suffrage to white men who did not own land and, assuming the legislature would be reapportioned, whether to count slaves for purposes of determining representation. Limiting the suffrage and counting slaves would allow a minority of eastern planters to control the state government. Led by the irascible John Randolph of Roanoke, their representatives openly repudiated the idea of majority rule. Littleton Walker Tazewell argued that only the upper classes could acquire the education necessary to participate intelligently in politics. Benjamin Watkins Leigh complained that the Tidewater and Piedmont would never agree to be ruled by the "peasantry of the West."[53]

Madison went to Richmond favoring an expansion of voting rights and inclined to compromise on the question of representation. He continued to believe that the diffusion of the slave population would gradually reduce the differences between the East and the West. His committee proposed that the suffrage be extended to householders and the heads of families, who presumably paid taxes, and Madison circulated among the delegates a memorandum supporting reform. The committee voted 13 to 11, with the former president in the majority, that slaves not be counted for purposes of determining representation in the lower house of the legislature. On the issue of representation in the senate, Madison changed sides, which produced a deadlock within the committee and prevented it from making a recommendation on the composition of the upper house. The committee's embrace of the "white basis," as it was called, for the lower house apparently surprised the conservatives—Madison was a substantial slave owner himself—and it drew howls of outrage.[54]

In response, Madison took to the floor on 2 December to give his one major speech of the convention. After a self-effacing introduction, he moved quickly to familiar themes. First, he said, "the rights of persons, and the rights of property are the objects for the protection of which Government was instituted." Next, as he had observed many times before, whatever the form of government, political power is forever subject to abuse, and "in republics, the great danger is, that the majority may not sufficiently respect the rights of the minority." "Our social feelings" or a "respect for character" could curb oppressive tendencies, "but they will not serve as a substitute for the coercive power belonging to Government and Law." Safeguards for minority rights had to be built into the political system.

Slavery, although he hesitated to use the word, divided Virginians. If power was placed "in the hands of a majority, who have no interest in this species of property . . . it may be oppressed by excessive taxation." Laying the foundation for a compromise that would count slaves in some fashion, he made what was by now an almost ritualized gesture on their behalf: slaves ought to be counted because "they should be considered, as much as possible, in the light of human beings, and not as mere property."

Madison proposed that the delegates count a slave as three-fifths of a free person, as was done in the federal Constitution. He seemed to prefer adopting the three-fifths rule in only one house of the legislature and ignoring slaves in the other. The nonslaveholders who would dominate the latter body "are apt to sympathize with the slaves" and would be disposed "to protect them from laws of an oppressive character." Madison's speech probably changed few minds. Few if any of the delegates worried very much about the welfare of the slaves; eastern delegates could easily dismiss that part of Madison's speech, but they readily embraced his larger point to argue that minority property rights deserved protection in both houses of the legislature. They saw no need to compromise, and many western delegates felt betrayed.[55]

Ultimately, the delegates extended the suffrage to long-term leaseholders and urban taxpayers, which allowed about two-thirds of adult white men to vote. For the most part, however, the convention left the status quo largely intact. The western counties received more seats in a new state House of Representatives under a formula that used a modified version of the three-fifths rule to enhance the influence of eastern slaveholders. An arbitrary division of senate seats between the East and the West gave the East a majority in that body. The new constitution left the county courts alone, rejected the popular election of the governor in lieu of a vote by the legislature, and created no procedure for adopting amendments. Virginians approved the document in a bitter election: over 80 percent of voters west of the Alleghenies voted against it. One modern study has placed Madison among a small group of rightward-leaning moderates who voted with the conservatives more often than not, and he accepted the results of the convention. In a letter to Lafayette written in February 1830, he concluded that compromise had been necessary. The largest slave owners were "most violent" against any step to restrict or burden slavery. Raising the issue of emancipation, as Lafayette had hoped Madison would do, "would have been a spark to a mass of gunpowder." Colonization remained a salve for troubled consciences. "Outlets for the freed blacks," Madison told his French friend, "are alone wanted for a rapid erasure of that blot from our Republican character.[56]

For Madison, compromise had become an end in itself. Keeping the republican system functioning was as important as the results it produced. Yet the arrangements of 1829–30 had not united Virginians, and they would not prevent West Virginia from breaking away after the rest of the state left the Union in 1861. Madison's earlier attacks on slavery had been largely rhetorical, but he had once recognized that slavery promoted aristocracy at the expense of popular rule. Otherwise, when it came to slavery, he could not face reality until eventually, toward the end of a distinguished career, he had come to confuse the need to protect legitimate minority rights with the acceptance of minority rule predicated on an institution he professed to despise. With enemies like Madison, slavery needed no defenders.

Madison had reason to doubt whether the constitutional order he had helped create would survive, and however ominous the issue of slavery might have appeared, in the last years of his life, the tariff controversy presented a more immediate threat to the Union. Many American businesspeople, especially textile mill owners in New England, wanted protection from foreign competition. Southern planters and western farmers tended to oppose higher tariffs, which made the manufactured goods they purchased more expensive. In 1824, Congress imposed new duties on imported woolen goods, but the tariff failed to eliminate British competition in the American market, and in February 1827, the House of Representatives passed a bill raising the tax on foreign woolens. In the Senate, South Carolina's John C. Calhoun, now vice president, cast a tie-breaking vote to kill it. Undeterred, a protectionist convention met in Harrisburg, Pennsylvania, in July 1827, and issued a call for higher tariffs. Meanwhile the tariff issue became entangled in presidential politics. In January 1828, supporters of Andrew Jackson introduced in the House of Representatives an ungainly bill to raise duties on several commodities while reducing the woolen tariff; they apparently hoped to embarrass President John Quincy Adams, a protectionist and a New Englander, by presenting him with a tariff that did little for his native region. Presumably, the self-interest of the real protectionists would be exposed when they refused to support a bill that protected every industry but textiles. To the Jacksonians' surprise, Congress passed the bill, and Adams signed it.[57]

The *Lynchburg Gazette* carried a story reporting that Madison had criticized the Virginia legislature for asserting that Congress lacked the constitutional authority to adopt a protective tariff. Mainly, however, Madison wanted to stay out of what promised to be an unusually nasty presidential campaign. Many of Madison's old admirers assumed he would oppose the candidacy of the rough-hewn Andrew Jackson. If, as Drew McCoy has written, Madison embodied "the classical principles of self-control and benevolence," the impulsive and imperious Old Hickory did not. Yet during the War of 1812, Madison had supported Jackson's promotion to major general, and later, despite their vast differences in temperament, Madison often seemed willing to give the general the benefit of the doubt. Madison rebuffed an effort to make him, along with James Monroe, an elector on an anti-Jackson ticket. As the Adams-Jackson contest raised political passions, Madison wrote Lafayette, "I am sorry that Virginia has caught too much of the prevailing fever."[58] Madison foresaw a time when the closing of the frontier, a shortage of foreign markets, and a surplus of staple crops would jeopardize his vision of an agrarian republic. Future generations would have to adapt republicanism to new conditions, but for him, the answer was not more partisanship.

Madison also found much of the controversy around the tariff misguided. Calling the 1828 bill the "Tariff of Abominations," politicians in the older southern states blamed it for the decline of the regional economy. Later historians have blamed slavery. Madison blamed the availability of cheap, fertile land in the West for falling crop prices and real estate values in Virginia. "I cannot but believe whatever well-founded complaints may be against the tariff, that, as a cause of the general sufferings of the country, it has been vastly overrated."[59]

Realizing that others disagreed, he feared during the summer of 1828 that discontent with the tariff could lead to secession, at least in South Carolina, the center of the antitariff movement. The crisis escalated in December when the South Carolina legislature formally condemned the Tariff of 1828 as unconstitutional, and Calhoun published his *Exposition and Protest*, setting out what came to be known as the nullification theory. Calhoun assumed that the Constitution was a compact among sovereign states, each of which retained for itself the right to pass judgment on the constitutionality of federal laws. Once a state had "nullified" a law it deemed to be unconstitutional, the law would be ineffective within the borders of the state. The state's decision could be overridden by a constitutional amendment granting Congress the contested power, but at that point the nullifying state would have a right to leave the Union.[60]

Advocates of nullification cited the Virginia and Kentucky Resolutions to support their theory. As the author of the Virginia Resolutions, Madison felt compelled to respond. He disagreed with Calhoun on two fundamental points. First, he believed the tariff was constitutional. The federal convention of 1787 had been called in large part to give Congress the power to regulate trade, and what was a protective tariff if not a commercial regulation? Second, Madison denied that ultimate sovereignty remained with the states, thus allowing them to nullify a federal statute. Federal and state governments retained sovereignty in their respective spheres, but the federal government enjoyed "a practical supremacy" through its power to interpret federal law.[61]

An ardent nationalist in the 1780s and a defender of states' rights in the 1790s, Madison frequently had to defend himself against charges of inconsistency. He admitted changing positions on the Bank of the United States, where there existed "an evidence of the Public Judgment, necessarily superseding individual opinions." He struggled, however, to reconcile his opposition to nullification with his authorship of the Virginia Resolutions, which seemed to interpose the state between its citizens and the federal Alien and Sedition Acts.[62]

In letters to Joseph Cabell, who led the fight against nullification in the Virginia senate, and to Edward Everett, then a Massachusetts congressman, Madison cited *Federalist No. 39* as evidence that when the Constitution was ratified, Americans understood that the Supreme Court would resolve conflicts between national and state authorities. He had written then: "In controversies relating to the boundaries between the two jurisdictions, the tribunal which is ultimately to decide, is to be established under the general government." Madison said he had assumed during the battle over the Alien and Sedition Acts, and he continued to maintain, that a state had a right to "interpose," or even secede, in extreme cases where fundamental liberties were at risk, but the Tariff of 1828 presented no such threat, and, in any event, the power of interposition was rooted in natural law, not in the Constitution. A tariff, moreover, had to be enforced everywhere in order to be effective. He also objected that nullification jeopardized the delicate balance among competing interests the Constitution had struck. If one state, or a minority of states, could impose its interpretation on a provision of the document, the political compromises on which it rested might unravel. Fundamentally, Madison thought, Calhoun had misread the Constitution: it was not a compact among sovereign states but an agreement among a sovereign people acting through the states. The Virginia Resolutions and Madison's 1800 report to the Virginia assembly did not recognize a constitutional right "to arrest by force the operation of a law of the U. S." Instead, they called on the states to organize in opposition to the Alien and Sedition Acts and to seek relief through the normal political process.[63]

Read literally, the Virginia Resolutions did not call for nullification, and

Madison often wrote with such subtlety and nuance as to make his actual intent almost impenetrable, but Jefferson's Kentucky Resolutions were harder to explain. Jefferson's original draft did assert the states' prerogative "to nullify of their own authority all assumptions of power by others within their limits." The Kentucky legislature deleted all reference to nullification in the final draft of the 1798 resolutions, but a year later Kentucky lawmakers had resurrected the idea, and Jefferson was raising the possibility of secession. To further confuse matters, in 1825 Jefferson penned a "Solemn Protest" condemning protective tariffs; it appeared in an 1829 edition of his writings. Jefferson's words put Madison on the defensive. In a letter to Nicholas Trist, he tried to explain Jefferson's more radical ideas as an example of his friend's tendency to overstate his case. Madison could also argue, more convincingly, that Jefferson had defended nullification as a matter of natural law, not a constitutional right.[64]

If Jefferson and the Kentucky legislature had encouraged the nullifiers, Madison did not want to encourage extreme nationalists like Senator Daniel Webster of Massachusetts. Madison denied that the preamble to the Constitution conferred any powers on the federal government, and he argued repeatedly that the general welfare and necessary and proper clauses did not grant Congress unlimited discretion. Yet as the debate dragged on through Jackson's first term, Madison worked tirelessly against nullification. He lobbied behind the scenes, wrote newspaper articles, and published an antinullification letter in the prestigious *North American Review*. Madison provided Virginia senator William Cabell Rives with material for speeches, and when his old friend Nicholas Trist became Jackson's private secretary, Trist helped spread Madison's ideas within the administration. Although the Virginia legislature joined South Carolina, Georgia, and Mississippi in condemning the tariff, Madison helped state senator Joseph Cabell kill the nullification movement in their home state.[65]

In July 1832, new legislation reduced tariff rates slightly, but South Carolina would not be appeased. In November, a South Carolina convention supposedly nullified both the 1828 and the 1832 tariffs, and the state began to prepare for war. Madison had feared nullification would lead to secession, which might sweep the South. Ambitious men, he wrote Henry Clay, would be tempted by the honors to be won "on a new political theatre." After Jackson sent Congress a request for a "force bill" authorizing him to use federal troops to collect the tariff, Clay proposed a compromise: a gradual reduction of tariff rates over ten years.[66]

Congress and the president readily accepted Clay's proposal, and South Carolina, with no other state prepared to follow it into civil war, grudgingly acquiesced. The immediate crisis had passed, but Madison worried about nullification for the rest of his life. Only a few months before his death, he wrote another long, and tedious, memorandum attempting to distance the Virginia Resolutions from the idea of nullification. He believed a widespread perception that irreconcilable interests had permanently divided the nation made the South vulnerable to the doctrines of nullification and secession. He did not predict a great civil war. Instead he feared a slow strangulation of republican liberty. Separate confederacies would lead to border wars, commercial rivalry, and smuggling. In their wake would come a more powerful executive, a standing army, higher taxes, and "entangling alliances with foreign powers."[67]

Madison expected slavery to create the occasion for the next sectional crisis. In January 1832, he seemed taken aback when a request from the Virginia Colonization Society—of which he was vice president—for state aid to resettle free blacks in Liberia drew criticism. Thomas R. Dew of William and Mary published a proslavery pamphlet attacking colonization, the former president's preferred remedy for America's most intractable problem. Nat Turner's rebellion and the rise of militant abolitionists like William Lloyd Garrison seemed to be pushing white southerners into more extreme positions.[68]

A step removed from the emerging political order, Madison hoped for consensus. Old friends continued to be perplexed at Madison's tolerance of Andrew Jackson, who had a far more capacious view of presidential power than did the majority of the founders. Madison, for example, told Edward Coles that Jackson's legally dubious diversion of federal revenues to his "pet banks" might constitute an "abuse" of power, but he could not call it a "usurpation." He denied that Jackson openly pursued the spoils system, although Jacksonian Democracy became synonymous with filling government jobs with political cronies. Madison deplored the partisanship of the parties that had arisen to support or oppose Jackson, the Democrats and the Whigs, respectively. He could undoubtedly appreciate the Whigs' commitment to self-improvement and their sense of civic duty while sharing the Democrats' belief in the strict construction of the Constitution. Convinced that the president's popularity was on the wane, he did not expect the new party system to outlive Jackson. For all his flaws, however, Jackson had taken a strong stand in favor of the Union, and Madison believed nullification and secession represented a greater threat to the nation than did the old general.[69]

Madison now faced all the tribulations of advancing age. Jefferson had died on 4 July 1826, and Madison dreaded the loss of James Monroe. His health failing and his finances in shambles, Monroe planned to move to New York, where he could live with his daughter. Fearful he would not see his old friend again, Madison urged Monroe to reconsider. "The pain I feel," the normally stoic Madison wrote in April 1831, "amounts to a pang which I cannot well express." Monroe died on 4 July. Madison observed to Jared Sparks that summer that since the death of William Few, he was the sole survivor of the Virginia convention of 1776 and of the revolutionary Congress and the last living signer of the U.S. Constitution. "Having outlived so many of my contemporaries, I ought not to forget that I may be thought to have outlived myself." On bad days rheumatism confined him to his room. Writing Andrew Stevenson to thank him for the gift of a cap and a pair of gloves, which he wore indoors to keep warm, he complained he needed "another article of clothing" which his "best friends cannot supply." He explained, "My bones have lost a sad portion of the flesh which clothed and protected them, and the digestive and nutritive organs which alone can replace it, are too slothful in their functions." In 1834, he retired as rector of the University of Virginia.[70]

His infirmities notwithstanding, Madison remained mentally alert and politically engaged. Andrew Jackson and Henry Clay visited Montpelier in 1832, and the following year, Madison became president of the American Colonization Society, a largely honorary position. He persisted with his surreal optimism about the prospects for emancipation, writing in 1831 that public land sales could finance large-scale colonization. Thomas Dew's essay attacking colonization forced Madison to consider its difficulties, including the problem of replacing slave workers. Madison claimed white immigration and less labor-intensive farming practices could eliminate the void. He suggested that the state purchase female slaves at birth and set them free after they had repaid the cost of their upbringing. Any number of sites could be colonized, and once the first settlements had been established, other blacks would follow enthusiastically.[71]

When Edward Coles urged Madison to speak out more forcefully against slavery, he minimized his own influence. Despite his well-known views, he explained that the Bank of the United States and the protective tariff re-

*Portrait by Joseph
Wood of Madison
in retirement.
According to one
observer, Madison
left the White House
as happy as "a
school boy on a long
vacation." (Virginia
Historical Society)*

mained unpopular, and that nullification seemed to be gaining support. Privately, Madison deplored the incendiary rhetoric of radicals in both the North and South. Charles Ingersoll of Philadelphia visited Madison a few weeks before he died and summarized his political temperament. Madison, he wrote, "is a man of medium, the middle way—avoiding all extremes, and perhaps fond of checks and balances; but he is in grain a genuine republican. You perceive directly that Mr. Jefferson is the god of his idolatry." Madison doubted that the majority of northern voters supported immediate abolition; the commercial interests of northern merchants, shippers, and manufacturers were better served by maintaining friendly relations with the South. In 1834, he dictated to Dolley Madison what was essentially his last public statement. In a two-paragraph message titled "Advice to My Country," he said that "the advice nearest to my heart and deepest in my convictions is that the Union of the States be cherished and perpetuated."[72]

The English writer Harriet Martineau interviewed Madison at Montpelier in 1834 and found him, she said, almost in despair about slavery. He rarely despaired, but he had reasons to be frustrated. In its eighteen-year history, the ACS had resettled no more than three thousand free blacks, while the country's slave population increased by sixty thousand annually. Virginia's whites faced being swamped by a deluge of surplus slaves. The black population was increasing faster than the white population because of "every slave girl being expected to be a mother by the time she is fifteen." Most of Montpelier's slaves were too young or too old to work. Trying to cut costs, Madison had sold several slaves after they refused to go to Liberia.

As Martineau recorded Madison's comments, slavery most victimized "conscientious southern women," who "know that their estates are surrounded by vicious free blacks, who induce thievery among the negroes, and keep the minds of the owners in a state of perpetual suspicion, fear, and anger." As to the slaves themselves, he believed their "intellects" had improved over time, and he knew they might appear happy. Visitors to Montpelier seemed surprised to see well-dressed slaves walking to church, "and, when a sprinkling of rain came, up went a dozen umbrellas." Madison, unlike slavery's apologists, believed appearances left a misleading impression. Montpelier's slaves, he reportedly told Martineau, were degraded in mind, careless with each other, and cruel to animals.[73]

For the last several months of his life, Madison was largely confined to bed. In April 1835, he wrote his will. He continued to enjoy good conversation. In April 1836, he wrote the noted historian George Bancroft to thank him for making a short visit to Montpelier. On the morning of 28 June, Sukey brought him his breakfast, but he could not swallow. As Paul Jennings remembered the conversation, Madison's niece Nelly Willis asked him, "What is the matter, Uncle James?" He replied, "Nothing more than a change of *mind*, my dear." His head dropped quickly, and in Jennings's words, "he ceased breathing as quickly as the snuff of a candle goes out." He was buried at Montpelier the next day.[74]

Madison had led Edward Coles to believe he would free his remaining slaves in his will, but he did not do it. He apparently concluded at the end that emancipating them would jeopardize Dolley's financial security. Charles Ingersoll noted after his last trip to Montpelier that the house was of "good design, but decayed and in need of considerable repairs, which, at a trifling expense would make a great difference." John Payne Todd's debts strained Madison's limited resources. Shortly before he died, Madison told a friend he had spent $40,000 on his stepson. He tried to hide the bills from Dolley, but Todd's debauchery was too flagrant to conceal. Madison's will provided simply that his slaves could not be sold without their consent or Dolley's.[75]

Madison never attempted to benefit financially from public service, except when it came to his papers. He had hoped his notes on the Constitutional Convention of 1787 could be sold after his death for as much as $100,000. John C. Payne, Payne Todd, and Edward Coles tried to find a private publisher, with no success. Unfamiliar with the publishing business, they made wholly unrealistic demands. Nicholas Trist eventually suggested to Dolley that she sell the documents to the federal government, and together they lobbied the Jackson administration to support the purchase. Trist knew the transaction might provoke opposition in Congress, partly because Madison's will left $2,000 to the ACS. A federal purchase of Madison's notes would allow Dolley to fulfill the bequest. When the measure reached the Senate floor, John C. Calhoun objected, arguing that Congress lacked the constitutional authority to purchase private papers. Calhoun failed, however, in his efforts to make the issue a referendum on slavery or on strict construction. Instead it became a vote on James Madison, and Madison won 32 to 14. The House concurred at a special session in March 1837. Dolley received $30,000. Madison's notes on the Philadelphia convention appeared in print three years later, and more than anything else, confirmed his place in American history.[76]

In 1848, Dolley sold the rest of the Madison papers she held to the federal government for $25,000. To keep the bulk of the money from Payne Todd, Dolley received $5,000, with $20,000 going into a trust fund from which she could draw an annuity. The Madison papers generated barely enough revenue to keep her solvent. In 1844, she had sold Montpelier and moved into a house on Lafayette Square in Washington, D.C. Official Washington still loved her. The House of Representatives reserved a special seat for her. She was an invited guest when Samuel F. B. Morse sent the first telegraph message: "What Hath God Wrought!" She attended the dedication of the cornerstone of the Washington Monument, and when she died on 12 July 1849, at the age of eighty-one, she received a virtual state funeral at St. John's Church. Yet she was never financially secure. Daniel Webster later bought Paul Jennings from Dolley, set him free, and hired him. Webster would send Jennings to the house on Lafayette Square with groceries, and Jennings recalled occasionally giving Dolley money himself. Payne Todd, who had never enjoyed much professional or personal success, contracted typhoid fever and died in January 1852.[77]

Thomas Jefferson had complained to James Madison in October 1814 that "it seems as if we should never find men for our public agencies with mind enough to rise above the little motives of pride and jealousy, and to do their duties in harmony, as the good of their country, and their own happiness would require."[78]

Madison undoubtedly passed Jefferson's test. Often criticized by modern scholars for inconsistency and for bowing to political expediency as president, he was for many years relatively neglected. Yet his fellow citizens never shunned or forgot him. According to one count, fifty-seven American towns and counties are named after him, the most of any president. Madison, to be sure, can easily be underestimated or misunderstood. As Irving Brant wrote years ago, "Among all the men who shaped the present government of the United States of America, the one who did the most is known the least."[79] Among historians, Brant's observation may be less true today, but the sheer length of Madison's career, the revolutionary times through which he lived, and his subtle approach to politics continue to make the essential Madison an elusive subject.

At a minimum, it seems fair to say that, over the long arc of his public life, Madison pursed a political golden mean. He sought to reconcile majority rule with individual rights, to strike a balance between state and federal power, and to find an accommodation between the values of his native Virginia and the welfare of the new nation. Interest in Madison will endure, in large measure because of his role in the adoption of the U.S. Constitution in 1787 and 1788; it is to be hoped that studies of his constitutional thought, which evolved over a lifetime, will not be limited to those years. Dealing in nuance and compromise, he left a remarkable but complex legacy, one that will be debated for years to come.

Notes

ABBREVIATIONS

ASP: FR   *American State Papers: Foreign Relations*, 38 vols. (Washington, D.C.: Gales & Seaton, 1832–61).

DHRC   Merrill Jensen et al., eds., *The Documentary History of the Ratification of the Constitution*, 20 vols. (Madison: State Historical Society of Wisconsin, 1976–).

DM   Dolley Madison

JM   James Madison

JMAN   Robert A. Rutland, ed., *James Madison and the American Nation, 1751–1836: An Encyclopedia* (New York: Simon & Schuster, 1994).

JMP   James Madison Papers, Manuscript Division, Library of Congress, Washington, D.C.

JMW   Jack N. Rakove, ed., *James Madison, Writings* (New York: Library of America, 1999).

LC   Manuscript Division, Library of Congress, Washington, D.C.

M & P   James D. Richardson, comp., *Messages and Papers of the Presidents, 1789–1902*, 20 vols. (Washington, D.C.: U.S. Government Printing Office, 1897–1917).

NA   National Archives, Washington, D.C.

PJM   William T. Hutchinson and William M. E. Rachel, eds., *The Papers of James Madison*, 17 vols. (Chicago: University of Chicago Press; Charlottesville: University of Virginia Press, 1962–91).

PJM, PS   Robert A. Rutland et al., eds., *The Papers of James Madison, Presidential Series*, 5 vols. (Charlottesville: University Press of Virginia, 1984–).

PJM, SS   Robert A. Rutland et al., eds., *The Papers of James Madison, Secretary of State Series*, 7 vols. (Charlottesville: University Press of Virginia, 1986–).

ROL   James Morton Smith, ed., *The Republic of Letters: The Correspondence between Thomas Jefferson and James Madison, 1776–1826*, 3 vols. (New York: W. W. Norton, 1995).

SLDPM   David B. Mattern and Holly C. Shulman, eds., *The Selected Letters of Dolley Payne Madison* (Charlottesville: University of Virginia Press, 2003).

WJM   Gaillard Hunt, ed., *The Writings of James Madison*, 9 vols. (New York: G. P. Putnam's Sons, 1900–1910).

PREFACE

1. Brant, *James Madison*, 2:268.

2. James Madison to J. K. Paulding, April 1831, *WJM*, 9:451–56.

3. For a comparison of Madison's and Jefferson's personalities, see Burstein and Isenberg, *Madison and Jefferson*, xiv–xvii, 470–71. Otto quoted in Brant, *James Madison*, 2:14. See also ibid., 2:301–2.

4. Estes, "The Voices of Publius and the Strategies of Persuasion in *The Federalist*," 555. See also Wood, *Revolutionary Characters*, 156.

5. See Burstein and Isenberg, *Madison and Jefferson*, 642. The scholarship on Madison's political thought is substantial, but McCoy, *The Elusive Republic*, provides an accessible introduction to his intellectual world. Equally insightful but more detailed is Banning, *The Sacred Fire of Liberty*.

6. Speech of 20 June 1788, *PJM*, 11:159–65; Ketcham, *Selected Writings of James Madison*, 71; Wright, *The Federalist*, 418.

7. Ketcham, *Selected Writings of James Madison*, xiv–xv; Wright, *The Federalist*, 351. On Madison and the role of public opinion, see generally Sheehan, *James Madison and the Spirit of Republican Self-Government*.

8. JM to Caleb Wallace, 23 August 1785, *PJM*, 8:350–58; JM to Ambrose Madison, 11 October 1787, ibid., 10:191–92; JM to Thomas Jefferson, 4 February 1790, ibid., 13:18–26; Ketcham, *Selected Writings of James Madison*, 65.

9. Burstein and Isenberg, *Madison and Jefferson*, 620; Ketcham, *James Madison*, 103; Gutzman, *Virginia's American Revolution*, 2, 83; Meyers, *The Mind of the Founder*, xviii.

10. See, for examples, Wood, *Revolutionary Characters*, 141–72; and Gibson, "The Madisonian Madison and the Question of Consistency." John P. Kaminski may exaggerate Madison's "remarkable consistency," but Kaminski is close to the truth in concluding that Madison's "focus was never on a particular type of government. Whenever he saw liberty and justice threatened by 'a change of circumstances,' he sought means to limit or eliminate the danger." Kaminski, *The Great Virginia Triumvirate*, 149–51.

CHAPTER ONE

1. *PJM*, 1:3–4; Brant, *James Madison*, 1:29. See also Ketcham, *James Madison*, 3–11; and Rakove, *James Madison and the Creation of the American Republic*, 1–2. According to the Julian calendar then used in the American colonies, Madison was born on 5 March 1750. England replaced the old calendar that year with the Gregorian calendar, and the colonies adopted the new system in 1752. It moved the last day of the year from 24 March to 31 December, and the calendar for 1752 skipped eleven days in September, making Madison's birthday 16 March 1751. On the history of the calendar, see Richards, *Mapping Time*.

2. Ketcham, *James Madison*, 8–14.

3. Madison quoted in Brant, *James Madison*, 1:60. See also Ketcham, *James Madison*, 19–23, 370; Swanson, *The Education of James Madison*, 20–25; and Sheldon, *The Political Philosophy of James Madison*, 3.

4. Brant, *James Madison*, 1:68; Ketcham, *James Madison*, 23–24.

5. Hutson, *Religion and the Founding of the American Republic*, 47; Noll, *Princeton and the Republic*, 32–36; Ketcham, *James Madison*, 38–44.

6. Miller, *The First Liberty*, 71.

7. Ketcham, *James Madison*, 23–24.

8. James Madison to Thomas Martin, 10 August 1769, *PJM*, 1:42–44; Ketcham, *James Madison*, 28–37; Miller, *The First Liberty*, 72–76.

9. JM to JM Sr., 30 September 1769, *PJM*, 1:45–48; JM to JM Sr., 23 July 1770, ibid., 1:49–51.

10. William Bradford to James Madison, 1 March 1773, ibid., 1:79–82; Brant, *James Madison*, 1:97–99, 106–9; Ketcham, *James Madison*, 45, 51–53, 89; Morrison, *John Witherspoon and the Founding of the American Republic*, 36–37.

11. Meade, *Old Churches, Ministers, and Families of Virginia*, 2:99–100; Ketcham, *James Madison*, 56–58; *PJM*, 1:32–42, 51–61.

12. JM to William Bradford, 9 November 1772, *PJM*, 1:74–77; JM to William Bradford, 28 April 1773, ibid., 1:83–85; JM to William Bradford, 25 September 1773, ibid., 1:95–97; JM to William Bradford, 1 July 1774, ibid., 1:114–17.

13. Ibid., 1:7, 17.

14. Ibid., 1:3–4; Edmund Randolph to JM, 18 March 1790, ibid., 13:108–9; Meade, *Old Churches, Ministers, and Families of Virginia*, 2:99–100; Ketcham, *James Madison*, 324; Holmes, *The Faiths of the Founding Fathers*, 91–98; Church, *So Help Me God*, 351–53.

15. Ketcham, "James Madison and Religion," 175–83; Matthew Jackson to JM, 6 February 1836, JMP; JM to Matthew Jackson, 20 February 1836, ibid.

16. Holmes, *The Faiths of the Founding Fathers*, 136, 141; Brant, *James Madison*, 1:112–20; Miller, *The First Liberty*, 91; Lambert, *The Founding Fathers and the Place of Religion in America*, 177; Mapp, *The Faiths of Our Fathers*, 47, 52–53; Hutson, *Religion and the Founding of the American Republic*, 62–64.

17. JM to William Bradford, 24 January 1774, *PJM*, 1:104–8; JM to William Bradford, 1 April 1774, ibid., 1:111–14; Curry, *The First Freedoms*, 135.

18. JM to William Bradford, 24 January 1774, *PJM*, 1:104–8.

19. Brant, *James Madison*, 1:85; Ketcham, *James Madison*, 59–65; Rakove, *James Madison and the Creation of the American Republic*, 9–11.

20. JM to William Bradford, 19 June 1775, *PJM*, 1:151–54; ibid., 1:163–64.

21. Ketcham, *James Madison*, 59–65; JM to William Bradford, 23 August 1774, *PJM*, 1:120–22; JM to William Bradford, 26 November 1774, ibid., 1:129–31; JM to William Bradford, 20 January 1775, ibid., 1:134–38; JM to William Bradford, 2 June 1775, ibid., 1:148–51; JM to William Bradford, 28 July 1775, ibid., 1:159–62.

22. Randolph, *History of Virginia*, 234–35.

23. As quoted in Ketcham, *James Madison*, 72–73. See also *PJM*, 1:170–73; Miller, *The First Liberty*, 99–100; and Buckley, *Church and State in Revolutionary Virginia*, 4.

24. *PJM*, 1:174–75.

25. See generally Miller, *The First Liberty*, 99–100; Brant, *James Madison*, 1:249; Wills, *James Madison*, 17–19; and Banning, *The Sacred Fire of Liberty*, 81–83. On the role of the dissenters, see Ragosta, "Fishing for Freedom."

26. Adair, "James Madison's Autobiography"; Brant, *James Madison*, 1:306–8, 314–15.

27. Council Order, 10 November 1778, *PJM*, 1:259–60; JM to Thomas Jefferson, 16 March 1784, ibid., 8:6–15; Ketcham, *James Madison*, 84–85.

28. JM to JM Sr., 20 March 1780, *PJM*, 2:3; ibid., 2:92 (n. 8); ibid., 7:217 (n. 2); Brant, *The Fourth President*, 115–16.

29. JM to Edmund Randolph, 3 June 1783, *PJM*, 7:107–8; David Jameson to JM, 24 May 1783, ibid., 7:71–72.

30. Ibid., 2:98 (n. 5); ibid., 3:114 (n. 1); ibid., 3:162 (n. 4); JM to JM Sr., 12 February 1782, ibid., 4:64–65; JM to JM Sr., 30 March 1782, ibid., 4:126–27; JM to JM Sr., 20 May 1782, ibid., 4:255–57. See also Brant, *James Madison*, 2:209–11.

31. JM to Edmund Randolph, 4 June 1782, *PJM*, 4:312–18; Arthur Lee quoted in Ketcham, *James Madison*, 132. Rodney quoted in Brant, *The Fourth President*, 49.

32. Edmund Randolph to JM, 19 April 1782, *PJM*, 4:159–62; Reverend James Madison to JM, 2 August 1782, ibid., 5:16–18; Luzerne quoted in Brant, *James Madison*, 2:14.

33. Brant, *James Madison*, 2:37–38, 179–80; Report on Retaliation, 1 October 1781, *PJM*, 3:271–73; Motion on Impressments, 18 May 1781, ibid., 3:124–25; JM to Edmund Pendleton, 30 October 1781, ibid., 3:296–99; Comments re Henry Laurens, 19 September 1782, ibid., 5:140–43; Notes on Debates, 5 November 1782, ibid., 5:236–38.

34. Brant, *James Madison*, 2:105–7; JM to Arthur Lee, 28 May 1782, *PJM*, 4:292–95.

35. Proposed Amendment, 12 March 1781, *PJM*, 3:17–20; JM to Thomas Jefferson, 16 April 1781, ibid., 3:71–73; Ketcham, *James Madison*, 113–15. Article 13 provided, in relevant part, that "every state shall abide by the determinations of the United States in Congress assembled, on all questions which by this confederation are submitted to them." Morison, *Sources and Documents Illustrating the American Revolution*, 185.

36. Notes on Debates, 23 January 1783, *PJM*, 6:115–17.

37. Virginia Delegates to Benjamin Harrison, 8 January 1782, ibid., 4:18–22; JM to Edmund Pendleton, 8 January 1782, ibid., 4:22–24.

38. Comments on Kentucky Petition, 27 August 1782, ibid., 5:82–84; Virginia Delegates to Benjamin Harrison, 10 April 1783, ibid., 6:446–49; JM to Edmund Pendleton, 28 July 1783, ibid., 7:254–55.

39. JM to Thomas Jefferson, 16 April 1781, ibid., 3:71–73; JM to Edmund Pendleton, 27 November 1781, ibid., 3:317–19; JM to Edmund Randolph, 26 November 1782, ibid., 5:328–34; JM to Edmund Randolph, 25 February 1783, ibid., 6:285–88. Banning, *The Sacred Fire of Liberty*, 26–34, provides a fair characterization of Madison's nationalism in the early 1780s.

40. "Money," *PJM*, 1:302–10; JM to Thomas Jefferson, 27 March 1780, ibid., 2:5–7; Thomas Jefferson to JM, 26 July 1780, ibid., 2:48–51.

41. JM to Thomas Jefferson, 6 May 1780, ibid., 2:19–20; JM to Joseph Jones, 24 October 1780, ibid., 2:144–48; JM to Edmund Pendleton, 7 November 1780, ibid., 2:165–68; JM to Joseph Jones, 21 November 1780, ibid., 2:190–93; Notes on Debates, 28 January 1783, ibid., 6:141–54.

42. Motion on Impost, 3 February 1781, ibid., 2:303–4; Notes on Debates, 21 February 1783, ibid., 6:270–77; Notes on Debates, 27 February 1783, ibid., 6:297–300; Report on Restoring Public Credit, 6 March 1783, ibid., 6:311–16; Report on Address to the States, 25 April 1783, ibid., 6:487–98; Joseph Jones to JM, 14 June 1783, ibid., 7:143–47.

43. Ibid., 6:xvii; Rutland, *James Madison, the Founding Father*, 80–81; Rakove, *The Beginnings of National Politics*, 321–24; Ketcham, *James Madison*, 118. For an argument that Hamilton later reconsidered his views on the value of public debt and had "set the revolutionary debt on the road to extinction before he left the Treasury," see Edling, "'So Immense a Power in the Affairs of War,'" 314.

44. JM to Edmund Randolph, 24 September 1782, *PJM*, 5:158–63; JM to Thomas Jefferson, 9 January 1781, ibid., 2:279–81; Benjamin Harrison to Virginia Delegates, 31 May 1783, ibid., 7:96–98.

45. Notes on Debates, 13 January 1783, ibid., 6:30–35; Notes on Debates, 20 June 1783, ibid., 7:167–70; Notes on Debates, 21–26 June 1783, ibid., 7:176–80.

46. Ibid., 7:217 (n. 2); JM to JM Sr., 30 August 1783, ibid., 7:294–95.

47. JM to Morris Anthony, 27 January 1826, *WJM*, 9:242–43. See also George Mason to JM, 2 August 1780, *PJM*, 2:52–54; and Editorial Note, ibid., 2:72–78.

48. Virginia Delegates to Thomas Nelson, 23 October 1781, ibid., 3:293–94; JM to Edmund Pendleton, 30 October 1781, ibid., 3:296–99; JM to Thomas Jefferson, 18 November 1781, ibid., 3:307–10; JM to Edmund Randolph, 1 May 1782, ibid., 4:195–200; JM to Arthur Lee, 7 May 1782, ibid., 4:217–18; Brant, *James Madison*, 2:93–103.

49. JM to Thomas Jefferson, 20 May 1783, *PJM*, 7:56–58; JM to Edmund Randolph, 10 June 1783, ibid., 7:133–36; JM to Thomas Jefferson, 20 September 1783, ibid., 7:352–56; Brant, *The Fourth President*, 84–85.

50. Comments on Edmund Randolph's "Facts and Observations," 16 August 1782, *PJM*, 5:56–57; JM to Edmund Randolph, 10 September 1782, ibid., 5:115–20; Onuf, "Toward Federalism."

51. JM to John Jay, 17 October 1780, *PJM*, 2:127–36; JM to Joseph Jones, 25 November 1780, ibid., 2:202–6; Instructions from General Assembly, 2 January 1781, ibid., 2:273; Motion on Mississippi Navigation, 1 February 1781, ibid., 2:302–3; Report on Instructions, 2 May 1781, ibid., 3:101–7; Brant, *James Madison*, 2:85–86.

52. Motion on Instructions, 29 June 1781, *PJM*, 3:168–70; Report on Instructions, 7 January 1782, ibid., 4:4–17; Report on Jay's Negotiations, 22 April 1782, ibid., 4:168–70; Motion re Peace Negotiations, 17 June 1782, ibid., 4:342–43; Comments on Instructions, 8 August 1782, ibid., 5:33–36; Notes on Debates, 30 December 1782, ibid., 5:466–72.

53. JM to Philip Mazzei, 7 July 1781, ibid., 3:176–83; Edmund Pendleton to JM, 27 May 1782, ibid., 4:276–78; Report on Cornwallis-Laurens Exchange, ibid., 5:163–65; Brant, *James Madison*, 2:159–60.

54. JM to Edmund Pendleton, 19 March 1782, *PJM*, 4:106–7; JM to Edmund Pendleton, 6 August 1782, ibid., 5:27–28; JM to Thomas Jefferson, 13 May 1783, ibid., 7:39–42; JM to Edmund Randolph, 20 May 1783, ibid., 7:59–64; JM to Edmund Randolph, 13 September 1783, ibid., 7:314–16; Brant, *James Madison*, 2:204–7.

55. JM to Edmund Pendleton, 3 September 1781, *PJM*, 3:247–48; Reverend James Madison to JM, 15 June 1782, ibid., 4:337–39; Edmund Randolph to JM, 18 July 1782, ibid., 4:422–26; JM to Edmund Randolph, 3 September 1782, ibid., 5:103–7; Edmund Randolph to JM, 15 January 1783, ibid., 6:43–46.

56. Notes on Debates, 6 January 1783, ibid., 6:15–16; Thomas Jefferson to JM, 17 June 1783, ibid., 7:156–58; Thomas Jefferson to JM, 25 April 1784, ibid., 8:23–28. See generally

Ketcham, *James Madison*, 100–103; and Brant, *James Madison*, 2:301–2, although Brant may somewhat exaggerate the extent of Madison's nationalism.

57. JM to Thomas Jefferson, 10 December 1783, *PJM*, 7:401–6; JM to Thomas Jefferson, 11 February 1783, ibid., 7:418; JM to Edmund Randolph, 10 March 1784, ibid., 8:3–6; JM to Thomas Jefferson, 22 January 1785, ibid., 8:236.

58. Deed of Gift, 19 August 1784, ibid., 8:99; Thomas Jefferson to JM, 20 February 1784, ibid., 7:422–35; JM to Thomas Jefferson, 7 September 1784, ibid., 8:113–14; Thomas Jefferson to JM, 8 December 1784, ibid., 8:177–82; JM to Thomas Jefferson, 27 April 1785, ibid., 8:265–72.

59. Editorial Note, ibid., 8:xx; Buckley, *Church and State in Revolutionary Virginia*, 77–78.

60. Rakove, *James Madison and the Creation of the American Republic*, 34–40; Leibiger, *Founding Friendship*, 11, 35–48; Bill Restricting Foreign Vessels, 8 June 1784, *PJM*, 8:64–66; Notes for Speech, circa 14 June 1784, ibid., 8:75–79; Bill for Courts of Assize, 2 December 1784, ibid., 8:163–72; Bill for James River Canal Company, 18 December 1784, ibid., 8:191–94.

61. Editorial Note, *PJM*, 8:47–48; Editorial Note, ibid., 8:389–99; JM to George Washington, 8 December 1785, ibid., 8:438–41; ibid., 8:446 (n. 3); JM to James Monroe, 22 January 1786, ibid., 8:482–84.

62. Jefferson quoted in Lambert, *The Founding Fathers and the Place of Religion in America*, 228. See also Buckley, *Church and State in Revolutionary Virginia*, 34–36, 81–82, 111; and Edmund Randolph to JM, 15 May 1783, *PJM*, 7:44–48.

63. Hutson, *Religion and the Founding of the American Republic*, 66; Risjord, *Chesapeake Politics*, 51–52; Beliles, "The Christian Communities, Religious Revivals, and Political Culture of the Central Virginia Piedmont," 4, 14.

64. John Blair Smith to JM, 21 June 1784, *PJM*, 8:80–83; JM to Thomas Jefferson, 3 July 1784, ibid., 8:92–96; Notes on Debates, 23–24 December 1784, ibid., 8:195–99.

65. Richard Henry Lee to JM, 26 November 1784, ibid., 8:149–52; JM to James Monroe, 27 November 1784, ibid., 8:156–58; JM to JM Sr., 6 January 1785, ibid., 8:216; JM to Thomas Jefferson, 9 January 1785, ibid., 8:222–34; JM to Richard Henry Lee, 14 November 1784, ibid., 9:430–31; Buckley, *Church and State in Revolutionary Virginia*, 106–7; Ketcham, *James Madison*, 162–65.

66. JM to James Monroe, 12 April 1785, *PJM*, 8:260–61.

67. George Nicholas to JM, 22 April 1785, ibid., 8:264–65; JM to James Monroe, 28 April 1785, ibid., 8:272–74; JM to James Monroe, 29 May 1785, ibid., 8:285–87.

68. Memorial and Remonstrance against Religious Assessments, circa 20 June 1785, ibid., 8:295–306; Noonan, *The Lustre of Our Country*, 74–75; Curry, *The First Freedoms*, 143; Buckley, *Church and State in Revolutionary Virginia*, 142–43.

69. JM to James Monroe, 21 June 1785, *PJM*, 8:306–9; JM to Thomas Jefferson, 20 August 1785, ibid., 8:344–47.

70. Bill for Religious Freedom, 31 October 1785, ibid., 8:399–402.

71. JM to Thomas Jefferson, 22 January 1786, ibid., 8:472–82; Isaac, *The Transformation of Virginia*, 284; Nelson, *A Blessed Company*, 298.

72. See generally Brant, *The Fourth President*, 35; Rakove, *James Madison and the Creation of the American Republic*, 225–33; Banning, *The Sacred Fire of Liberty*, 81–85; and

Banning, "James Madison, the Statute for Religious Freedom, and the Crisis of Republican Convictions."

73. *National Gazette*, 29 March 1792, in *JMW*, 516; "Observations on the 'Draught of a Constitution,'" circa 15 October 1788, ibid., 412; Buckley, *Church and State in Revolutionary Virginia*, 69–70.

74. Lambert, *The Founding Fathers and the Place of Religion in America*, 259; Rutland, *James Madison, the Founding Father*, 46–48; Miller, *The First Liberty*, 119–21; Noonan, *The Lustre of Our Country*, 78–79; JM to Thomas Jefferson, 17 October 1788, *JMW*, 420–21; Constitutional Amendments, 8 June 1789, ibid., 442–43; Ketcham, *James Madison*, 355.

75. Virginia Resolutions, 21 December 1798, *JMW*, 589–91.

76. First Inaugural Address, 4 March 1801, ibid., 681; Veto Message, 21 February 1811, ibid., 683; *PJM, PS*, 2:383 (n. 1); Rutland, *The Presidency of James Madison*, 77. For Madison's religious proclamations as president, see Proclamation of 9 July 1812, in *M & P*, 2:498; Proclamation of 13 July 1813, ibid., 2:517–18; Proclamation of 16 November 1814, ibid., 2:543; and Proclamation of 4 March 1815, in Gales, *Annals of Congress*, 13th Congress, 3rd session, 1830–32.

77. Hutson, *Religion and the Founding of the American Republic*, 84–89.

78. See, for examples, Noonan, *The Lustre of Our Country*, 85–87; and Lindsay, "James Madison on Religion and Politics."

79. Vices of the Political System of the United States, April 1781, *JMW*, 77–79; JM to Wilson Cary Nicholas, 26 November 1814, ibid., 706–7; JM to Robert Walsh, 2 March 1819, ibid., 723–27; Hutson, *Religion and the Founding of the American Republic*, 68–69; Church, *So Help Me God*, 330–35.

80. Detached Memorandum, 1819, *JMW*, 762–66; JM to Edward Livingston, 10 July 1822, ibid., 786–89; Hutson, *Religion and the Founding of the American Republic*, 53–54; Lambert, *The Founding Fathers and the Place of Religion in America*, 268–72.

81. Detached Memorandum, 1819, *JMW*, 756–62; JM to Edward Everett, 19 March 1823, ibid., 794–98; JM to Chapman Johnson, 1 May 1828, JMP.

CHAPTER TWO

1. JM to William Cogswell, 10 March 1834, *WJM*, 9:533–34; Brant, *The Fourth President*, 197–98.

2. McDonald, *Novus Ordo Seclorum*, 203.

3. Miller, *The Business of May Next*, 103, 142–43; Rutland, *James Madison, the Founding Father*, 14–18.

4. As quoted in Ketcham, *James Madison*, 189. See also Ellis, *American Creation*, 100; and Banning, *The Sacred Fire of Liberty*, 187.

5. Farrand, *The Records of the Federal Convention of 1787*, 3:94.

6. Beard, *An Economic Interpretation of the Constitution of the United States*. The historiography on the intent of the founders is a book unto itself, to wit, Gibson, *Interpreting the Founding*.

7. Morris, *The Forging of the Union*, 130–44; Edling, *A Revolution in Favor of Government*, 84–85.

8. Morris, *The Forging of the Union*, 151; Brown, *Redeeming the Republic*, 12, 19.

9. JM to Thomas Jefferson, 3 October 1785, *PJM*, 8:373–76; JM to Ambrose Madison, 7 August 1786, ibid., 9:89–90; JM to Thomas Jefferson, 12 August 1786, ibid., 9:93–100; Morris, *The Forging of the Union*, 157.

10. Morris, *The Forging of the Union*, 38–39, 253–54; Resolutions of the House of Delegates, 28 June 1784, *PJM*, 8:89–90; Richard Henry Lee to JM, 26 November 1784, ibid., 8:149–52; JM to Richard Henry Lee, 25 December 1784, ibid., 8:201; JM to James Monroe, 22 January 1786, ibid., 8:482–84; Daniel Carroll to JM, 13 March 1786, ibid., 8:496–97.

11. JM to James Monroe, 14 March 1786, *PJM*, 8:497–98; JM to Thomas Jefferson, 18 March 1786, ibid., 8:500–504; JM to James Monroe, 19 March 1786, ibid., 8:504–6; JM to James Monroe, 13 May 1786, ibid., 9:54–57; Ford, *Journals of the Continental Congress*, 30:230.

12. JM to James Monroe, 21 June 1786, *PJM*, 9:82–85; James Monroe to JM, 30 August 1786, ibid., 9:109–10; Ford, *Journals of the Continental Congress*, 31:397, 601, 604–7; Morris, *The Forging of the Union*, 232–44; Marks, *Independence on Trial*, 29–35.

13. JM to Thomas Jefferson, 12 August 1786, *PJM*, 9:93–100; James Monroe to JM, 14 August 1786, ibid., 9:104; Ketcham, *James Madison*, 178–79.

14. JM to Thomas Jefferson, 18 March 1786, *PJM*, 8:500–504; JM to James Monroe, 9 April 1786, ibid., 9:25–26; JM to Thomas Jefferson, 12 May 1786, ibid., 9:48–54.

15. JM to Thomas Jefferson, 18 March 1786, ibid., 8:500–504; William Grayson to JM, 22 March 1786, ibid., 8:508–11; JM to James Monroe, 5 October 1786, ibid., 9:140–42; Ketcham, *James Madison*, 175, 181.

16. JM to Caleb Wallace, 23 August 1785, *PJM*, 8:350–58.

17. JM to James Monroe, 7 August 1785, ibid., 8:333–36; Richard Henry Lee to JM, 11 August 1785, ibid., 8:339–41; Thomas Jefferson to JM, 8 February 1786, ibid., 8:485–89; Thomas Jefferson to JM, 30 January 1787, ibid., 9:247–52.

18. McCoy, *The Elusive Republic*, 120–35.

19. Holton, *Unruly Americans and the Origins of the Constitution*, 214–15.

20. JM to Thomas Jefferson, 19 June 1786, *PJM*, 9:76–81; Edmund Pendleton to JM, 9 December 1786, ibid., 9:201–4; JM to Edmund Pendleton, 9 January 1787, ibid., 9:243–46.

21. McCoy, *The Elusive Republic*, 120–21, 131–32.

22. JM to Thomas Jefferson, 12 May 1786, *PJM*, 9:48–54; JM to Thomas Jefferson, 17 June 1786, ibid., 9:76–81; Thomas Jefferson to JM, 30 January 1787, ibid., 9:247–52.

23. JM to Thomas Jefferson, 16 March 1784, ibid., 8:6–15; JM to Thomas Jefferson, 18 March 1786, ibid., 8:500–504; "Notes on Ancient & Modern Confederacies," circa April–June 1786, ibid., 9:3–24; Ketcham, *James Madison*, 183–87; Miller, *The Business of May Next*, 19–20.

24. Editorial Note, *PJM*, 9:115–19; Address of the Annapolis Convention, 13 September 1786, in Syrett and Cooke, *The Papers of Alexander Hamilton*, 3:686–90; Brant, *The Fourth President*, 136; Rakove, *Original Meanings*, 33–40.

25. Editorial Note, *PJM*, 9:147–51; Bill Concerning the Collection of Duties, 8 January 1787, ibid., 9:232–42; JM to Thomas Jefferson, 15 February 1787, ibid., 9:267–70.

26. Bill Providing for Delegates to the Convention of 1787, ibid., 9:163–64; JM to Thomas Jefferson, 4 December 1786, ibid., 9:189–92; Ellis, *American Creation*, 93–98.

27. JM to Edmund Pendleton, 30 November 1786, *PJM*, 9:185–87; JM to Thomas Jefferson, 19 March 1787, ibid., 9:317–22; Edmund Randolph to JM, 22 March 1787, ibid., 9:328–29.

28. JM to Eliza House Trist, 10 February 1787, ibid., 9:259–60; JM to Edmund Randolph, 25 February 1787, ibid., 9:299–300; Notes on Debates, 30 March 1787, ibid., 9:340–41; William Short to JM, 7 May 1787, ibid., 9:411–13.

29. James Monroe to JM, 12 September 1786, ibid., 9:122–24; JM to Eliza House Trist, 19 March 1787, ibid., 9:323–24.

30. Abraham Clark to JM, 23 November 1786, ibid., 9:177–78; William Grayson & JM to Edmund Randolph, 5 March 1787, ibid., 9:302–3; Notes on Debates, 13 March 1787, ibid., 9:309–11; JM to Thomas Jefferson, 19 March 1787, ibid., 9:317–22; Resolution of 18 April 1787, ibid., 9:388–90; Notes on Debates, 26 April 1787, ibid., 9:407; Ford, *Journals of the Continental Congress*, 32:217–20.

31. JM to George Washington, 7 December 1786, *PJM*, 9:199–200; Edmund Randolph to JM, 7 March 1787, ibid., 9:303–4.

32. George Washington to JM, 18 November 1786, *PJM*, 9:170–71; George Washington to JM, 16 December 1786, ibid., 9:215–18; JM to George Washington, 24 December 1786, ibid., 9:224–26; Edmund Randolph to JM, 7 March 1787, ibid., 9:303–4; Edmund Randolph to JM, 4 April 1787, ibid., 9:364–66; JM to Edmund Randolph, 15 April 1787, ibid., 9:378–80; George Washington to Edmund Randolph, 28 March 1787, in Fitzpatrick, *The Writings of George Washington*, 39:186–88.

33. Henry Lee to JM, 19 October 1786, *PJM*, 9:143–45; JM to JM Sr., 1 November 1786, ibid., 9:153–56; George Washington to JM, 5 November 1786, ibid., 9:161–62; William Grayson to JM, 22 November 1786, ibid., 9:173–74; JM to George Muter, 7 January 1787, ibid., 9:230–31; JM to Edmund Pendleton, 9 January 1787, ibid., 9:243–46.

34. *PJM*, 9:144–45 (n. 3); Thomas Jefferson to JM, 30 January 1787, ibid., 9:247–52; JM to George Washington, 21 February 1787, ibid., 9:285–86; Ford, *Journals of the Continental Congress*, 32:39. On Shays's Rebellion, see Richards, *Shays's Rebellion*, and Szatmary, *Shays's Rebellion*.

35. JM to Edmund Randolph, 11 March 1787, *PJM*, 9:307–8; JM to Thomas Jefferson, 19 March 1787, ibid., 9:317–22; JM to Edmund Pendleton, 22 April 1787, ibid., 9:394–96; Edmund Randolph to Virginia Delegates, 4 April 1787, ibid., 9:366–67; John Dawson to JM, 15 April 1787, ibid., 9:381–82; JM to James Monroe, 30 April 1787, ibid., 9:407–8; Adair, "'Experience Must Be Our Only Guide.'"

36. JM to Edmund Pendleton, 24 February 1787, *PJM*, 9:294–96; JM to Edmund Randolph, 25 February 1787, ibid., 9:299–300; JM to JM Sr., 1 April 1787, ibid., 9:358–61. Nathaniel Gorham of Massachusetts reportedly suggested recruiting Prince Henry of Prussia to become king of the United States. See Holton, *Unruly Americans and the Origins of the Constitution*, 179.

37. Thomas Jefferson to JM, 16 December 1786, ibid., 9:210–14; Morris, *The Forging of the Union*, 120–23; Edling, *A Revolution in Favor of Government*, 6–8; Rosen, *American Compact*, 126–28. See generally Rakove, *James Madison and the Creation of the American Republic*, 49–60.

38. JM to Thomas Jefferson, 19 March 1787, *PJM*, 9:317–22; JM to Edmund Randolph, 8 April 1787, ibid., 9:368–71; JM to George Washington, 16 April 1787, ibid., 9:382–87; Banning, *The Sacred Fire of Liberty*, 142–43.

39. See Holton, *Unruly Americans and the Origins of the Constitution*, 4–5; and Banning, *The Sacred Fire of Liberty*, 120–21.

40. "The Vices of the Political System of the United States," circa February–April 1787, *PJM*, 9:345–58. See also Sheehan, *James Madison and the Spirit of Republican Self-Government*, 93 (n. 25).

41. Adair, "That Politics May Be Reduced to a Science"; Sheldon, *The Political Philosophy of James Madison*, 13–15; Peterson, *James Madison*, 136. On Witherspoon, see Morrison, *John Witherspoon and the Founding of the American Republic*.

42. JM to JM Sr., 27 May 1787, *PJM*, 10:10–11; Reverend James Madison to JM, 1 August 1787, ibid., 10:120–21; Banning, *The Sacred Fire of Liberty*, 113–15; Morris, *The Forging of the Union*, 277; Leibiger, *Founding Friendship*, 81.

43. Quoted in Peterson, *James Madison*, 131–32. See also Brant, *James Madison*, 3:19–22.

44. JM to JM Sr., 12 August 1787, *PJM*, 10:146–47; Brant, *The Fourth President*, 149; Brant, *James Madison*, 3:115–16, 147.

45. JM to Ambrose Madison, 11 October 1787, *PJM*, 10:191–92.

46. The Virginia Plan, 29 May 1787, ibid., 10:12–18; Brant, *James Madison*, 3:32.

47. JM to Edmund Pendleton, 27 May 1787, *PJM*, 10:11–12; Banning, *The Sacred Fire of Liberty*, 113.

48. JM's Notes, 30 May 1787, *PJM*, 10:18–19; JM's Notes, 7 July 1787, ibid., 10:96; Morris, *The Forging of the Union*, 86; Miller, *The Business of May Next*, 69–70. Jack Rakove has suggested that the Virginia Plan "implied" each state would have at least one vote in the upper house but that Madison "had not thought through" the implications of proportional representation. Rakove, *Original Meanings*, 60–62.

49. JM's Notes, 7 June 1787, *PJM*, 10:39–40; JM's Notes, 30 June 1787, ibid., 10:91–92; Banning, *The Sacred Fire of Liberty*, 153; Burstein and Isenberg, *Madison and Jefferson*, 154–55.

50. JM's Notes, 14 July 1787, *PJM*, 10:100–102. See Brant, *James Madison*, 3:67–69.

51. JM's Notes, 6 June 1787, *PJM*, 8:32–34; Brant, *James Madison*, 3:43; Ketcham, *James Madison*, 200–201.

52. Rakove, *Original Meanings*, 62–63; JM's Notes, 4 June 1787, *PJM*, 10:25–26; JM's Notes, 6 June 1787, ibid., 10:35–36; Melvin Urofsky, "Federal Convention," *JMAN*, 139.

53. Farrand, *The Records of the Federal Convention of 1787*, 1:242–45; Rakove, *Original Meanings*, 63; Ketcham, *James Madison*, 204–5; Urofsky, "Federal Convention," *JMAN*, 139.

54. JM's Notes, 19 June 1757, *PJM*, 10:55–63.

55. JM's Notes, 28 June 1787, ibid., 10:79–83; JM's Notes, 29 June 1787, ibid., 10:86–88; JM's Notes, 30 June 1787, ibid., 10:89–92.

56. Broadwater, *George Mason, Forgotten Founder*, 172–76.

57. JM's Notes, 5 July 1787, *PJM*, 10:92–94; JM's Notes, 14 July 1787, ibid., 10:100–102; Banning, *The Sacred Fire of Liberty*, 158.

58. JM's Notes, 8 June 1787, *PJM*, 10:41–42; JM's Notes, 8 September 1787, ibid., 10:165; JM's Notes, 12 September 1787, ibid., 10:166; Beeman, *Plain, Honest Men*, 237–38. See generally Rakove, *James Madison and the Creation of the American Republic*, 65–78.

59. JM's Notes, 31 May 1787, *PJM*, 10:19–20; JM's Notes, 12 June 1787, ibid., 10:48–50; JM's Notes, 11 July 1787, ibid., 10:98–100; JM's Notes, 26 July 1787, ibid., 10:117–18; JM's Notes, 9 August 1787, ibid., 10:142; Miller, *The Business of May Next*, 80–81; Leibiger, *Founding Friendship*, 74–77; Beeman, *Plain, Honest Men*, 280–84.

60. JM to Thomas Jefferson, 18 July 1787, *PJM*, 10:105–6.

61. JM's Notes, 5 June 1787, ibid., 10:27; JM's Notes, 23 July 1787, ibid., 10:112–13; Morris, *The Forging of the Union*, 300.

62. JM's Notes, 19 July 1787, *PJM*, 10:107–8; JM's Notes, 21 July 1787, ibid., 10:110–11; Miller, *The Business of May Next*, 78–90; Banning, *The Sacred Fire of Liberty*, 167–68; Brant, *James Madison*, 3:41, 122; Beeman, *Plain, Honest Men*, 233–34, 257; Burstein and Isenberg, *Madison and Jefferson*, 160–64.

63. JM's Notes, 31 May 1787, *PJM*, 10:20–22; JM's Notes, 6 August 1787, ibid., 10:151–52; JM's Notes, 29 August 1787, ibid., 10:158–59; Banning, *The Sacred Fire of Liberty*, 159–70, 179–80; Brant, *The Fourth President*, 174.

64. JM's Notes, 23 June 1787, *PJM*, 10:74–75; JM's Notes, 25 July 1787, ibid., 10:115–17; JM's Notes, 7 August 1787, ibid., 10:138–39; JM's Notes, 25 August 1787, ibid., 10:157; Brant, *James Madison*, 3:32–34.

65. JM to Thomas Jefferson, 6 September 1787, *PJM*, 10:163–65; JM to Thomas Jefferson, 24 October 1787, ibid., 10:205–20.

66. Edward Carrington to JM, 23 September 1787, ibid., 10:172–73; John Dawson to JM, 25 September 1787, ibid., 10:173–74; Ford, *Journals of the Continental Congress*, 33:540–42; Brant, *James Madison*, 3:72–73, 145, 152.

67. Reverend James Madison to JM, 1 October 1787, *PJM*, 10:183–85; Joseph Jones to JM, 29 October 1787, ibid., 10:227–29; James McClurg to JM, 31 October 1787, ibid., 10:233–34.

68. James Monroe to JM, 13 October 1787, ibid., 10:192–94; JM to Edmund Pendleton, 28 October 1787, ibid., 10:223–25; Edmund Randolph to JM, 29 October 1787, ibid., 10:229–31; JM to Ambrose Madison, 8 November 1787, ibid., 10:243–45; John Dawson to JM, circa 10 November 1787, ibid., 10:247–49.

69. JM to William Short, 6 June 1787, ibid., 10:31–32.

70. Thomas Jefferson to JM, 20 June 1787, ibid., 10:63–67; Brant, *James Madison*, 3:129.

71. Archibald Stuart to JM, 9 November 1787, *PJM*, 10:245–47.

CHAPTER THREE

1. Rutland, *James Madison, the Founding Father*, 29; Beeman, *Plain, Honest Men*, 357; Brant, *James Madison*, 3:161; Ford, *Journals of the Continental Congress*, 33:549. Ironically, one of Lee's amendments provided for proportional representation in both houses of Congress, but Madison feared that debating amendments at that stage in the process would open a Pandora's box. See Maier, *Ratification*, 54–58.

2. Editorial Note, *PJM*, 10:259–63; Meyerson, *Liberty's Blueprint*, 84–87.

3. Meyerson, *Liberty's Blueprint*, 79–80; Joseph Jones to JM, 18 December 1787, *PJM*, 10:329–30; Wright, *The Federalist*, 8; Ketcham, *James Madison*, 239.

4. Meyerson, *Liberty's Blueprint*, 88–97; Kramnick, *The Federalist Papers*, 11, 75–76. Jefferson quoted in ibid., 11.

5. Detached Memorandum on *The Federalist*, circa 1819, in *JMW*, 768–70; Editorial Note, *PJM*, 10:259–63; JM to Thomas Jefferson, 10 August 1788, ibid., 11:225–27; Meyerson, *Liberty's Blueprint*, 88–97.

6. Hamilton quoted in Kramnick, *The Federalist Papers*, 35. See also Ketcham, *James*

Madison, 240–41, 299–301; Wright, *The Federalist*, 17; and Banning, *The Sacred Fire of Liberty*, 232. Adrienne Koch noted differences between Madison and Hamilton in *Jefferson and Madison*, 53–54, but recent scholarship suggests those differences may have been more stylistic and strategic than substantive. See Estes, "The Voices of Publius and Strategies of Persuasion in *The Federalist*."

7. Rakove, *Original Meanings*, 218–21, 311–16; JM to George Washington, 14 December 1787, *PJM*, 10:327; JM to Thomas Jefferson, 20 December 1787, ibid., 10:331–33.

8. Brant, *James Madison*, 3:174–76, Banning, *The Sacred Fire of Liberty*, 209–17; JM to Philip Mazzei, 8 October 1788, *PJM*, 11:278–79; Rakove, *Original Meanings*, 139–40. For a critical view of Madison as a classical liberal, see Matthews, *If Men Were Angels*. More sympathetic is Rosen, *American Compact*.

9. Thomas Jefferson to JM, 20 December 1787, *PJM*, 10:335–40; George Lee Turberville to JM, 11 December 1787, ibid., 10:315–18.

10. JM to Thomas Jefferson, 9 December 1787, ibid., 10:310–15; JM to Archibald Stuart, 14 December 1787, ibid., 10:325–27; JM to Edmund Randolph, 10 January 1788, ibid., 10:354–57; JM to Edmund Pendleton, 21 February 1788, ibid., 10:532–34.

11. *Federalist No. 10*, 22 November 1787, *JMW*, 160–67; Wright, *The Federalist*, 50.

12. *Federalist No. 14*, 30 November 1787, *JMW*, 168–73.

13. *Federalist No. 18*, 7 December 1787, ibid., 174–79; *Federalist No. 19*, 8 December 1787, ibid., 180–85; *Federalist No. 20*, 11 December 1787, ibid., 186–90.

14. Archibald Stuart to JM, 14 January 1788, *PJM*, 10:373–75; Tench Coxe to JM, 16 January 1788, ibid., 10:375; *Federalist No. 37*, 11 January 1788, *JMW*, 194–201.

15. *Federalist No. 38*, 12 January 1788, *JMW*, 202–10.

16. *Federalist No. 40*, 18 January 1788, ibid., 218–25.

17. *Federalist No. 41*, 19 January 1788, ibid., 226–34.

18. *Federalist No. 42*, 22 January 1788, ibid., 235–42.

19. *Federalist No. 43*, 23 January 1788, ibid., 243–51.

20. *Federalist No. 44*, 25 January 1788, ibid., 252–59.

21. *Federalist No. 39*, 16 January 1788, ibid., 211–17; *Federalist No. 44*, 25 January 1788, ibid., 252–59; *Federalist No. 45*, 26 January 1788, ibid., 260–65; *Federalist No. 46*, 29 January 1788, ibid., 266–72.

22. *Federalist No. 42*, 22 January 1788, ibid., 235–42; *Federalist No. 54*, 12 February 1788, ibid., 310–14.

23. *Federalist No. 62*, 27 February 1788, ibid., 338–44; *Federalist No. 63*, 1 March 1788, ibid., 345–52.

24. *Federalist No. 47*, 30 January 1788, ibid., 273–80.

25. *Federalist No. 48*, 1 February 1788, ibid., 281–85. See also *Federalist No. 55*, 13 February 1788, ibid., 315–20.

26. *Federalist No. 51*, 6 February 1788, ibid., 294–98.

27. Ibid.; Rakove, *Original Meanings*, 176, 328–29; Wright, *The Federalist*, 63.

28. Nathaniel Gorham to JM, 27 January 1788, *PJM*, 10:435–36; Rufus King to JM, 27 January 1788, ibid., 10:436–37. In reality, many mechanics and artisans in cities like Boston and Philadelphia supported the Constitution because they believed a stronger national government would promote American trade. See Beeman, *Plain, Honest Men*, 378–79, 389.

29. *Federalist No. 49*, 2 February 1788, *JMW*, 286–90; *Federalist No. 50*, 5 February 1788, ibid., 291–93.

30. *Federalist No. 52*, 8 February 1788, ibid., 299–303; *Federalist No. 53*, 9 February 1788, ibid., 304–9; *Federalist No. 55*, 13 February 1788, ibid., 315–20; *Federalist No. 56*, 16 February 1788, ibid., 321–25; *Federalist No. 58*, 20 February 1788, ibid., 332–37.

31. *Federalist No. 55*, 13 February 1788, ibid., 315–20; *Federalist No. 57*, 19 February 1788, ibid., 326–31.

32. JM to George Washington, 15 February 1788, *PJM*, 10:510–11; JM to Edmund Pendleton, 3 March 1788; ibid., 10:554; Kramnick, *The Federalist Papers*, 37–38.

33. JM to George Washington, 8 February 1788, *PJM*, 10:481–82; Benjamin Hawkins to JM, 14 February 1788, ibid., 10:508–9.

34. Edmund Randolph to JM, 27 December 1787, ibid., 10:346–47; George Washington to JM, 10 January 1788, ibid., 10:357–58; Edward Carrington to JM, 18 January 1788, ibid., 10:382–84; Thomas Jefferson to JM, 6 February 1788, ibid., 10:473–75; JM to Thomas Jefferson, 19 February 1788, ibid., 10:518–21.

35. JM Sr. to JM, 30 January 1788, ibid., 10:446–48; William Moore to JM, 31 January 1788, ibid., 10:454–55; James Gordon Jr. to JM, 17 February 1788, ibid., 10:515–16; John Dawson to JM, 18 February 1788, ibid., 10:517–18; JM to George Washington, 20 February 1788, ibid., 10:526–27; Joseph Spencer to JM, 28 February 1788, ibid., 10:540–42.

36. Madison quoted in Kramnick, *The Federalist Papers*, 81. See also Tench Coxe to JM, 6 February 1788, *PJM*, 10:473; Reverend James Madison to JM, 9 February 1788, *PJM*, 10:478–86; Rakove, *James Madison and the Creation of the American Republic*, 86–87; and Maier, *Ratification*, xi, 84, 257. Kramer, "Madison's Audience," argues that *Federalist No. 10* was too esoteric to be of immediate political value. See also Burstein and Isenberg, *Madison and Jefferson*, 174.

37. JM to Eliza House Trist, 25 March 1788, *PJM*, 11:5–6; Ketcham, *James Madison*, 251–52.

38. Cyrus Griffin to JM, 14 April 1788, *PJM*, 11:22–23; Rutland, *The Ordeal of the Constitution*, 184–86.

39. Grayson quoted in Rutland, *The Ordeal of the Constitution*, 230–31. See also ibid., 249–50; Ketcham, *James Madison*, 266–68; Banning, *The Sacred Fire of Liberty*, 261–63; Maier, *Ratification*, 237; and JM to John Brown, 27 May 1788, *PJM*, 11:59–60.

40. JM to Thomas Jefferson, 22 April 1788, *PJM*, 11:27–29; Brant, *James Madison*, 3:191–92, 196; Rutland, *James Madison, the Founding Father*, 15; Ketcham, *James Madison*, 255–56.

41. Ketcham, *James Madison*, 260–61, 266–68; John Brown to JM, 12 May 1788, *PJM*, 11:42–44.

42. JM to George Nicholas, 17 May 1788, *PJM*, 11:44–51.

43. JM to George Washington, 10 April 1788, ibid., 11:20–21; Tench Coxe to JM, 19 May 1788, ibid., 11:51–52; Alexander Hamilton to JM, 19 May 1788, ibid., 11:53–54.

44. JM to George Washington, 4 June 1788, ibid., 11:77; Labunski, *James Madison and the Struggle for the Bill of Rights*, 67–68. For a succinct survey of the Virginia convention, see Briceland, "Virginia."

45. Editorial Note, *PJM*, 11:72–76; Labunski, *James Madison and the Struggle for the Bill of Rights*, 73.

46. JM to Tench Coxe, 11 June 1788, *PJM*, 11:102–3; Speech of 12 June 1788, ibid., 11:121–29; JM to Rufus King, 18 June 1788, ibid., 11:152; George Washington to JM, 23 June 1788, ibid., 11:170. Grigsby quoted in Brant, *James Madison*, 3:199–200.

47. Speech of 6 June 1788, *PJM*, 11:78–88; Speech of 7 June 1788, ibid., 11:90–98; Speech of 11 June 1788, ibid., 11:107–19; Speech of 12 June 1788, ibid., 11:121–29; JM to Rufus King, 13 June 1788, ibid., 11:133–34.

48. Speeches of 13 June 1788, ibid., 11:129–33, 135–39.

49. JM to Alexander Hamilton, 20 June 1788, ibid., 11:157; Speech of 20 June 1788, ibid., 11:158–65; Maier, *Ratification*, 289.

50. Speech of 12 June 1788, *PJM*, 11:129–33; Brant, *James Madison*, 3:205.

51. Speech of 16 June 1788, *PJM*, 11:144–47; Speech of 17 June 1788, ibid., 11:150–51; Speech of 18 June 1788, ibid., 11:153–55; Speech of 24 June 1788, ibid., 11:172–77.

52. Speech of 6 June 1788, ibid., 11:78–80; Speech of 14 June 1788, ibid., 11:142–44; JM to Alexander Hamilton, 16 June 1788, ibid., 11:144; Speech of 20 June 1788, ibid., 11:158–65.

53. George Nicholas to JM, 5 April 1788, ibid., 11:8–10; JM to George Nicholas, 8 April 1788, ibid., 11:11–15; Alexander Hamilton to JM, 19 July 1788, ibid., 11:188; JM to Alexander Hamilton, 20 July 1788, ibid., 11:189.

54. JM to Alexander Hamilton, 22 June 1788, ibid., 11:166; JM to Rufus King, 22 June 1788, ibid., 11:167; Maier, *Ratification*, 292–93.

55. The best source on the debates of 23–25 June is *DHRC*, 10:1464–1563. Madison quoted in ibid., 10:1504.

56. *DHRC*, 10:1556–57; Speech of 24 June 1788, *PJM*, 11:172–77; JM to George Washington, ibid., 11:182–83; Maier, *Ratification*, 293–309; Banning, "Virginia," 282.

57. JM to Rufus King, 25 June 1788, *PJM*, 11:178; John Page to JM, 6 August 1788, ibid., 11:225; Martin Oster to Comte de la Luzerne, 28 June 1788, *DHRC*, 10:1689–91; Brant, *James Madison*, 3:227.

58. JM to Tench Coxe, 30 July 1788, *PJM*, 11:210; Edmund Randolph to JM, 13 August 1788, ibid., 11:231–32; JM to Edmund Randolph, 22 August 1788, ibid., 11:237–38; JM to George Washington, 24 August 1788, ibid., 11:240–42; McCoy, "James Madison and Visions of American Nationality in the Confederation Period"; Rutland, *The Ordeal of the Constitution*, 208–9, 263–66.

59. Thomas Jefferson to JM, 31 July 1788, *PJM*, 11:210–14; JM to Thomas Jefferson, 23 August 1788, ibid., 11:238; JM to Edmund Pendleton, 20 October 1788, ibid., 11:306–7; JM to Thomas Mann Randolph, 13 January 1789, ibid., 11:415–16; Tench Coxe to JM, 18 March 1789, ibid., 12:20–22; JM to Thomas Jefferson, 29 March 1789, ibid., 12:37–40. See generally Hutson, "The Drafting of the Bill of Rights."

60. JM to Thomas Jefferson, 17 October 1788, *PJM*, 11:295–300.

61. Levy, *Origins of the Bill of Rights*, 33; Rakove, *Original Meanings*, 289–306, 328–29; Banning, *The Sacred Fire of Liberty*, 278–81; Alexander White to JM, 16 August 1788, *PJM*, 11:232–34; Thomas Jefferson to JM, 15 March 1789, ibid., 12:13–17; Speech of 17 June 1789, ibid., 12:238.

62. JM to Edmund Randolph, 17 October 1788, *PJM*, 11:304–5; Edward Carrington to JM, 9 November 1788, ibid., 11:336–38; Edmund Randolph to JM, 10 November 1788, ibid., 11:338–39; Edward Carrington to JM, 15 November 1788, ibid., 11:345–46; Henry Lee to

JM, 19 November 1788, ibid., 11:355–57; JM to Edmund Randolph, 23 November 1788, ibid., 11:362–64.

63. George Lee Turberville to JM, 13 November 1788, ibid., 11:343–44; Rakove, *James Madison and the Creation of the American Republic*, 91–92.

64. JM to George Washington, 2 December 1788, *PJM*, 11:376–78; JM to Thomas Jefferson, 8 December 1788, ibid., 11:381–84; Burgess Ball to JM, 8 December 1788, ibid., 11:385–86; George Lee Turberville to JM, 14 December 1788, ibid., 11:396–98.

65. JM to George Washington, 14 January 1789, ibid., 11:417–18; JM to George Thompson, 29 January 1789, ibid., 11:433–37; Ketcham, *James Madison*, 277.

66. JM to George Eve, 2 January 1789, *PJM*, 11:404–6; Benjamin Johnson to JM, 19 January 1789, ibid., 11:423–24; ibid., 11:438 (n. 1); Rutland, *James Madison, the Founding Father*, 47–48.

67. JM to Edmund Randolph, 1 March 1789, *PJM*, 11:453–54.

68. Brant, *James Madison*, 3:246; First Inaugural Address, 30 April 1789, *PJM*, 12:120–24; George Washington to JM, 5 May 1789, ibid., 12:131–32; Address to the President, 5 May 1789, ibid., 12:132–34.

69. Ketcham, *James Madison*, 287.

70. Speech of 11 May 1789, *PJM*, 12:154–56.

71. Speech of 16 July 1789, ibid., 12:293.

72. Editorial Note, ibid., 12:52–64; Speech of 16 June 1789, ibid., 12:225–29; Speech of 18 June 1789, ibid., 12:244–45.

73. Editorial Note, ibid., 12:52–64; Speech of 25 April 1789, ibid., 12:110–13; Speech of 4 May 1789, ibid., 12:125–29; JM to Thomas Jefferson, 30 June 1789, ibid., 12:267–72.

74. JM to Henry Lee, 30 November 1788, ibid., 11:371–72; JM to Thomas Jefferson, 29 March 1789, ibid., 12:37–40; James Monroe to JM, circa 26 April 1789, ibid., 12:113–14; JM to Edmund Randolph, 31 May 1789, ibid., 12:189–91; JM to JM Sr., 5 July 1789, ibid., 12:278–79.

75. JM to Edmund Randolph, 12 April 1789, ibid., 12:75–77; JM to Edmund Randolph, 31 May 1789, ibid., 12:189–91; JM to Thomas Jefferson, 9 May 1789, ibid., 12:142–44; JM to Thomas Jefferson, 30 June 1789, ibid., 12:267–72.

76. Quoted in Ketcham, *James Madison*, 272–73.

77. Ames quoted in Brant, *James Madison*, 3:249. Sedgwick quoted in Labunski, *James Madison and the Struggle for the Bill of Rights*, 208–9. See also Tench Coxe to JM, 10 September 1788, *PJM*, 11:248–50; and Editorial Note, ibid., 12:53.

78. Labunski, *James Madison and the Struggle for the Bill of Rights*, 228–29.

79. Brant, *James Madison*, 3:264, Labunski, *James Madison and the Struggle for the Bill of Rights*, 189–91; JM to Richard Peters, 19 August 1789, *PJM*, 12:346–48; Goldwin, *From Parchment to Power*, 72–74, 101–2.

80. Rakove, *Original Meanings*, 330–38; Goldwin, *From Parchment to Power*, 11.

81. JM to Thomas Jefferson, 27 May 1789, *PJM*, 12:185–87; Speech of 8 June 1789, ibid., 12:196–210; Debates of 8 June 1789, Veit et al., *Creating the Bill of Rights*, 63–95.

82. Rutland, *James Madison, the Founding Father*, 59–60; Brant, *James Madison*, 3:265; Veit et al., *Creating the Bill of Rights*, xii–xv. See generally Leibiger, "James Madison and Amendments to the Constitution."

83. Veit et al., *Creating the Bill of Rights*, 11–14; Speech of 8 June 1789, *PJM*, 12:197–210; Labunski, *James Madison and the Struggle for the Bill of Rights*, 198–200.

84. Speech of 8 June 1789, *PJM*, 12:208–10. See generally Rakove, *Original Meanings*, 330–38.

85. Tench Coxe to JM, 18 June 1789, *PJM*, 12:239–41; Edward Stevens to JM, 25 June 1789, ibid., 12:261; Edmund Randolph to JM, 30 June 1789, ibid., 12:273–74; Archibald Stuart to JM, 31 July 1789, ibid., 12:319–20.

86. John Dawson to JM, 28 June 1789, ibid., 12:263–65; Reverend James Madison to JM, 15 August 1789, ibid., 12:337–38; George Mason to John Mason, 31 July 1789, Rutland, *The Papers of George Mason*, 3:1162–68; George Mason to Samuel Griffin, 8 September 1789, ibid., 3:1170–73.

87. George Washington to JM, circa 31 May 1789, *PJM*, 12:191; William R. Davie to JM, 10 June 1789, ibid., 12:210–12; Hugh Williamson to JM, 2 July 1789, ibid., 12:274–75; Benjamin Hawkins to JM, 3 July 1789, ibid., 12:275–76. See generally Bowling, "'A Tub to the Whale.'"

88. Veit et al., *Creating the Bill of Rights*, 5–11; Schwartz, *The Roots of the Bill of Rights*, 5:1054–61, 1122–26.

89. Veit et al., *Creating the Bill of Rights*, 150–59, 180, 199–201; Schwartz, *The Roots of the Bill of Rights*, 5:1114–20; Labunski, *James Madison and the Struggle for the Bill of Rights*, 230–31.

90. Rutland, *The Birth of the Bill of Rights*, 197–98; Veit et al., *Creating the Bill of Rights*, 12, 158–59; Speech of 15 August 1789, *PJM*, 12:339; Labunski, *James Madison and the Struggle for the Bill of Rights*, 230–31; Brant, *James Madison*, 3:269–71.

91. JM to Richard Peters, 19 August 1789, *PJM*, 12:346–48; JM to Edmund Randolph, 21 August 1789, ibid., 12:348–49.

92. Speech of 17 August 1789, ibid., 12:344; Veit et al., *Creating the Bill of Rights*, 5–11; Schwartz, *The Roots of the Bill of Rights*, 5:1146–59; Brant, *James Madison*, 3:275.

93. Billings, "'That All Men Are Born Equally Free and Independent.'"

94. Veit et al., *Creating the Bill of Rights*, xvi; Labunski, *James Madison and the Struggle for the Bill of Rights*, 257–58; Edward Carrington to JM, 9 September 1789, *PJM*, 12:392–94; Goldwin, *From Parchment to Power*, 175; Rutland, *The Birth of the Bill of Rights*, 210; Levy, *Origins of the Bill of Rights*, 43.

CHAPTER FOUR

1. Jefferson quoted in Hofstadter, *The Idea of a Party System*, 122–23. See also ibid., 11–24. Abigail Adams quoted in Burstein and Isenberg, *Madison and Jefferson*, 418.

2. Hofstadter, *The Idea of a Party System*, 80–85, 118–19; Elkins and McKitrick, *The Age of Federalism*, 484–88; Wilentz, *The Rise of American Democracy*, 52–53.

3. Hofstadter, *The Idea of a Party System*, 88–89; Rakove, *James Madison and the Creation of the American Republic*, 107–21; Rutland, *James Madison, the Founding Father*, 140; Cunningham, *The Jeffersonian Republicans*, 54–55; Sharp, *American Politics in the Early Republic*, 72–74, 90–91.

4. JM to Thomas Jefferson, 8 August 1791, *PJM*, 14:69–70; Memorandum on a Discussion of the President's Retirement, circa 5 May 1792, ibid., 14:299–303; *National Gazette*,

20 December 1792, ibid., 14:426–27; Cunningham, *The Jeffersonian Republicans*, 75–76; Elkins and McKitrick, *The Age of Federalism*, 263–68; Sharp, *American Politics in the Early Republic*, 1–12.

5. Memorandum from John Taylor, 11 May 1794, *PJM*, 15:328–31; Edmund Randolph to JM, 1 November 1795, ibid., 16:117–18.

6. Bell, *Party and Faction in American Politics*, 98; Wilentz, *The Rise of American Democracy*, 50–51; Sharp, *American Politics in the Early Republic*, 58–60; Cunningham, *The Jeffersonian Republicans*, 256. Party labels remained in flux. Although historians usually refer to Madison's faction as the Republican Party, which should not be confused with its modern namesake, the terms *Republican*, *Democrat*, and *Democratic-Republican* were sometimes used interchangeably. See Jonathan Dayton to JM, circa 17 September 1812, *PJM, PS*, 5:325–28; and JM to William Eustis, 22 May 1823, *WJM*, 9:135–37.

7. Fischer, "Patterns of Partisan Allegiance"; Henderson, "The Continental Congress and the Genesis of Parties"; Charles, *The Origins of the American Party System*, 21–31; Nichols, *The Invention of American Political Parties*, 167–69.

8. Cunningham, *The Jeffersonian Republicans*, 22–23; Buel, *Securing the Revolution*, 1–6; Risjord and DenBoer, "The Evolution of Political Parties in Virginia"; Sharp, *American Politics in the Early Republic*, 44–47.

9. Wilentz, *The Rise of American Democracy*, 41–42; Sharp, *American Politics in the Early Republic*, 100–104.

10. Cunningham, *The Jeffersonian Republicans*, 9–19, 63–87; Charles, *The Origins of the American Party System*, 81–84; Hofstadter, *The Idea of a Party System*, 54.

11. Ferguson, "The Nationalists of 1781–1783"; Elkins and McKitrick, *The Age of Federalism*, 117–23; Banning, *The Sacred Fire of Liberty*, 309–16; Rakove, *James Madison and the Creation of the American Republic*, 138–39.

12. Speech of 11 February 1790, *PJM*, 13:34–39.

13. Speech of 18 February 1790, ibid., 13:47–56; Elkins and McKitrick, *The Age of Federalism*, 117.

14. Speech of 24 February 1790, *PJM*, 13:60–62.

15. Ferguson, "The Nationalists of 1781–1783," 123.

16. John Nicholson to JM, 17 February 1790, *PJM*, 13:45; Charles, *The Origins of the American Party System*, 17–18.

17. George Nicholas to JM, 3 May 1790, *PJM*, 13:186–87; Edmund Randolph to JM, 20 May 1790, ibid., 13:224–25; Beverly Randolph to JM, 26 May 1790, ibid., 13:230; John Dawson to JM, 4 July 1790, ibid., 13:262–63.

18. Joseph Jones to JM, 26 March 1790, ibid., 13:123–24; Edward Carrington to JM, 27 March 1790, ibid., 13:124–27; Henry Lee to JM, 13 April 1790, ibid., 13:147–48.

19. Banning, *The Sacred Fire of Liberty*, 316; Elkins and McKitrick, *The Age of Federalism*, 26–28, 68–71, 136–53; Charles, *The Origins of the American Party System*, 45; Brant, *James Madison*, 3:301–5; McCoy, *The Elusive Republic*, 172–78.

20. JM to Thomas Jefferson, 24 January 1790, *PJM*, 13:3–5.

21. Brant, *James Madison*, 3:351. Sedgwick quoted in Ketcham, *James Madison*, 311. Madison could argue that Hamilton had been the one who had changed. The New Yorker, like Madison, had supposedly supported constitutional reform in part to establish a national government strong enough to protect American trade from British mercantile polices. His

new duties as secretary of the treasury, according to one theory, led him to favor appeasement of Great Britain. See Schwarz, "The Great Divergence Reconsidered."

22. JM to Alexander Hamilton, 19 November 1789, *PJM*, 12:449–51; Banning, *The Sacred Fire of Liberty*, 294–97; Elkins and McKitrick, *The Age of Federalism*, 107–14.

23. Hamilton quoted in Elkins and McKitrick, *The Age of Federalism*, 125. See also Wood, *Revolutionary Characters*, 125–39; and Sharp, *American Politics in the Early Republic*, 214–17, 234–35.

24. JM to JM Sr., 27 February 1790, *PJM*, 13:66–67; Sharp, *American Politics in the Early Republic*, 35–41.

25. JM to Edmund Pendleton, 4 March 1790, *PJM*, 13:85–87; JM to Edmund Pendleton, 22 June 1790, ibid., 13:252–53; Banning, *The Sacred Fire of Liberty*, 322–24.

26. Editorial Note, *PJM*, 13:243; JM to JM Sr., 31 July 1790, ibid., 13:284–85.

27. Speech of 3 September 1789, ibid., 12:369–70; Benjamin Rush to JM, 27 February 1790, ibid., 13:67–70; Henry Lee to JM, 4 March 1790, ibid., 13:87–91; JM to Benjamin Rush, 7 March 1790, ibid., 13:93–94.

28. See Rutland, *James Madison, the Founding Father*, 88–89.

29. Speech of 2 February 1791, *PJM*, 13:372–82.

30. Elkins and McKitrick, *The Age of Federalism*, 224–42; Banning, *The Sacred Fire of Liberty*, 327–31; Draft Veto, 21 February 1791, *PJM*, 13:395–96; JM to Edward Carrington, 26 February 1791, ibid., 13:398–400.

31. JM to Thomas Jefferson, 10 July 1791, *PJM*, 14:42–44.

32. JM to Thomas Jefferson, 24 July 1791, ibid., 14:52–54; JM to Edmund Randolph, 13 September 1792, ibid., 14:364–65; Pasley, *"The Tyranny of Printers,"* 64–66.

33. Smith quoted in *PJM*, 14:396–401. See also Thomas Jefferson to JM, 21 June 1792, ibid., 14:324–25; Thomas Jefferson to JM, 29 June 1792, ibid., 14:333–34; John Beckley to JM, 10 September 1792, ibid., 14:361–63; and JM to Benjamin Rush, 1 October 1792, ibid., 14:372–73.

34. Speech of 24 March 1792, ibid., 14:262; Memorandum by JM, 9 May 1792, ibid., 14:303; George Washington to JM, 20 May 1792, ibid., 14:310–12; JM to George Washington, 20 June 1792, ibid., 14:319–24.

35. Editorial Note, ibid., 14:110–12; *National Gazette*, circa 19 December 1791, ibid., 14:170; *National Gazette*, 18 February 1792, ibid., 14:233–34; *National Gazette*, 3 December 1791, ibid., 14:137–39; *National Gazette*, 4 February 1792, ibid., 14:217–19.

36. *National Gazette*, 3 March 1792, ibid., 14:244–46; *National Gazette*, 20 March 1792, ibid., 14:257–59; *National Gazette*, 27 March 1792, ibid., 14:266–68. Jefferson actually referred to "those who labour in the earth." Peterson, *The Portable Thomas Jefferson*, 217.

37. *National Gazette*, 22 September 1792, *PJM*, 14:370–72.

38. Maclay quoted in Brant, *James Madison*, 3:298–99.

39. Morison, *A Concise History of the American Republic*, 1:160.

40. Elkins and McKitrick, *The Age of Federalism*, 79.

41. See generally ibid., 68–71, 130–31, 376–87.

42. Speech of 7 December 1791, *PJM*, 14:142–43; Speech of 6 February 1792, ibid., 14:220–24; JM to Edmund Pendleton, 21 February 1792, ibid., 14:235–36; Speech of 13 November 1792, ibid., 14:405–7; Speech of 19 November 1792, ibid., 14:413–17; ibid., 15:341 (n. 2).

43. Samuel Dexter Jr. to JM, 3 February 1795, ibid., 15:462–63; JM to Samuel Dexter Jr., 5 February 1795, ibid., 15:466; Wood, *Revolutionary Characters*, 142–72.

44. Brant, *James Madison*, 3:330–31; Elkins and McKitrick, *The Age of Federalism*, 229–34.

45. George Lee Turberville to JM, 28 January 1793, *PJM*, 14:444–45; Ketcham, *James Madison*, 369.

46. Walter Jones to JM, 15 September 1789, *PJM*, 12:403–4; Elkins and McKitrick, *The Age of Federalism*, 88–92. See generally McCoy, *The Elusive Republic*.

47. *PJM*, 13:220–21; Joseph Jones to JM, 2 March 1792, ibid., 14:243–44; Joseph Jones to JM, 6 April 1792, ibid., 14:279–80; Elkins and McKitrick, *The Age of Federalism*, 279–80.

48. *National Gazette*, 27 March 1792, *PJM*, 14:266–68; Ketcham, *James Madison*, 319–23; Ellis, *American Creation*, 174–78; Trees, *The Founding Fathers and the Politics of Character*, 107–27.

49. See generally Read, *Power versus Liberty*, 2–30.

50. JM to Tench Coxe, 28 March 1790, *PJM*, 13:128–29.

51. Editorial Note, ibid., 14:126–27; Speech of 22 March 1792, ibid., 14:261–63; JM to Henry Lee, 28 March 1792, ibid., 14:269–70.

52. Editorial Note, ibid., 15:145–54; Speech of 1 March 1793, ibid., 14:455–69; JM to George Nicholas, 15 March 1793, ibid., 14:472–73; Detached Memorandum, *JMW*, 752–54; Thomas Jefferson to JM, circa 21–27 February 1793, *ROL*, 2:763–64; Burstein and Isenberg, *Madison and Jefferson*, 267; Schultz, *James Madison*, 104. Federalists defeated in 1793 included Alexander White of Virginia, whom Madison had persuaded to vote for assumption as part of the Compromise of 1790. See JM to Thomas Jefferson, 12 April 1793, *PJM*, 15:6–9.

53. Thomas Jefferson to JM, 28 August 1789, *PJM*, 12:360–65; JM to Edmund Pendleton, 18 December 1791, ibid., 14:156–57; George Lee Turberville to JM, 28 January 1793, ibid., 14:444–45; James Monroe to JM, 18 December 1794, ibid., 15:416–17.

54. JM to George Nicholas, 15 March 1793, ibid., 14:472–73; Editorial Note, ibid., 15:76–80.

55. Speech of 13 May 1790, ibid., 13:211–15; Speech of 14 May 1790, ibid., 13:216–20; Speech of 25 June 1790, ibid., 13:255–57; Speech of 14 January 1794, ibid., 15:182–200; Speech of 30 January 1794, ibid., 15:210–24; Speech of 31 January 1794, ibid., 15:224–43.

56. Proclamation of Neutrality, 22 April 1793, in Rhodehamel, *George Washington, Writings*, 840; JM to Thomas Jefferson, 13 June 1793, *PJM*, 15:28–30; JM to Thomas Jefferson, 19 June 1793, ibid., 15:33–34; Thomas Jefferson to JM, 7 July 1793, ibid., 15:43.

57. JM to Thomas Jefferson, 18 July 1793, *PJM*, 15:44–45; Thomas Jefferson to JM, 3 August 1793, ibid., 15:50–51; Thomas Jefferson to JM, 11 August 1793, ibid., 15:56–69; Editorial Note, ibid., 15:64–66; JM to Archibald Stuart, 1 September 1793, ibid., 15:87–88.

58. *Helvidius No. 4*, 14 September 1793, ibid., 15:106–10; JM to Thomas Jefferson, 30 July 1793, ibid., 15:48–49; Ketcham, *James Madison*, 347–48.

59. Leibiger, *Founding Friendship*, 178; Editorial Note, *PJM*, 15:145–54; Speech of 3 January 1794, ibid., 15:167–71; JM to Thomas Jefferson, 3 April 1794, ibid., 15:301–2.

60. JM to Thomas Jefferson, 2 March 1794, ibid., 15:269–71.

61. "Political Observations," 20 April 1795, ibid., 15:511–34; ibid., 16:12 (n. 2).

62. Address to the President, 27 November 1794, ibid., 15:390–93; JM to Thomas Jeffer-

son, 30 November 1794, ibid., 15:396–98; JM to James Monroe, 4 December 1794, ibid., 15:405–9; Gales, *Annals of Congress*, 2:1933–34.

63. JM to Thomas Jefferson, 21 December 1794, *PJM*, 15:419–21.

64. Gerard Clarfield, "Jay's Treaty," *JMAN*, 209–10; Ketcham, *James Madison*, 351–65; Brant, *James Madison*, 3:424–25; Rakove, *James Madison and the Creation of the American Republic*, 139–45. For criticism of the Jay Treaty, see Banning, *The Sacred Fire of Liberty*, 374–84; Charles, *The Origins of the American Party System*, 118–19; and Wilentz, *The Rise of American Democracy*, 67–68. More sympathetic are Elkins and McKitrick, *The Age of Federalism*, 410–14; and Ellis, *American Creation*, 194–201. James Roger Sharp, by contrast, concludes that "it is difficult to see why it was so controversial." *American Politics in the Early Republic*, 117.

65. Pierce Butler to JM, 12 June 1795, *PJM*, 16:14–16; James Monroe to JM, 30 June 1795, ibid., 16:32–34; Robert R. Livingston to JM, 6 July 1795, ibid., 16:34–36; Reverend James Madison to JM, 25 July 1795, ibid., 16:40–41; JM to James Monroe, 20 December 1795, ibid., 16:168–71.

66. Editorial Note, ibid., 16:62–69; Petition to the General Assembly of the Commonwealth of Virginia, 12 October 1795, ibid., 16:95–104.

67. Speech of 7 March 1796, ibid., 16:254–55; JM to Thomas Jefferson, 4 April 1796, ibid., 16:285–87; Ketcham, *James Madison*, 358–59.

68. Speech of 6 April 1796, *PJM*, 16:290–301.

69. Speech of 15 April 1796, ibid., 16:313–27.

70. JM to Thomas Jefferson, 1 May 1796, ibid., 16:342–43.

71. JM to James Monroe, 20 December 1795, ibid., 16:168–71; JM to Thomas Jefferson, 23 April 1796, ibid., 16:335–36; JM to Hubbard Taylor, 10 May 1796, ibid., 16:353–54; Charles, *The Origins of the American Party System*, 47; Wills, *James Madison*, 43.

72. Clarfield, "Jay's Treaty," *JMAN*, 211.

73. Charles, *The Origins of the American Party System*, 99; Cunningham, *The Jeffersonian Republicans*, 82–88; Sharp, *American Politics in the Early Republic*, 133–35; Editorial Note, *PJM*, 16:142–43. See generally Estes, *The Jay Treaty Debate, Public Opinion, and the Development of American Political Culture*.

74. JM to Robert R. Livingston, 10 August 1795, *PJM*, 16:46–49.

75. JM to James Monroe, 18 April 1796, ibid., 16:332–34; Leibiger, *Founding Friendship*, 154–55, 189–209.

76. Smith and Livingston quoted in Ketcham, *James Madison*, 360. See also Bell, *Party and Faction in American Politics*, 55–57, 146–48.

77. JM to James Monroe, 7 April 1796, *PJM*, 16:301–4; JM to James Monroe, 14 May 1796, ibid., 16:356–59; JM to Thomas Jefferson, 22 May 1796, ibid., 16:363–65.

78. Thomas Jefferson to JM, 28 December 1794, ibid., 15:426–29; JM to Thomas Jefferson, 23 March 1795, ibid., 15:493–94; Thomas Jefferson to JM, 27 April 1795, ibid., 16:1–3; JM to James Monroe, 26 February 1796, ibid., 16:232–34; Cunningham, *The Jeffersonian Republicans*, 107.

79. JM to James Monroe, 29 September 1796, *PJM*, 16:403–5; Thomas Jefferson to JM, 17 December 1796, ibid., 16:431–32.

80. JM to Thomas Jefferson, 19 December 1796, ibid., 16:432–34; JM to Thomas Jefferson, 15 January 1797, ibid., 16:455–57; Thomas Jefferson to JM, 30 January 1797, ibid.,

16:479–80; Banning, *The Sacred Fire of Liberty*, 341; Sharp, *American Politics in the Early Republic*, 143–59, Ellis, *Passionate Sage*, 29–31.

81. Sharp, *American Politics in the Early Republic*, 164–65.

82. See generally Deconde, *The Quasi-War*; and Stinchcombe, *The XYZ Affair*.

83. Thomas Jefferson to JM, 10 May 1798, *PJM*, 17:128–30; Thomas Jefferson to JM, 17 May 1798, ibid., 17:132–33; Henry Tazewell to JM, 28 June 1798, ibid., 17:158–59.

84. JM to Thomas Jefferson, 15 April 1798, ibid., 17:112–15; JM to Thomas Jefferson, 29 April 1798, ibid., 17:122–23.

85. JM to Thomas Jefferson, circa 18 February 1798, ibid., 17:82–83; JM to Thomas Jefferson, 21 January 1798, ibid., 17:69–71; JM to Thomas Jefferson, 2 April 1798, ibid., 17:104–5; Wills, *James Madison*, 48. By the time Washington left office, Madison was convinced the president was "completely in the snares of the British faction." See JM to James Monroe, 29 September 1796, *PJM*, 16:403–5. For an argument for Hamilton's moderation, see Coleman, "'A Second Bounaparty?'"

86. JM to Thomas Jefferson, 20 May 1798, *PJM*, 17:133; Wilentz, *The Rise of American Democracy*, 81; James Morton Smith, "Alien and Sedition Acts of 1798," *JMAN*, 10; Bradburn, "A Clamor in the Public Mind."

87. Editorial Note, *PJM*, 17:185–91; Thomas Jefferson to JM, 17 November 1798, ibid., 17:175–81; Sharp, *American Politics in the Early Republic*, 187–200, 223–24; Rakove, *James Madison and the Creation of the American Republic*, 151–54.

88. Virginia Resolutions, 21 December 1798, *JMW*, 589–91; Rosen, *American Compact*, 140–41; Brant, *James Madison*, 3:463, 470–71; Elkins and McKitrick, *The Age of Federalism*, 719–26; Banning, *The Sacred Fire of Liberty*, 387–90.

89. "Foreign Influence," 23 January 1799, *PJM*, 17:214–20; "Political Reflections," 23 February 1799, ibid., 17:237–43.

90. Speech of 6 December 1799, ibid., 17:286–87; JM to Thomas Jefferson, 29 December 1799, ibid., 17:297–99; Editorial Note, ibid., 17:303–7.

91. "Report of 1800," 7 January 1800, ibid., 17:307–31; Banning, *The Sacred Fire of Liberty*, 387–91; Ketcham, *James Madison*, 396–403.

92. Editorial Note, *PJM*, 17:303–7; Elkins and McKitrick, *The Age of Federalism*, 719–26.

93. James Monroe to JM, 4 June 1800, *PJM*, 17:391; Editorial Note, ibid., 17:415–17; Hofstadter, *The Idea of a Party System*, 111–12; Sharp, *American Politics in the Early Republic*, 228–47; Schultz, *James Madison*, 137.

94. David Gelston to JM, 21 November 1800, *PJM*, 17:438; Cunningham, "The Election of 1800."

95. John Dawson to JM, 4 May 1800, *PJM*, 17:386.

96. JM to Thomas Jefferson, 10 January 1801, ibid., 17:453; Thomas Jefferson to JM, 18 February 1801, ibid., 17:467–68; Sharp, *The Deadlocked Election of 1800*, 133–39.

97. Rutland, *James Madison, the Founding Father*, 168. Hamilton quoted in Sharp, *American Politics in the Early Republic*, 259.

CHAPTER FIVE

1. Martha Bland to Mrs. St. George Tucker, 30 March 1781, *PJM*, 2:196 (n. 3). Coles quoted in Ketcham, *James Madison*, 407. For a typical report of Madison's health problems,

see JM to Levi Lincoln, 25 July 1801, *PJM, SS*, 1:475–76. John Kaminski believes that what Madison referred to as "bilious lax" would today be diagnosed as irritable bowel syndrome. Kaminski, *The Great Virginia Triumvirate*, 154–55.

2. Rutland, *The Presidency of James Madison*, 21. George Tucker quoted in Brant, *James Madison*, 4:47. Margaret Bayard Smith quoted in Brant, *The Fourth President*, 59. See also Perkins, *Prologue to War*, 42–44; and Foster, *Jeffersonian America*, 155.

3. Ketcham, *James Madison*, 272; Brant, *James Madison*, 2:341, 3:343; Burstein and Isenberg, *Madison and Jefferson*, 192–93.

4. Ketcham, *James Madison*, 108–11; Brant, *James Madison*, 2:158; Thomas Jefferson to JM, 14 April 1783, *PJM*, 6:459–60.

5. JM to Thomas Jefferson, 22 April 1783, *PJM*, 6:481–83; ibid., 6:498 (n. 2).

6. JM to Thomas Jefferson, 11 August 1783, ibid., 7:268–72; Thomas Jefferson to JM, 31 August 1783, ibid., 7:298–99.

7. Rutland, *James Madison, the Founding Father*, 67–68; *PJM*, 6:182 (n. 28); ibid., 6:482 (n. 7).

8. On Dolley Madison's early years, see Allgor, *A Perfect Union*, 15–21; and Cote, *Strength and Honor*, 15–41.

9. Allgor, *A Perfect Union*, 19; Cote, *Strength and Honor*, ix–x.

10. Allgor, *A Perfect Union*, 22–26; *SLDPM*, 10–17.

11. Will of Dolley Payne Todd, 13 May 1794, *SLDPM*, 26–27; Catherine Coles to Dolley Payne Todd, 1 June 1794, ibid., 27–28; Ketcham, *James Madison*, 278–79; Allgor, *A Perfect Union*, 27–33.

12. William W. Wilkins to Dolley Payne Todd, 22 August 1794, *SLDPM*, 29–31; Dolley Payne Todd to Eliza Collins Lee, 16 September 1794, ibid., 31–32.

13. Ibid., 17; Editorial Note, *PJM*, 15:152; JM to JM Sr., 14 December 1794, ibid., 15:414–15; John Swanwick to JM, 14 June 1795, ibid., 16:21–23.

14. Brant, *James Madison*, 4:41–42; Allgor, *A Perfect Union*, 41–59.

15. Foster, *Jeffersonian America*, 104.

16. Foster quoted in Brant, *James Madison*, 4:163. See also Allgor, *A Perfect Union*, 69.

17. Thomas Jefferson to JM, 12 March 1801, *PJM, SS*, 1:12–13; Allgor, *Parlor Politics*, 17–27, 31; Morris, *The Forging of the Union*, 190–91. See generally Zagarri, *Revolutionary Backlash*.

18. Foster quoted in *SLDPM*, 38. See also Allgor, *A Perfect Union*, 63–77; Ketcham, *James Madison*, 408–49; and *ROL*, 3:1412.

19. DM to JM, 1 November 1805, *SLDPM*, 70.

20. DM to Anna Cutts, 22 May 1805, ibid., 60–61; Allgor, *A Perfect Union*, 247–48. See generally ibid., 49–61.

21. Martha Jefferson Randolph to DM, 15 January 1808, *SLDPM*, 83–84; Mary Randolph to DM, 10 February 1808, ibid., 84; Allgor, *A Perfect Union*, 6–7, 55, 233–46.

22. Peder Blicherolsen to JM, 21 June 1803, *PJM, SS*, 5:109–10; Allgor, *A Perfect Union*, 247–48, 251.

23. DM to Anna Cutts, May–June 1804, *SLDPM*, 57–58; JM to DM, 31 October 1805, ibid., 69–70; Allgor, *A Perfect Union*, 181.

24. DM to Anna Cutts, 29 July 1805, *SLDPM*, 62–63; DM to Anna Cutts, 19 August 1805,

ibid., 63–64; DM to Eliza Collins Lee, 26 February 1808, ibid., 84–85; Allgor, *A Perfect Union*, 108–20.

25. Brant, *James Madison*, 4:241–42.

26. Allgor, *Parlor Politics*, 35–38.

27. Rufus King to JM, 30 April 1802, *PJM, SS*, 3:118–19; James Monroe to JM, 18 September 1808, ibid., 5:446.

28. James Monroe to JM, 3 March 1804, ibid., 6:536–39; Lester, *Anthony Merry Redivivus*, 1–20; Allgor, *A Perfect Union*, 92–101; Ketcham, *James Madison*, 432–33.

29. Allgor, *Parlor Politics*, 37–38; Foster, *Jeffersonian America*, 52. For a view more favorable to the administration, see Rutland, *James Madison, the Founding Father*, 179.

30. JM to James Monroe, 19 January 1804, *PJM, SS*, 6:361–66; Lester, *Anthony Merry Redivivus*, 36; Allgor, *Parlor Politics*, 38–39.

31. JM to James Monroe, 16 February 1804, *PJM, SS*, 6:484–86; Allgor, *Parlor Politics*, 35–37; Allgor, *A Perfect Union*, 92–101. Merry quoted in Lester, *Anthony Merry Redivivus*, 36.

32. DM to Anna Cutts, 25 May 1804, *SLDPM*, 56–57; DM to Anna Cutts, 4 June 1805, ibid., 61–62.

33. JM to Rufus King, 18 December 1803, *PJM, SS*, 6:186–87; Rufus King to JM, 22 December 1803, ibid., 6:197–99; JM to James Monroe, 19 January 1804, ibid., 6:361–66.

34. Ibid., 7:xxiii; Anthony Merry to JM, 4 May 1804, ibid., 7:150–52; Anthony Merry to JM, 20 May 1804, ibid., 7:233–34; JM to Anthony Merry, 22 May 1804, ibid., 7:238–40; JM to James Monroe, 21 July 1804, ibid., 7:498–99; Foster, *Jeffersonian America*, 22–23.

35. James Monroe to JM, 26 April 1804, *PJM, SS*, 7:114–16; James Monroe to JM, 28 June 1804, ibid., 7:384–90; James Monroe to JM, 1 July 1804, ibid., 7:402–5; Lester, *Anthony Merry Redivivus*, 37.

36. JM to Thomas Jefferson, 28 August 1804, *PJM, SS*, 7:645; JM to James Monroe, 12 September 1804, ibid., 8:35–36; Lester, *Anthony Merry Redivivus*, 76–87.

37. Noah Webster to JM, 18 July 1801, *PJM, SS*, 1:436; Charles Pinckney to JM, 22 July 1801, ibid., 1:458–59; Cunningham, *The Process of Government under Jefferson*, 87–88; Ketcham, *James Madison*, 410–14.

38. Brant, *James Madison*, 4:48–49; Rutland, *James Madison, the Founding Father*, 176–77; White, *The Jeffersonians*, 189–90.

39. Brant, *James Madison*, 4:321; Jacob Wagner to JM, 30 April 1802, *PJM, SS*, 3:168.

40. Cunningham, *The Process of Government under Jefferson*, 87–97.

41. Ibid.; JM to Joseph Jones, 14 July 1804, *PJM, SS*, 7:449; Editorial Notes, ibid., 2:xxv–xxxiii, 4:xxv–xxix, and 6:xiii–xxxi.

42. JM to Thomas Jefferson, 11 August 1802, ibid., 3:473; JM to Thomas Jefferson, 15 May 1808, *ROL*, 3:1519–20; Brant, *James Madison*, 4:43–44, 303–4; Rutland, *James Madison, the Founding Father*, 169.

43. Meyers, *The Mind of the Founder*, 277–78; JM to John Armstrong, 6 June 1805, *WJM*, 7:183–90; JM to William Jarvis, 17 December 1802, *PJM, SS*, 4:196; Rutland, *James Madison, the Founding Father*, 173; Rakove, *James Madison and the Creation of the American Republic*, 161.

44. Ketcham, *James Madison*, 469–73; Brant, *James Madison*, 4:274–76.

45. William Eaton to Secretary of State, 10 April 1801, *PJM, SS*, 1:78–81; William Eaton to JM, 25 May 1801, ibid., 1:227; John Quincy Adams to JM, 25 June 1801, ibid., 1:348–49; William Eaton to JM, 28 June 1801, ibid., 1:355–56; James Leander Cathcart to JM, 2 July 1801, ibid., 1:370–72; JM to Richard O'Brien, 30 March 1803, ibid., 4:459–60; James Leander Cathcart to JM, 15 December 1803, ibid., 6:172–74.

46. Editorial Note, ibid., 1:197–99; JM to James Leander Cathcart, 18 April 1802, ibid., 3:135–36; JM to James Leander Cathcart, 10 May 1802, ibid., 3:202; JM to James Leander Cathcart, 9 April 1803, ibid., 4:494–96.

47. Ebenezer Stevens to JM, 24 June 1801, ibid., 1:347–48; George Davis to JM, 17 November 1803, ibid., 6:58–59; Tobias Lear to JM, 7 May 1804, ibid., 7:171–85.

48. Thomas Jefferson to JM, 27 April 1804, ibid., 7:116–18; JM to Tobias Lear, 6 June 1804, ibid., 7:287–91; Tina H. Sheller, "Barbary States," *JMAN*, 30–31; Brant, *James Madison*, 4:305–9.

49. JM to Robert R. Livingston, 11 July 1801, *PJM, SS*, 1:402–4. See Brant, *James Madison*, 4:93; and Rutland, *James Madison, the Founding Father*, 175.

50. Louis-André Pichon to JM, 9 March 1804, *PJM, SS*, 6:569–73; Louis-André Pichon to JM, 7 May 1804, ibid., 7:185–89; Samuel Smith to JM, 17 May 1804, ibid., 7:225–26. For a view from Boston that is similar to Smith's, see Richard Cutts to JM, 8 June 1804, ibid., 7:296–97.

51. Ketcham, *James Madison*, 416–17; Tina H. Sheller, "Santo Domingo," *JMAN*, 373.

52. JM to Charles Pinckney, 9 June 1801, *PJM, SS*, 1:273–79; ibid., 1:403 (n. 1); JM to Robert R. Livingston, 28 September 1801, ibid., 2:142–47; Robert R. Livingston to JM, 24 March 1802, ibid., 3:25–30; Charles Pinckney to JM, 1 July 1802, ibid., 3:353–55; Ketcham, *James Madison*, 417–26.

53. JM to Charles Pinckney, 25 September 1801, *PJM, SS*, 2:131–32; JM to Robert R. Livingston, 18 May 1802, ibid., 3:174–77.

54. William E. Hulings to JM, 18 October 1802, ibid., 4:30; JM to Carlos Martínez de Yrujo, 25 November 1802, ibid., 4:139–40; JM to James Monroe and Robert R. Livingston, 2 March 1803, ibid., 4:364–79; James Monroe to JM, 7 March 1803, ibid., 4:395–97; Thomas McKean Thompson to JM, 21 March 1803, ibid., 4:440.

55. Brant, *James Madison*, 4:133–34; Robert R. Livingston to JM, 30 July 1802, *PJM, SS*, 3:443–45; Robert R. Livingston to JM, 20 May 1803, ibid., 5:18–20; Robert R. Livingston and James Monroe to JM, 7 June 1803, ibid., 5:66–72.

56. Brant, *James Madison*, 4:66; JM to Charles Pinckney, 11 May 1802, *PJM, SS*, 3:215–16; James Monroe to JM, 14 May 1803, ibid., 4:610–16; JM to Robert R. Livingston and James Monroe, 29 July 1803, *JMW*, 671–73.

57. Robert R. Livingston to JM, 10 August 1802, *PJM, SS*, 3:467–70; Robert R. Livingston to JM, 13 February 1804, ibid., 6:471–72.

58. Rakove, *James Madison and the Creation of the American Republic*, 163–65; Brant, *James Madison*, 4:141–43, 156; Proposed Constitutional Amendment, circa 9 July 1803, *PJM, SS*, 5:156; Thomas Jefferson to JM, 18 August 1803, ibid., 5:323–24.

59. JM to Robert R. Livingston, 17 December 1802, ibid., 4:197–98; JM to James Monroe and Robert R. Livingston, 2 March 1803, ibid., 4:364–79; JM to James Monroe and Robert R. Livingston, 18 April 1803, ibid., 4:527–32; JM to James Monroe, 25 June 1803,

ibid., 5:117–19; Thomas Jefferson to JM, 17 July 1803, ibid., 5:191; JM to William C. C. Claiborne, 31 October 1803, ibid., 5:589–92.

60. Carlos Martínez de Yrujo to JM, 4 September 1803, ibid., 5:378–79; JM to Thomas Jefferson, 12 September 1803, ibid., 5:403; Sylvanus Burke to JM, 2 February 1804, ibid., 6:424–25; Robert R. Livingston to JM, 31 March 1804, ibid., 6:648–55; Charles Pinckney to JM, 20 July 1804, ibid., 7:486.

61. Carlos Martínez de Yrujo to JM, 7 March 1804, ibid., 6:557–63; JM to Charles Pinckney, 10 April 1804, ibid., 7:28–31; Brant, *James Madison*, 4:190–98.

62. JM to James Monroe, 15 April 1804, *PJM, SS,* 7:51–61; Thomas Jefferson to JM, 11 October 1805, *ROL,* 3:1391; Editorial Notes, ibid., 3:1354–55 and 1404–6; Spivak, *Jefferson's English Crisis,* 49; Tucker and Hendrickson, *Empire of Liberty,* 183–87.

63. Thomas Jefferson to JM, 9 July 1806, *ROL,* 3:1426–27; Thomas Jefferson to JM, 16 August 1807, ibid., 3:1485–86; JM to James Bowdoin, 25 May 1807, Bowdoin-Temple Collection, Massachusetts Historical Society, Boston, Mass.; JM to John Armstrong and James Bowdoin, 15 July 1807, *WJM,* 7:460–62; Tucker and Hendrickson, *Empire of Liberty,* 180.

64. JM to Rufus King, 24 July 1801, *PJM, SS,* 1:464–70; George W. Erving to JM, 6 June 1803, ibid., 5:63–64; Thomas Jefferson to JM, 24 August 1803, ibid., 5:339–41; JM to the Speaker of the House, 19 January 1805, ibid., 8:486–87; Perkins, *Prologue to War,* 85–86.

65. Albert Gallatin to JM, 13 April 1807, Rives Collection, JMP; JM to Thomas Jefferson, 17 April 1807, *ROL,* 3:1467–68; Thomas Jefferson to JM, 21 April 1807, ibid., 3:1469–70.

66. JM to Rufus King, 10 December 1801, *PJM, SS,* 2:299; JM to Rufus King, 22 December 1801, ibid., 2:331–36; Rutland, *James Madison, the Founding Father,* 182–86.

67. Donald R. Hickey, "Rule of 1756," *JMAN,* 368; JM to Edward Thornton, 27 October 1803, *PJM, SS,* 5:580–82.

68. Plumer quoted in Rutland, *James Madison, the Founding Father,* 185. See also Brant, *James Madison,* 4:297–301; JM to James Monroe, 24 September 1805, *WJM,* 7:176–83; and "An Examination of the British Doctrine" (1806), ibid., 7:204–375.

69. Perkins, *Prologue to War,* 113; JM to James Monroe and William Pinkney, 17 May 1806, *WJM,* 7:375–95; JM to Thomas Jefferson, 22 September 1806, *ROL,* 3:1439–40; Thomas Jefferson to JM, 23 September 1806, ibid., 3:1440; Ketcham, *James Madison,* 448–52; Rakove, *James Madison and the Creation of the American Republic,* 166–70; Rutland, *James Madison, the Founding Father,* 186–89.

70. See generally Hickey, "The Monroe-Pinkney Treaty of 1806."

71. Hickey, "The Monroe-Pinkney Treaty," 82; JM to James Monroe and William Pinkney, 3 February 1807, *WJM,* 7:395–404; Samuel Smith to JM, 3 April 1807, Samuel Smith Papers, LC; James Monroe to John Taylor, 9 January 1809, Hamilton, *The Writings of James Monroe,* 5:87–90; Perkins, *Prologue to War,* 132–39, 188. Spivak, *Jefferson's English Crisis,* 57–62, is somewhat more sympathetic to the administration. See also Brant, *James Madison,* 4:377; and Rakove, *James Madison and the Creation of the American Republic,* 169–72.

72. Ketcham, *James Madison,* 448–57; JM to James Monroe and William Pinkney, 20 May 1807, *WJM,* 7:406–46; JM to James Monroe, 25 May 1807, JMP; John Jay to JM, 4 July 1807, RG 59, ML, NA; William Pinkney and James Monroe to JM, 23 July 1807, James Monroe Papers, LC.

73. Thomas Matthews to JM, 23 June 1807, RG 59, ML, NA; David Erskine to JM, 14 Sep-

tember 1807, RG 59, NFL, Great Britain, vol. 5, NA; Charles E. Brodine Jr., "*Chesapeake-Leopard* Affair," *JMAN*, 67–68; Perkins, *Prologue to War*, 190.

74. John Dawson to JM, 28 June 1807, JMP; Tench Coxe to JM, 30 June 1807, ibid.; John G. Jackson to JM, 5 July 1807, ibid.; Tench Coxe to JM, 2 July 1807, ibid.; JM to James Monroe, 25 July 1807, ibid.; *ROL*, 3:1477–79.

75. JM to James Monroe, 6 July 1807, *WJM*, 7:454–60; Spivak, *Jefferson's English Crisis*, 81–85, 92.

76. JM to Richard Peters, 5 September 1807, Historical Society of Pennsylvania, Philadelphia, Pa.; James Monroe to JM, 10 October 1807, RG 59, DD, Great Britain, vol. 12, NA; "Negotiations with Mr. Rose," 1 February 1808, *WJM*, 8:1–11; JM to William Pinkney, 8 March 1808, ibid., 8:19–21; Brant, *James Madison*, 4:384–401, 415, Perkins, *Prologue to War*, 196. On impressment and American public opinion, see Brunsman, "Subjects vs. Citizens."

77. JM to James Monroe, 17 July 1807, *WJM*, 7:463–64.

78. William Riggin to JM, 30 June 1807, RG 59, CD, Trieste, vol. 1, NA; Frederick Jacob Wichelhausen to JM, 4 July 1807, RG 59, CD, Bremen, vol. 1, NA; Thomas Appleton to JM, 9 July 1807, RG 59, CD, Leghorn, vol. 2, NA; Robert Montgomery to JM, 24 July 1807, RG 59, CD, Alicante, vol. 1, NA; John Armstrong to JM, 24 July 1807, RG 59, DD, France, Vol. 10, NA; Abraham Gibbs to JM, 24 September 1808, RG 59, CD, Palermo, vol. 1, NA; Hans Rudolph Saabye to JM, 25 September 1807, RG 59, CD, Copenhagen, vol. 1, NA.

79. Rakove, *James Madison and the Creation of the American Republic*, 172–73; Wood, *Empire of Liberty*, 646.

80. JM to Thomas Jefferson, 7 February 1796, *PJM*, 16:214–16; John Quincy Adams to Secretary of State, 14 March 1801, *PJM, SS*, 1:20–22; Rufus King to JM, 1 May 1801, ibid., 1:132–35; Elbridge Gerry to JM, 19 February 1806, Elbridge Gerry Papers, LC; James Monroe to JM, 14 August 1807, Monroe Papers, LC; Morgan Lewis to JM, 9 January 1808, JMP; *ROL*, 3:1503–5; Rutland, *James Madison, the Founding Father*, 194; Tucker and Hendrickson, *Empire of Liberty*, 204–5.

81. Brant, *James Madison*, 4:394–403; Spivak, *Jefferson's English Crisis*, 108–17; *ROL*, 3:1503–15; *National Intelligencer*, 23 December 1807.

82. *National Intelligencer*, 25 December 1807; ibid., 28 December 1807.

83. Thomas Jefferson to JM, 11 March 1808, *ROL*, 3:1514–15.

84. Ibid., 3:1507–10; JM to Thomas Jefferson, 10 August 1808, ibid., 3:1531–32; Ketcham, *James Madison*, 458–62; Wood, *Empire of Liberty*, 654.

85. DM to Anna Cutts, 28 August 1808, *SLDPM*, 87–88; Peterson, *James Madison*, 267.

86. Brant, *James Madison*, 4:159; Ketcham, *James Madison*, 466. Historians have traditionally interpreted Jefferson's decision to drop Burr from the Republican ticket as a response to the latter's alleged coyness during the electoral deadlock in 1800. Burr's demise, however, may have had more to do with the future than the past. The Clinton machine in New York wanted to eliminate Burr as a possible rival, while southern Republicans hoped to clear a path for Madison. See Isenberg, *Fallen Founder*, 245–51. There was also reason to question Burr's commitment to republican principles. See Wood, *Revolutionary Characters*, 223–42.

87. James Taylor to JM, 3 April 1807, JMP; Wilentz, *The Rise of American Democracy*, 105–7; Brant, *James Madison*, 4:234–40; Ketcham, *James Madison*, 433–39.

88. JM to Isaac Hite, 22 June 1803, *PJM, SS*, 5:112; Robert R. Livingston to JM, 12 July 1807, Rives Collection, JMP. See generally Brant, "The Election of 1808."

89. Smith quoted in Allgor, *Parlor Politics*, 84.

90. Mitchill quoted in ibid., 70. See also ibid., 90; Allgor, *A Perfect Union*, 121–27; and Rutland, *James Madison, the Founding Father*, 190.

91. Pinckney quoted in Allgor, *Parlor Politics*, 70–71. See also Brant, *James Madison*, 4:419–68; and Wilentz, *The Rise of American Democracy*, 132.

92. Albert Gallatin and JM to Thomas Jefferson, 15 November 1808, *ROL*, 3:1557–58; Thomas Jefferson to Charles Pinckney, 8 November 1808, in Bergh, *The Writings of Thomas Jefferson*, 11:190; Thomas Jefferson to James Monroe, 28 January 1809, ibid., 11:240–43.

93. Cook quoted in *ROL*, 3:1553. See also ibid., 13:1548–54; JM to William Pinkney, 3 January 1809, *WJM*, 8:40–42, Peterson, *James Madison*, 269–70; and Spivak, *Jefferson's English Crisis*, 189.

94. Ketcham, *James Madison*, 463–69; Rakove, *James Madison and the Creation of the American Republic*, 172–75; Peterson, *James Madison*, 271–72.

95. Wood, *Empire of Liberty*, 650–54; Perkins, *Prologue to War*, 50–51.

96. See generally Perkins, *Prologue to War*, 24–27; and Tucker and Hendrickson, *Empire of Liberty*, 178–79, 190–203.

97. Wood, *Empire of Liberty*, 624–29; Perkins, *Prologue to War*, 28.

CHAPTER SIX

1. Thomas Jefferson to JM, 17 March 1809, *PJM, PS*, 1:59–60; Wills, *James Madison*, 1–2, 165 (n. 1).

2. First Inaugural Address, 4 March 1809, *M & P*, 1:451–53.

3. See generally Rakove, *James Madison and the Creation of the American Republic*, 180–93; Perkins, *Prologue to War*, 260; Ketcham, *James Madison*, 530–32; and Wills, *James Madison*, 153–55.

4. See, for examples, First Annual Message, 29 November 1809, *M & P*, 1:458–62; and Special Session Message, 25 May 1813, ibid., 2:511–15.

5. Wills, *James Madison*, 154–55.

6. Rutland, *The Presidency of James Madison*, 32–36; Ketcham, *James Madison*, 478–81; Thomas Jefferson to JM, 25 March 1810, *PJM, PS*, 2:285–86; JM to Thomas Jefferson, 2 April 1810, ibid., 2:293; JM to Tobias Lear, 26 October 1811, ibid., 3:501–2.

7. Quoted in Brant, *James Madison*, 5:14. See also Allgor, *Parlor Politics*, 71; and Burstein and Isenberg, *Madison and Jefferson*, 478–79.

8. Bledsoe quoted in Stagg, *Mr. Madison's War*, 319. See also ibid., 49–52; Wills, *James Madison*, 69–70; and Ketcham, *James Madison*, 538.

9. Wills, *James Madison*, 62–67; Rutland, *The Presidency of James Madison*, 15–17; Wilson Cary Nichols to JM, 3 March 1809, *PJM, PS*, 1:10–11.

10. Ketcham, *James Madison*, 482–83; Rutland, *The Presidency of James Madison*, 32–36.

11. Rutland, *The Presidency of James Madison*, 146; Ketcham, *James Madison*, 569–70; Caleb Atwater to JM, 20 December 1809, *PJM, PS*, 2:138–39; George Jackson to JM, 24 November 1810, ibid., 3:25.

12. Isaac Coles to JM, 29 December 1809, *PJM, PS*, 2:150–51; Thomas Jefferson to JM, 7 April 1811, ibid., 3:249–51.

13. Thomas Jefferson to JM, 30 November 1809, ibid., 2:95–97; John McKinley to JM, 1 June 1812, ibid., 4:440–41; Rutland, *The Presidency of James Madison*, 57–59; C. Edward Skeen, "James Wilkinson," *JMAN*, 449–51.

14. Thomas Jefferson to JM, 15 October 1810, *PJM, PS*, 2:580–82; JM to Levi Lincoln, 2 January 1811, ibid., 3:91; John Quincy Adams to JM, 17 August 1811, ibid., 3:421–22; Wills, *James Madison*, 70–73.

15. Brant, *James Madison*, 5:168–69; Rutland, *The Presidency of James Madison*, 55–57; Donald O. Dewey, "Gabriel Duvall," *JMAN*, 116–17; Caesar Rodney to JM, 5 December 1811, *PJM, PS*, 4:50–51.

16. See G. Kurt Piehler, "Albert Gallatin," *JMAN*, 160–63.

17. Thomas Jefferson to JM, 30 March 1809, *PJM, PS*, 1:91–92; Thomas Jefferson to JM, 30 November 1809, ibid., 2:95–97; Albert Gallatin to JM, 7 March 1811, ibid., 3:208–12; Wills, *James Madison*, 90–91.

18. C. Edward Skeen, "John R. Armstrong," *JMAN*, 17–18; Perkins, *Prologue to War*, 311–12.

19. Quoted in Rutland, *The Presidency of James Madison*, 21. See also Allgor, *A Perfect Union*, 139–45; Allgor, *Parlor Politics*, 82; *SLDPM*, 92–100; and John Graham to JM, 10 September 1810, *PJM, PS*, 2:534–35.

20. Allgor, *A Perfect Union*, 182–201; Allgor, *Parlor Politics*, 71–73; Wood, *Empire of Liberty*, 663.

21. Allgor, *A Perfect Union*, 188–94; Allgor, *Parlor Politics*, 78–83.

22. Rutland, *The Presidency of James Madison*, 125. See generally Allgor, *A Perfect Union*, 155–72.

23. Ketcham, *James Madison*, 551; Thomas B. Jackson to DM, 11 March 1809, *SLDPM*, 109–10; Jane O'Bryan to DM, 27 January 1811, ibid., 134–36; Abigail Adams to DM, 14 May 1815, ibid., 200–201.

24. DM to Ruth Barlow, 15 November 1811, *SLDPM*, 150–51; DM to Anna Cutts, 8 April 1812, ibid., 158–60; DM to Hannah Gallatin, 29 July 1813, ibid., 179.

25. Second Annual Message, 5 December 1810, *M & P*, 2:470; Brant, *James Madison*, 5:224. For criticisms of the Cabinet as an institution, see *PJM, PS*, 3:359 (n. 1); and Baptist Irvine to JM, 9 August 1811, ibid., 3:404–10.

26. Rutland, *The Presidency of James Madison*, 68–70.

27. Hickey, *The War of 1812*, 9.

28. Ibid., 10–11; Norman A. Graebner, "Orders in Council," *JMAN*, 327–28.

29. Norman A. Graebner, "Continental System," *JMAN*, 101–2.

30. Donald R. Hickey, "Blockades by France and England," ibid., 43.

31. Madison quoted in Brant, *James Madison*, 5:37. See also Schultz, *James Madison*, 150.

32. Brant, *James Madison*, 5:43–44; David Erskine to Robert Smith, 17 April 1809, *ASP: FR*, 3:295.

33. Brant, *James Madison*, 5:46; David Erskine to Robert Smith, 18 April 1809, *ASP: FR*, 3:296; Robert Smith to David Erskine, 18 April 1809, ibid., 3:296; Proclamation of 19 April 1809, *M & P*, 1:457.

34. David Erskine to Robert Smith, 17 April 1809, *ASP: FR*, 3:295; Brant, *James Madison*, 5:39; JM to Thomas Jefferson, 9 April 1809, *PJM, PS*, 1:107–8; JM to Thomas Jefferson, 1 May 1809, ibid., 1:149; JM to Congress, 23 May 1809, ibid., 1:199–202.

35. JM to Thomas Jefferson, 12 June 1809, *PJM, PS*, 1:239–40; David Erskine to Robert Smith, 15 June 1809, *ASP: FR*, 3:297.

36. Perkins, *Prologue to War*, 208–19; Proclamation of 9 August 1809, *M & P*, 1:458.

37. Perkins, *Prologue to War*, 222; William Pinkney to JM, 3 May 1809, *PJM, PS*, 1:161; Brant, *James Madison*, 5:66.

38. Robert Smith to JM, 24 July 1809, *PJM, PS*, 1:303; JM to Albert Gallatin, 28 July 1809, ibid., 1:309–10; JM to Albert Gallatin, 20 July 1809, ibid., 1:311–13.

39. Caesar Rodney to JM, 6 September 1809, ibid., 1:357–59; Albert Gallatin, 11 September 1809, ibid., 1:371; JM to Thomas Jefferson, 11 September 1809, ibid., 1:370–71; Thomas Jefferson to JM, 12 September 1809, ibid., 1:374; Peterson, *James Madison*, 282–83.

40. JM to Thomas Jefferson, 30 May 1809, *PJM, PS*, 1:213–14; Daniel Baldwin to JM, 13 September 1809, ibid., 1:384–85; John F. Price to JM, 18 September 1809, ibid., 1:385–86; William Duane to JM, 1 December 1809, ibid., 2:97–103; John Tyler to JM, 15 January 1809, ibid., 2:179. On Jackson, see Brant, *James Madison*, 5:83–101.

41. JM to David Gelston, 24 November 1809, *PJM, PS*, 2:81.

42. Perkins, *Prologue to War*, 241–43; JM to William Pinkney, 20 January 1810, *PJM, PS*, 2:194–96; Proposal to Renew Non-intercourse, circa 5 April 1810, ibid., 2:294–95; JM to Thomas Jefferson, 23 April 1810, ibid., 2:321–22.

43. Brant, *James Madison*, 5:138–47; JM to William Pinkney, 23 May 1810, *PJM, PS*, 2:347–49.

44. James Wilkinson to JM, 1 May 1809, *PJM, PS*, 1:155–56; JM to Thomas Jefferson, 19 October 1810, ibid., 2:585–87; Proclamation of 27 October 1810, *M & P*, 1:465–66; Brant, *James Madison*, 5:175–89; Ketcham, *James Madison*, 500–502; Rutland, *The Presidency of James Madison*, 60–62; Stagg, *Borderlines in Borderlands*, 59–79.

45. John Mahon, "Florida," *JMAN*, 147–48; Rutland, *The Presidency of James Madison*, 67–68; Stagg, *Borderlines in Borderlands*, 89–110, 120–33.

46. Brant, *James Madison*, 5:210–11; William Pinkney to Robert Smith, 18 August 1810, *ASP: FR*, 3:364; William Pinkney to Robert Smith, 21 August 1810, ibid., 3:364–65.

47. Napoleon quoted in Brant, *James Madison*, 5:151.

48. Ibid., 5:218.

49. Ketcham, *James Madison*, 504–7; Marquis de Lafayette to JM, 25 August 1810, *PJM, PS*, 2:507–8; JM to Caesar Rodney, 30 September 1810, ibid., 2:565–66; JM to Thomas Jefferson, 19 October 1810, ibid., 2:585–87.

50. Proclamation of 2 November 1810, *M & P*, 1:466–67.

51. DM to James Taylor, 10 November 1810, *SLDPM*, 133–34.

52. Brant, *James Madison*, 5:261; Lord Wellesley to William Pinckney, 4 December 1810, *ASP: FR*, 3:376; William Pinkney to JM, 17 December 1810, *PJM, PS*, 3:71–74.

53. Robert Smith to JM, 11 December 1810, *PJM, PS*, 3:64–65; Draft of Robert Smith to Louis-Charles-Barbé Sérurier, 20 February 1811, ibid., 3:174–75; Brant, *James Madison*, 5:310.

54. William Jones to JM, 21 February 1811, *PJM, PS*, 3:177–78; George Irving to JM, 10 March 1811, ibid., 3:212–14; JM to Thomas Jefferson, 18 March 1811, ibid., 3:224–25; Memorandum on Robert Smith, circa 11 April 1811, ibid., 3:255–65.

55. Paul Hamilton to JM, 23 July 1810, ibid., 2:432–33; JM to the Inhabitants of New Haven, 24 May 1811, ibid., 3:316–18; JM to Richard Cutts, 16 June 1811, ibid., 3:342–43; JM to Richard Cutts, 23 July 1811, ibid., 3:388–89; Brant, *James Madison*, 5:314–19.

56. JM to Henry Dearborn, 23 July 1811, *PJM, PS*, 3:390; Brant, *James Madison*, 5:343, 367.

57. James Monroe to Joel Barlow, 26 July 1811, *ASP: FR*, 3:509–12; James Monroe to Joel Barlow, 21 November 1811, ibid., 3:513–15; Joel Barlow to Jonathan Russell, 2 March 1812, ibid., 3:518–19; Joel Barlow to Duke of Bassano, 12 March 1812, ibid., 3:520; JM to Albert Gallatin, 14 September 1811, *PJM, PS*, 3:460–61.

58. Memorandum from Albert Gallatin, circa 1 November 1811, *PJM, PS*, 3:533–39.

59. Brant, *James Madison*, 5:361; Perkins, *Prologue to War*, 290–91; Third Annual Message, 5 November 1811, *M & P*, 2:476–81.

60. Joseph Allen to JM, 23 November 1811, *PJM, PS*, 4:31–33. See also Resolutions of the General Assembly of Pennsylvania, 20 December 1811, ibid., 4:79–82; John Geddes to JM, 22 December 1811, ibid., 4:83–87; JM to Congress, 22 January 1812, ibid., 4:144–47; Resolutions of the Virginia General Assembly, 25 January 1812, ibid., 4:155–57; John Quincy Adams to JM, 7 February 1812, ibid., 4:170–72; David Fay to JM, 25 February 1812, ibid., 4:209–12; Petition from the Inhabitants of Richmond, Manchester, and Vicinity, 30 May 1812, ibid., 4:429–30; and DM to Anna Cutts, 22 December 1811, *SLDPM*, 153–54.

61. Samuel Harrison to JM, 11 May 1812, *PJM, PS*, 4:374–77. See also Petition from the Inhabitants of Troy, New York, 7 May 1812, ibid., 4:369–70.

62. JM to Joel Barlow, 17 November 1812, ibid., 4:19–23; ibid., 4:117 (n. 1); Stagg, *Mr. Madison's War*, 97; Perkins, *Prologue to War*, 373.

63. JM to Thomas Jefferson, 3 April 1812, *PJM, PS*, 4:286–89; ibid., 4:280 (n. 1); Brant, *James Madison*, 5:449.

64. Henry Dearborn to JM, 6 April 1812, *PJM, PS*, 4:298–303; JM to Thomas Jefferson, 24 April 1812, ibid., 4:345–46; Ketcham, *James Madison*, 524–33; Brant, *James Madison*, 5:476.

65. Address to Congress, 1 June 1812, *M & P*, 2:484–90; Schultz, *James Madison*, 159–60; Brant, *James Madison*, 5:464.

66. Stagg, *Mr. Madison's War*, 110–15; Rutland, *The Presidency of James Madison*, 102–4.

67. See Perkins, *Prologue to War*, 326, 339–40, 425–26; and JM to Henry Wheaton, 26 February 1827, in Peterson, *James Madison*, 301–2.

68. JM to Thomas Jefferson, 23 July 1809, *PJM, PS*, 1:298–99; Rutland, *The Presidency of James Madison*, 105; Burstein and Isenberg, *Madison and Jefferson*, 537.

69. John Armstrong to JM, 6 June 1809, *PJM, PS*, 1:228–31; Caesar Rodney to JM, 16 January 1809, ibid., 2:181–86; JM to Thomas Jefferson, 25 May 1812, ibid., 4:415; Thomas Jefferson to JM, 30 May 1812, ibid., 4:426; Perkins, *Prologue to War*, 393–94.

70. JM to House of Representatives, 6 July 1812, *PJM, PS*, 4:568; Peterson, *James Madison*, 288.

71. John Armstrong to JM, 18 September 1809, *PJM, PS*, 1:382–84; JM to Thomas Jefferson, 22 June 1810, ibid., 2:388–89; Schultz, *James Madison*, 107.

72. See, for examples, William Bellinger Bullock to JM, 4 June 1812, *PJM, PS*, 4:451–52; Petition from the Citizens of Cecil County, 13 June 1812, ibid., 4:478–79; and Petition from Republican Citizens of Milledgeville, 13 June 1812, ibid., 4:479–82. See generally Gilje, "'Free Trade and Sailors' Rights.'"

73. William Pinkney to JM, 10 December 1809, *PJM, PS*, 2:121–24.

74. On the problem of weak British leadership, see ibid., 2:56 (n. 3); and William Pinkney to JM, 13 August 1810, ibid., 2:478–83.

75. JM to John Geddes, 8 January 1812, ibid., 4:122–24; Wood, *Empire of Liberty*, 667–70; Brant, *James Madison*, 5:403.

76. Christopher Ellery to JM, 24 June 1812, *PJM, PS*, 4:505–6; Wood, *Empire of Liberty*, 692–700; Rutland, *The Presidency of James Madison*, 141; Fourth Annual Message, 4 November 1812, *M & P*, 2:499–506.

77. Memorandum of a Conversation with Augustus John Foster, 23 June 1812, *PJM, PS*, 4:501–2; JM to Joel Barlow, 11 August 1812, ibid., 5:144–46; Brant, *James Madison*, 6:33–35, 70–72; 118–19; Rutland, *The Presidency of James Madison*, 128–31.

78. Perkins, *Prologue to War*, 437; Brant, *James Madison*, 6:39.

79. Albert Gallatin to JM, 18 May 1809, *PJM, PS*, 1:191–92; William Eustis to JM, 30 November 1810, ibid., 3:39–40; William Eaton to JM, 25 October 1811, ibid., 3:499–500; Ketcham, *James Madison*, 498–99; Stagg, *Mr. Madison's War*, 141–42.

80. Message to Congress, 3 January 1810, *PJM, PS*, 2:158; Message to Congress, 5 November 1811, *M & P*, 2:479; Perkins, *Prologue to War*, 298, 356–65; Ketcham, *James Madison*, 514–15.

81. JM to Thomas Jefferson, 7 February 1812, *PJM, PS*, 4:168–69; Thomas Jefferson to JM, 19 February 1812, ibid., 4:195–96; JM to Thomas Jefferson, 6 March 1812, ibid., 4:228–29; Albert Gallatin to JM, 5 March 1813, ibid., 6:90–91; Message to Congress, 25 May 1813, ibid., 6:339–43; Wood, *Empire of Liberty*, 672–74.

82. Jefferson quoted in Heidler and Heidler, *The War of 1812*, 58. See also JM to John Nichols, 2 April 1813, *PJM, PS*, 6:175–76; Stagg, *Mr. Madison's War*, 174–76; and Rutland, *The Presidency of James Madison*, 105–10.

83. James Monroe to JM, 6 September 1812, *PJM, PS*, 5:281; William Eustis to JM, 8 September 1812, ibid., 5:289.

84. Brant, *James Madison*, 6:79.

85. JM to Henry Dearborn, 9 August 1812, *PJM, PS*, 5:133–34; Henry Dearborn to JM, 15 August 1812, ibid., 5:157–58; Henry Dearborn to JM, 30 September 1812, ibid., 5:364–66; Henry Dearborn to JM, 24 October 1812, ibid., 5:410–11; Brant, *James Madison*, 6:51–54; Stagg, *Mr. Madison's War*, 244–46, 252–53.

86. Peterson, *James Madison*, 523–25.

87. Rakove, *James Madison and the Creation of the American Republic*, 191; Brant, *James Madison*, 6:97–99.

88. Jonathan Dayton to JM, circa 28 December 1812, *PJM, PS*, 5:528–31; Allgor, *A Perfect Union*, 290–91; Rutland, *The Presidency of James Madison*, 118–19; Wills, *James Madison*, 115–18.

89. William Eustis to JM, 3 December 1812, *PJM, PS*, 5:477; ibid., 5:535 (n. 1); Rutland, *The Presidency of James Madison*, 120.

90. JM to James Monroe, 10 September 1812, *PJM, PS*, 5:295–96; James Monroe to JM, 10 September 1812, ibid., 5:297–98; ibid., 5:552 (n. 2); Albert Gallatin to JM, 7 January 1813, ibid., 5:557–58; Brant, *James Madison*, 6:128.

91. Henry Dearborn to JM, 13 March 1813, *PJM, PS*, 6:113–14; ibid., 6:461 (n. 1).

92. Ketcham, *James Madison*, 560–61; JM to Senate, 6 July 1813, *PJM, PS*, 6:406–7;

ibid., 6:487 (n. 1); JM to Albert Gallatin, 2 August 1813, ibid., 6:491–94; JM to Congress, 20 July 1813, ibid., 6:449–50; JM to William Jones, 14 August 1813, ibid., 6:526.

93. JM to William Wirt, 30 September 1813, *PJM, PS*, 6:663–65.

94. *ROL*, 3:1731.

95. *PJM, PS*, 6:194 (n. 1); William Jones to JM, 27 August 1813, ibid., 6:563–64; Walter Jones to JM, 8 November 1813, JMP; William Jones to JM, 9 March 1814, RG59, ML, NA; William Jones to JM, 25 May 1814, William Jones Papers, Historical Society of Pennsylvania, Philadelphia, Pa.

96. D.C. Militia Officers to JM, 22 September 1813, *PJM, PS*, 6:649–51; Walter Jones to JM, 8 November 1813, JMP; JM to James Monroe, 21 May 1814, James Monroe Papers, LC.

97. Brant, *James Madison*, 6:128; James Monroe to JM, 25 February 1813, *PJM, PS*, 6:67–68; James Monroe to JM, 27 December 1813, Rives Collection, JMP; James Monroe to JM, September 1814, Monroe Papers, LC.

98. JM to John Armstrong, 25 May 1814, JMP; JM to John Armstrong, 12 August 1814, *Letters and Other Writings of James Madison*, 3:416; JM to John Armstrong, 11 August 1814, *JMW*, 697–700.

99. JM to DM, 23 August 1814, *SLDPM*, 192; Ketcham, *James Madison*, 583–86; Stagg, *Mr. Madison's War*, 409–18.

100. Memorandum on the Battle of Bladensburg, 24 August 1814, *JMW*, 700–703; Proclamation, 1 September 1814, *M & P*, 2:530–31; Hickey, *The War of 1812*, 197–98; Mahon, *The War of 1812*, 299.

101. Memorandum by JM, 29 August 1814, *WJM*, 8:300–304; Brant, *James Madison*, 6:321–22; Allgor, *A Perfect Union*, 312–29.

102. William Jones to JM, 1 September 1814, Jones Papers, Historical Society of Pennsylvania, Philadelphia, Pa.; Thomas Leiper to JM, 1 September 1814, JMP; Stagg, *Mr. Madison's War*, 431–36; Allgor, *A Perfect Union*, 321–29; Annual Message, 20 September 1814, *M & P*, 2:532–36. For an argument that Federalist partisanship badly undermined U.S. diplomacy, see Buel, *America on the Brink*.

103. Jones quoted in Brant, *James Madison*, 6:329. Madison quoted in Ketcham, *James Madison*, 586.

104. Speech of 29 June 1787, *PJM*, 10:86–87; Speech of 11 May 1789, *JMW*, 433–34.

105. James Monroe to JM, 4 August 1812, *PJM, PS*, 5:114–15.

106. Randolph quoted in Brant, *James Madison*, 6:229. See also Samuel Thurber to JM, 27 July 1812, *PJM, PS*, 5:91–92; and Elbridge Gerry to JM, 15 August 1812, ibid., 5:158–62.

107. Thomas Leiper to JM, 16 August 1812, *PJM, PS*, 5:164.

108. Connecticut General Assembly to JM, 25 August 1812, ibid., 5:194–96; William Montgomery to JM, 25 August 1812, ibid., 5:199–200; Samuel Spring to JM, 26 August 1812, ibid., 5:208–9.

109. Andrew Hull Jr. to JM, 7 August 1812, ibid., 5:125–26; Unidentified Correspondent to JM, 4 November 1812, ibid., 5:436–37; Jonathan Dayton to JM, circa 28 December 1813, ibid., 5:528–31; Unidentified Correspondent to JM, 6 February 1812, ibid., 5:648; Burstein and Isenberg, *Madison and Jefferson*, 511.

110. Joseph Story to William Pinkney, 26 June 1812, *PJM, PS*, 4:561–62.

111. Mathew Carey to JM, 12 August 1812, ibid., 5:148–50; Mathew Carey to JM, 21 Janu-

ary 1813, ibid., 5:601–3; Mathew Carey to JM, 15 December 1813, JMP; Mathew Carey to JM, 16 November 1814, ibid.

112. JM to Richard Cutts, 8 August 1812, *PJM, PS*, 5:127–28; JM to Mathew Carey, 19 September 1812, ibid., 5:335; JM to David Humphreys, 23 March 1813, ibid., 6:148–50; JM to William Plumer, 14 April 1813, ibid., 6:197–98; JM to Thomas Jefferson, 10 May 1814, *ROL*, 3:1742–43.

113. Brant, *James Madison*, 6:233; JM to Congress, 5 November 1812, *PJM, PS*, 5:438.

114. Wirt quoted in Brant, *James Madison*, 6:342–43. See also ibid., 6:359; Wilson Cary Nicholas to JM, 11 November 1814, Rives Collection, JMP; and JM to Wilson Cary Nicholas, 26 November 1814, *JMW*, 706–7.

115. Brant, *James Madison*, 6:260–61.

116. Cabinet Memorandum, 23–24 and 27 June 1814, *WJM*, 8:280–81; JM to Thomas Jefferson, 10 October 1814, *ROL*, 3:1745–46; Rutland, *The Presidency of James Madison*, 176–79, 188; Norman A. Graebner, "Treaty of Ghent," *JMAN*, 407–9.

117. Wilson Cary Nicholas to JM, 18 December 1814, JMP; John G. Jackson to JM, 10 January 1815, ibid.; William A. Burwell to JM, 1 February 1815, ibid.; Major General Parker et al. to JM, 12 February 1815, Letters Received by the Sec. of War, Registered Series, M 221:66, T-120 (8), NA.

118. JM to Congress, 18 February 1815, *M & P*, 2:537–39; James Taylor to JM, 21 February 1815, JMP; David Jones to JM, 8 March 1815, Rives Collection, ibid. For the argument that Great Britain would have honored the Treaty of Ghent even if it had won the Battle of New Orleans, see Carr, "The Battle of New Orleans and the Treaty of Ghent."

119. JM to Congress, 23 February 1815, *M & P*, 2:539; Rutland, *The Presidency of James Madison*, 190–93.

120. JM to Henry Dearborn, 4 March 1815, *WJM*, 8:331–32.

121. John Nicholas to JM, 4 May 1813, *PJM, PS*, 6:276–79. On the administrative inadequacies of the American state, see Stagg, *Mr. Madison's War*, 504–9.

122. Annual Message, 5 December 1815, *M & P*, 2:547–54.

123. Peterson, *James Madison*, 359. Madison left office pleading for improvements in the militia. See Annual Message, 3 December 1817, *M & P*, 2:561.

124. Veto Message, 30 January 1815, *M & P*, 2:540–42; Annual Message, 5 December 1815, ibid., 2:547–54; Veto Message, 3 March 1817, ibid., 2:569–70.

125. Schultz, *James Madison*, 1–14; McCoy, "James Madison," 49–50; Rutland, *The Presidency of James Madison*, 208. Wills, *Henry Adams and the Making of America*, takes a different approach, arguing that later historians exaggerated Adams's hostility to Madison.

126. Abigail Adams quoted in Rakove, *James Madison and the Creation of the American Republic*, 206. See also John Adams to Thomas Jefferson, 2 February 1817, in Cappon, *The Adams-Jefferson Letters*, 2:508; Ketcham, *James Madison*, 597–99; and Peterson, *James Madison*, 364.

127. Wills, *James Madison*, 153–58, 164; *ROL*, 3:1761. Blake quoted in Brant, *James Madison*, 6:418–19.

128. Rutland, *The Presidency of James Madison*, 207.

CHAPTER SEVEN

1. JM to Robert Walsh Jr., 22 December 1827, JMP; Peterson, *James Madison*, 366–68; Ketcham, *The Madisons at Montpelier*, 14–21, 99–100.

2. JM to John Payne Todd, 26 April 1827, JMP; JM to Chester Bailey, 12 May 1826, ibid.; Ketcham, *The Madisons at Montpelier*, 9–14.

3. Peterson, *James Madison*, 366–68; Jennings, *A Colored Man's Reminiscences*, 15–19.

4. Hyland, *Montpelier and the Madisons*, 43–64; Ketcham, *The Madisons at Montpelier*, 33–35.

5. Ketcham, *The Madisons at Montpelier*, 103–5; JM to Charles J. Ingersoll, 4 January 1818, *WJM*, 8:407–8; JM to Jacob Gideon, 28 January 1819, ibid., 8:408–11; JM to Henry Wheaton, 11 July 1824, ibid., 9:192–96; JM to Henry Lee, 16 February 1827, ibid., 9:277–81; JM to Jonathan Elliot, 14 February 1827, JMP.

6. Brant, *James Madison*, 6:434–35; JM to Joseph Gales, 26 August 1821, *WJM*, 9:68–70; JM to John G. Jackson, 27 December 1821, ibid., 9:70–77.

7. JM to John Adams, 22 May 1817, *WJM*, 8:390–92; JM to John G. Jackson, 27 December 1821, ibid., 9:70–77; Joseph Ficklin to JM, 9 August 1823, JMP.

8. JM to Richard Peters, 22 February 1819, *WJM*, 8:423–25; JM to James Monroe, 30 October 1823, ibid., 9:157–60; JM to James Barbour, 5 December 1823, ibid., 9:171–73; JM to Thomas Jefferson, 14 January 1824, *ROL*, 3:1890–91.

9. JM to James Monroe, 29 November 1817, *WJM*, 8:397–98; JM to Spencer Roane, 2 September 1819, *JMW*, 733–37; JM to Spencer Roane, 6 May 1821, ibid., 772–77; JM to Thomas Jefferson, 27 June 1823, *ROL*, 3:1867–70; JM to Henry Clay, 24 April 1824, *WJM*, 9:183–87.

10. JM to Thomas Jefferson, 17 February 1825, *ROL*, 3:1927–28; JM to Martin Van Buren, 20 September 1826, *WJM*, 9:251–55; McCoy, *The Last of the Fathers*, 65–68.

11. JM to William T. Barry, 4 August 1822, *JMW*, 790–94; JM to Marquis de Lafayette, November 1826, *WJM*, 9:261–66.

12. JM to Edward Everett, 19 March 1823, *JMW*, 794–98; JM to Thomas Jefferson, 10 September 1824, *ROL*, 3:1898–1901; JM to Frederick Beasley, 22 December 1824, *WJM*, 9:210–13; JM to Thomas Jefferson, 31 December 1824, *ROL*, 3:1913–14; JM to Thomas Jefferson, 15 January 1825, ibid., 3:1921.

13. JM to Richard Rush, 17 April 1824, JM Papers, University of Virginia, Charlottesville, Va.; Thomas Jefferson to JM, 6 October 1824, *ROL*, 3:1903–4; JM to Thomas Jefferson, 9 October 1824, ibid., 3:1904–5; JM to Thomas Jefferson, 3 December 1824, ibid., 3:1909–10.

14. *ROL*, 3:1883–91; Brant, *James Madison*, 6:451–52.

15. Thomas Jefferson to JM, 1 February 1825, *ROL*, 3:1923–24; JM to Thomas Jefferson, 8 February 1825, ibid., 3:1924–25; Thomas Jefferson to JM, 12 February 1825, ibid., 3:1926; Thomas Jefferson to JM, 17 February 1826, ibid., 3:1964–67; Brant, *James Madison*, 6:453–54. The problem of retaining instructors and the prejudice against American applicants persisted. Nicholas Trist later warned Madison that appointing "any of our native professors" to the university faculty would have the effect of "sealing the doom of this noble institution." Nicholas P. Trist to JM, 1 February 1827, Nicholas P. Trist Album Book, Virginia Historical Society, Richmond, Va.

16. JM to Richard Rush, 10 May 1819, *WJM*, 8:433–38; Ketcham, *James Madison*, 623–24.

17. JM to Richard Cutts, 1 September 1823, JMP; JM to George Graham, 30 October 1823, ibid.; JM to George Graham, 27 March 1824, ibid.; JM to Hubbard Taylor, 29 July 1826, ibid.

18. JM to Nicholas Biddle, 16 April 1825, *WJM*, 9:221; JM to James K. Paulding, 10 March 1827, ibid., 9:281–83; Nicholas Biddle to JM, 26 April 1825, JMP.

19. Ticknor quoted in Peterson, *James Madison*, 368. See also Thomas Jefferson to JM, 17 February 1826, *ROL*, 3:1964–67; JM to Thomas Jefferson, 24 February 1826, ibid., 3:1967–68; and Ketcham, *The Madisons at Montpelier*, 33–38.

20. JM to Clarkson Crolius, December 1819, *WJM*, 9:15–20.

21. See McCoy, *The Last of the Fathers*, 179–202.

22. Ketcham, *The Madisons at Montpelier*, 159–64; Dunn, *Dominion of Memories*, 11–14. See generally Gutzman, *Virginia's American Revolution*.

23. Hyland, *Montpelier and the Madisons*, 14–15, 37; Kaminski, *James Madison*, 34; JM to John G. Jackson, 27 December 1821, *WJM*, 9:70–77.

24. JM to Edmund Pendleton, 6 August 1782, *PJM*, 5:27–28; JM to Edmund Pendleton, 3 September 1782, ibid., 5:101–3; JM to Edmund Pendleton, 24 September 1782, ibid., 5:157–58; JM to Edmund Randolph, 26 July 1785, ibid., 8:327–29.

25. Instructions for the Montpelier Overseers, circa 8 November 1790, ibid., 13:302–4; JM to Thomas Jefferson, 3 October 1801, *PJM, SS*, 2:154; Hyland, *Montpelier and the Madisons*, 82–83; Ketcham, *The Madisons at Montpelier*, 45.

26. Thomas Jefferson to JM, 4 April 1800, *PJM*, 17:378–79; Burstein and Isenberg, *Madison and Jefferson*, 124, 200–202, 230.

27. JM to JM Sr., 8 September 1783, *PJM*, 7:304–5; JM to JM Sr., 27 December 1795, ibid., 16:174; Ketcham, *James Madison*, 374; Ketcham, *The Madisons at Montpelier*, 7, 76–77.

28. JM to JM Sr., 27 July 1788, *PJM*, 11:208; JM to JM Sr., 6 September 1788, ibid., 11:247–48; Ketcham, *The Madisons at Montpelier*, 24; Brant, *James Madison*, 6:443–44; Jennings, *A Colored Man's Reminiscences*, 15.

29. JM to William Bradford, 19 June 1775, *PJM*, 1:151–54; JM to Joseph Jones, 28 November 1780, ibid., 2:209–11.

30. Motion on Slaves Taken by the British, 10 September 1782, ibid., 5:111–13; Report on Property Recaptured on Land, 23 December 1782, ibid., 5:432–36; JM to Thomas Jefferson, 13 May 1783, ibid., 7:39–42; Notes on Debates, 26 May 1783, ibid., 7:80.

31. JM to George Washington, 11 November 1785, ibid., 8:403–5; JM to Ambrose Madison, 15 December 1785, ibid., 8:442–44; JM to Thomas Jefferson, 22 January 1786, ibid., 8:472–82; Ketcham, *James Madison*, 148–49.

32. Notes on Debates, 28 March 1783, *PJM*, 6:407–9; Notes on Debates, 25 August 1787, ibid., 10:157; Notes on Debates, 1 April 1783, ibid., 6:424–26; Brant, *James Madison*, 2:234; Rakove, *Original Meanings*, 77–78.

33. Notes on Debates, 6 June 1787, *PJM*, 10:32–34; Notes on Debates, 25 August 1787, ibid., 10:157; Kester, *The Haunted Philosophe*, 103.

34. *JMW*, 235–42; ibid., 310–14; Rutland, *The Papers of George Mason*, 3:1086.

35. Notes on Debates, 13 May 1789, *PJM*, 12:160–63; Brant, *James Madison*, 3:250–51.

36. Memorandum on an African Colony for Freed Slaves, circa 20 October 1789, *PJM*, 12:437–38.

37. Notes on Debates, 11 February 1790, ibid., 13:32–33; Notes on Debates, 12 February 1790, ibid., 13:39–40.

38. JM to Benjamin Rush, 20 March 1790, ibid., 13:109; JM to Edmund Randolph, 21 March 1790, ibid., 13:110; Notes on Debates, 23 March 1790, ibid., 13:116–18; Kaminski, *The Great Virginia Triumvirate*, 169–71; Ellis, *American Creation*, 175.

39. JM to John Parish, 6 June 1790, *PJM*, 13:240; Robert Pleasants to JM, 6 June 1791, ibid., 14:30–31; Robert Pleasants to JM, 8 August 1791, ibid., 14:70; JM to Robert Pleasants, 30 October 1791, ibid., 14:91–92.

40. "Population and Emigration," *National Gazette*, 19 November 1791, ibid., 14:117–22; Notes for the *National Gazette* Essays, circa 19 December 1791–3 March 1792, ibid., 14:157; Notes on Debates, 1–2 January 1795, ibid., 15:432–35.

41. Officers of the Second Regiment, Virginia Militia, to JM, 2 June 1812, *PJM, PS*, 4:446–47; James Monroe to JM, 24 March 1815, Rives Collection, JMP; James Monroe to JM, 22 April 1815, ibid.; Burstein and Isenberg, *Madison and Jefferson*, 397–99. On the spread of slavery, see Rothman, *Slave Country*.

42. JM to Robert Walsh, 2 March 1819, *JMW*, 723–25; JM to Richard Rush, 21 April 1821, *WJM*, 9:44–45; Answers to Questions Concerning Slavery, 28 March 1823, ibid., 9:134.

43. JM to Robert J. Evans, 15 June 1819, *JMW*, 728–33; JM to Marquis de Lafayette, no date, *WJM*, 9:85; JM to Marquis de Lafayette, November 1826, ibid., 9:261–66.

44. JM to Edward Coles, 3 September 1819, *WJM*, 8:453–55; JM to Francis Corbin, 26 November 1820, ibid., 9:38–41; JM to Frances Wright, ibid., 9:224–29.

45. JM to Robert Walsh, 27 November 1819, *JMW*, 737–43; Answers to Questions Concerning Slavery, 28 March 1823, *WJM*, 9:132.

46. Notes on Debates, 12 February 1790, *PJM*, 13:39–40; JM to James Monroe, 10 February 1820, *JMW*, 771–72; JM to James Monroe, 23 February 1820, *WJM*, 9:23–26.

47. JM to James Monroe, 19 November 1820, *WJM*, 9:30–35; JM to Marquis de Lafayette, 25 November 1820, ibid., 9:35–38; Forbes, *The Missouri Compromise and Its Aftermath*, 108–18.

48. Jefferson quoted in *ROL*, 3:1821; JM to James Monroe, 28 December 1820, *WJM*, 9:41–44; McCoy, *The Last of the Fathers*, 108–14; Dunn, *Dominion of Memories*, 43–45.

49. Jonathan and Mary Bull, circa 1821, *JMW*, 779–86; Burstein and Isenberg, *Madison and Jefferson*, 580.

50. Dunn, *Dominion of Memories*, 151.

51. Ibid., 152–54.

52. JM to James Monroe, 26 March 1829, JMP; Ketcham, *The Madisons at Montpelier*, 58–61; Speech in the Virginia Constitutional Convention, 2 December 1829, *JMW*, 824–27.

53. Sutton, *Revolution to Secession*, 72–77, 80, 90; Bruce, *The Rhetoric of Conservatism*, 32–33; Peterson, *James Madison*, 388–90; Dunn, *Dominion of Memories*, 158–61. Leigh quoted in Alison Goodyear Freehling, *Drift toward Dissolution*, 56.

54. JM to Joseph C. Cabell, 5 January 1829, JMP; Notes on Suffrage, *Letters and Other Writings of James Madison*, 4:28; Bruce, *The Rhetoric of Conservatism*, 60–61; Ketcham, *The Madisons at Montpelier*, 62–65.

55. Speech in the Virginia Constitutional Convention, 2 December 1829, *JMW*, 824–27; Dunn, *Dominion of Memories*, 166–67.

56. JM to Marquis de Lafayette, 1 February 1830, in Peterson, *James Madison*, 394–96; Dunn, *Dominion of Memories*, 168–69; Bruce, *The Rhetoric of Conservatism*, 36, 63, 66–68. In expanding the suffrage beyond freeholders the convention may have strengthened the connection between the possession of political rights and the ownership of slaves. See Curtis, "Reconsidering Suffrage Reform in the 1829–1830 Virginia Constitutional Convention."

57. The classic study of the tariff controversy is William W. Freehling, *Prelude to Civil War*.

58. "Paper on Relations with Andrew Jackson," December 1823, JM Papers, University of Virginia; JM to Fletcher & Toler, 10 October 1827, JMP; Joseph C. Cabell to JM, 12 January 1828, ibid.; JM to Marquis de Lafayette, 20 February 1828, *WJM*, 9:306–12; McCoy, *The Last of the Fathers*, 34.

59. JM to Nicholas Trist, 26 January 1829, *WJM*, 9:301–5; JM to Reynolds Chapman, 6 January 1831, ibid., 9:429–37.

60. JM to Thomas Lehre, 2 August 1828, ibid., 9:314–16.

61. JM to Joseph Cabell, 18 September 1828, *JMW*, 813–23; Memorandum on Sovereignty, no date, *WJM*, 9:568–73.

62. JM to Nicholas Trist, December 1831, *WJM*, 9:471–77; Peterson, *James Madison*, 397–98.

63. JM to Joseph C. Cabell, 16 August 1829, *WJM*, 9:341–44; JM to Joseph C. Cabell, 7 September 1829, ibid., 9:346–51; JM to Edward Everett, 25 August 1830, ibid., 9:383–403; *Federalist No. 39*, *JMW*, 216.

64. JM to Robert Y. Hayne, 3–4 April 1830, *WJM*, 9:383–94; JM to Edward Everett, 20 August 1830, ibid., 9:394–95; *ROL*, 3:1981; Read, "Madison's Response to Nullification," 269–83; McCoy, *The Last of the Fathers*, 143–51; James Morton Smith, "Virginia and Kentucky Resolutions," *JMAN*, 421–23.

65. JM to M. L. Harlbert, May 1830, *WJM*, 9:370–75; JM to Andrew Stevenson, 27 November 1830, ibid., 9:411–24; Ketcham, *James Madison*, 640–46.

66. JM to Henry Clay, 22 March 1832, *WJM*, 9:477–78; JM to Nicholas Trist, 29 May 1832, ibid., 9:480–82.

67. JM to Edward Coles, 29 August 1834, ibid., 9:536–42; JM to Daniel Drake, 12 August 1835, ibid., 9:546–47; Notes on Nullification, circa 1835–36, ibid., 9:573–607.

68. Brant, *James Madison*, 6:509–11; *ROL*, 3:1998.

69. JM to Charles J. Ingersoll, 2 February 1831, *WJM*, 9:437–39; JM to Edward Coles, 29 August 1834, ibid., 9:536–42; Burstein and Isenberg, *Madison and Jefferson*, 588–90; McCoy, *The Elusive Republic*, 255.

70. JM to James Monroe, 21 April 1831, *WJM*, 9:457–59; JM to Jared Sparks, 1 June 1831, *JMW*, 857; JM to Tench Ringgold, 12 July 1831, *WJM*, 9:460–62; JM to Andrew Stevenson, 20 November 1832, ibid., 9:488–89.

71. JM to R. R. Gurley, 28 December 1831, *WJM*, 9:468–70; JM to Thomas R. Dew, 23 February 1833, ibid., 9:498–502; Dew, *Review of the Debate in the Virginia Legislature of 1831 and 1832*.

72. JM to Henry Clay, June 1833, *WJM*, 9:515–18; Advice to My Country, 1834, *JMW*, 866; Brant, *James Madison*, 6:517–18; McCoy, *The Last of the Fathers*, 161; Ingersoll quoted in Ketcham, *The Madisons at Montpelier*, 168.

73. Peterson, *James Madison*, 376–79.

74. JM to George Bancroft, 13 April 1836, JMP; Jennings, *A Colored Man's Reminiscences*, 13–19.

75. Madison's Will, 19 April 1835, *WJM*, 9:548–52; Ketcham, *James Madison*, 629; Ketcham, *The Madisons at Montpelier*, 9–14. Ingersoll quoted in ibid., 165.

76. Houpt, "Securing a Legacy"; Shulman, "A Constant Attention."

77. Ann L. Miller, "Dolley Madison," *JMAN*, 253–58; Jennings, *A Colored Man's Reminiscences*, 14–15; Ketcham, *The Madisons at Montpelier*, 9–14.

78. Thomas Jefferson to JM, 13 October 1814, *ROL*, 3:1747–48.

79. Brant, *James Madison*, 1:ii. See also Rutland, *The Presidency of James Madison*, 209–13; and Church, *So Help Me God*, 350.

Bibliography

PRIMARY SOURCES

Manuscript Collections

Bowdoin-Temple Collection, Massachusetts Historical Society, Boston, Mass.

Consular Records, Record Group 59, National Archives, Washington, D.C.

Elbridge Gerry Papers, Manuscript Division, Library of Congress, Washington, D.C.

William Jones Papers, Historical Society of Pennsylvania, Philadelphia, Pa.

James Madison Papers, Manuscript Division, Library of Congress, Washington, D.C.

James Madison Papers, University of Virginia, Charlottesville, Va.

James Monroe Papers, Manuscript Division, Library of Congress, Washington, D.C.

Daniel Parker Papers, Historical Society of Pennsylvania, Philadelphia, Pa.

Secretary of War Letters, Registered Series, National Archives, Washington, D.C.

Samuel Smith Papers, Manuscript Division, Library of Congress, Washington, D.C.

Nicholas Trist Papers, Virginia Historical Society, Richmond, Va.

Published Works

Adair, Douglass, ed. "James Madison's Autobiography." *William and Mary Quarterly*, 3rd ser., 2 (April 1945): 191–209.

American State Papers: Foreign Relations. 38 vols. Washington, D.C.: Gales & Seaton, 1832–61.

Bergh, Albert, ed. *The Writings of Thomas Jefferson*. 20 vols. Washington, D.C.: Thomas Jefferson Memorial Association, 1907.

Cappon, Lester J., ed. *The Adams-Jefferson Letters: The Complete Correspondence between Thomas Jefferson and Abigail and John Adams*. 2 vols. Chapel Hill: University of North Carolina Press, 1959.

Dew, Thomas R. *Review of the Debate in the Virginia Legislature of 1831 and 1832*. Richmond, Va.: T. H. White, 1832; reprint, Westport, Conn.: Negro Universities Press, 1970.

Farrand, Max, ed. *The Records of the Federal Convention of 1787*. Rev. ed., 4 vols. New Haven, Conn.: Yale University Press, 1937.

Fitzpatrick, John C., ed. *The Writings of George Washington*. 39 vols. Washington, D.C.: U.S. Government Printing Office, 1931–44.

Ford, Washington C., ed. *Journals of the Continental Congress, 1776–1789*. 34 vols. Washington, D.C.: U.S. Government Printing Office, 1931–34.

Foster, Augustus John. *Jeffersonian America: Notes on the United States of America*. San Marino, Calif.: Huntington Library, 1954.

Gales, Joseph, ed. *Annals of Congress: Proceedings and Debates, 1789-1824.* 18 vols. Washington, D.C.: Gales & Seaton, 1834.

Hamilton, Stanislaus Murray, ed. *The Writings of James Monroe.* 7 vols. New York: G. P. Putnam's Sons, 1896–1903.

Hunt, Gaillard, ed. *The Writings of James Madison.* 9 vols. New York: G. P. Putnam's Sons, 1900–1910.

Hutchinson, William T., and William M. E. Rachel, eds. *The Papers of James Madison.* 17 vols. Chicago: University of Chicago Press; Charlottesville: University of Virginia Press, 1962–91.

Jennings, Paul. *A Colored Man's Reminiscences of James Madison.* Brooklyn, N.Y.: George C. Beadle, 1865.

Jensen, Merrill, et al., eds. *The Documentary History of the Ratification of the Constitution.* 20 vols. Madison: State Historical Society of Wisconsin, 1976– .

Ketcham, Ralph, ed. *Selected Writings of James Madison.* Indianapolis: Hackett, 2006.

Kramnick, Isaac, ed. *The Federalist Papers.* New York: Penguin, 1987.

Kurland, Philip B., and Ralph Lerner, eds. *The Founders' Constitution.* 4 vols. Chicago: University of Chicago Press, 1987.

Letters and Other Writings of James Madison. Cong ed., 4 vols. New York: R. Worthington, 1884.

Mattern, David B., and Holly C. Shulman, eds. *The Selected Letters of Dolley Payne Madison.* Charlottesville: University of Virginia Press, 2003.

Meade, William. *Old Churches, Ministers, and Families of Virginia.* 2 vols. Philadelphia: J. B. Lippincott, 1857.

Meyers, Marvin, ed. *The Mind of the Founder: Sources of the Political Thought of James Madison.* Rev. ed. Waltham, Mass.: Brandeis University Press, 1981.

Morison, Samuel Eliot, ed. *Sources and Documents Illustrating the American Revolution, 1764-1788.* 2nd ed. New York: Oxford University Press, 1929.

Peterson, Merrill D., ed. *The Portable Thomas Jefferson.* New York: Penguin, 1975.

Rakove, Jack N., ed. *James Madison, Writings.* New York: Library of America, 1999.

Randolph, Edmund. *History of Virginia.* Edited by Arthur Shaffer. Charlottesville: University Press of Virginia, 1970.

Rhodehamel, John, ed. *George Washington, Writings.* New York: Library of America, 1997.

Richardson, James D., comp. *Messages and Papers of the Presidents, 1789-1902.* 20 vols. Washington, D.C.: U.S. Government Printing Office, 1897–1917.

Rutland, Robert A., ed. *The Papers of George Mason, 1725-1792.* 3 vols. Chapel Hill: University of North Carolina Press, 1970.

Rutland, Robert A., et al., eds. *The Papers of James Madison, Presidential Series.* 6 vols. Charlottesville: University Press of Virginia, 1984– .

———. *The Papers of James Madison, Secretary of State Series.* 7 vols. Charlottesville: University Press of Virginia, 1986– .

Schwartz, Bernard, ed. *The Roots of the Bill of Rights.* 5 vols. New York: Chelsea House, 1980.

Smith, James Morton, ed. *The Republic of Letters: The Correspondence between Thomas Jefferson and James Madison, 1776-1826.* 3 vols. New York: W. W. Norton, 1995.

Syrett, Harold C., and Jacob E. Cooke, ed. *The Papers of Alexander Hamilton*. 27 vols. Columbia: New York University Press, 1961–87.

Veit, Helen C., et al., eds. *Creating the Bill of Rights: The Documentary Record of the First Federal Congress*. Baltimore: Johns Hopkins University Press, 1991.

Wright, Benjamin F., ed. *The Federalist*. Cambridge: Harvard University Press, 1961.

SECONDARY SOURCES

Books

Allgor, Catherine. *Parlor Politics: In Which the Ladies of Washington Help Build a City and a Government*. Charlottesville: University Press of Virginia, 2000.

———. *A Perfect Union: Dolley Madison and the Creation of the American Nation*. New York: Henry Holt, 2006.

Banning, Lance. *The Sacred Fire of Liberty: James Madison and the Founding of the Federal Republic*. Ithaca, N.Y.: Cornell University Press, 1995.

Beard, Charles A. *An Economic Interpretation of the Constitution of the United States*. New York: Macmillan, 1913.

Beeman, Richard. *Plain, Honest Men: The Making of the American Constitution*. New York: Random House, 2009.

Bell, Rudolph M. *Party and Faction in American Politics: The House of Representatives, 1789–1810*. Westport, Conn.: Greenwood, 1973.

Brant, Irving. *The Fourth President: A Life of James Madison*. Indianapolis: Bobbs-Merrill, 1970.

———. *James Madison*. 6 vols. Indianapolis: Bobbs-Merrill, 1941–61.

Broadwater, Jeff. *George Mason, Forgotten Founder*. Chapel Hill: University of North Carolina Press, 2006.

Brown, Roger H. *Redeeming the Republic: Federalists, Taxation, and the Origins of the Constitution*. Baltimore: Johns Hopkins University Press, 1993.

Bruce, Dickson D., Jr. *The Rhetoric of Conservatism: The Virginia Constitutional Convention of 1829–30 and the Conservative Tradition in the South*. San Marino, Calif.: Huntington Library, 1982.

Buckley, Thomas E. *Church and State in Revolutionary Virginia, 1776–1787*. Charlottesville: University of Virginia Press, 1977.

Buel, Richard, Jr. *America on the Brink: How the Political Struggle over the War of 1812 Almost Destroyed the Young Republic*. New York: Palgrave Macmillan, 2005.

———. *Securing the Revolution: Ideology in American Politics, 1789–1815*. Ithaca, N.Y.: Cornell University Press, 1972.

Burstein, Andrew, and Nancy Isenberg. *Madison and Jefferson*. New York: Random House, 2010.

Charles, Joseph. *The Origins of the American Party System*. New York: Harper & Brothers, 1956.

Church, Forrest. *So Help Me God: The Founding Fathers and the First Great Battle over Church and State*. Orlando, Fla.: Harcourt, 2007.

Cote, Richard N. *Strength and Honor: The Life of Dolley Madison*. Mt. Pleasant, S.C.: Corinthian, 2005.

Cunningham, Noble E., Jr. *The Jeffersonian Republicans: The Formation of Party Organizations, 1789–1801*. Chapel Hill: University of North Carolina Press, 1957.

———. *The Process of Government under Jefferson*. Princeton, N.J.: Princeton University Press, 1978.

Curry, Thomas J. *The First Freedoms: Church and State in America to the Passage of the First Amendment*. New York: Oxford University Press, 1986.

Deconde, Alexander. *The Quasi-War: The Politics and Diplomacy of the Undeclared Naval War with France, 1797–1801*. New York: Scribner, 1966.

Dunn, Susan. *Dominion of Memories: Jefferson, Madison, and the Decline of Virginia*. New York: Basic Books, 2007.

Edling, Max M. *A Revolution in Favor of Government: Origins of the U.S. Constitution and the Making of the American State*. New York: Oxford University Press, 2003.

Elkins, Stanley, and Eric McKitrick. *The Age of Federalism: The Early American Republic, 1788–1800*. New York: Oxford University Press, 1993.

Ellis, Joseph J. *American Creation: Triumphs and Tragedies at the Founding of the Republic*. New York: Alfred A. Knopf, 2007.

———. *Passionate Sage: The Character and Legacy of John Adams*. New York: W. W. Norton & Co., 1993.

Estes, Todd. *The Jay Treaty Debate, Public Opinion, and the Development of American Political Culture*. Amherst: University of Massachusetts Press, 2006.

Forbes, Robert P. *The Missouri Compromise and Its Aftermath: Slavery and the Meaning of America*. Chapel Hill: University of North Carolina Press, 2007.

Freehling, Alison Goodyear. *Drift toward Dissolution: The Virginia Slave Debate of 1831–1832*. Baton Rouge: Louisiana State University Press, 1982.

Freehling, William W. *Prelude to Civil War: The Nullification Crisis in South Carolina, 1816–1836*. New York: Harper & Row, 1965.

Gibson, Alan. *Interpreting the Founding: A Guide to the Enduring Debates over the Origins and Foundations of the American Republic*. Lawrence: University Press of Kansas, 2006.

Goldwin, Robert A. *From Parchment to Power: How James Madison Used the Bill of Rights to Save the Constitution*. Washington, D.C.: AEI Press, 1997.

Gutzman, Kevin R. C. *Virginia's American Revolution: From Dominion to Republic, 1776–1840*. Lanham, Md.: Lexington, 2007.

Heidler, David S., and Jeanne T. Heidler. *The War of 1812*. Westport, Conn.: Greenwood, 2002.

Hickey, Donald R. *The War of 1812: A Forgotten Conflict*. Urbana: University of Illinois Press, 1989.

Hofstadter, Richard. *The Idea of a Party System: The Rise of Legitimate Opposition in the United States, 1780–1840*. Berkeley: University of California Press, 1970.

Holmes, David L. *The Faiths of the Founding Fathers*. New York: Oxford University Press, 2006.

Holton, Woody. *Unruly Americans and the Origins of the Constitution*. New York: Hill & Wang, 2007.

Hutson, James H. *Religion and the Founding of the American Republic.* Washington, D.C.: Library of Congress, 1998.

Hyland, Matthew G. *Montpelier and the Madisons: House, Home and the American Heritage.* Charleston, S.C.: History Press, 2007.

Isaac, Rhys. *The Transformation of Virginia, 1740–1790.* Chapel Hill: University of North Carolina Press, 1982.

Isenberg, Nancy. *Fallen Founder: The Life of Aaron Burr.* New York: Viking, 2007.

Kaminski, John P. *The Great Virginia Triumvirate: George Washington, Thomas Jefferson, and James Madison in the Eyes of Their Contemporaries.* Charlottesville: University of Virginia Press, 2010.

———. *James Madison: Champion of Liberty and Justice.* Madison, Wis.: Parallel, 2006.

Kester, Scott J. *The Haunted Philosophe: James Madison, Republicanism, and Slavery.* Lanham, Md.: Lexington, 2008.

Ketcham, Ralph. *James Madison: A Biography.* Charlottesville: University Press of Virginia, 1990.

———. *The Madisons at Montpelier: Reflections on the Founding Couple.* Charlottesville: University of Virginia Press. 2009.

Koch, Adrienne. *Jefferson and Madison: The Great Collaboration.* New York: Alfred A. Knopf, 1950.

Labunski, Richard. *James Madison and the Struggle for the Bill of Rights.* New York: Oxford University Press, 2006.

Lambert, Frank. *The Founding Fathers and the Place of Religion in America.* Princeton, N.J.: Princeton University Press, 2003.

Leibiger, Stuart. *Founding Friendship: George Washington, James Madison, and the Creation of the American Republic.* Charlottesville: University Press of Virginia, 1999.

Lester, Malcolm. *Anthony Merry Redivivus: A Reappraisal of the British Minister to the United States, 1803–1806.* Charlottesville: University Press of Virginia, 1978.

Levy, Leonard W. *Origins of the Bill of Rights.* New Haven, Conn.: Yale University Press, 1999.

Mahon, John K. *The War of 1812.* Gainesville: University of Florida Press, 1972.

Maier, Pauline. *Ratification: The People Debate the Constitution, 1787–1788.* New York: Simon & Schuster, 2010.

Mapp, Alf J. *The Faiths of Our Fathers: What America's Founders Really Believed.* Lanham, Md.: Rowman & Littlefield, 2003.

Marks, Frederick W., III. *Independence on Trial: Foreign Affairs and the Making of the Constitution.* Wilmington, Del.: Scholarly Resources, 1986.

Matthews, Richard K. *If Men Were Angels: James Madison and the Heartless Empire of Reason.* Lawrence: University Press of Kansas, 1995.

McCoy, Drew R. *The Elusive Republic: Political Economy in Jeffersonian America.* New York: W. W. Norton, 1980.

———. *The Last of the Fathers: James Madison and the Republican Legacy.* New York: Cambridge University Press, 1989.

McDonald, Forrest. *Novus Ordo Seclorum: The Intellectual Origins of the Constitution.* Lawrence: University Press of Kansas, 1985.

Meyerson, Michael I. *Liberty's Blueprint: How Madison and Hamilton Wrote the Federalist*

Papers, Defined the Constitution, and Made Democracy Safe for the World. New York: Basic Books, 2008.

Miller, William Lee. *The Business of May Next: James Madison and the Founding.* Charlottesville: University Press of Virginia, 1992.

———. *The First Liberty: America's Foundation in Religious Freedom.* Washington, D.C.: Georgetown University Press, 2003.

Morison, Samuel Eliot, et al. *A Concise History of the American Republic.* 2 vols. New York: Oxford University Press, 1977.

Morris, Richard B. *The Forging of the Union, 1781–1789.* New York: Harper & Row, 1987.

Morrison, Jeffrey H. *John Witherspoon and the Founding of the American Republic.* South Bend, Ind.: University of Notre Dame Press, 2005.

Nelson, John K. *A Blessed Company: Parishes, Parsons, and Parishioners in Anglican Virginia, 1690–1776.* Chapel Hill: University of North Carolina Press, 2001.

Nichols, Roy F. *The Invention of American Political Parties.* New York: Macmillan, 1967.

Noll, Mark A. *Princeton and the Republic, 1768–1822: The Search for a Christian Enlightenment in the Era of Samuel Stanhope Smith.* Princeton, N.J.: Princeton University Press, 1989.

Noonan, John T., Jr. *The Lustre of Our Country: The American Experience of Religious Freedom.* Berkeley: University of California Press, 1998.

Pasley, Jeffrey L. *"The Tyranny of Printers": Newspaper Politics in the Early American Republic.* Charlottesville: University Press of Virginia, 2003.

Perkins, Bradford. *Prologue to War: England and the United States, 1805–1812.* Berkeley: University of California Press, 1961.

Peterson, Merrill D. *James Madison: A Biography in His Own Words.* New York: Harper & Row, 1974.

Rakove, Jack N. *The Beginnings of National Politics: An Interpretive History of the Continental Congress.* New York: Alfred A. Knopf, 1979.

———. *James Madison and the Creation of the American Republic.* 2d ed. New York: Longman, 2002.

———. *Original Meanings: Politics and Ideas in the Making of the Constitution.* New York: Alfred A. Knopf, 1997.

Read, James H. *Power versus Liberty: Madison, Hamilton, and Jefferson.* Charlottesville: University of Virginia Press, 2000.

Richards, E. G. *Mapping Time: The Calendar and Its History.* New York: Oxford University Press, 1998.

Richards, Leonard L. *Shays's Rebellion: The American Revolution's Final Battle.* Philadelphia: University of Pennsylvania Press, 2002.

Risjord, Norman K. *Chesapeake Politics, 1781–1800.* New York: Columbia University Press, 1978.

Rosen, Gary. *American Compact: James Madison and the Problem of Founding.* Lawrence: University Press of Kansas, 1999.

Rothman, Adam. *Slave Country: American Expansion and the Origins of the Deep South.* Cambridge: Harvard University Press, 2005.

Rutland, Robert A. *The Birth of the Bill of Rights, 1776–1791.* Chapel Hill: University of North Carolina Press, 1955.

———. *James Madison, the Founding Father.* New York: Macmillan, 1987.

———. *The Ordeal of the Constitution: Antifederalists and the Ratification of the Constitution.* Boston: Northeastern University Press, 1983.

———. *The Presidency of James Madison.* Lawrence: University Press of Kansas, 1980.

———, ed. *James Madison and the American Nation, 1751–1836: An Encyclopedia.* New York: Simon & Schuster, 1994.

Schultz, Harold S. *James Madison.* New York: Twayne, 1970.

Sharp, James Roger. *American Politics in the Early Republic: The New Nation in Crisis.* New Haven, Conn.: Yale University Press, 1993.

———. *The Deadlocked Election of 1800: Jefferson, Burr, and the Union in the Balance.* Lawrence: University Press of Kansas, 2010.

Sheehan, Colleen A. *James Madison and the Spirit of Republican Self-Government.* New York: Cambridge University Press, 2009.

Sheldon, Garret Ward. *The Political Philosophy of James Madison.* Baltimore: Johns Hopkins University Press, 2001.

Spivak, Burton. *Jefferson's English Crisis: Commerce, Embargo, and the Republican Revolution.* Charlottesville: University of Virginia Press, 1979.

Stagg, J. C. A. *Borderlines in Borderlands: James Madison and the Spanish-American Frontier, 1776–1821.* New Haven, Conn.: Yale University Press, 2009.

———. *Mr. Madison's War: Politics, Diplomacy, and Warfare in the Early American Republic.* Princeton, N.J.: Princeton University Press, 1983.

Stinchcombe, William C. *The XYZ Affair.* Westport, Conn.: Greenwood, 1980.

Sutton, Robert P. *Revolution to Secession: Constitution Making in the Old Dominion.* Charlottesville: University Press of Virginia, 1989.

Swanson, Mary-Elaine. *The Education of James Madison.* Montgomery, Ala.: Hoffman Center, 1992.

Szatmary, David P. *Shays's Rebellion: The Making of an Agrarian Insurrection.* Amherst: University of Massachusetts Press, 1980.

Trees, Andrew S. *The Founding Fathers and the Politics of Character.* Princeton, N.J.: Princeton University Press, 2004.

Tucker, Robert, and David C. Hendrickson. *Empire of Liberty: The Statecraft of Thomas Jefferson.* New York: Oxford University Press, 1990.

White, Leonard D. *The Jeffersonians: A Study in Administrative History.* New York: Macmillan, 1956.

Wilentz, Sean. *The Rise of American Democracy: Jefferson to Lincoln.* New York: W. W. Norton, 2005.

Wills, Garry. *Henry Adams and the Making of America.* Boston: Houghton Mifflin, 2005.

———. *James Madison.* New York: Henry Holt, 2002.

Wood, Gordon S. *Empire of Liberty: A History of the Early Republic, 1789–1815.* New York: Oxford University Press, 2009.

———. *Revolutionary Characters: What Made the Founders Different?* New York: Penguin, 2006.

Zagarri, Rosemarie. *Revolutionary Backlash: Women and Politics in the Early American Republic.* Philadelphia: University of Pennsylvania Press, 2007.

Articles and Essays

Adair, Douglass. "'Experience Must Be Our Only Guide': History, Democratic Theory and the United States Constitution." In *Fame and the Founding Fathers: Essays by Douglass Adair*, edited by Trevor Colburn, 164–69. Indianapolis: Liberty Fund, 1998.

———. "'That Politics May Be Reduced to a Science': David Hume, James Madison, and the Tenth Federalist." In *Fame and the Founding Fathers: Essays by Douglas Adair*, edited by Trevor Colburn, 132–51. Indianapolis: Liberty Fund, 1998.

Banning, Lance. "James Madison, the Statute for Religious Freedom, and the Crisis of Republican Convictions." In *The Virginia Statute for Religious Freedom: Its Evolution and Consequences in American History*, edited by Merrill D. Peterson and Robert C. Vaughn, 109–38. New York: Cambridge University Press, 1988.

———. "Virginia: Sectionalism and the General Good." In *Ratifying the Constitution*, edited by Michael A. Gillespie and Michael Lienesch, 261–99. Lawrence: University Press of Kansas, 1989.

Beliles, Mark A. "The Christian Communities, Religious Revivals, and Political Culture of the Central Virginia Piedmont, 1737–1813." In *Religion and Political Culture in Jefferson's Virginia*, edited by Garret Ward Sheldon and Daniel Dreisbach, 3–40. Lanham, Md.: Rowman & Littlefield, 2000.

Billings, Warren M. "'That All Men Are Born Equally Free and Independent': Virginia and the Origins of the Bill of Rights." In *The Bill of Rights and the States: The Colonial and Revolutionary Origins of American Liberties*, edited by Patrick Conley and John P. Kaminski, 335–69. Madison, Wis.: Madison House, 1992.

Bowling, Kenneth R. "'A Tub to the Whale': The Founding Fathers and the Adoption of the Federal Bill of Rights." *Journal of the Early Republic* 8 (Fall 1988): 223–51.

Bradburn, Douglas. "A Clamor in the Public Mind: Opposition to the Alien and Sedition Acts." *William and Mary Quarterly*, 3rd ser., 65 (July 2008): 565–600.

Brant, Irving. "The Election of 1808." In *History of American Presidential Elections, 1789–1968*, 4 vols., edited by Arthur M. Schlesinger Jr. and Fred L. Israel, 1:185–246. New York: Chelsea House, 1971.

Briceland, Alan V. "Virginia: Cement of the Union." In *The Constitution and the States: The Role of the Original Thirteen in the Framing and the Adoption of the Constitution*, edited by Patrick T. Conley and John P. Kaminski, 201–23. Madison, Wis.: Madison House, 1988.

Brunsman, Denver. "Subjects vs. Citizens: Impressment and Identity in the Anglo-American Atlantic." *Journal of the Early Republic* 30 (Winter 2010): 557–86.

Carr, James A. "The Battle of New Orleans and the Treaty of Ghent." *Diplomatic History* 3 (1979): 273–82.

Coleman, Aaron N. "'A Second Bounaparty?' A Reexamination of Alexander Hamilton during the Franco-American Crisis." *Journal of the Early Republic* 28 (Summer 2008): 183–214.

Cunningham, Noble E. "The Election of 1800." In *History of American Presidential Elections, 1789–1968*, 4 vols., edited by Arthur M. Schlesinger Jr. and Fred L. Israel, 1:59–98. New York: Chelsea House, 1971.

Curtis, Christopher M. "Reconsidering Suffrage Reform in the 1829–30 Virginia Constitutional Convention." *Journal of Southern History* 84 (February 2008): 89–124.

Edling, Max M. "'So Immense a Power in the Affairs of War': Alexander Hamilton and the Restoration of the Public Credit." *William & Mary Quarterly*, 3rd ser., 65 (April 2007): 287–326.

Estes, Todd. "The Voices of Publius and the Strategies of Persuasion in *The Federalist*." *Journal of the Early Republic* 28 (Winter 2008): 523–58.

Ferguson, E. James. "The Nationalists of 1781–1783 and the Economic Interpretation of the Constitution." In *After the Constitution: Party Conflict in the New Republic*, edited by Lance Banning, 106–27. Belmont, Calif.: Wadsworth, 1989.

Fischer, David Hackett. "Patterns of Partisan Allegiance, 1800." In *After the Constitution: Party Conflict in the New Republic*, edited by Lance Banning, 143–70. Belmont, Calif.: Wadsworth, 1989.

Gibson, Alan. "The Madisonian Madison and the Question of Consistency: The Significance and Challenge of Recent Research." *Review of Politics* 64 (Spring 2002): 311–39.

Gilje, Paul A. "'Free Trade and Sailors' Rights': The Rhetoric of the War of 1812." *Journal of the Early Republic* 30 (Spring 2010): 1–23.

Henderson, H. James. "The Continental Congress and the Genesis of Parties." In *After the Constitution: Party Conflict in the New Republic*, edited by Lance Banning, 128–39. Belmont, Calif.: Wadsworth, 1989.

Hickey, Donald R. "The Monroe-Pinkney Treaty of 1806: A Reappraisal." *William & Mary Quarterly*, 3rd ser., 44 (January 1987): 65–88.

Houpt, David W. "Securing a Legacy: The Publication of James Madison's Notes from the Constitutional Convention." *Virginia Magazine of History and Biography* 118, no. 1 (2010): 5–39.

Hutson, James H. "The Drafting of the Bill of Rights: Madison's 'Nauseous Project' Reexamined." *Benchmark* 3 (November–December 1987): 309–20.

Ketcham, Ralph. "James Madison and Religion: A New Hypothesis." In *James Madison and Religious Liberty*, edited by Robert S. Alley, 175–83. Buffalo, N.Y.: Prometheus, 1985.

Kramer, Larry D. "Madison's Audience." *Harvard Law Review* 112 (1999): 611–79.

Leibiger, Stuart. "James Madison and Amendments to the Constitution, 1787–1789: Parchment Barriers." *Journal of Southern History* 59 (August 1993): 441–68.

Lindsay, Thomas. "James Madison on Religion and Politics: Rhetoric and Reality." *American Political Science Review* 85 (December 1991): 1321–38.

McCoy, Drew R. "James Madison." In *The Amercian Presidency*, edited by Alan Brinkley and Davis Dyer, 48–58. Boston: Houghton Mifflin, 2004.

———. "James Madison and Visions of American Nationality in the Confederation Period: A Regional Perspective." In *Beyond Confederation: Origins of the Constitution and American National Identity*, edited by Richard Beeman, Stephen Botein, and Edward C. Carter II, 226–58. Chapel Hill: University of North Carolina Press, 1987.

Onuf, Peter S. "Toward Federalism: Virginia, Congress and the Western Lands." *William & Mary Quarterly*, 3rd ser., 34 (July 1977): 353–74.

Ragosta, John A. "Fishing for Freedom: Virginia's Dissenters' Struggle for Religious Liberty during the American Revolution." *Virginia Magazine of History and Biography* 116, no. 3 (2008): 227–61.

Read, James H. "Madison's Response to Nullification." In *James Madison: Philosopher, Founder, and Statesman*, edited by John R. Vile, William D. Pederson, and Frank J. Williams, 269–83. Athens: Ohio University Press, 2008.

Risjord, Norman K., and Gordon DenBoer. "The Evolution of Political Parties in Virginia, 1782–1800." In *After the Constitution: Party Conflict in the New Republic*, edited by Lance Banning, 190–214. Belmont, Calif.: Wadsworth, 1989.

Schwarz, Michael. "The Great Divergence Reconsidered: Hamilton, Madison, and U.S.-British Relations, 1783–1789." *Journal of the Early Republic* 27 (Fall 2007): 407–36.

Shulman, Holly C. "A Constant Attention: Dolley Madison and the Publication of the Papers of James Madison." In *Virginia Magazine of History and Biography* 118, no. 1 (2010): 41–70.

Index

Note: JM = James Madison.

Gallatin, Albert, 147, 165; estimates U.S. reliance on British seamen, 131; on Embargo Act, 136–37; background of, 149; supports Bank of the United States, 152; on causes of War of 1812, 158; reservations about declaration of war, 159–60; favors increased defense spending, 164; recommends Daniel Tompkins as secretary of war, 167; as delegate to Ghent peace conference, 176

Gallatin, Hannah Nicholson, 118, 122

Garrison, William Lloyd, 205

Gelston, David, 111

General Assessment Bill, 21–24

Genet, Edmund, 99

Gerry, Elbridge, 53, 106, 136, 166

Giles, William Branch, 147, 198; proposes censure of Alexander Hamilton, 98

Gilmer, Francis Walker, 184–85

Gordon, James, Jr., 67

Governor's Council (Virginia), 9–10

Granger, Gideon, 147, 148

Grayson, William, 33, 39, 53, 57, 75

Greene, Nathanael, 11

Griffin, Cyrus, 67

Hamilton, Alexander, 63, 69, 72, 85, 100, 101, 189; opposes 1783 import plan, 14; views compared to JM's, 41–42; at Annapolis Convention, 57; works with JM on *Federalist* essays, 57–59, 65, 67; submits First Report on the Public Credit, 87–88; surprised by JM's opposition, 89–90; agrees to Compromise of 1790, 91; proposes creation of Bank of the United States, 92; attempt to censure, 98; criticizes Aaron Burr, 112; on national debt, 215 (n. 43); on British mercantile policies, 227 (n. 21)

Hamilton, Paul, 147, 167, 168

Hampton, Wade, 168

Hanson, Alexander, 173

Harrison, William Henry, 167

Hartford Convention, 175

Henry, John: letters of, 160

Henry, Patrick, 8, 38, 53; supports general assessment bill, 21; at Virginia ratifying convention, 70–72; calls for second constitutional convention, 74; creates gerrymandered congressional district for JM, 76

House, Mary, 10

Hull, William, 165–66

Hume, David, 43–44, 90

Impressment, 130–31, 133, 135–36, 164, 176

Ingersoll, Charles J., 207, 208; calls JM "Father of the Constitution," 29

Jackson, Andrew, 177, 201–2, 205–6

Jackson, Francis James, 155

Jackson, James, 80

Jay, John, 17, 38, 57, 58. *See also* Jay-Gardoqui Treaty and Jay Treaty

Jay-Gardoqui Treaty, 32–33, 34, 37–38, 39, 41, 68–69

Jay Treaty, 85, 101–5, 230 (n. 64)

Jefferson, Thomas, xi–xii, 19, 31, 32, 38, 41, 81, 124; collaboration with JM begins, 10; and Bill for Religious Freedom, 20, 23–24; describes European poor, 35; buys books for JM, 36; discusses Buffon's theories with JM, 36; and Jay-Gardoqui Treaty, 39; on Shays's Rebellion, 40; criticizes congressional veto, 54; praises *The Federalist*, 58; advocates bill of rights, 60, 74–75; on political parties, 85; as party leader, 86–87, 93; and Compromise of 1790, 91; opposes Bank of the United States, 92; and attempts to censure Alexander Hamilton, 98; urges JM to reply to Hamilton, 99; resigns as secretary of state, 100; in election of 1796, 105–6; writes Kentucky Resolutions, 108, 204; in election of 1800, 110–12; praises Kitty Floyd, 114; and Dolley Madison, 117–18; and Merry affair, 120–23; and Louisiana Purchase, 127–29; on impressment, 131; rejects Monroe-Pinkney Treaty, 133–34; and *Chesapeake* affair, 135–36; and Em-

CPSIA information can be obtained at www.ICGtesting.com
Printed in the USA
LVOW11s1831240216

476551LV00003B/164/P